I0824284

Gullah Images
The Art of Jonathan Green

GULLAH IMAGES
The Art of Jonathan Green

UNIVERSITY OF SOUTH CAROLINA PRESS

For Richard D. Weedman

Published in Columbia, South Carolina, by the
University of South Carolina Press

www.uscpress.com

Printed in China

26 25 24 23 22 13 12 11 10 9

Library of Congress Cataloging-in-Publication Data

Green, Jonathan, 1955–
Gullah images: the art of Jonathan Green
p. cm.
Includes index.
ISBN 1-57003-145-2 (cloth)
1. Green, Jonathan, 1955– —Themes, motives. 2. Gullahs in art.
I. Title
ND237.G6169A4 1996
759. 13—dc20 96–25200

ISBN-13: 978-1-57003-145-8

Contents

Foreword

Pat Conroy

When Jonathan Green came into the world, he brought with him an inescapable sign of his specialness. He was born wearing a caul, an inner fetal membrane that covered his head at birth. In some societies, this is interpreted as a token of great luck or that this child will never know death by drowning. But in the Gullah society along the South Carolina coast, it insures that the child is touched by an uncommonness and magic that will bring inordinate grace to the community. From the beginning, Jonathan Green was marked and grew up known as "the child of the veil."

Jonathan Green, an artist indigenous to Beaufort County, South Carolina, is in the middle of a career that finds him painting the autobiography of his childhood. He paints what made him, the source he issued out of, the forms that inspired his rare sensibility. It is this singular, unshakable vision that gives his work its aura of astonishing originality. Each one of his paintings looks as though it were a commemorative stamp imagined out of the backcountry of Jonathan Green's unconscious. He is the immaculate, real thing, and his art is a cry of pure love for his community, his family, and the geography of the Carolina Sea Islands.

In his art, Jonathan Green is that rarest of twentieth-century painters in that he dares to tell a story. There is a strong narrative flow that binds his work to a central theme. By capturing the essence of the Gullah culture that raised him, there is a sense of both celebration and rediscovery to all his work. His paintings contain some of the primitive, raw beauty I once saw when I visited the cave paintings of our Cro-Magnon ancestors in the Dordogne Valley of France. They possess that kind of mythic grace and nameless grandeur that I observed in those thrilling, ill-lit French caves filled with fabulous images over ten thousand years old. Like those anonymous cave painters, Jonathan Green paints what he considers sacred and essential and mysterious in his own life. It remains a primitive urge for the artist to search for a definition of self that he can live by, and Jonathan Green chose to illuminate the life of his community along Highway 21 from Gardens Corner to Yemassee. By narrowing his vision so finely, he discovered himself as an artist and made his works both magisterial and universal. By returning to the source, he discovered the inexhaustible mainstream of his life's work. Because he so fully understands what he is doing and why, there is never a false note registered on his canvases. Few painters can match Jonathan Green's shining authenticity.

If you study his work carefully, you can detect the peacock-tail love of color found among Haitian painters, then on a much deeper level, you begin to sense the timelessness of Africa. The influence of African culture is still found today in Beaufort County in rich and delightful ways and the imprint of the lost and scattered tribes is still written on the faces of the Gullah people. Jonathan Green himself possesses a face of exceptional beauty that makes you think of exiled princes. When he speaks of his dreams, you know that he sometimes paints from images stolen from his sleeping life. You also know that he dreams in fabulous colors. His use of bright colors is reckless enough that he could easily land a job painting new species of parrots and songbirds in some undiscovered rain forest. The Gullah people depicted in Jonathan Green's world look like they got dressed while staring at rainbows. His art is a love song to his past. You imagine him singing as he paints, an ode to joy and the bright astonishment of memory.

In the South where Jonathan Green and I were born, we could not have sat together on the same bus, drunk from the same water fountain, attended the same school, sat in the same waiting room at a doctor's office, worshiped the same God together, or voted in the same election. It was a hard, unregenerate South we were born into, one obsessed by race, and it was the one part of the country where a white man would never be asked to write an introduction to a book praising a black man's art. Both of us came of age during the Civil Rights movement and both of us lived in Beaufort when Martin Luther King and his lieutenants came to Penn Center on St. Helena's Island to plan the marches and demonstrations that would change our part of the world. The Ku Klux Klan would meet along the same Highway 21 where most of Jonathan's paintings have their origin. I attended an all-white Beaufort High School, yet he graduated from that same school, fully integrated, ten years later. Both of us share an ardent love of Beaufort County and both believe it is one of the loveliest parts of the planet, but our Beauforts are still two different places, worlds apart in both texture and time.

I had been a fan of Jonathan Green's work, having admired his paintings in Elayne Scott's Red Piano Too Gallery on St. Helena's Island long before I met him. His work reminded me with startling clarity of the one year I spent teaching black children on Daufuskie Island, the first year that white teachers were sent to formerly all-black schools. My stay on the island had ended badly when the superintendent fired me one Friday night, but he could not dim the powerful associations I had built up between my students and their parents. I had fallen in love with the people of Daufuskie Island and I wrote my book *The Water Is Wide* to give voice to that love. Jonathan Green's art took me directly back to that time when I steered a boat out across the marshes of Beaufort County to teach everyday. Here were the oystermen I passed in the river, the baptisms in the small creeks, the yards full of children and chickens and dogs, the companionship of women, the wisdom of old men, the dignity of cattle and hogs—all of it coming out in a great tide of artistic labor. He was painting the life that he had led and the one I had been allowed to visit for a single year of my life, and like a fine novelist, Jonathan Green was getting all the details right.

One Saturday in March of 1996, I drove Jonathan Green through the lowcountry that we both cherish and both use as the basis for our art. I wanted to see his Beaufort and he showed it to me as we rode out toward Yemassee to his father's trailer and an amazing yard filled with derelict cars and bizarre, oddball collections of castaway fencing and building supplies, as hunting beagles barked at us from homemade pens.

His grandmother's trailer was nearby and she welcomed us inside and instantly we were engulfed in color as though we had entered into a Byzantine tent in a story of the Arabian nights. An artist was destined to come from a family with such passion for color and sense of form.

Then we drove among his mother's people and I learned where Jonathan came by his extraordinary gentleness, his all-encompassing serenity. Many were farmers and they lived in simple but lovely houses off the main highway with wood-burning stoves and pictures of Jesus on the wall. I sat with his mother and aunt in Burton, South Carolina, and they talked about the early signs of Jonathan's artistry surfacing throughout the long, growing seasons of his childhood. In many of the houses we entered, there was an original oil painting that Jonathan had given to some of his favorite relatives as a gift.

We paid a special visit to his maternal grandmother's grave near the church of his childhood and he showed me the remnants of that church that had been destroyed during Hurricane Gracie. Jonathan described the rituals of total immersion in the saltwater creek near the church and the fasting for seven days and nights in the lowcountry woods that his congregation required of any candidate for baptism. He was telling me that his art had a spiritual origin intimately related to his mission as an artist to preserve the Gullah culture that had nurtured and cherished and brought him into manhood. No one we met that day, as we went from house to house along the country road off Highway 21, had any doubts about the great talent of Jonathan Green. Most had been there or close by on the day of his birth and knew that his gift had come preordained, that his artistry was written into the symbols and myths surrounding his birth, and that extraordinary things were expected of the "child of the veil" by the Gullah people who knew how to read the secret signs of the lowcountry.

Jonathan Green in Motion

Gullah Anointed

Bettye J. (Mbitha) Parker Smith

Each bristle of Jonathan Green's paintbrush seems tempered by an ancestral presence that has been marinating for centuries in Gold Coast West African liquidity. When he walks to face his canvas, Jonathan Green does not make the trek alone. Surrounded by oscillating echoes of things past, he is clairvoyant and prescriptive. He gives honor to a higher force; one of his familiar. Each brush stroke responds to the residual sounds of Congo drums beating delicately against the lowering Daufuski sunset. Enveloped in mystery and history, how often has he responded to the whispered advice of the Mandingo warrior on the mixing of purples and oranges and blues? What about, one may wonder, the swaying of women's hips that are laid to rest on Jonathan's vibrating canvas—over and over again? Is it the presence of the Tshi elder who ensures his exactness of motion; who steals his privacy in the middle of the night and guides the hip-swaying moves which are present in the formula of this young artist? Where else did he secure the patent on his vivid display of "hands-on-hips," on canvas?

Maybe. Maybe the water sounds heard quietly splashing against the rowboat's edges of his painting space were once intermixed with Sierra Leonean river tidal waves. Or, maybe this perplexity that hovers over Jonathan Green is much less complicated than the intricacies which his images project. After all, he could have just transferred onto his masonite the "laying-on-of-hands" rituals practiced by elders from the Liberian hinterlands. Of course, the Gola may have unleashed their century-stored blessings which have been banked along the Atlantic Sea waves, straight onto Jonathan Green's vividly portrayed pray-house (or, as it is sometimes known, praise-house) pews. Could what one sees, feels, and breathes, when in the presence of Jonathan Green's paintings, very well be prime ingredients of another world wonder, called Gullah?

Gullah is an appellative used to describe a population of Africans who were taken against their will from the Gold Coast of West Africa and transferred permanently, with a culture intact, to the Americas—specifically to the coastal region of South Carolina and Georgia. These New World inhabitants were accorded residence on fertile islands in this region that have made deep indentations into the sea. Among other important items which they carted across the Middle Passage with them were their keen agrarian skills and an inexhaustible pride. To this end, these well-endowed Africans became refined indigo tillers, superior rice producers, and farmers who grew cotton of the purest quality. These islands, whose temperaments were well suited for their new guests, graciously received the Africans who became known as Gullah. The islands are often referred to as Sea Islands and were geographically acceptable to South Carolina slavers who wished to raise an isolated, noninterfering slave populace. Excluded from the mainland by creeks, rivers, and marshes, the islands could only be reached by boat. Most of them did not have conveyance to the mainland until 1940. While not all of the islands are currently inhabited, some which are do not have mainland access still. They number about 1,000 and are situated between Georgetown on the north and Port Royal and St. Helena Sound on the south. They were so well insulated from the mainland—by about twenty miles or so—that none bothered to notice the continued importation of slaves long after this North American institutional holocaust was deemed illegal by the Slave Trade Act of 1808. According to J. Herman Blake in "The Sea Island as a Cultural Resource" (*Black Scholar,* March 1974), Africans continued to be brought onto the Sea Islands until 1858. Upon arriving in this new space, the newly displaced Africans found communities of other Africans, although obviously many generations were now American born. Indeed, Gullah born. To demonstrate the extent of the Gullah-populated islands, Blake writes: "in 1800 there were 2,150 whites and 12,400 slaves in the Georgetown district and by 1840 the same region contained 2,200 whites and 18,000 slaves."

These Gold Coast West Africans who became indentured slaves were a unique entity within the North American slavery system. South Carolina slave owners used their legal system to shape their slave community. This is demonstrated in the amount of duty tax imposed on the cargo of individual traders. In the first place, South Carolina and Georgia catalogue-ordered their slaves directly from the West African Coast, particularly those areas that range from Senegal to Angola and also include Gambia, Sierra Leone, and Nigeria. In 1721, an act was imposed that required a duty of ten pounds on Africans brought directly from Africa, while for those brought into the state en route from another state in America, an additional thirty pounds was imposed. In 1722, another law required a duty of one hundred and fifty pounds on any slave of Spanish background entering the state. A South Carolina Act of 1803, quoted in Lorenzo Dow Turner's *Africanisms in the Gullah Dialect* (1949), forbade the importation of all slaves from the West Indies, and all others "over fifteen years of age from other parts of the United States except under certificate of good character." Early on, to further ensure the importation of pure, unadulterated Africans, a very low tax of only three pounds was imposed on those directly from Africa and on those who were over four feet tall.

By selecting their slaves specifically from the Gold Coast of West Africa, the slave owners were attempting to strategically limit ethnic diversity in their slave communities. However, some of the Gold Coast areas had well-developed secret societies which constituted an admixture of ethnic groups and kinship systems, and these different societies were only mistaken as one because of their demonstrated allegiances. The initiation rites into these secret societies prepared Africans in the region to protect themselves and their communities from invaders and instructed them in ways to survive against the most difficult odds. So when captured by the interlopers, and after surviving the Middle Passage and being taken off to the isolated Sea Islands in the New World, the Africans who had now become initiated slaves were better prepared than other Africans who were cast into multilingual, multiethnic, and less homogeneous groupings. Their strong religious manifestations provided psychological and physical protection. And by virtue of their isolation and the small number of whites who lived on the islands, the Gullah received little acculturation into the ways of North America, and particularly of the antebellum South. The climate in the region was not friendly to whites—their immune systems were not strong enough to protect them against the extreme heat, malaria, and humidity—and often the only white inhabitants on the islands were those in charge of overseeing the management of the plantations. Turner informs us: "It is said that there were two Negro families to every one white family in many sections of coastal South Carolina. On many plantations, there were no white overseers. Here the work of the field slaves was directed entirely by Negro drivers."

Therefore, the geographical isolation which characterized the newly transplanted Africans, the state of South Carolina's insistence on importing Africans directly from the Gold Coast of West Africa, and the small numbers of whites able to survive the climate and conditions of these Sea Islands created a sort of petri dish for preserving African cultural tenets and for the development of a unique African American culture. Further, as the Slave Trade Act of 1808 was ignored, Africans continued to be transported into the established slave communities, which allowed for the refueling and strengthening of existing Africanisms. Clearly, it was not the intent of the slave owners, even in the state of South Carolina, to establish a system which would promote African pride. In fact, the intent was to destroy all sense of self-worth and fashion a submissive people. But for the South Carolina Sea Island slaves, the human spirit was strengthened by isolation. The history and practice of a self-sustaining community, which they had packaged well and brought with them to their new world, produced attitudes of selflessness and pride which would extend into perpetuity. As devastating and wrenching as the North American slave system was, it is difficult to annihilate the inner lining of a human being's spirit. The Africans whose spirit later designed the Gullah culture understood at the beginning of this atrocity something that those who chose to destroy them did not know: they were equipped to maintain control of their collectivity and, according to Margaret Washington Creel in *A Peculiar People* (1988), they "possessed a proclivity for rising above their near-tragic situation for the sake of community."

Africanisms which permeate the Gullah culture carry the velocity and intensity of the history and culture of their antecessors. Out of their common and multifaceted African cultures, and the limited access they had with the English language, the newly ascribed Gullah were able to blend a language that allowed for communication, and therefore were better able to retain their cultural canons. An examination of some of these Africanisms is essential to a deeper appreciation of the art of Jonathan Green.

The unique geographical seclusion which the Gullah people experienced at the onset of their new life in America spared them the inundation of American Protestant proselytization at the level that their sisters and brothers elsewhere experienced. In fact, the Gullah received their major introduction to Christianity from Methodists and Baptists over a hundred years after their own system was stabilized, and by this time they had already effected their own African ontological spiritual system into their community structure. The Southern Christian exhortations were intended to encourage obedience and loyalty to the slave-master structure and build a belief system, the subscriptions of which were prerequisite to a heavenly home in the afterlife; or, certainly a reward for earthly subjugation. And, while much of the preachings did in fact change some of the coloring of their own system, religious efforts were never able to destroy the historical beliefs of these Africans. Indeed, parts of what they revered were synthesized into their own traditional African world view.

It is the custom for the Gullah to believe strongly in a set of values that identify the community as the focal point from which their existence is anchored. John Mbiti, renowned scholar on African religions, informs us in *African Religions and Philosophy* (1969) that in traditional societies, "to be human is to belong to the whole community. . . . A person cannot detach himself from the religion of his group, to do so is to be severed from his roots, his foundation, his context of security, his kinship. . . . African people do not know how to exist without religion." This African worldview engenders ceremonies and rituals for all aspects of living, including birth, death, fishing practices, motor movement, and styles of dress, especially among women.

Further, the Gullah people, in keeping with their heritage, engaged in a combined spiritual and nonecclesiastical formula that again was driven by their devotion to their African heritage. Like their African neighbors, the West Africans from the Gold Coast were proponents of initiations which had ethereal ingredients. A belief in the spirit world as a natural extension of their declaration of faith provided for a cyclical acceptance of nature. They remained closely connected to their ancestors and felt assured that their movements were indeed overseen and protected by their spirits. A part of the ritualistic ceremonies was the wearing of very sophisticated and often highly adorned masks. Of course, these rituals were approved by God, who reigned always at the apex of the belief system, and those who had earned the right to be ceremonial participants were anointed by God. The majority of Africans who were brought to America were associated with initiation processes. This custom was known to the Methodists and Baptists, who were frustrated by the practices and were determined to dismantle the duality within the Gullah spiritual base: they identified this religious facet as paganistic. The independent worship centers, the pray houses, sheltered and effectuated the beliefs and practices of the Gullah people.

To be sure, the population of human beings characterized as Gullah continue to live along the coastal region of South Carolina and Georgia, and they are phenomenal indeed. The retention of their African history and culture has sustained them, and their long-identifiable lineage makes them unique among African Americans whose specific African connection is, more often than not, difficult to identify. While there have been concerted efforts over the past twenty years by scholars and artists to collect, preserve, and capture this culture, much work is left to be completed. In a 1974 article in *Black Scholar,* J. Herman Blake appealed to young scholars, particularly African Americans and those interested in collecting oral history, to seize the moment and consider this area for fresh research and scholarship. That prospect is not as likely today and will be less so as South Carolina structures its move toward the twenty-first century. The isolation and independence which the inhabitants of these islands have enjoyed for so long is soon to give way to modernistic advances, especially as related to urban renewal and resort development. Communicating in modern terms and adjusting to a new system of life management—rent, mortgages,

ATM machines, bridges, upscale boats, and shops—certainly create serious problems of psychological and physical adaptation for a people who have made their own rules and managed their lives in their own defined space. National debate on issues of crime and criminal justice, public health facilities, and treatment of the elderly will be even heavier burdens to bear.

The human situation herein described represents the formation, the history, and the linkages which gave rise to Jonathan Green's valued ancestry. Jonathan Green, tall, angular, graphically astute, and enveloped in a wide-angled quietude, is an artist par excellence, and he shadows the warrior often seen walking about on West African soil making demands with his very presence. Actually, he is equally akin to the South Carolinian Gullah patrician, seen standing at the edge of the waterway emphatically and aesthetically measuring the distance between the colors in the rainbow. These parallels depict a presence that is perpetual; one that exudes motion and remnants of a distant past. And, vibrating all around him are ancestral acclamations, because after all, he has colored new links in the Gullah's long chain of pride. Using his talents wisely and claiming his place as a Gullah native son, Jonathan Green has transfixed his ancestry in time: his paintings are highly informed by African retentions, especially his deep association with and respect for community as the foundation of Gullah life. While this is clearly an instinctive train present in Jonathan Green the man, it is also a display of conscious depth. In this regard, he has theorized in a statement included in Alan Gussow's *The Artist as Native* (1993): "How a man tills the soil in silent labor depicts a sense of purpose and functional movement that brings sustenance and well-being to the family and community."

However, this sense of divine revelation about the culture that is Jonathan Green, and which now encompasses the essence of his work, was not an easily determined recognition. On a conscious level, even though Jonathan Green grew up walking hand in hand with the corporeal and the intangible cultural edifices of his surroundings, the realization and appreciation for their imitable value evolved over time. Examining human existence outside his Gullah environment set up transparencies which gave him strength and assisted in bringing balance to a conscious and subliminal position regarding the "certain uniqueness" to which he subscribes. Having accepted his connection with the richness of his heritage, Jonathan Green's work endorses the community as the substructure to the Gullah system of living; an Africanism well preserved by these South Carolina islanders.

The first visual artist from the Gullah community to be academically trained and achieve national and international prominence, Jonathan Green has accepted the calling of his ancestors and is on a mission to preserve the magnificence of their way of life. Through a series of some one hundred and fifty paintings, he has indeed exacted the finiteness of their touch, their strength, their determination, their drive, and the rawness of their sensibilities; and through his own ordination, he has endowed them with power. He is very clear about his mission, articulated in a 1993 article in the *Naples (Fla.) Daily News*: "The only power-stronghold blacks have is their ethnicity. They have nothing else. A white man can take a bath, put on a nice shirt and immediately get respect—that's power."

So the power inherent in communities which the West Africans took on their journey through the Middle Passage is the link which welded the Gullah culture, and it is that power which is highly evident in Jonathan Green's art. Piece by piece, one sees this power vividly entrenched in the religious activities associated with pray houses, in the contrariety of his faces, and in the stance and unity of his figures. It comes through in the washing and hanging of clothes, the cooking of food, the sharing of tasks in the workplaces; in dressing up, slowdragging, and hanging out. The multidimensionality of power vibrates through the fabric of pride on which his figures step, sashay, quilt, flirt, carry their pocketbooks, and bury their dead. And this special strain of power gets deeper on his waterways where the heavy vibrations compete with the calmness of the water and resound an admixture of ancestral pain and laughter and blood, and offer visual transportation from a sacred old life to a vibrant but unsettled new one. Actually, his stories on canvas produce the aftermath of an African griot story.

The timing of Jonathan Green the artist, and the level of momentum to which he subscribes, is not just one of happenstance. Indeed, while he may not have arrived in swaddling clothing, it is perhaps safe to say that he carries the sign of one anointed. He responds tenebrifically to the culture which has virtually maintained its virginity for so many years now and is in fact becoming quickly semenized by the tentacles of modernism. In an interview article for *American Visions* (February 1990), Carroll Greene, Jr., writes: "He seeks to recall the feel, texture and color of a way of life he knows is rapidly disappearing. And quite literally on some of the islands near his mother's home, a way of life is being bulldozed out of existence in the name of progress: condos, highways, fast food chains and displacement of people."

Progress notwithstanding, Jonathan Green, like his forebears, is equipped to manage in the face of adversity. And like them he feels secure; even powerful, as Carroll Greene reports: "I know I can't save a whole culture . . . but as an artist I can help create greater awareness, perhaps. All of the change is not bad. But, are they throwing out the baby with the bath?" The question is academic. The baby is now impaled. Richard Weedman, longtime friend and a Jonathan Green collector, assures us in an unpublished biographical statement on Green, that through his art, "Jonathan has the unique and gifted ability to afford the viewer a sense of space and silence to unobtrusively observe and participate."

Jonathan Green is realistic about the uncertainty of the future for a quarter of a million Gullahs who reside along the coastal region of South Carolina. For them the page has indeed turned again. This time there is no slave ship waiting at a safe distance to be loaded with human cargo and venture off into the deep waters to an unknown land. There are no auction blocks erected on the new land to insult their humanity. There is no overseer to whip them, or branding iron to indent foreign initials onto their skin. There is no forced division of families through a selling and buying process. There is no big house or master, in the thralldom sense. But, on this new page of progress to which they are forced to turn, is a series of questions whose answers just might be as surreal as the "forty-acres-and-a-mule" oddity.

Are the carriers of this generation of misplaced Africans strong enough to manage their African Americanness, while at the same time continuing to protect this heritage and secure it for their children? What, one may question, is the potency level of their power? While these answers are clearly unknowns, if one is to respect the system which places ancestry at an important level in a people's belief system, then perhaps the power level is active. Certainly, with Jonathan Green, the artist and the man, the power is the people.

The poet Mari Evans footnotes Jonathan Green's notion in this regard:

Daufuskie: Jake

Jake the best damn cap'n in the world
O gaaahd
the best damn cap'n in the world
just been runnin the boat
for the last twenny years
for the last twenny years
O gaaahd

He boat turn over with he wife
You tell'm
He ride the breakers sideways
in the storm
Smooth as m'hand I say that Jake
and he caint swim

But he the best damn cap'n in the world
O gaaahd
the best damn cap'n in the world.

Sources

Compton, Rick. "Artist Jonathan Green Puts the Community on Canvas," *Ambience Magazine, Naples Daily News,* November 1993, 30–31.

Creel, Margaret Washington. *A Peculiar People: Slave Religion and Community-Culture among the Gullahs.* New York: New York University Press, 1988.

Cunningham, Irma Aloyce Ewing. *A Syntactic Analysis of Sea Island Creole.* Greensboro: University of North Carolina, 1992.

Evans, Mari. *Nightstar 1973–1978.* Los Angeles: University of California, 1981.

Greene, Carroll, Jr. "Coming Home Again: Artist Jonathan Green Returns to His Roots," *American Visions,* 5 (February 1990): 44–52.

Gussow, Alan. *The Artist as Native: Reinventing Regionalism.* Rohnert Park, Calif.: Pomegranate Artbooks, 1993.

Jackson, Juanita, Sabna Slaughter, and J. Herman Blake. "The Sea Island as a Cultural Resource," *Black Scholar* (March 1974): 32.

Mbiti, John. *African Religions and Philosophy.* New York: Praeger, 1969.

I am grateful to the following persons for bringing significant pieces of literature on the Gullah culture to my attention: Ayana Karanja, Herman Blake, Israel Tribble, Jr., and Joy O'Shields.

Walking with His Peers

The African American Artist in the South

Lynn Robertson

> *My approach to art is greatly influenced by my heritage as an African American. The images and subject matter reveal black images, but in many cases I try to make these images universal. . . . What I try to show in my work is what I feel within, the ideals of higher truth and peace.*
>
> *Louis Delsarte*

Twentieth-century American art has been examined largely in terms of differences. Because of the perceived dominance of Europe in all things cultural, the post–World War II emergence of an art that not only looked different but also captured the unique aspects of the mood of America was heralded with a renewed declaration of independence. Since the end of colonial status American artists had been engaged in a battle to prove their sovereignty. The negative side to this heady new dominance of the international art world was that a large number of creative individuals who worked outside of the modernist mainstreams remained unaccepted.

What is far more interesting about this phenomenon than the creation of a new definition for American art is the compulsion to search for an identity, the need to construct a sense of self distinguishable from the rest of the world. The same search, although on a different scale, has unfolded in the various geographic regions within the United States. In the South, however, the creation of identity has taken on an unusual dimension in that many of the attributes accepted as southern have come from outside the region. Sensing that the landscape below the Mason-Dixon line was vastly different from their own, outsiders created their own versions of the South. The many missionaries who came at various times to improve the economic state of poor blacks and whites espoused the nobility of those who lived on the land, and therefore they sought to create a moral uplifting as well as bring financial improvement through reviving traditional crafts. More recently, popular writers and filmmakers have created images either of a land of moonlight and magnolias where men were chivalrous and women genteel or of a backwoods peopled with bigoted small-town lawmen out to arrest the wrong person.

While others busy themselves with creating a "national" image of the South, those who dwell there have been quietly communicating among themselves. Family folklore, community legends, and the prose and poetry of southern writers capture the essence of local life. The literary storytellers of this century have garnered much public attention: Eudora Welty, Tennessee Williams, Carson McCullers, William Faulkner, Flannery O'Connor, and, more recently, Peter Taylor, Pat Conroy, and Josephine Humphries, among others. But lesser known visual artists, William H. Johnson, Elliott Dangerfield, Alice Ravenel Huger Smith, Romare Bearden, and, now, Jonathan Green, equally possess talent to create vivid and moving stories about the people and places they know. And, although the strong narrative tradition has served southern writers well, it has placed visual artists outside of the national creative mainstream where abstract intellectual explorations and technical inventiveness dominate.

Steeped in deep-rooted customs, clinging to its history and sense of place, the South persists as a stronghold of representational traditions. Folktales from various cultures have long been a staple of southern life, their narratives imparting traditional wisdom to each new generation. An agricultural economy has provided minimal financial rewards for those individuals who worked the land and served not only to keep people within their communities but also to make them mindful of the dominance of land and weather in their lives. The recent influx of immigrants to the Sunbelt and newfound land wealth has only reinforced the reliance on narrative. Now, it serves to call forth memories of earlier times. As has been recognized by art historian and writer Estill Pennington in *Look Away: Reality and Sentiment in Southern Art,* memory and nostalgia have assumed an important role in southern thought. "The past continues to exert a strong influence upon the present, because Southerners do not forget. Indeed, they yearn to remember, to recall, to reflect."

Jonathan Green has successfully woven together the central themes of southern art—memory, narrative, place, and community—in his paintings. He nostalgically tells a story that is clearly rooted in a love of land and of the families who inhabited it. Educated in Chicago and currently living in coastal Florida, Green repeatedly draws on his rural South Carolina childhood for his artistic vision. Born in 1955 near Beaufort, South Carolina, he seeks not only to re-create the look and feel of his early years but also to convey the significance of these events in deeply human terms. Using his narrative skills, Green makes us care about the individuals depicted in his lowcountry scenes. In so doing, the scenes are transformed into celebrations of the life experience.

This celebratory aspect is especially significant. Celebrations have played a vital role in the life of black communities for generations. They affirm the identity of the community and create strong ties to it as well as providing settings for social interaction. Because many aspects of southern life continued to be segregated well into this century, black communities have perpetuated their rites of celebration. River baptisms, weddings, revival meetings, Decoration Day parades, harvest dinners, and family homecomings are examples of some formal observances. In addition to these are many spontaneous social activities such as beach outings and lounge dances. Along with numerous occupational activities such as oyster tonging and spring planting, these events make up the subject and spirit of Jonathan Green's work.

The artist's own memories of small-town South Carolina life are vividly reproduced through his art work. Though many of Green's paintings are personal recollections of the 1960s, the traditions he speaks to have remained largely the same throughout most of this century. Paintings such as *Shucking Oysters* and *Braiding Hair* depict the continuation of rural social and occupational traditions. However, the years since the 1960s have brought many changes. In Green's words, "I can remember things as a child that are now gone—hair wrapping, men weaving fish nets, farming and hunting. There are very little of these activities going on now. What fishing and hunting that goes on is mainly for sport and not out of necessity as before. Food used to be preserved in various ways . . . drying, canning, smoking. Now, only gardening seems to continue."

While Green's narrative ability and the use of memory expressed in his art work places him strongly within the southern artistic tradition shared by black and white artists, his sense of mission and community responsibility ties him to the world of contemporary African American art. Green wants us to appreciate and respect the multicultural heritage of the South, particularly the traditions of African Americans whose past is often interpreted narrowly, with a focus on the institution of slavery rather than the rich cultural heritage that survived those years. Green's work emphasizes the Gullah traditions carried on by the community and their link with an African past.

The traditions he depicts are not the only link with Africa. According to certain anthropologists, the most fundamental tribal legacy to African American life is the belief that personal strength and well-being come through the use of skillful communication and cooperative community involvement. An examination of Green's work, as well as of the work of other significant black artists, discloses a common desire to communicate the deeper significance of life experiences shared within the African American community. Such an examination is not easy, however, because most American art histories have had little to present on black artists. Until such efforts as the 1993 exhibition at the National Museum of American Art entitled *Free within Ourselves* (accompanied by Regina Perry's excellent catalogue) and the publication the same year of Romare Bearden and Harry Henderson's encyclopedic volume, *A History of African-American Artists,* little recognition had been given to this significant group of artists. In his introduction Henderson comments on the lack of even primary archival and documentary material from which he and Bearden could work to construct a chronology of artists: "In our view we have sketched little more than an outline and washed away some of the old varnish that has contributed to the denial of recognition of African American artists and their participation in American Art."

Beyond the problems of primary research, the identification of a clearly African American aesthetic is still difficult. The work of early black artists, like that of other Americans, can only be looked at in the context of European-inspired styles. As Charles Eldridge, former director of the National Museum of American Art, has pointed out, "Recognition was slow, but when it came . . . it was won not in a separate category, but in the wide field of international competition." By the end of the nineteenth century things had begun to change, and the idea that art could and should reflect a more localized point of view began to surface. A number of artists from the South, however, were especially instrumental in creating a visual genre that responded to the region's vernacular culture and strong community focus. Four, in particular, deserve recognition for generating a national appreciation of the African American experience: William H. Johnson, Archibald Motley, Jr., Ellis Wilson, and Romare Bearden. Their success in creating a way to convey visually the spirit of their communities makes them important in understanding the contribution made by Jonathan Green to contemporary American art.

William H. Johnson, a South Carolina native, was one of a number of African American artists who first gained professional success outside of the United States.

After training at the National Academy of Design in New York City, he traveled to France in hopes of broadening his experience through first-hand knowledge of the contemporary European art scene. He was influenced by the work of the Postimpressionists, especially Paul Gauguin, and several of the younger expressionist artists. He traveled, exhibited his work, and sought to establish a style uniquely his own. The larger critical and financial successes he envisioned eluded him, and in 1938, after more than ten years in Europe, Johnson returned to the United States in search of a new beginning to his career. While teaching for the WPA (Work Projects Administration), he began to draw on his own experiences in a simple and direct format and to experiment with a new style rooted in his southern past. The childlike simplicity of the works of this period disguises their sophisticated composition and use of color. Johnson is sometimes criticized for developing a forced primitivism to convey his subject matter. Yet, the ability of his work to speak to contemporary audiences cannot be denied. He was one of the first African American artists to seek a way to depict scenes from everyday southern rural life, as well as those in Harlem, that conveyed both the occupations and the inner strength of the individuals portrayed. Johnson's contribution was in his use of European expressionist technique to create a style through which he could convey the importance that everyday life within an African American community had for him.

If Johnson was successful in conveying the full range of the black community he experienced, Archibald Motley, Jr., was the most accomplished at creating a clear vision of a vibrant African American social life. Born in 1891 in New Orleans, Motley grew up in Chicago and attended The Art Institute of Chicago. Like many artists of the period, he was influenced by the American realist painters and their insistence that the subjects of everyday life made for high art. The nightclubs, restaurants, and jazz bars frequented by urban blacks soon became the subject of his most ambitious paintings. Like Johnson, Motley traveled to France, but he went as a mature artist with a well developed sense of his own style and subject matter. His participation in the WPA was a significant contribution toward the program's success in Illinois. He was one of the most respected black artists of the 1920s, but, more important, he excelled at producing sophisticated and exciting paintings that celebrated the social interactions of urban black life.

As the number of black artists exhibiting on a national level throughout the 1940s and 1950s grew, so did the question of racial consciousness. This development mirrored the larger changes in U.S. society and the increasing popularity of ethnic awareness. Bound on one side by the WPA and on the other by the Black Pride movement, this period was one in which a number of artists integrated experimental techniques with a continuing desire to convey community mores.

South Carolina life became an unexpected source of inspiration for Ellis Wilson, who grew up amid the rolling tobacco-producing lands of Kentucky. Inspired by his father's interest in art and accomplishments as an amateur painter, Wilson eventually made his way to The Art Institute of Chicago, where he studied commercial art for four years. After a short design career in Chicago, he moved to New York and worked for the WPA. In 1944 he received a Guggenheim fellowship that allowed him to travel throughout the South sketching scenes of everyday life in black communities. South Carolina held particular fascination for him. At the market in Charleston, South Carolina, Wilson observed black people from the Sea Islands off the Carolinas. Bearden and Henderson comment on his discovery of the dignity of these people who walked erectly like Africans and balanced baskets on their heads. In Beaufort, South Carolina, he spent time with the families who earned their livelihood shrimping and fishing the Atlantic waters. At home in New York, Wilson turned his many preliminary sketches and memories into finished paintings. The scenes of Charleston were especially successful. Bearden and Henderson theorize that these "promptly sold because they evoked memories of such markets among southerners of all races." In his later years Wilson turned to Haiti for inspiration. The agricultural markets and religious celebrations of the island people became favorite subjects. In striving to capture the positive spirit of community traditions and celebrations, Wilson's style became increasingly flat with an emphasis on repeated silhouette, shape, and color. These relationships not only enhanced the decorative aspects of the work but also created a rhythmic, almost musical, pattern.

As a successful artist of the 1950s, Ellis Wilson drew on first-hand observations of black communities. Equally successful, Romare Bearden looked toward his African heritage and experimented with new artistic techniques to tell his stories. Born in 1912 in Charlotte, North Carolina, Bearden, like Motley, grew up in an urban setting, first in New York City and then in Pittsburgh. He graduated from New York University with a degree in mathematics. Within a short period, from 1935 to 1945, he attended the Art Students League in New York, worked as a social services case worker, and served in the army, all the while developing his interest in becoming a professional artist. Like Motley he was interested in music, and through discussions with other artists, he began to visualize a relationship between painting and jazz. Throughout the 1950s he experimented with collage techniques and within ten years was producing his signature photomontages. According to Regina Perry in a description of African American artists in the collection of the National Museum of Art, in the late 1960s "Bearden produced some of his largest and most innovative works. Memories of Mecklenburg County, North Carolina, abound, reaffirming Bearden's roots in the rural South." His nostalgic and emotive scenes of remembered relatives and childhood activities bring him clearly into the sphere of southern artists. During his career he also produced works linking the narratives of classical mythology with African themes. Bearden was a tireless lecturer, exhibition organizer, researcher, and community activist.

Although these four individuals were acclaimed artists more than fifty years ago, their contributions to the contemporary art scene are still felt. They created the visual vocabulary that Jonathan Green draws upon in presenting views of his world. During the 1960s a number of black artists sought national acceptance through abstract art. This phenomenon did not erase their concerns for social well-being, however. Politically influenced groups such as Africobra emerged and focused on black issues. But political statement was not the aim of a host of other gifted artists, some southern, some not, who continued to focus on the meaning of community and personal identity. Such artists as John Biggers, Betty Saar, and Leo Twiggs steadily carried on the narrative tradition and created an acceptance of African American subject matter. Today Jonathan Green, Faith Ringgold, and Carrie May Weems take fresh looks at what it means to grow up amid black traditions in America. Each of these artists extracts the essence of family memories and life's early lessons to make a life-affirming statement. Another artist featured in the National Museum of American Art's 1993 exhibition, Frederick James Brown, espouses the strength of narrative painting not only in reaching an expanding African American audience but also in presenting his message to a broader public. "People are not conceptual to the aunts and neighbors of my youth, if you said you could cook . . . you don't go there and mess up the food. If you say you can sing, you have to sing like Muddy Waters. . . . If I can lend any credence to anything that is African American I am willing to do that. But I am an artist and I would like to see my things in a global situation."

Perhaps this is the strongest message of Jonathan Green's paintings. Instead of reinforcing the presumption that African American art can speak only to blacks, his work speaks equally to all people. He draws upon his own experiences and the richness of coastal Gullah culture to create a vocabulary that touches all of us. Like other successful artists, Jonathan Green has the ability to move beyond the moment he depicts and to convey a timeless and universal message, reminding us of the importance of memory shared, of community, of celebrating life.

Gathering Light in the Gray City

The Chicago Years

Ronne Hartfield

Jonathan Green, painter, began his artistic journey in a world of color and light. His paintings reflect subjects seen, observed, remembered, suffused with sunlight: black fishermen setting their nets at dawn to escape the sun's oncoming heat; lines of immaculate, sun-bleached bed linen, barely catching the faintest wind from the sea; women crowded into narrow church pews, replete with wide-brimmed hats and the South's inevitable fans, crucial shade, and respite from an unremitting sun.

For Jonathan Green, light is essential to the human experience of the world.The Mexican poet and Nobel laureate Octavio Paz writes of this power of light, alluding to the experience of seeing as one of sense and beyond sense. In a poem entitled simply "Hay Luz / There is Light," Paz responds to the biblical commandment "Let there be Light" with the artist's hunger to *see beyond sight.* "There is light. We neither see nor touch it. / . . . / I see with my fingertips / what my eyes touch" (*Octavio Paz: The Collected Poems, 1957–1987,* trans. Eliot Weinberger).

Jonathan Green sees with his fingertips. For Green, as for Paz, light is critical to the human experience of the world. From his memories of light and his formation in a universe where meanings and mysteries, literal and metaphoric, were lived and communicated through light and shadow, he creates paintings that are filled with the precision of personal recollection. But more, his paintings are rich with the look and feel and smell of the lowcountry. In the African American religiocultural vernacular, these paintings do more than record a certain kind of world: they *testify.*

In "My Soul Looks Back," James Cone, African American theologian, locates this experience within the black logos: "Testimony is an integral part of the black religious tradition. It is the occasion where the believer stands before the community of faith in order to give account of the hope that is in him or her. Although testimony is unquestionably personal, and primarily an individual story, it is also a story accessible to others in the community of faith. Indeed, the purpose of testimony is not only to strengthen an individual's faith, but also to build a faith of the community."

Where does this concept of *testimony* reside, this understanding of the individual story as inextricable from its role in weaving the collective tapestry? Drawing on the deepest sources of a solitary journey inward, it resides in the private vision of the black artist, but it is always informed by an aggregate *communal* history. Seeking images that express a *personal* sensibility, the black artist finds that his or her metaphors are necessarily rooted in, bound to, and reflective of a larger psychocultural discourse. When the African American paints, the act is at once a private risk to express an intimate, personal response to the world, and, inevitably, homage to the ancestors. Because this revisiting of the story is also a setting straight of the record, the aesthetic heritage of the black American artist is always consonant with the cultural heritage, a powerful assertion of spirit over circumstance. The past is always present, darkness behind and beneath the light.

The work of Jonathan Green, perhaps more explicitly than that of many of his contemporaries, expresses this dual concern, this double consciousness of isolated experience rooted in and strengthened by the communal. Green himself, in a biographical statement for Alan Gussow's *The Artist as Native,* has said, "I am drawn to rural environments that afford a sense of space and silence and an opportunity to unobtrusively observe daily functions of others as we all pursue life's mission of work, love and belonging. . . . It is the small, but critical tasks of daily life that I find most stimulating and reflective of the quality of essential, personal, community, and social values." Thus the brilliant colors and lyrical movement in Green's paintings cannot be dismissed as sheerly representational. Like the British painter Howard Hodgkin, noted for his use of color, Green employs color and the particularity of domestic moments to allude to *shared* human experiences. Hodgkin has said, "I am a representational painter, but not of appearances. I paint representational pictures of emotional situations." Green's representations of the daily life he observed as a child in rural South Carolina cannot be considered apart from his understandings of "situations," moments not so much emotionally as *culturally* charged. His explorations of Gullah traditions are, on one level, documentation of the daily rituals of people's lives in a traditional African American community unmarked by the process of assimilation into modernity. The community that Green documents is the southern coastal community into which he was born and where he grew to be a man. In that sense the work is undeniably *testament.* His paintings introduce us to forms, rituals, and styles present in a particular part of the world at a particular time.

On a larger plane, these Sea Island representations are also *testimony*. That is to say, as much as they tell personal stories, each story is always in dialogue with the mutual experience of the community. The community in this instance is not simply a lowcountry village; it is a *black* village, a group of people severed involuntarily from their homes and from their identities as Africans, coping with the new and unforeseen world of America while somehow stubbornly retaining something of Africanness in their way of life. This task of creating wholeness from fragmentation, of locating a center amid such complexity, is, in the words of Ralph Ellison, "a discipline teaching its own insights into the human condition." In Green's work, the resilient strength of a people becomes manifest through the talent and expressive skill of one of their own.

The imperative for continuity and connection, so vital to emotional and spiritual survival in the black world, is in counterpoint with much of the discourse of modernism and postmodernism. Beginning to work seriously as an artist when he came to Chicago to study at The School of The Art Institute of Chicago (SAIC) in 1976, Jonathan Green found himself thrust into the middle of puzzling debates about modernity. *Modernity* is not a term simply or easily defined. What impelled interest in it, and in all that it implied, among many young artists at that moment was their sense that modernity promised a liberating—and empowering—separation from the past, an exciting sense of being on the threshold of something entirely new. In the midst of a frenzy of bicentennialism as the United States celebrated its 200th birthday, the prototypical art student eschewed inherited traditions in a passionate search for a unique, individual voice. As Todd Gitlin has written in an article entitled "Dissent: Postmodernism Defined, at Last": "In modernism . . . artists set out to remake life. Audacious individual style threw off the dead hand of the past, . . . continuity was disrupted, the individual subject dislocated."

In one sense, U.S. history itself is a history of modernism, for the American adventure celebrated in that bicentennial year is in actuality one continuum of dislocation and relocation. In a 1992 article entitled "Who and What is American?," Lewis H. Lapham, *Harper's Magazine* editor, writes: "Who else is the American hero if not a wandering pilgrim who goes forth on a perpetual quest?" Lapham quotes founding father John Quincy Adams, who wrote in the 1820s about certain prospective émigrés and the requirements for success in the new world: "They must look forward to their posterity rather than backwards to their ancestors." Elsewhere in the same article, Lapham discusses the *invention* of self as an essential feature of the American character.

The problem in this *ex nihilo* notion of what it means to be an American is that it simply does not fit for the black American. Africans were brought violently to these shores, torn from a world in which individual identity formation was profoundly rooted in and inseparable from the collective ancestral heritage. Rather than seeking the invention of a new self, the new world African yearned backwards toward a barely remembered past when the self resonated with reflected value. African Americans, therefore, as both an individual and group necessity, have sought *recovery* of the past rather than discovery of the future.

In an unpublished memoir Mississippi scholar and blues poet Sterling Plumpp, whose Chicago years were simultaneous with Jonathan Green's, describes his own aesthetic, at once personal and inseparable from historical circumstance: "For me, blues has always been and will always be ancestral. It is my heritage. It is my legacy. It is my culture. . . . It is there among the pathos, gestures, uncertain rhythm of seasons, and deaf ears of heaven that I came to know Black life and my ancestral heritage. It is a specific lineage with strange places and exotic cosmologies. By the time I was born, already several generations had lived their lives out working the land and getting nothing in return except their tales and a will to live another day. They had been born, lived, left children and grandchildren behind by the time of my arrival. They had also taught, prayed, sung, danced, cried, hollered, and told their stories to one another, to neighbors, and even to strangers. . . . The blues stem from depths of Afro-American souls when uttered or gestured to combat something unbalanced or painful or threatening so as to control it, handle it, place it before the community in a lyrical expression of mastery."

It is this "lyrical expression of mastery" that Jonathan Green seemed to be struggling to call up in his work in the late 1970s when he first encountered the harsh gray realities of the urban north. The School of The Art Institute of Chicago was at that time firmly in the mainstream of modernism. The ideational scaffolding of ancestral heritage and recovery of communal life seemed romantic if not soft-headed and sentimental. Students were discouraged from such perspectives, encouraged to dismantle former constructs and to explore subject matter and art forms that were radically new. African American students who were desperately seeking to root themselves in an imagined African past were urged to turn away from these concerns and to engage the abstract, the nonrepresentational, the avant-garde. This tension between the aggregate resource of one's own lived experience, frequently rural and homogeneous, and the challenge to become an artist within a contemporary urban context presented black students at SAIC and other such institutions with particular difficulties. With diminished opportunity for self-reflectiveness through positive role models and lacking a forum for shared cultural perspectives, many black students found themselves clinging together. Although this communality strengthened them in some ways, it also tempted them to reject some of what the larger campus experience might add to their skills and knowledge.

This situation was potentially dangerous, especially for the growing, developing black artist. Any artist has a need to define and understand whatever might be meant by the term *self,* because the act of art-making is necessarily one of self-investigation. Further, artists need to develop clear social and cultural perspectives, to engage and to think about the larger world. Between these poles of self and other, the tasks of educating oneself as an artist are multiple. An art student must develop technical knowledge, skill, and aesthetic aptitude; he or she must learn art history, that of others as well as that indigenous to one's own background. Art education should expose students to the best artistic products of Western and pre-Western civilizations, as well as to the sociohistorical contexts of both; students should have access to fine museums and to good contemporary galleries representing widely diverse traditions; there should be contact with stimulating, innovative visiting artists and opportunities for students to engage in creative dialogue about new issues as well as about enduring, classical questions.

Green's experience at SAIC fits all of the criteria described above. The School in the 1970s was central to the growth and development of some of the most exciting African American artists working today. Among them are sculptor Lorenzo Pace, painters Robert Dilworth and Maurice Wilson, fiber artist Venus Blue, and painter-photographer Leslee Stadford. These students worked and learned within an atmosphere of great paradox. The School was a place of incredible artistic ferment and tremendous excitement, and yet black students had to overcome their sense of alienation and even loneliness. Sympathetic faculty such as painter Tony Phillips, Rufino Silva and his wife Iola Rigacci, visual anthropologist Marilyn Houlberg, and art therapist Don Seiden were important influences for Green. Nonetheless, there were only two full-time black visual artists on the faculty. Frank DeBose, a visual communications expert, nurtured many students, and expressionist painter Emilio Cruz brought New York sensibilities and a level of intellectual inquiry that were stimulating to nearly all SAIC students, not just to the young black students who sat at his feet and patterned their lexicons, both visual and verbal, after his. Among part-time faculty, Barbara Jones-Hogu, a member of the Chicago school of the 1960s known as the Africobra movement, brought a politically conscious dimension to SAIC, and artist and critic Keith Morrison visited and encouraged many students.

Beyond these and a few other exceptions, the vocabulary and history of black America seemed largely unreflected, and there were few opportunities to study African American art. Almost as few options for serious study of African art existed. Socially, although the gallery scene was burgeoning, black students felt isolated from many of the contemporary shows passing through the city.

Jonathan Green experienced some of this isolation. As a displaced southerner, removed from the sights and sounds that had constituted the bedrock of his artistic sources, Green found himself in a time of self-questioning and redefinition. Impelled by a ceaseless artistic curiosity, he investigated all of Chicago's art worlds. He speaks of his time in Chicago as "one big discovery." In ever widening circles, he met numbers of citizens active in Chicago's civic life, including Essee Kupcinet, wife of the journalist Irv Kupcinet. With Essee's encouragement, Green became an active supporter of the Chicago Academy, a private high school for students seeking to become professionals in the fields of visual and performing arts. Later he met several important Chicago patrons of the arts, including the collector Ruth Horwich, who took an interest in his work. All the while, he was studying intensely. As a student in my classes, Green immersed himself in the imaginative literatures of Africa and the Caribbean, Mexico and South America. Class discussions explored both literary considerations and their ideological contexts. Students examined questions designed to help them think about their own lives within a wider cultural framework, questions such as how individual identities and personal visions are formed within close-knit traditional communities; how communal undergirdings can collapse as individualism emerges; how universal mythologies can be imaged in local manifestations; how conflicting value systems can add both positive and negative tension to cultural expression. Such contextual reflection was useful for artists-in-the-making, providing a language structure for locating and naming that elusive thing called identity. As Anna Deavere Smith has remarked in *Fires in the Mirror,* "In America identity is always being negotiated; . . . the inevitable tension in America is the tension of identity in motion, the tension of identity in contrast with an old idea, but a resonant idea, of America."

For black people, becoming American has been less about Lewis Lapham's invention of self than about the integration of past, present, and future. For us, the experience of America has been less what Lapham termed "a hopeful pilgrimage" than a fearful canoe trip, weighted with ancestral memory and with, frequently, only a drinking gourd constellation of stars to guide us. We have felt, as a people, the tenuous but magnetic pull of assimilation's inevitable cultural syncretism; we have known its disappointments, imaged by Marcus Garvey's resonating calls to make the journey back to African homelands. For us, the need and commitment to preserve that which is culturally specific, indigenous—if you will, pure—informs the task of our artists. The group's understanding of itself is imaged by our artists who, by taking events *out* of history and giving them form, can help us to create pragmatic formal meanings for living *within* history.

What has helped to sustain and shape our self-understandings through centuries of suffering and survival? An image system from Old Testament poetry; a profound sense of transcendence over unimaginable odds; a respect for history and for lessons of the past much deeper than any academic understanding can communicate; a delight in children and an appreciation for the wisdom of our elders; a love for the word, a love of color and music and dance; an ability to laugh in the worst of circumstances, and, at the other end of the spectrum, enough pragmatism to know that, in the words of an old black spiritual, "we gotta keep moving until we move on in."

We have, inevitably, a profound need to remember. In the theological sense, this re/membering is about both recollection and the putting back together of that which has been severed. Our memory bank is in large part in the eyes and hands of our artists. Africans and African Americans have an inherent and irrevocable respect for our artists. We respect them because our lives are less about *discovery* than about *recovery*. We respect them because we know that it is artists who carry the truthful messages of the past and the prophetic possibilities of our futures. We do not see our artists as marginal iconoclasts to be tolerated; we *need* them in order to know who we were and who we are. It is our artists who create the semantic space within which these revelations occur. The African consciousness emerged within cultures of revelation, if you will, shamanistic cultures. As contemporary shamans, our artists have the vocation to create a climate for understanding, even for healing. They are the mediators and prophets, the listeners and truthsayers in whom we invest the cultural authority to speak.

Jonathan Green is just such a truth teller. His paintings function as a marriage of the communal and the personal, the conceptual and the experiential. His skill, his gift, is to take images of ordinariness, filter them through his metaphoric lens, and return them to us as extraordinary icons of our heritage. He inverts the contemporary polarization self and other, removing his Gullah subjects from the marginality assigned by modernity to their own self-defined centrality. The paintings of Jonathan Green strip the encounter between the larger world and his simple rural subjects from any limiting connotations of social hierarchy, drawing the viewer into authentic and enlarging human contact: in the words of W. E. B. Du Bois from *The Souls of Black Folk,* "these crooked marks on a fragile leaf . . . turn the tangle straight."

The work of Jonathan Green presents us with a new world of cultural, ideological, and creative parity, an America re/membered and reimagined, a vision formed in the sun-saturated colors of South Carolina and refined amid the gray stone fortresses of Chicago. His luminous paintings affirm his early beginnings and the winnowing years; as viewers we reap the harvest of darkness and light in true and delicate balance.

Gullah Images

The Art of Jonathan Green

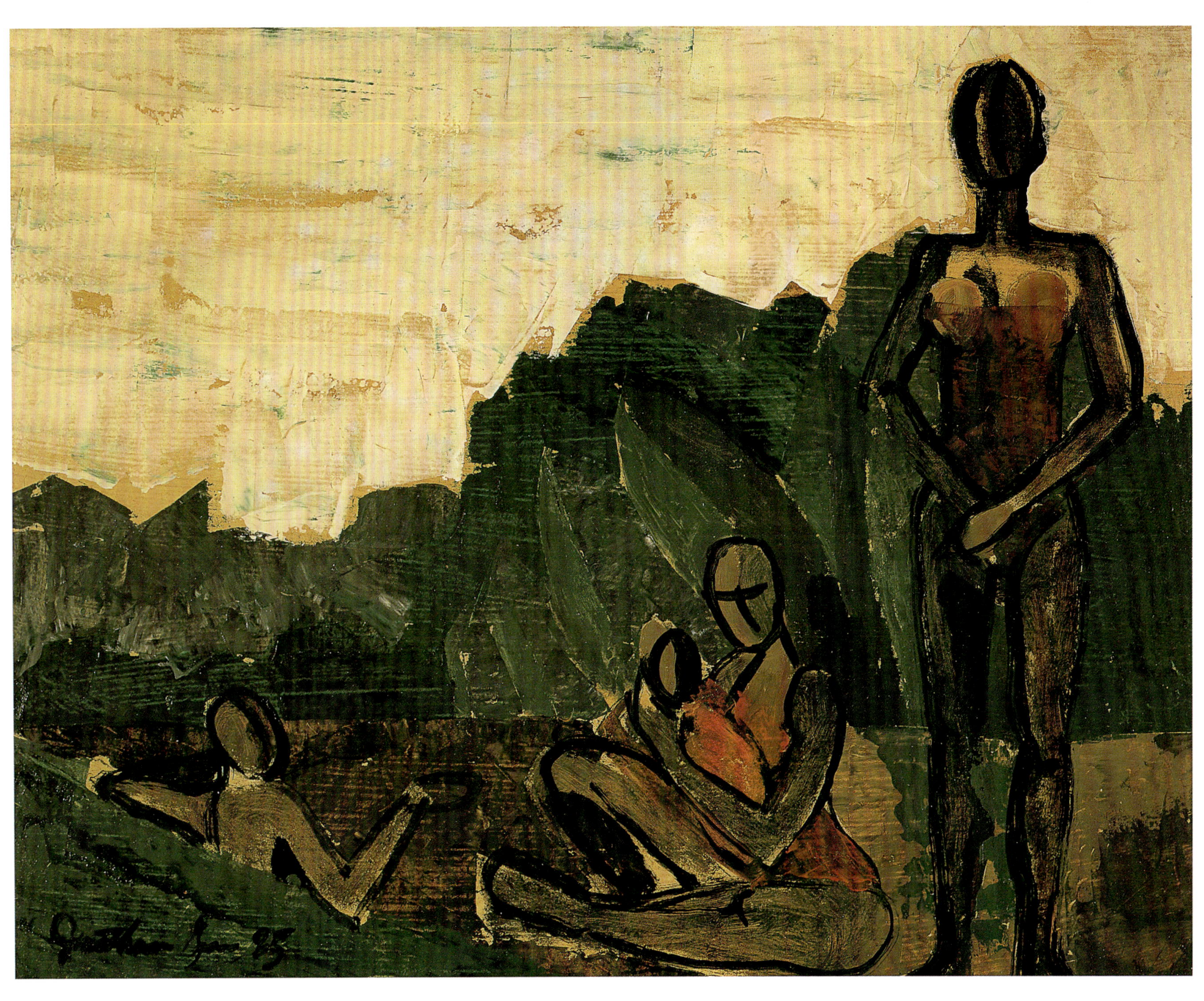

Family, 1985. Oil on masonite, 11 x 15".
Collection of the artist. Photograph by Tim Stamm.

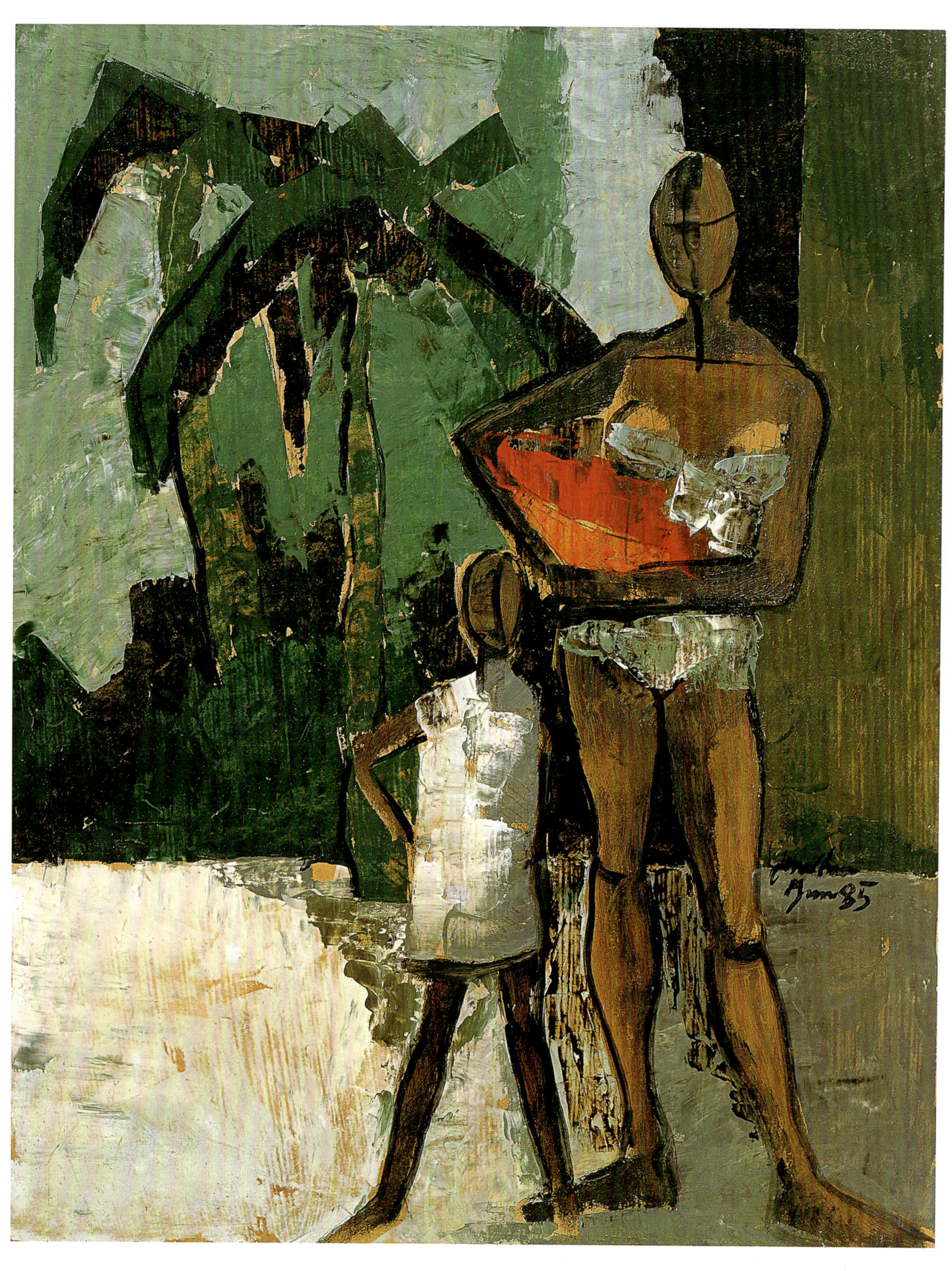

Fruit Pickers, 1985. Oil on masonite, 14 x 12".
Courtesy of Tra Halloway Boxer. Photograph by Tim Stamm.

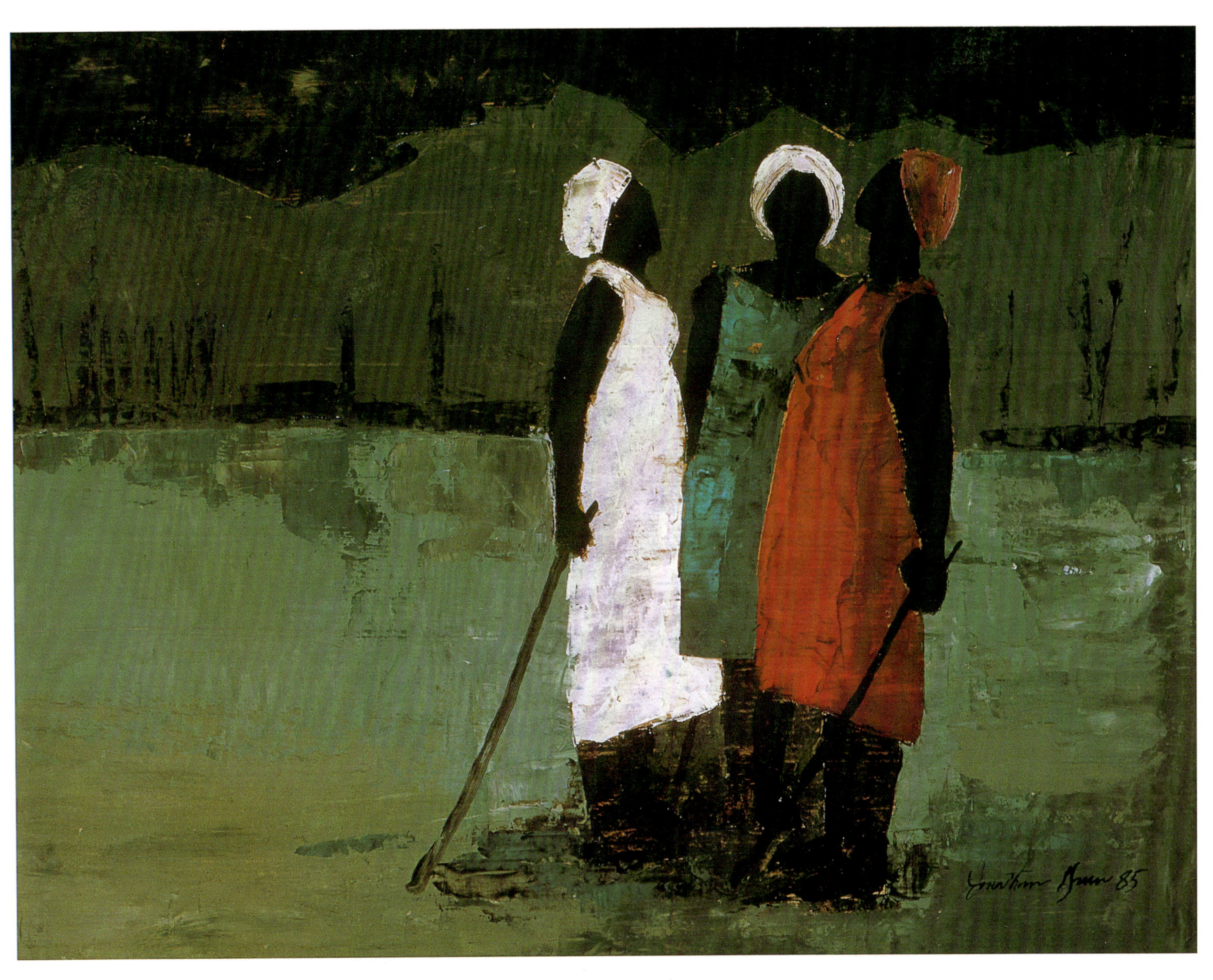

Three Sisters, 1985. Oil on masonite, 11 x 14".
Courtesy of Richard Weedman. Photograph by Tim Stamm.

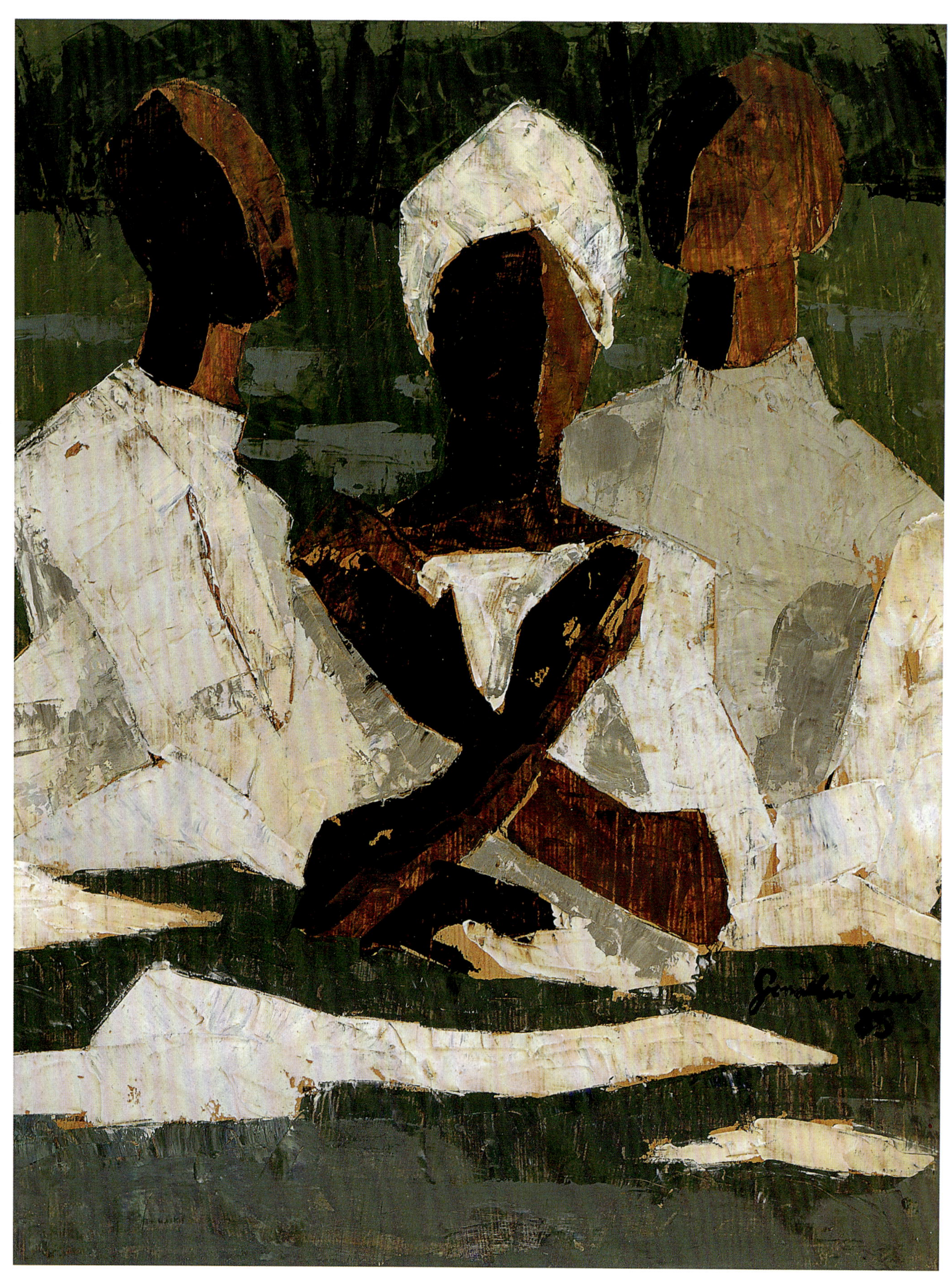

The Baptism, 1985. Oil on masonite, 14 x 11".
Collection of the artist. Photograph by Tim Stamm.

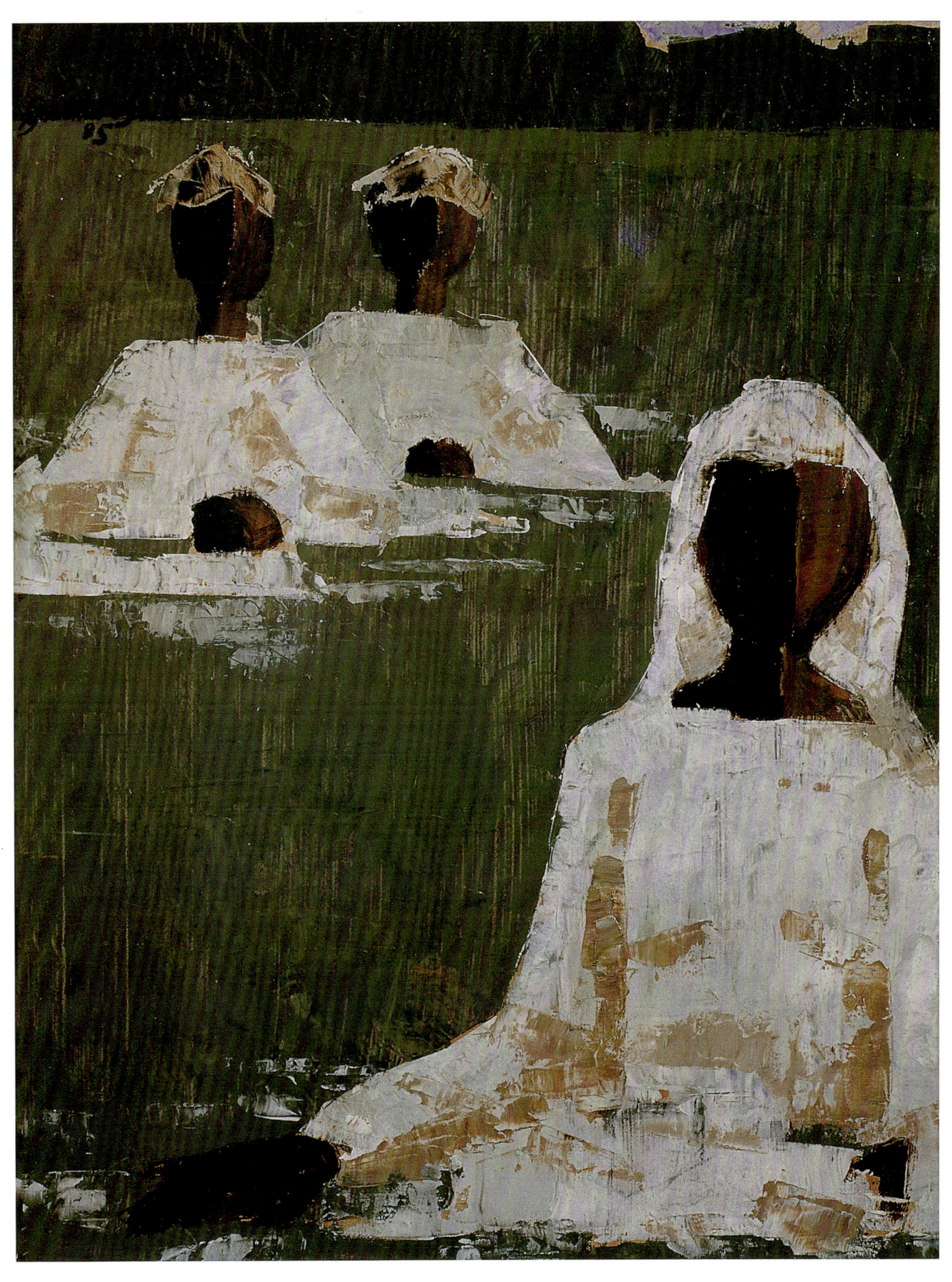

River Baptism, 1985. Oil on masonite, 14 x 11".
Courtesy of Tracy Schalk. Photograph by Tim Stamm.

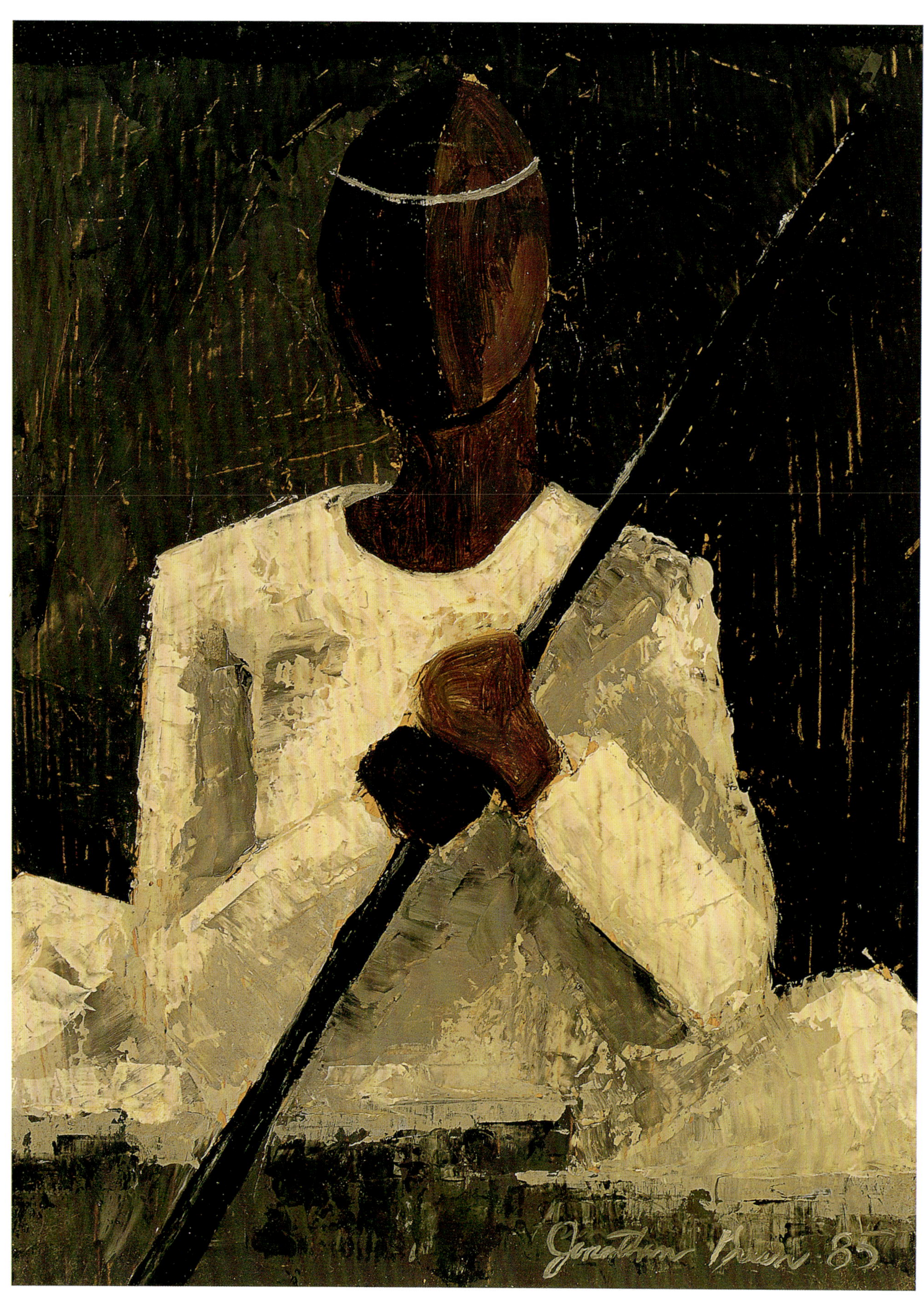

The Poleman, 1985. Oil on masonite, 8 x 6".
Courtesy of Julia J. Norrell. Photograph by Tim Stamm.

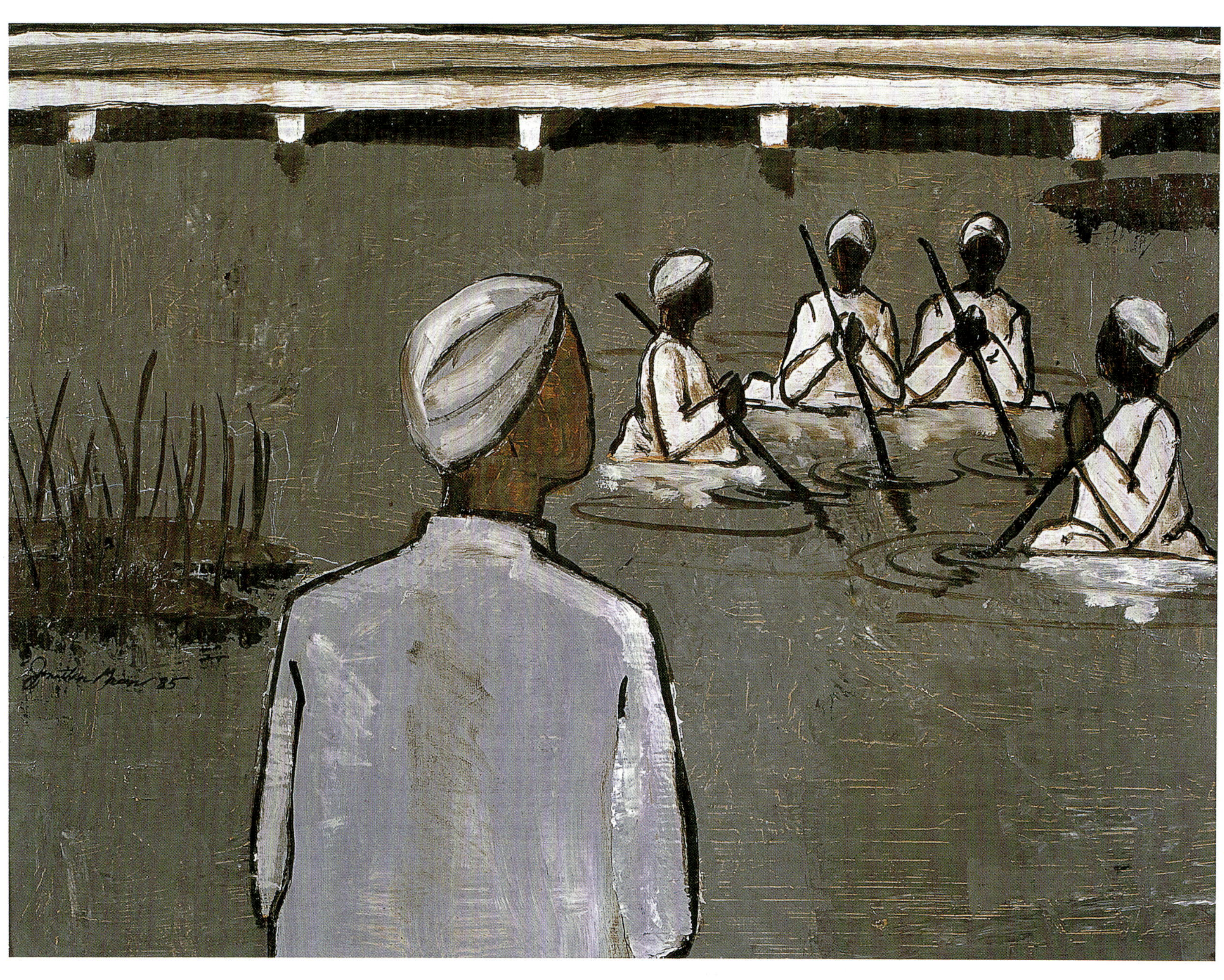

Baptism by the Bridge, 1985. Oil on masonite, 16 x 22".
Courtesy of Bernadette Anderson. Photograph by Tim Stamm.

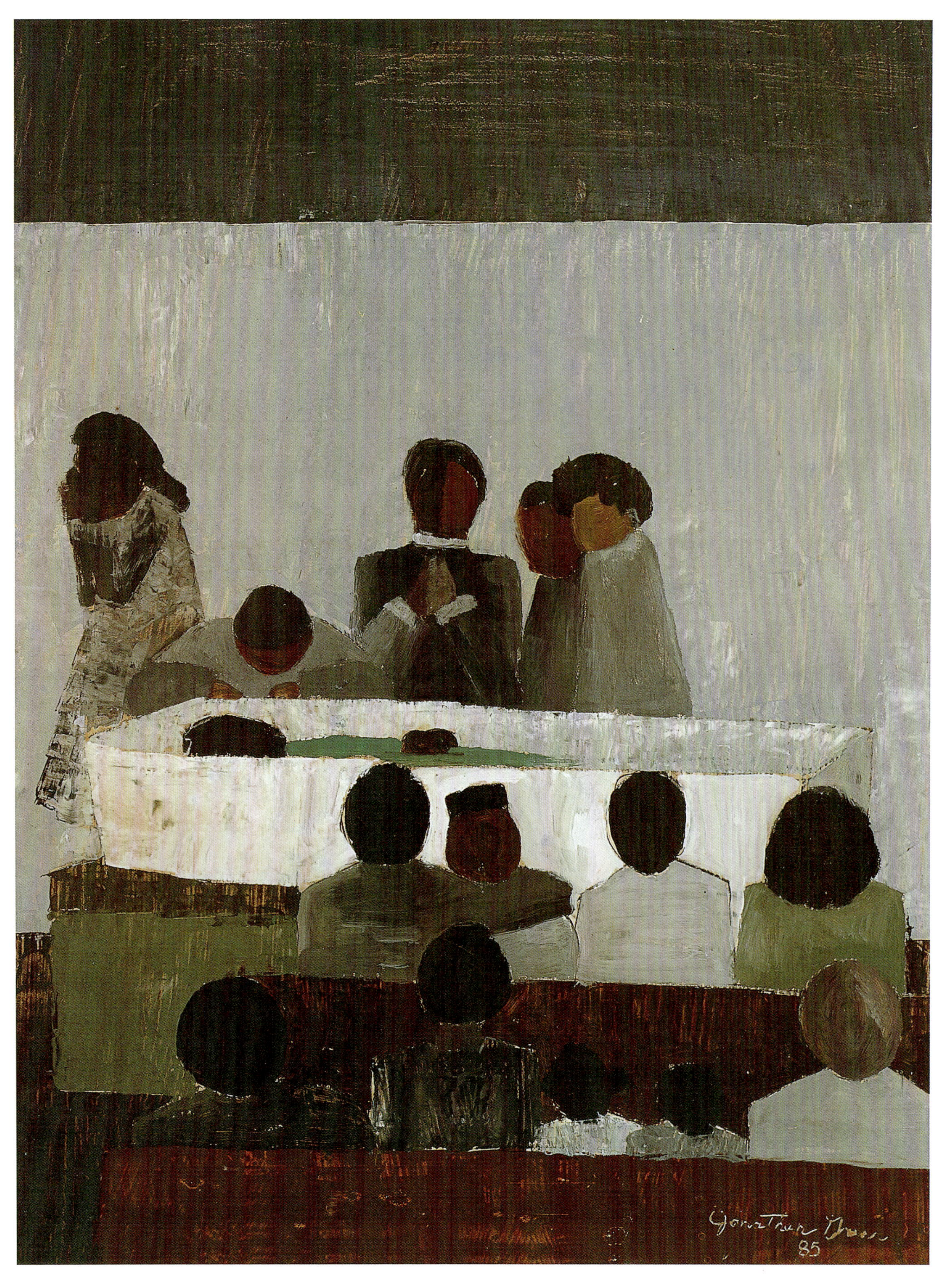

The Wake, 1985. Oil on masonite, 18 x 11".
Courtesy of Michael and Mary James. Photograph by Katherine Wetzel.

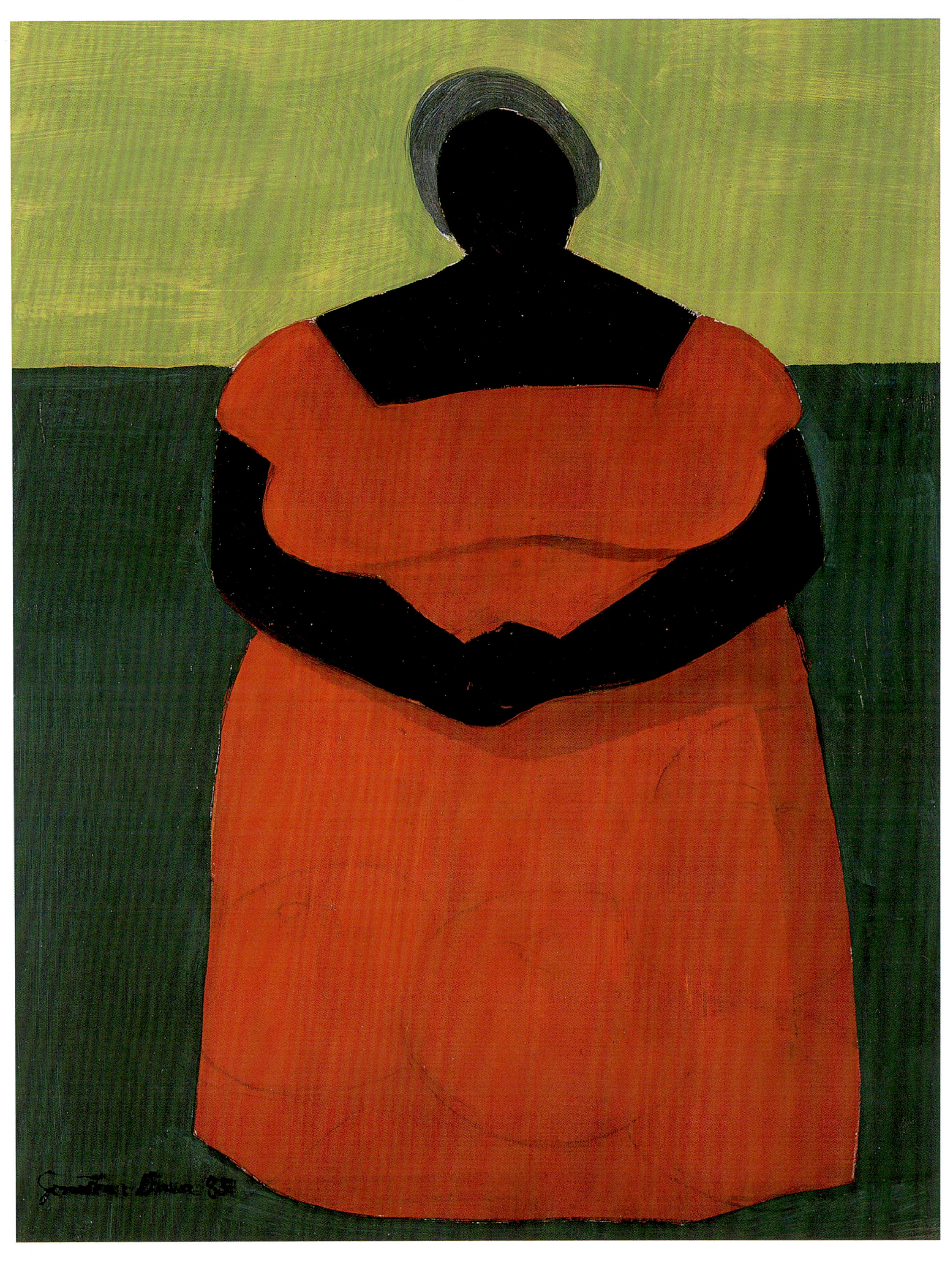

Woman in Red, 1985. Oil on masonite, 12 x 10".
Courtesy of Michael and Mary James. Photograph by Tim Stamm.

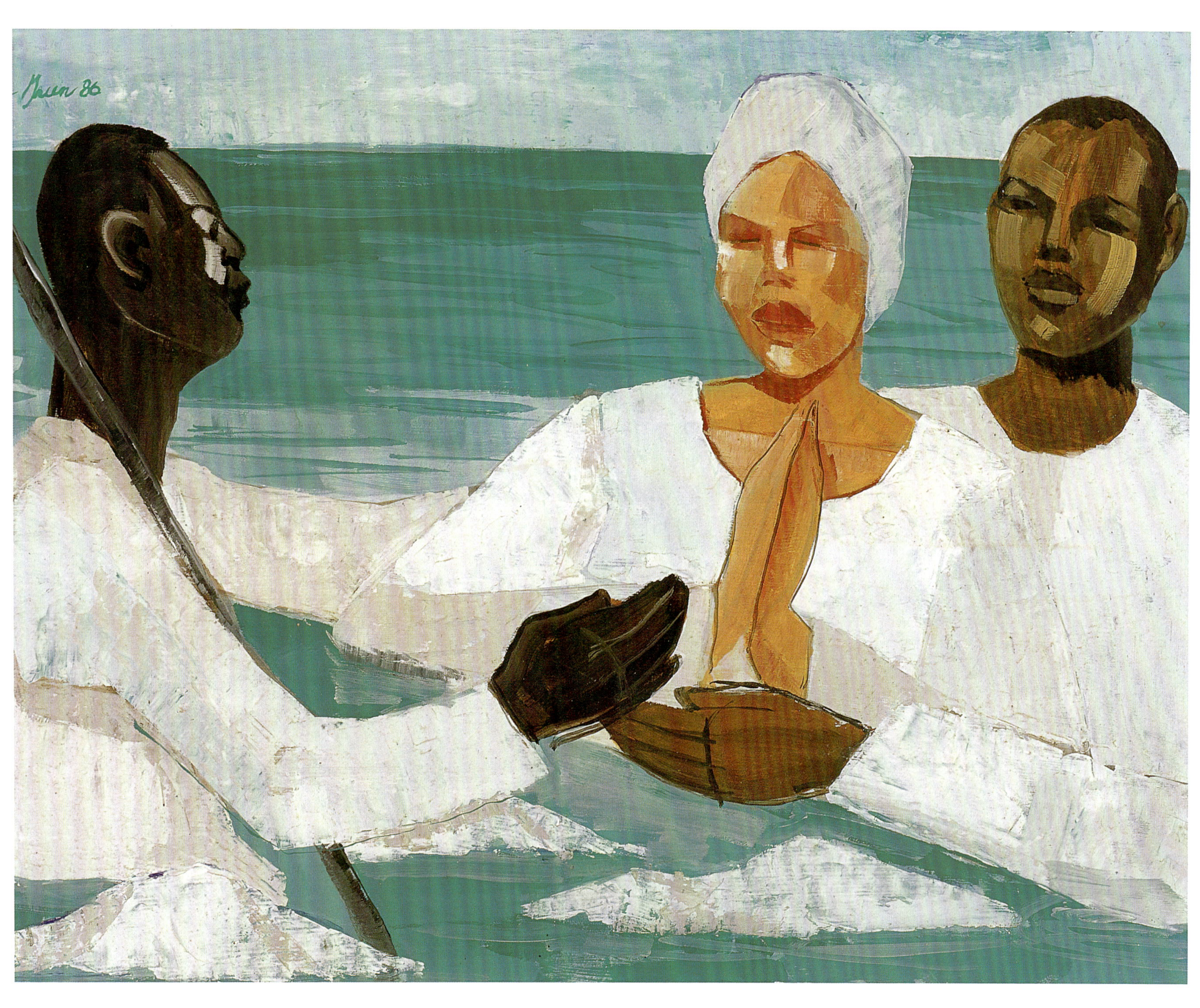

Baptism of Susie Mae, 1986. Oil on masonite, 16 x 20".
Courtesy of Ruth J. Green. Photograph by Katherine Wetzel.

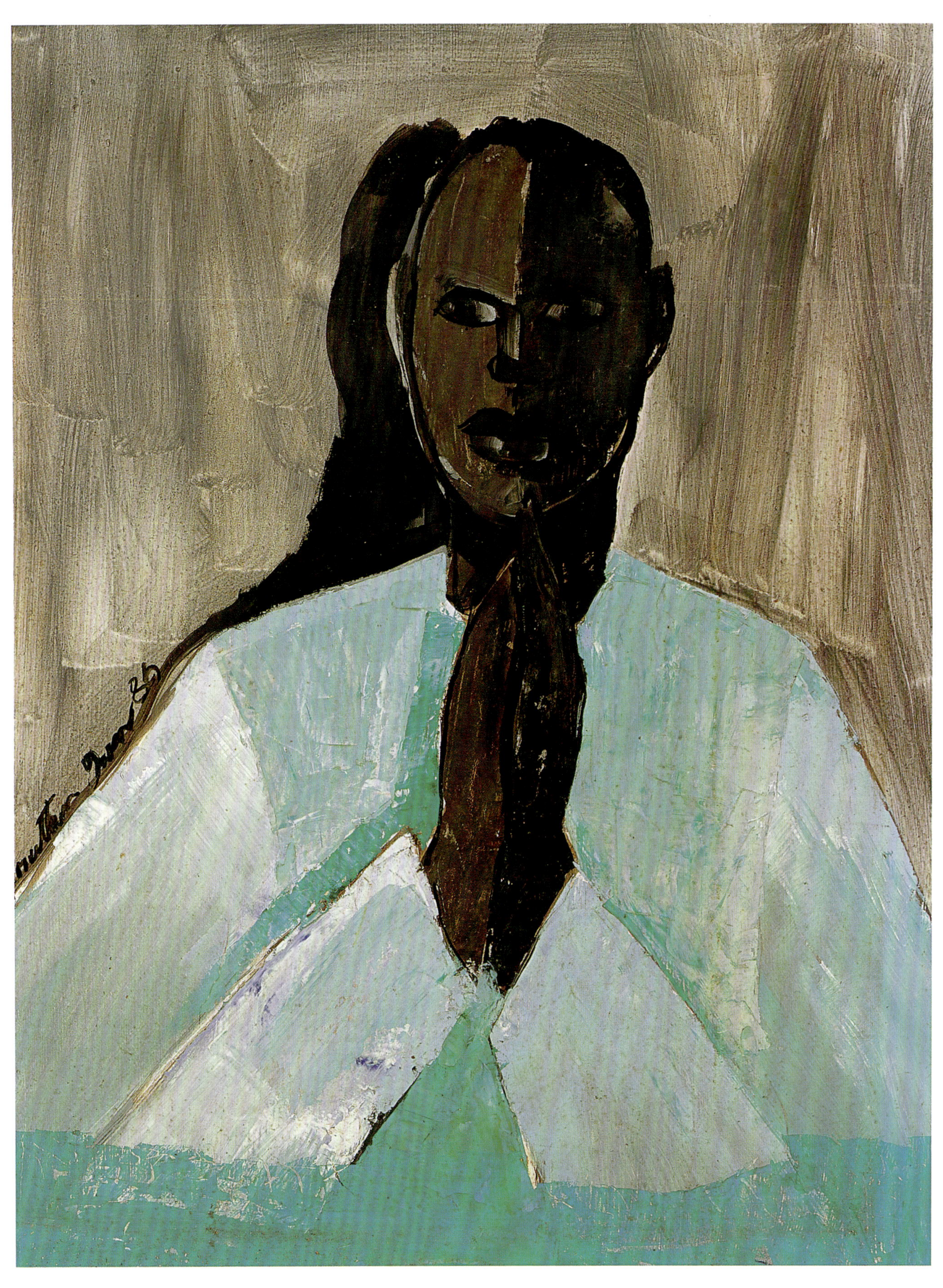

David, 1986. Oil on masonite, 18 x 15".
Courtesy of Annette Green. Photograph by Tim Stamm.

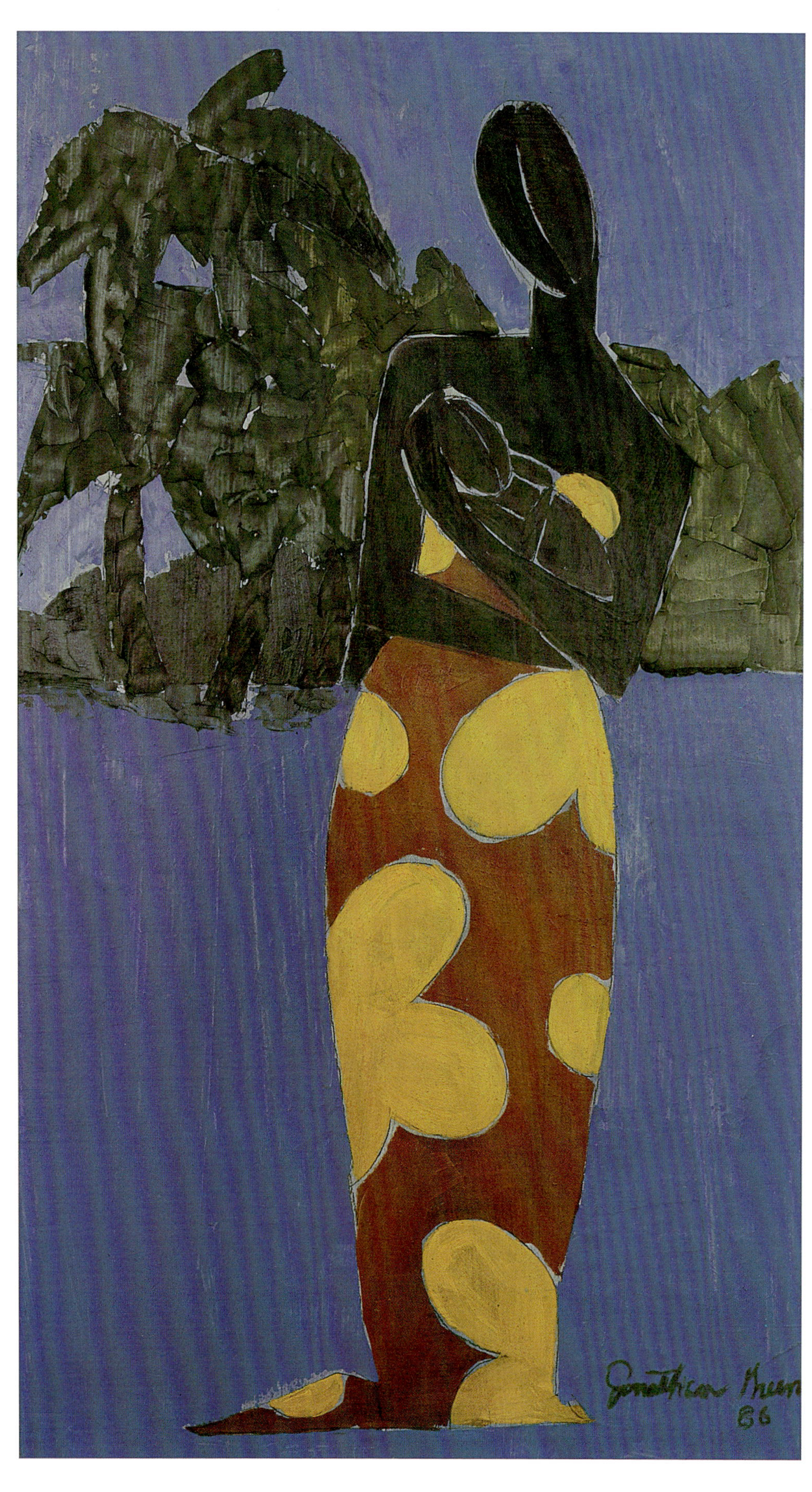

Woman and Child, 1986. Oil on masonite, 19 x 12".
Courtesy of Sam and Dona Scott. Photograph by Isadore Howard.

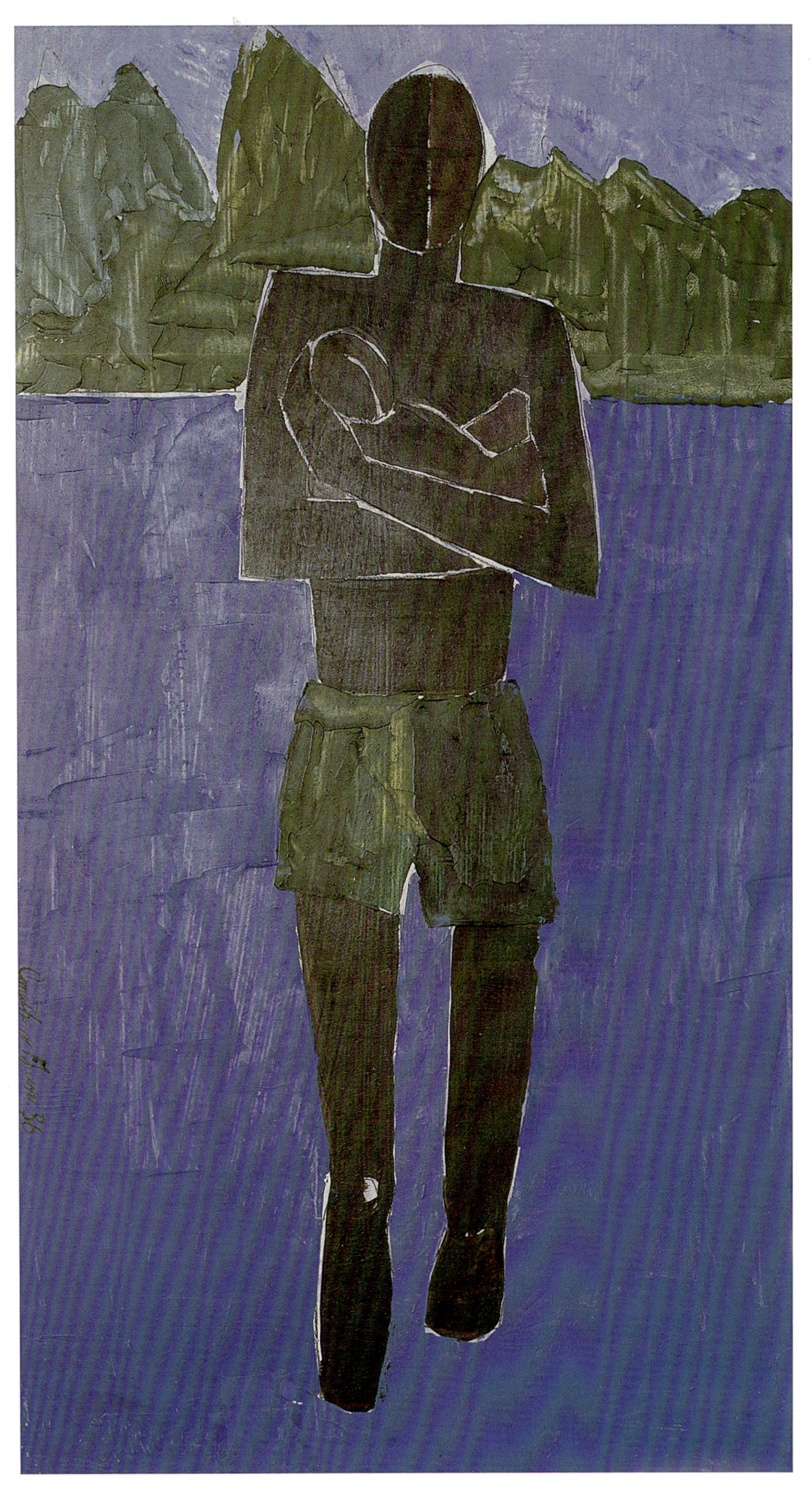

Man and Child, 1986. Oil on masonite, 19 x 12".
Courtesy of Sam and Dona Scott. Photograph by Isadore Howard.

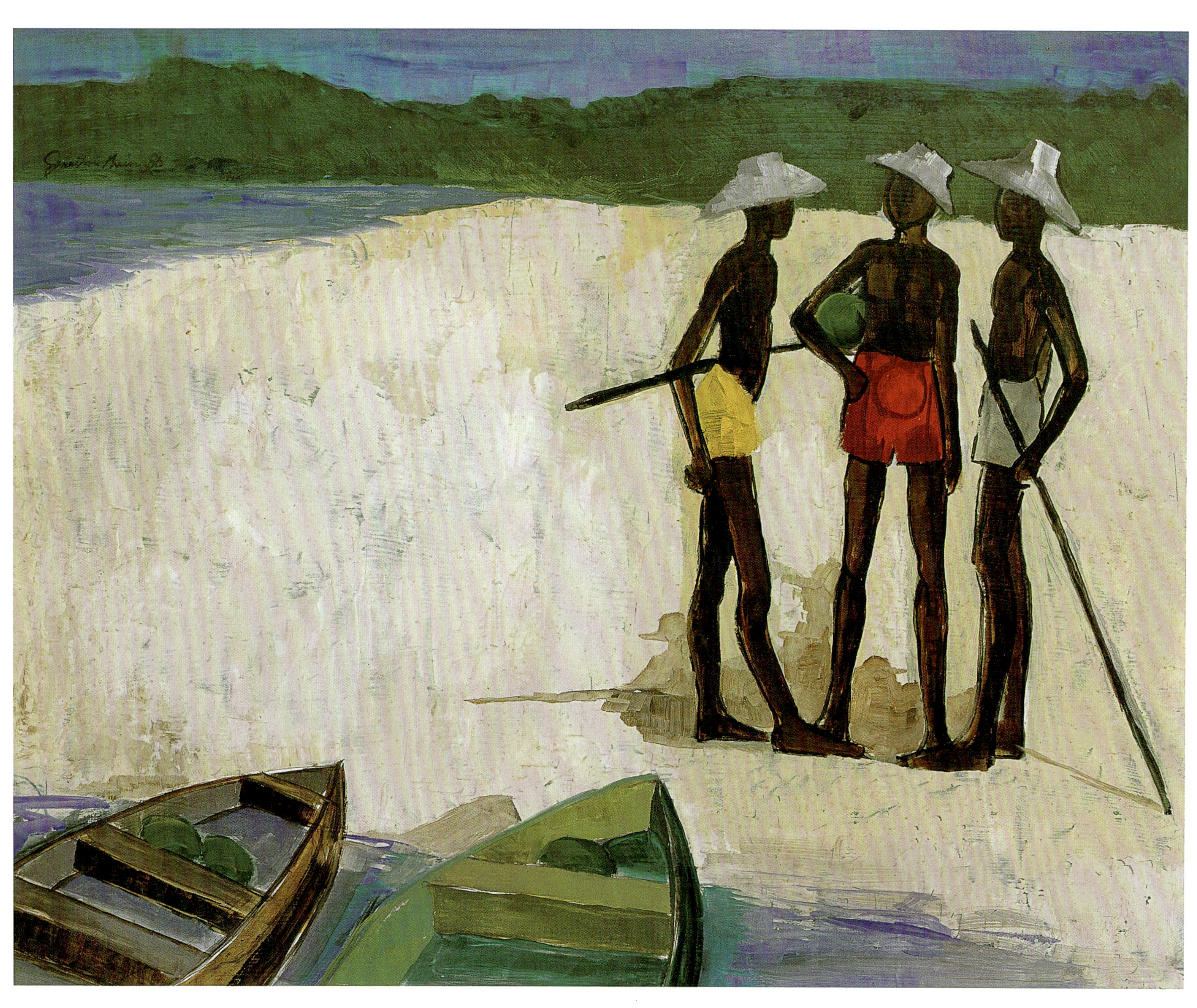

Boat Men, 1986. Oil on masonite, 16 x 20".
Courtesy of Norman E. Pendergraft. Photograph by Tim Stamm.

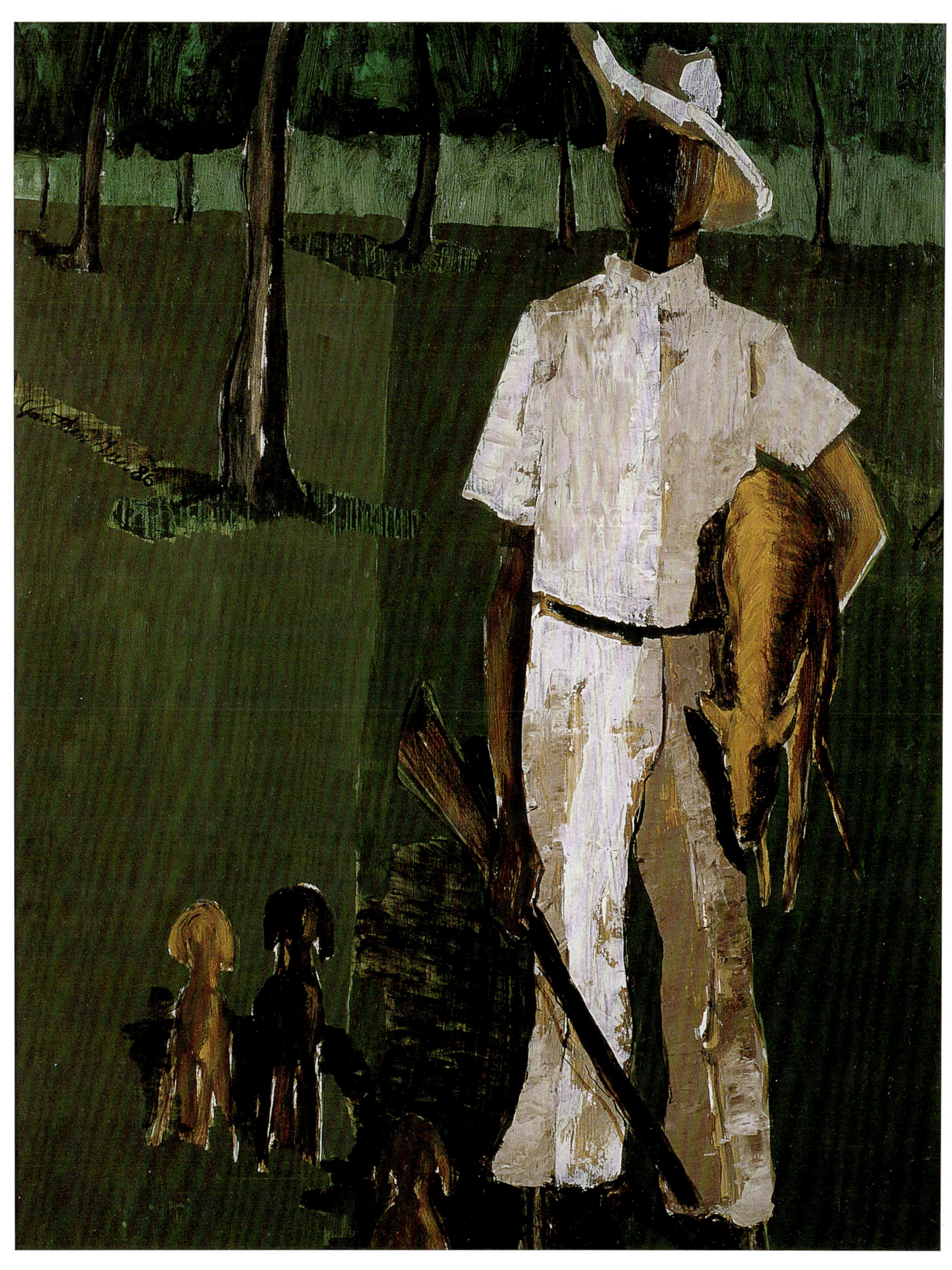

Low Country Hunter, 1986. Oil on masonite, 20 x 16".
Courtesy of Mary E. Stewart. Photograph by Tim Stamm.

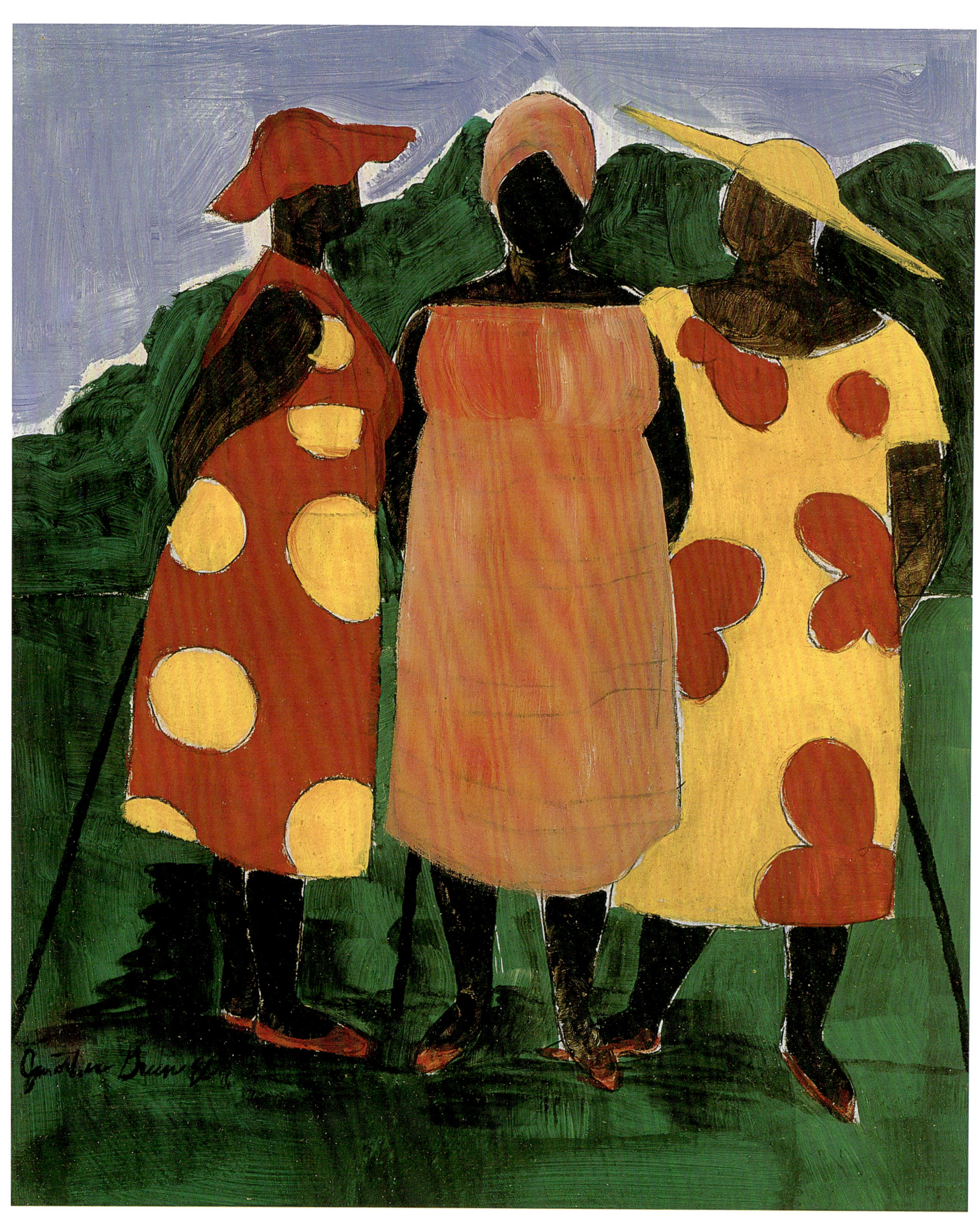

Three Neighbors, 1986. Oil on masonite, 14 x 11".
Courtesy of Dori Wilson. Photograph by John Riley.

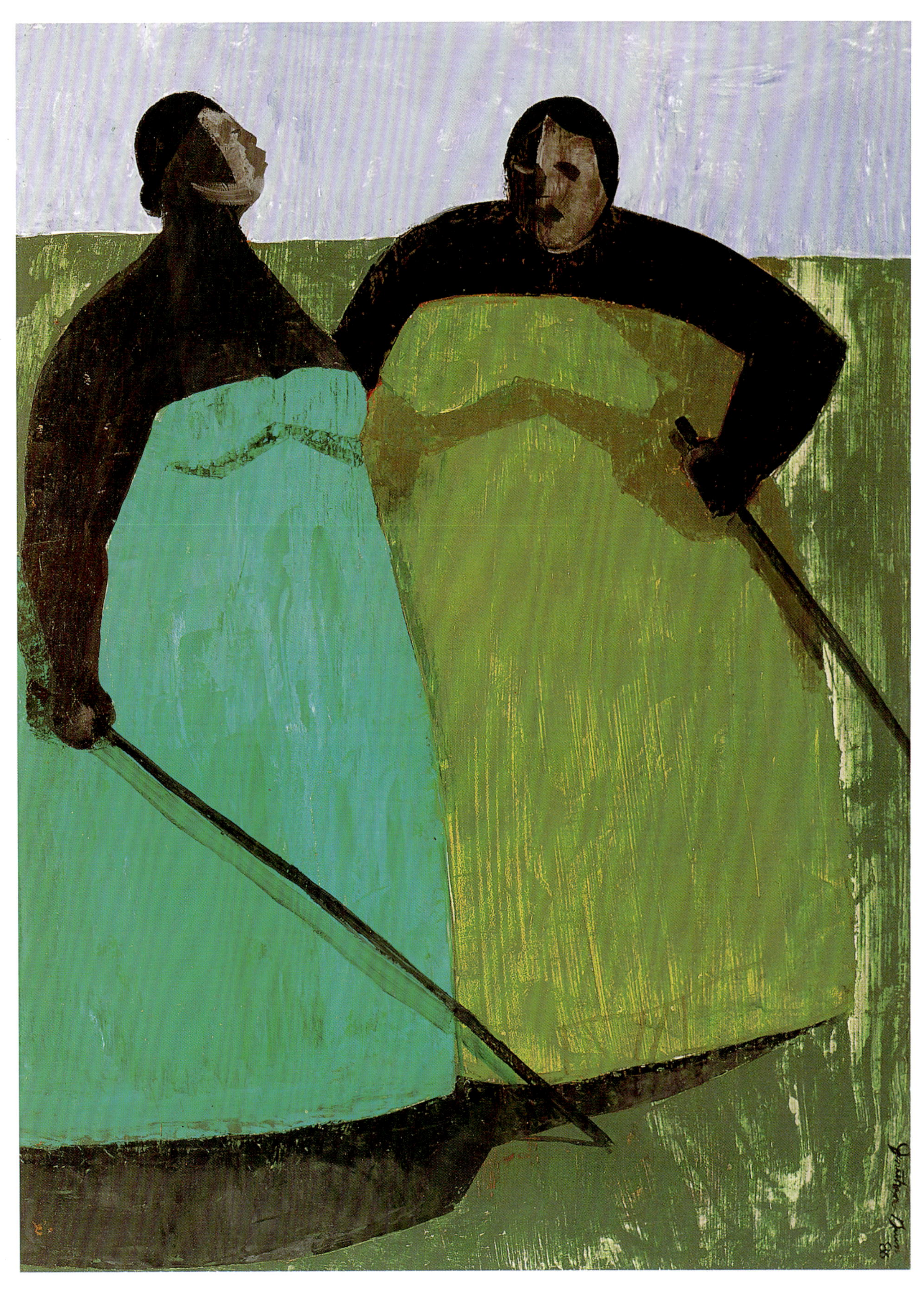

Sisters, 1986. Oil on masonite, 24 x 18".
Courtesy of Mary Mack. Photograph by Tim Stamm.

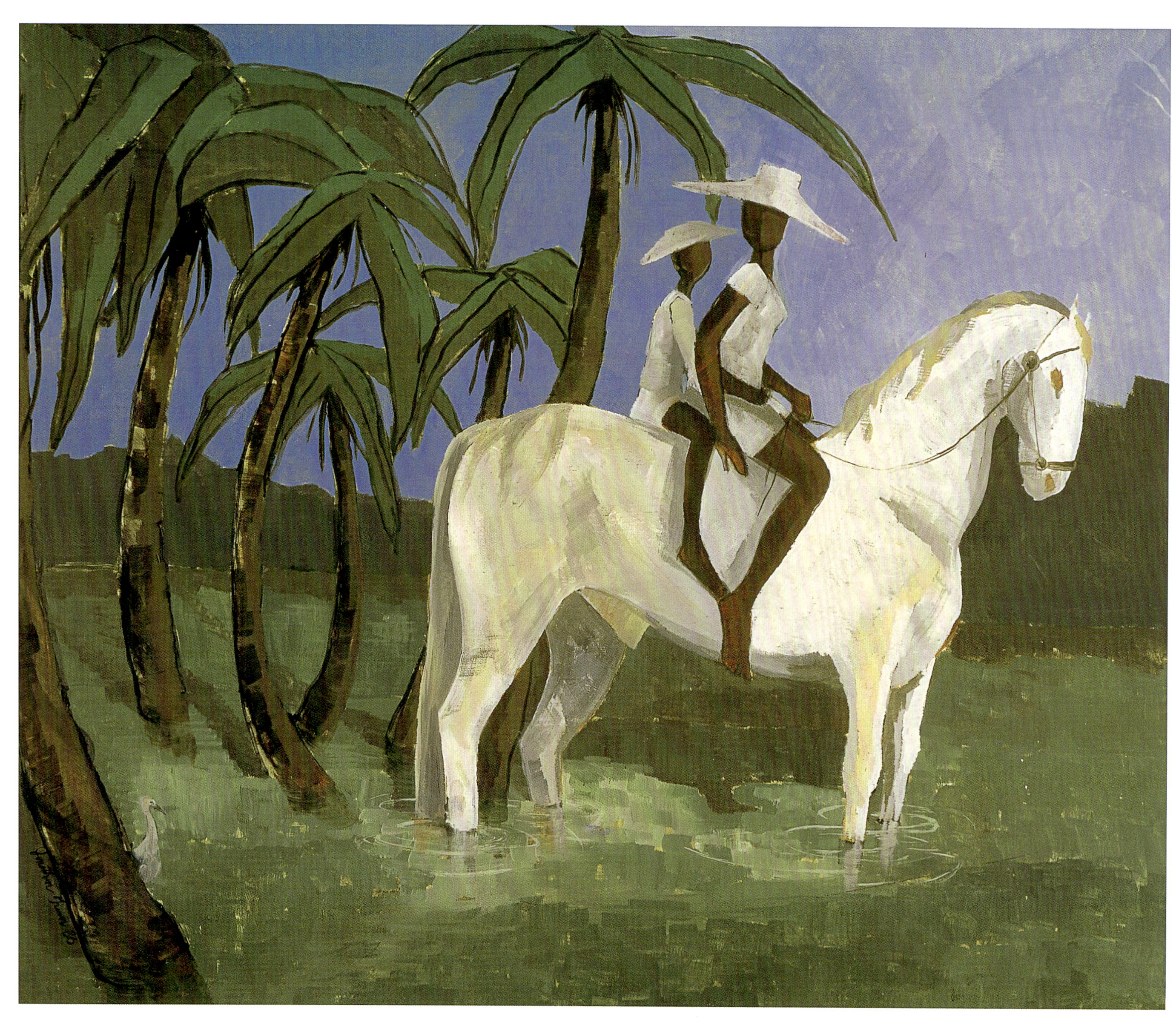

Youths on White Horse, 1986. Oil on masonite, 14 x 18".
Courtesy of Richard Weedman. Photograph by Tim Stamm.

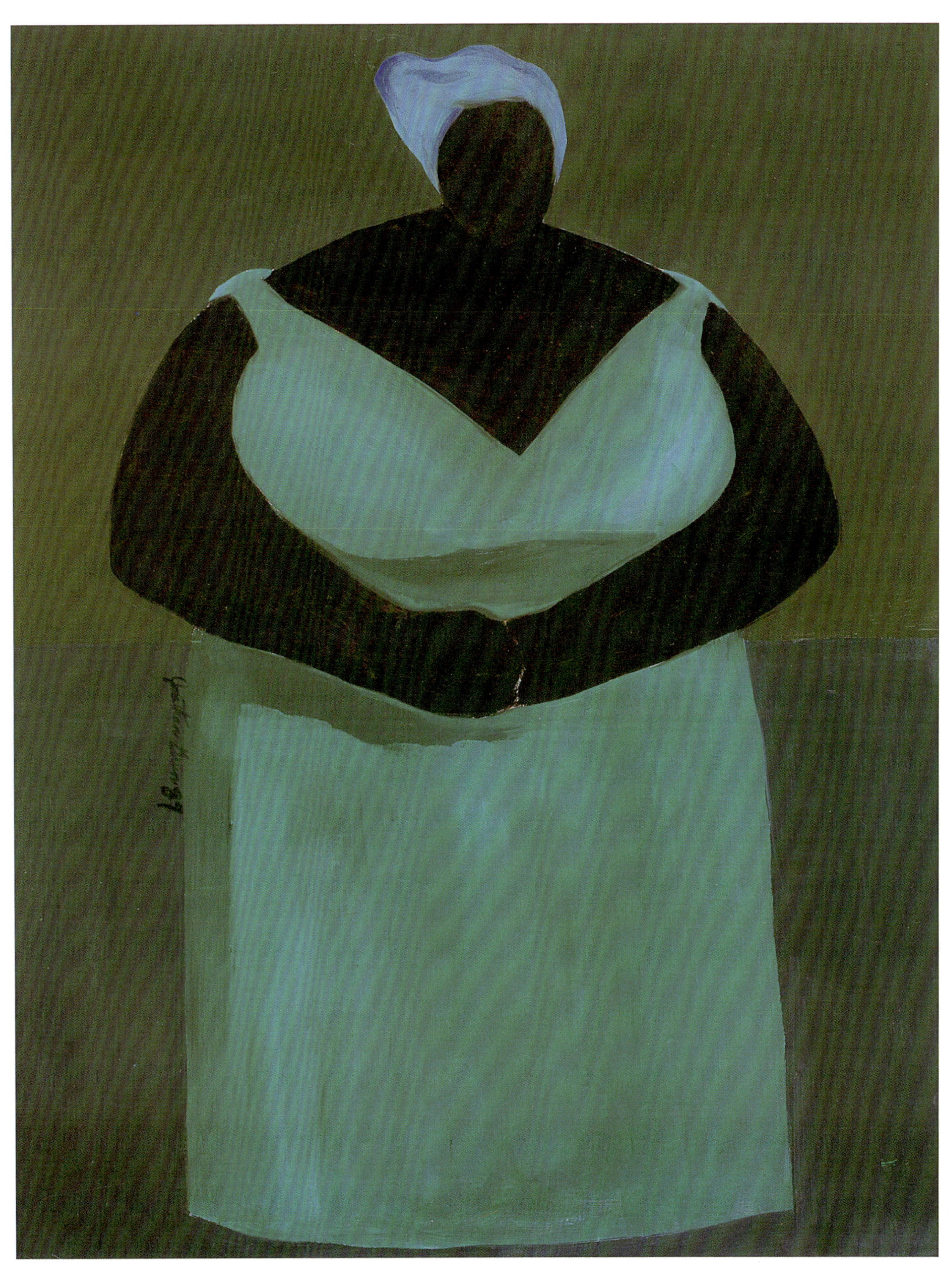

Recital, 1987. Oil on masonite, 22 x 20".
Courtesy of Diane Chandler. Photograph by Tim Stamm.

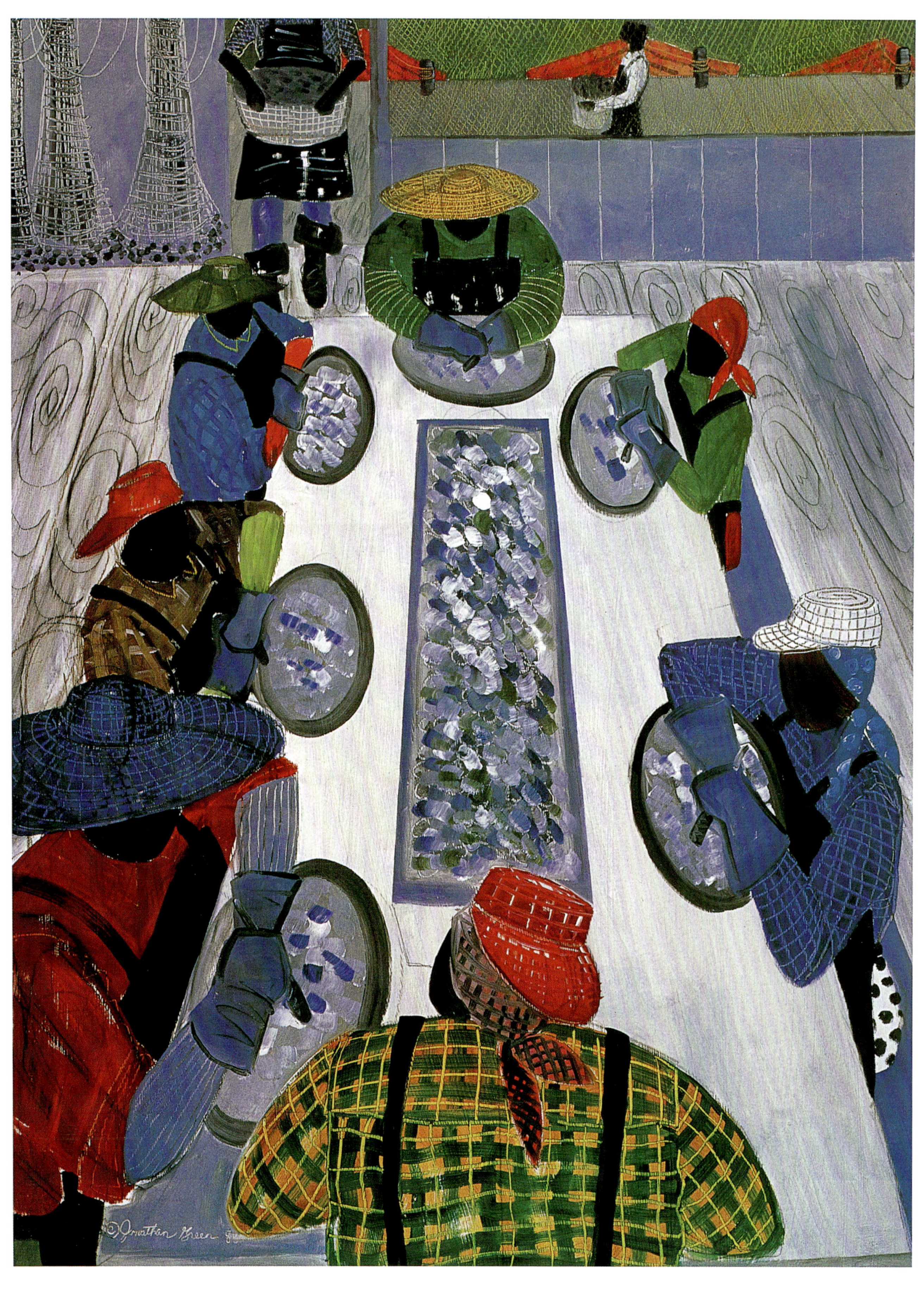

Shucking Oysters, 1988. Oil on masonite, 32 x 24".
Private Collection. Photograph by Tim Stamm.

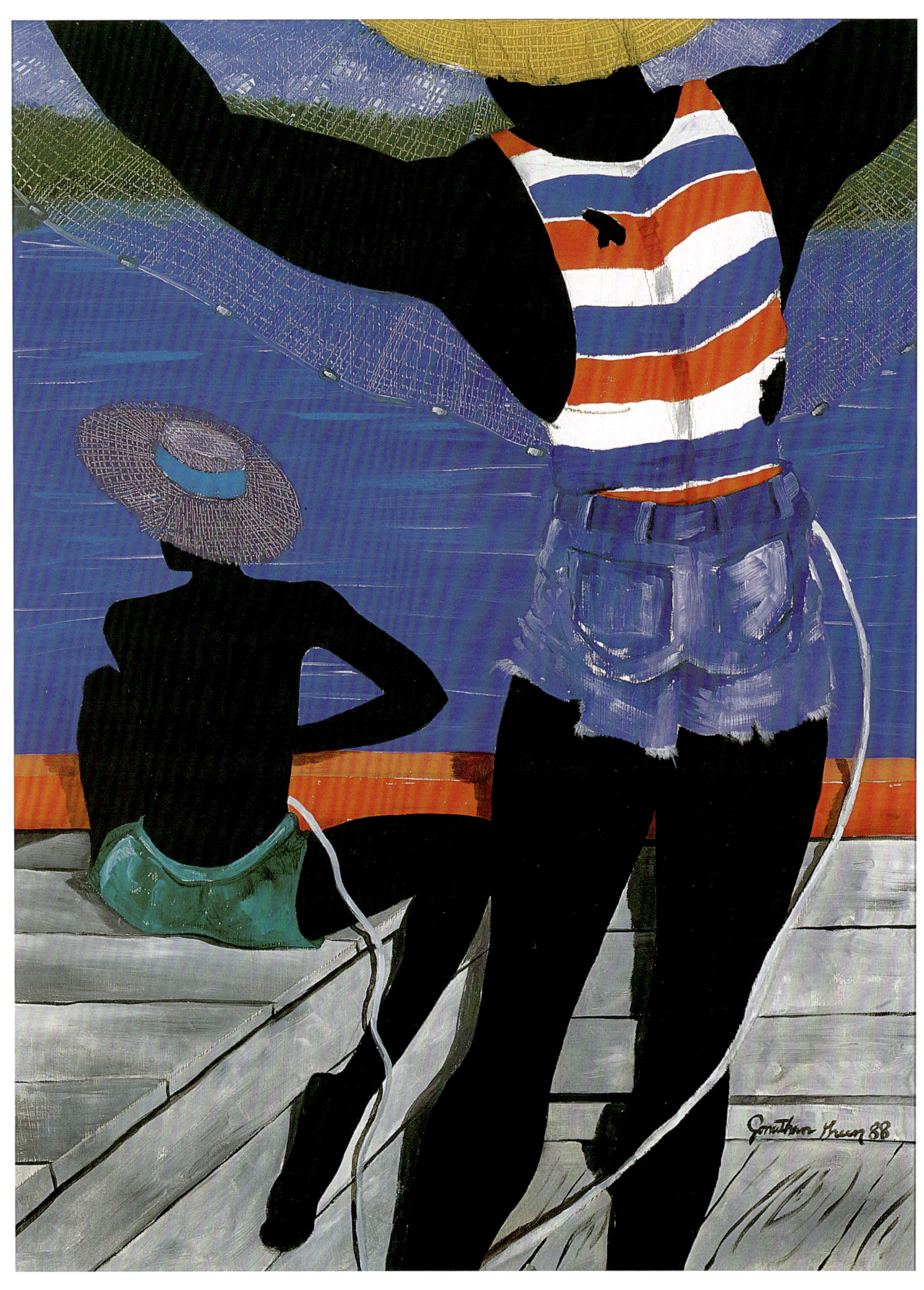

Fishing, 1988. Oil on masonite, 32 x 24".
Courtesy of Mr. and Mrs. Gerald Hillian. Photograph by Katherine Wetzel.

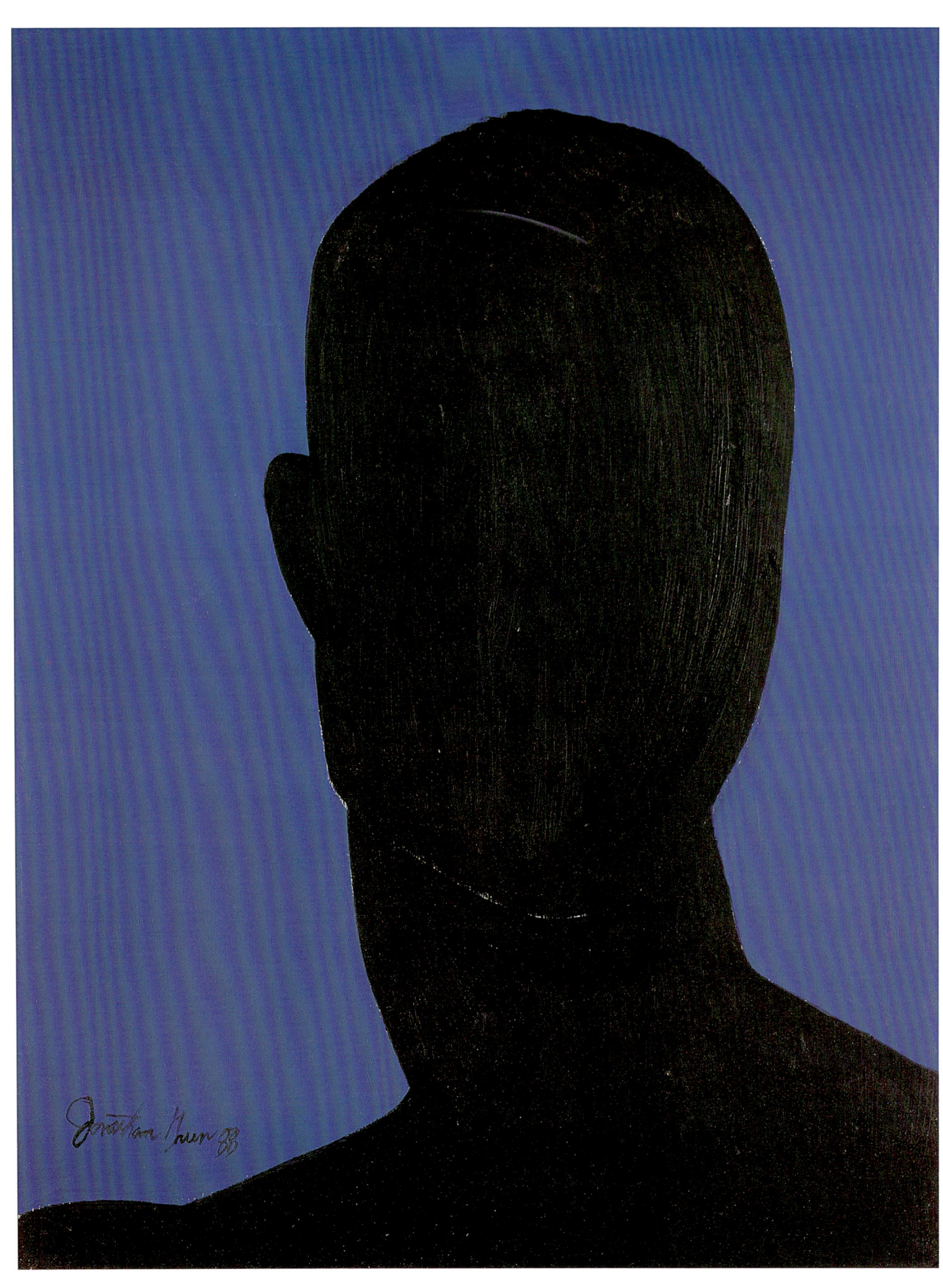

Neptune, 1988. Oil on canvas, 14 x 11".
Collection of the artist. Photograph by Tim Stamm.

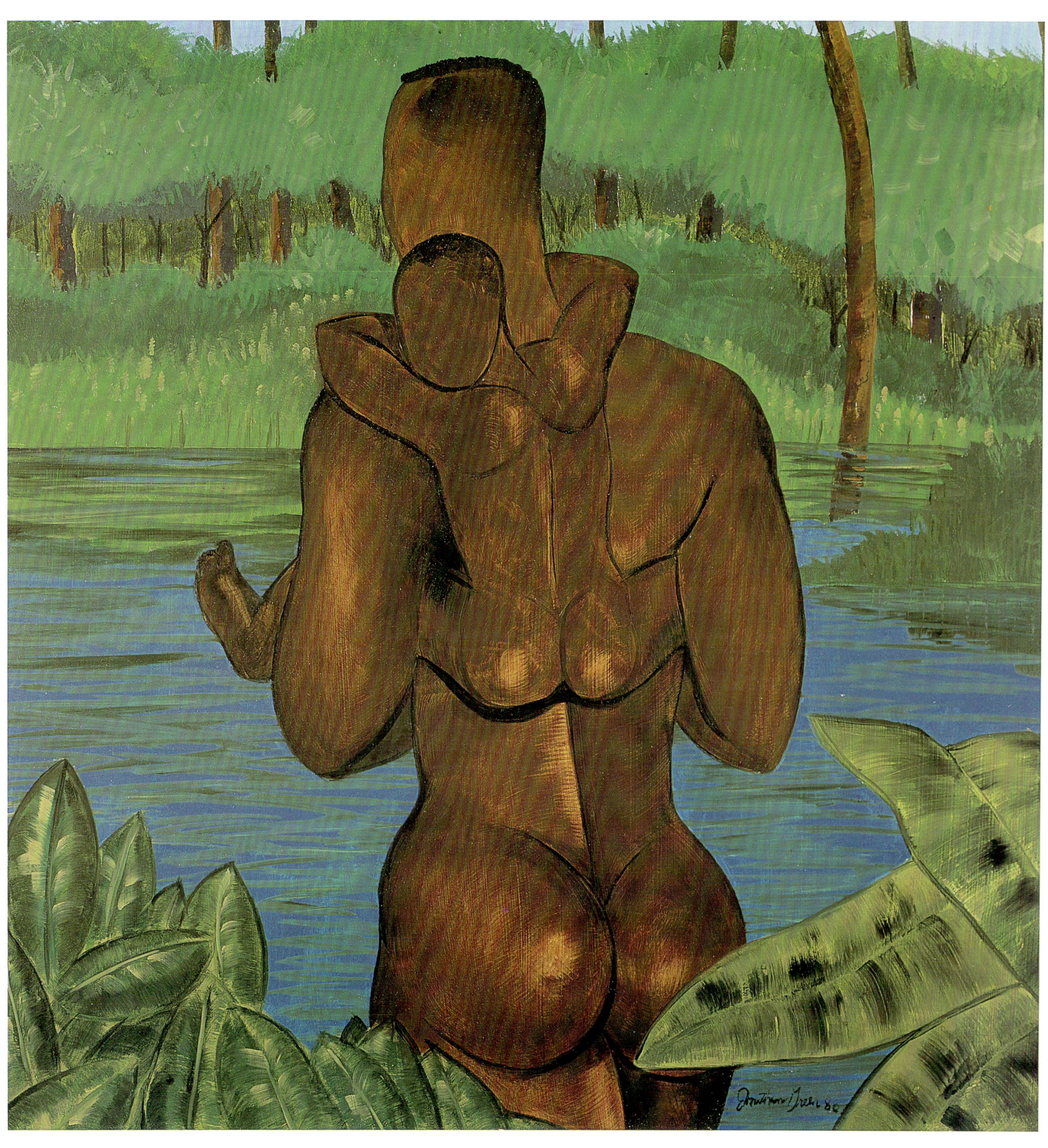

First Swim, 1988. Oil on masonite, 23 x 23".
Courtesy of Robert and Tina Weiss. Photograph by Tim Stamm.

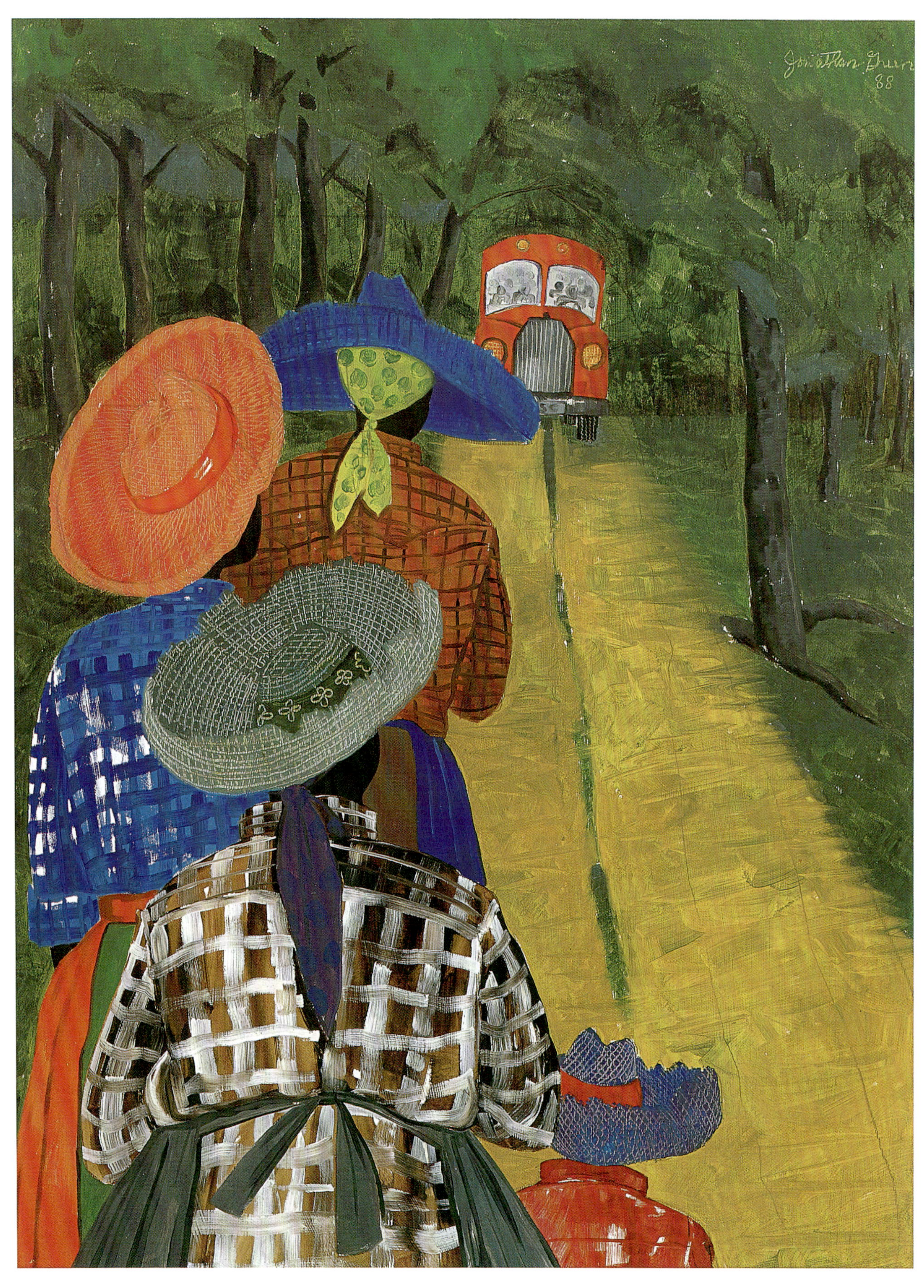

Field Hands, 1988. Oil on masonite, 32 x 24".
Courtesy of Bernard and Shirley Kinsey. Photograph by Tim Stamm.

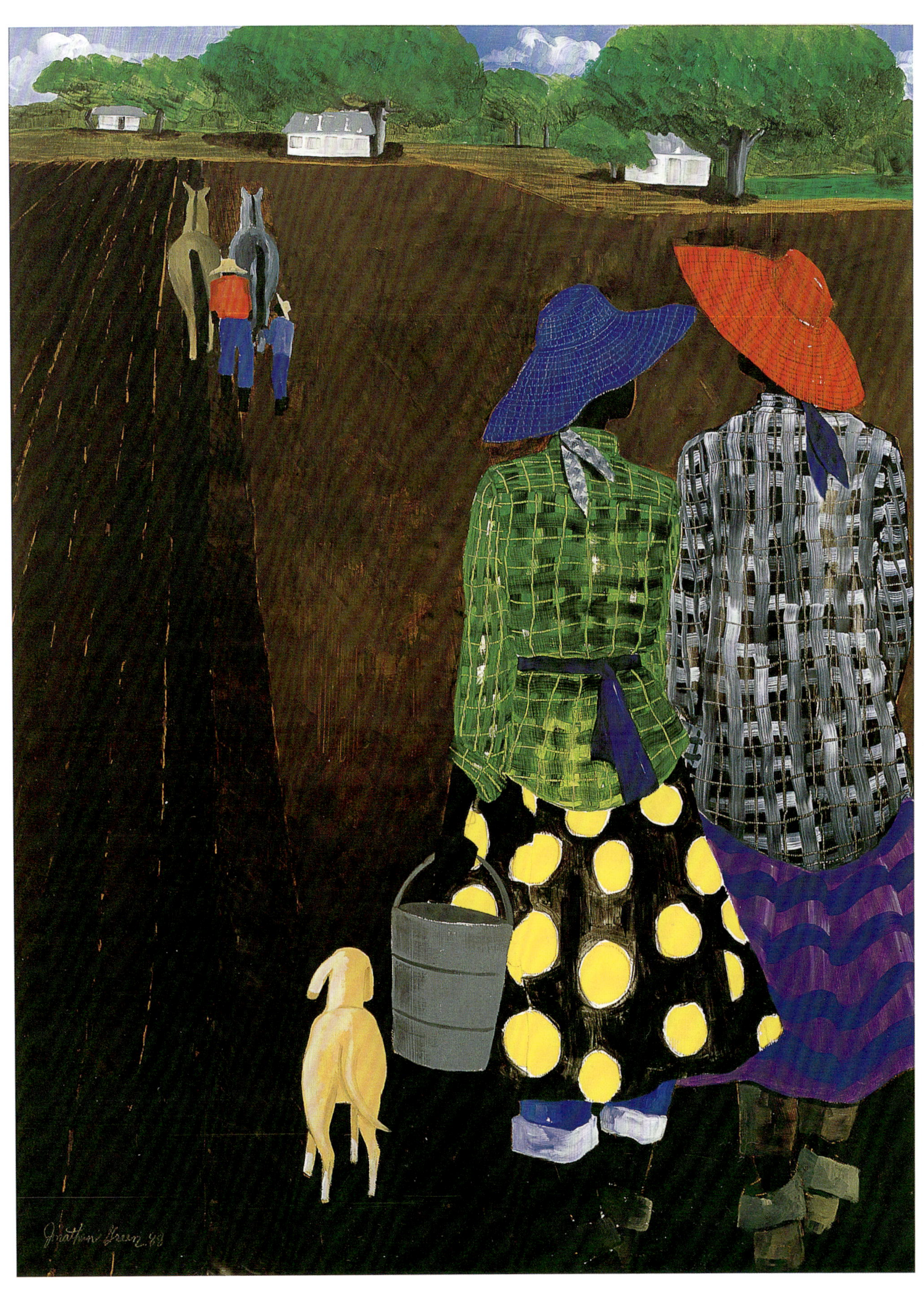

Family at Work, 1988. Oil on masonite, 32 x 24".
Private Collection. Photograph by Katherine Wetzel.

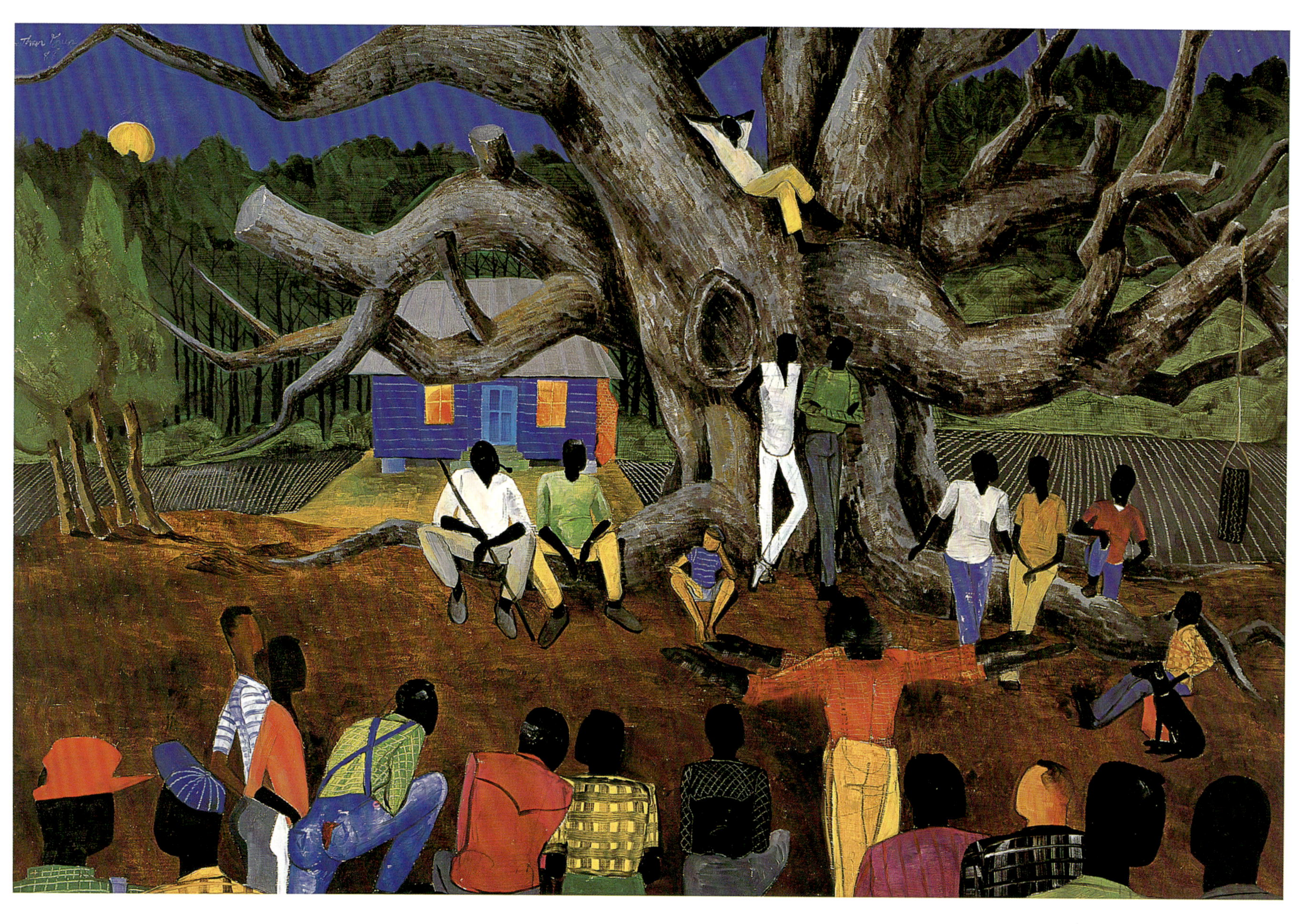

Tales, 1988. Oil on masonite, 24 x 36".
Courtesy of Richard Weedman. Photograph by Tim Stamm.

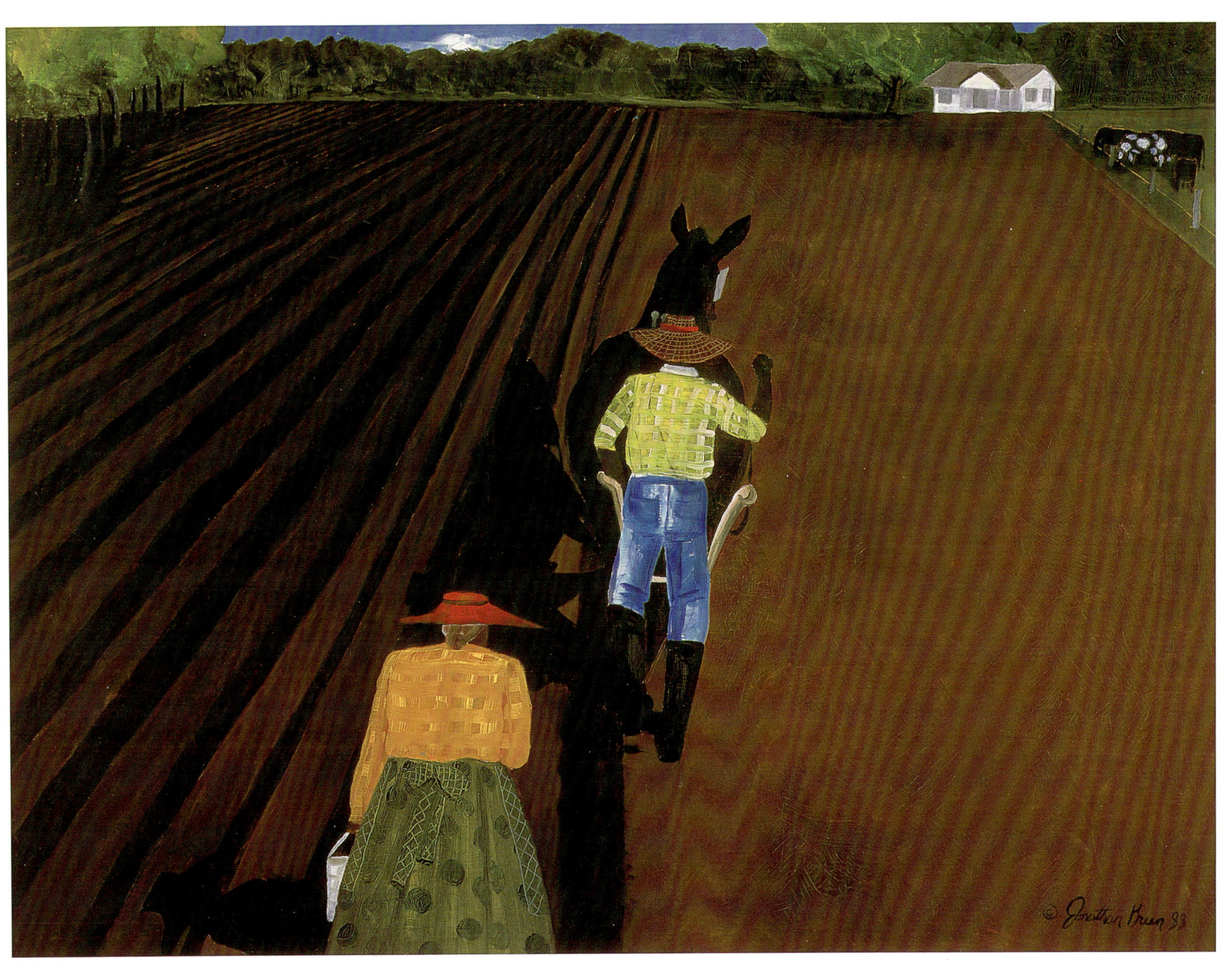

Spring Planting, 1988. Oil on masonite, 24 x 32".
Collection of the artist. Photograph by Tim Stamm.

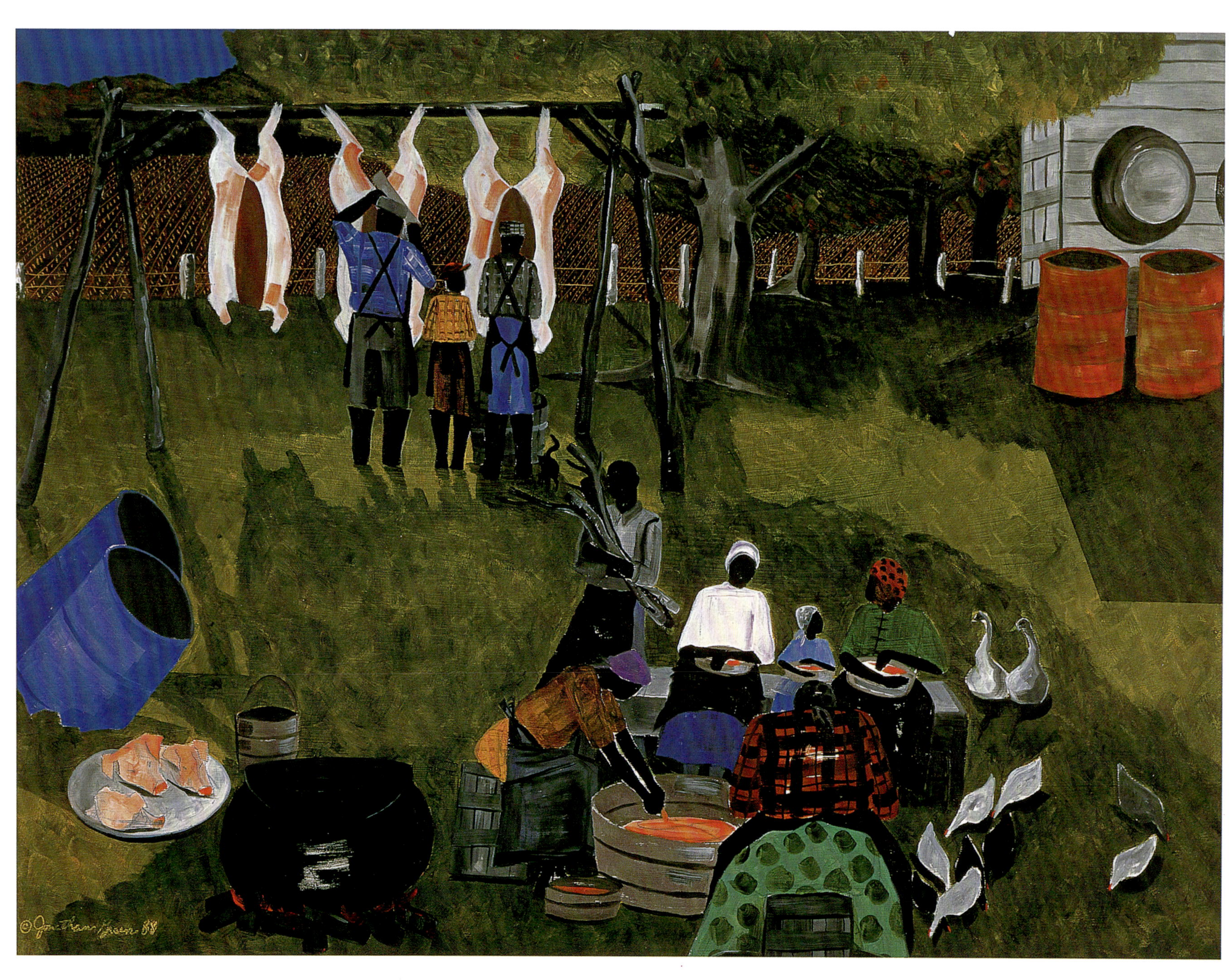

Holiday Preparation, 1988. Oil on masonite, 24 x 32".
Courtesy of Ann H. Hughes. Photograph by Tim Stamm.

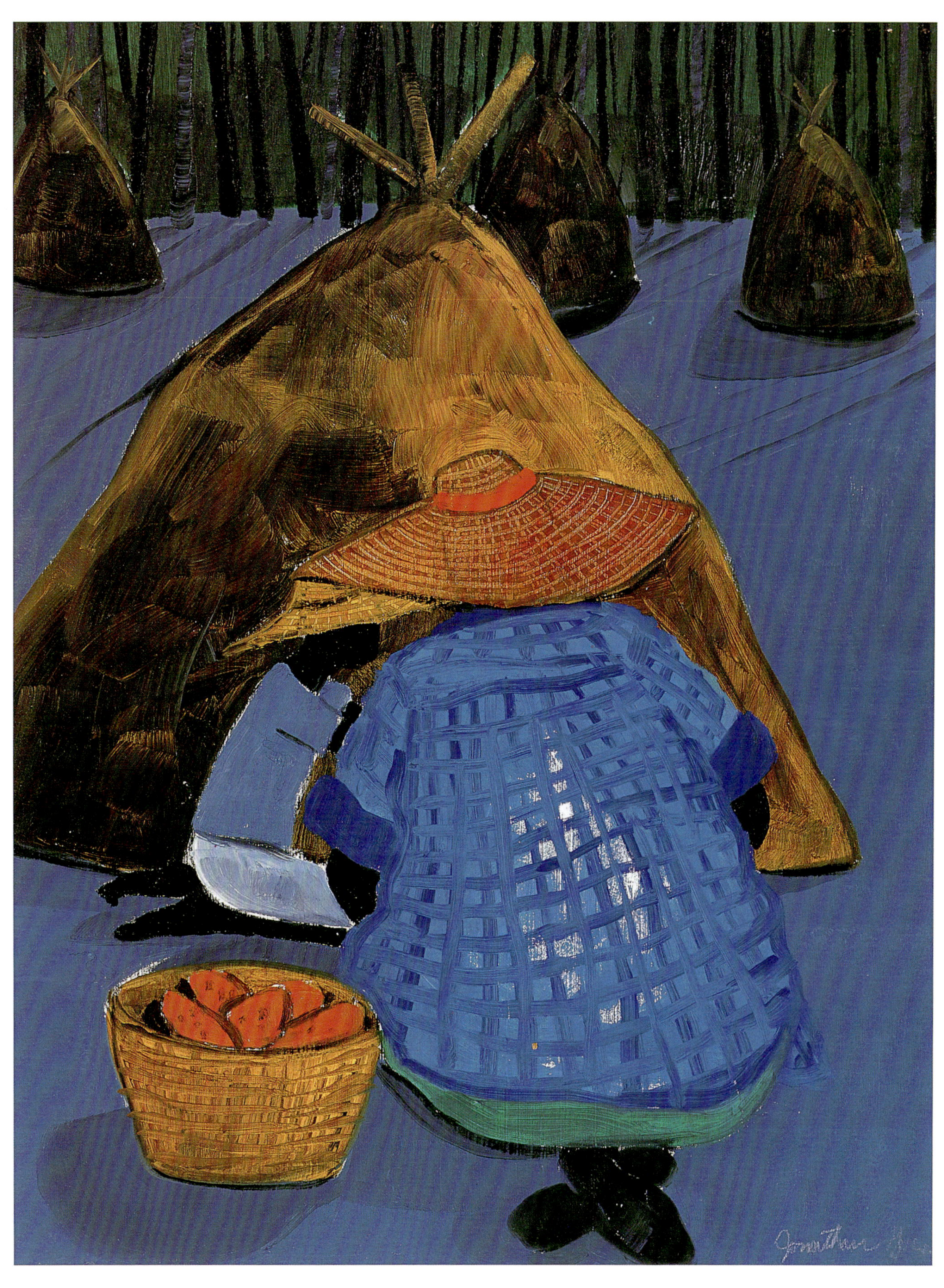

Banking Yams, 1988. Oil on canvas, 14 x 11".
Courtesy of Richard Weedman. Photograph by Tim Stamm.

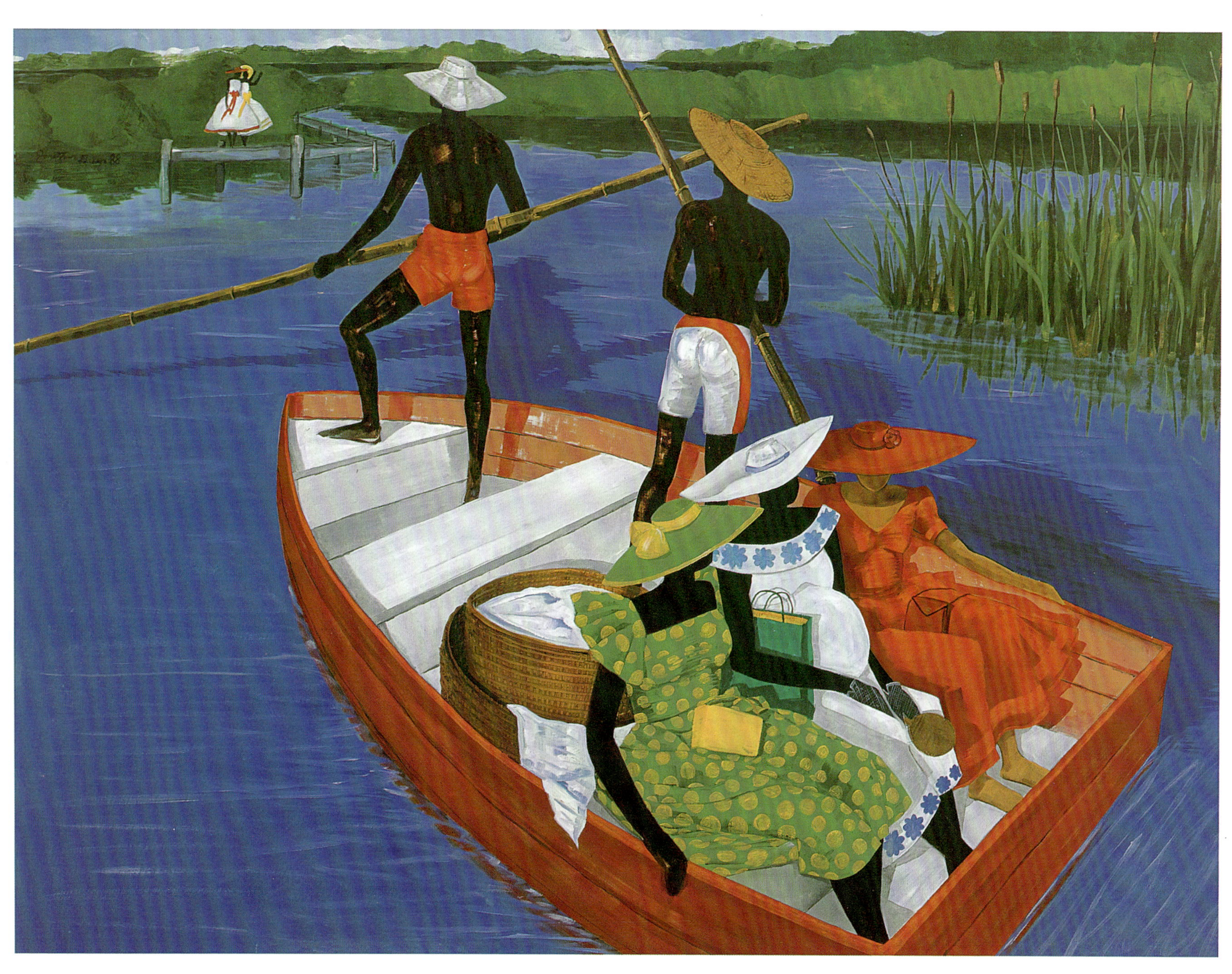

The Escorting of Ruth, 1988. Oil on masonite, 36 x 48".
Courtesy of Arnold Rampersad. Photograph by Katherine Wetzel.

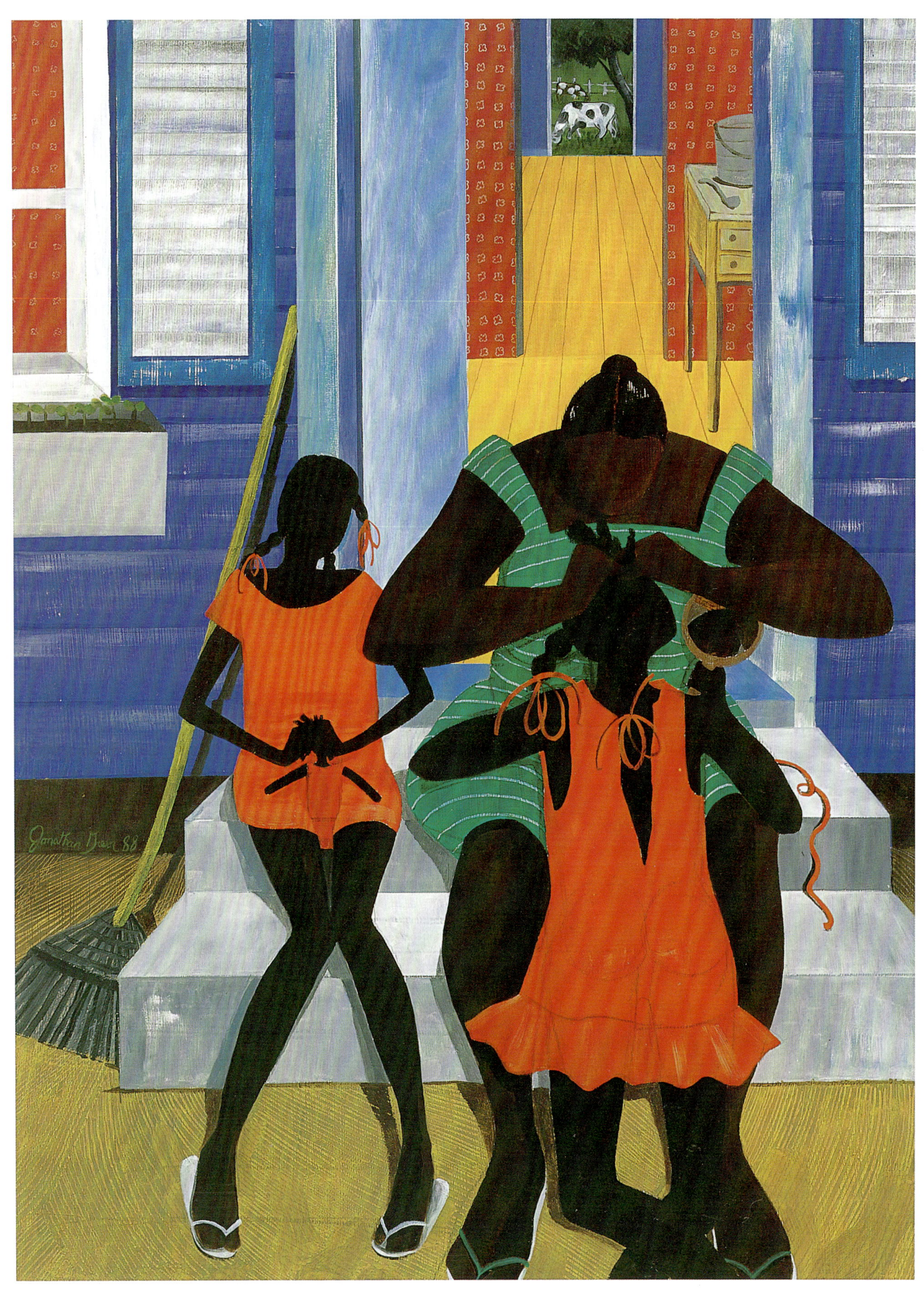

Braiding Hair, 1988. Oil on masonite, 32 x 24".
Courtesy of Vanessa G. Niles. Photograph by Katherine Wetzel.

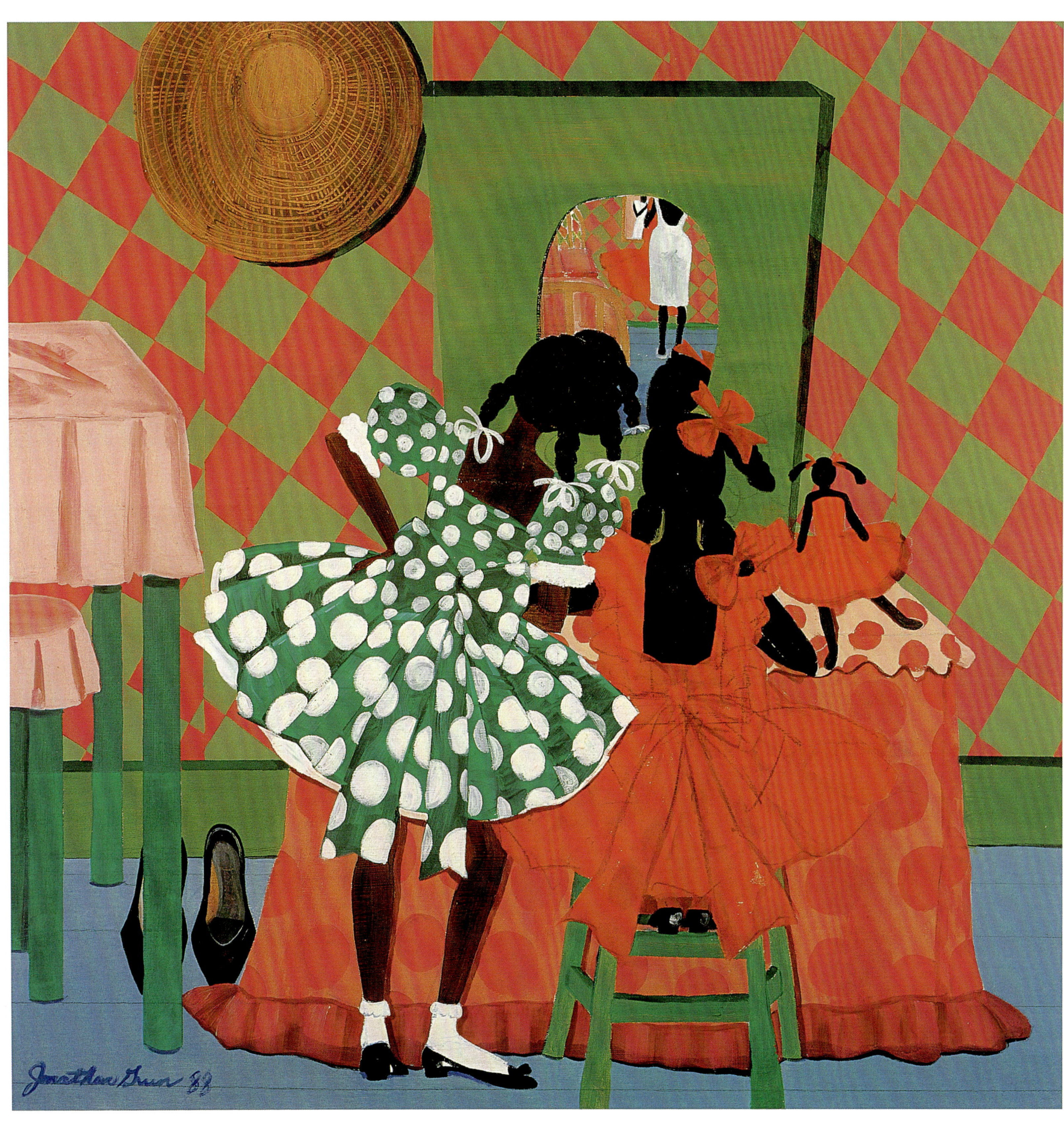

Dressing Up, 1988. Oil on masonite, 23 x 23".
Courtesy of Carole A. Parks. Photograph by Ron Breazeale.

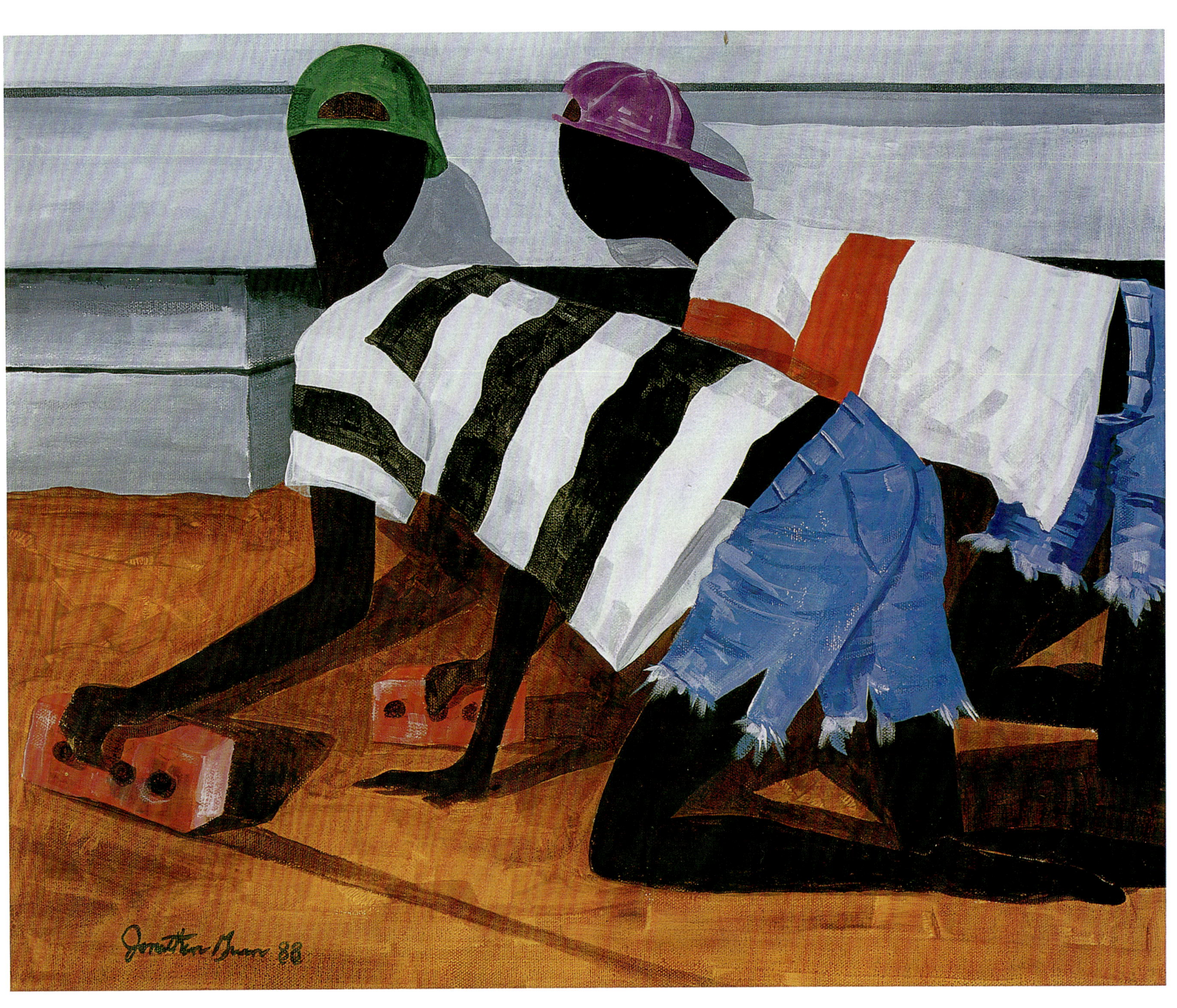

Red Brick Greyhounds, 1988. Acrylic on canvas, 16 x 20".
Courtesy of Louis and Marlene Osteen. Photograph by Katherine Wetzel.

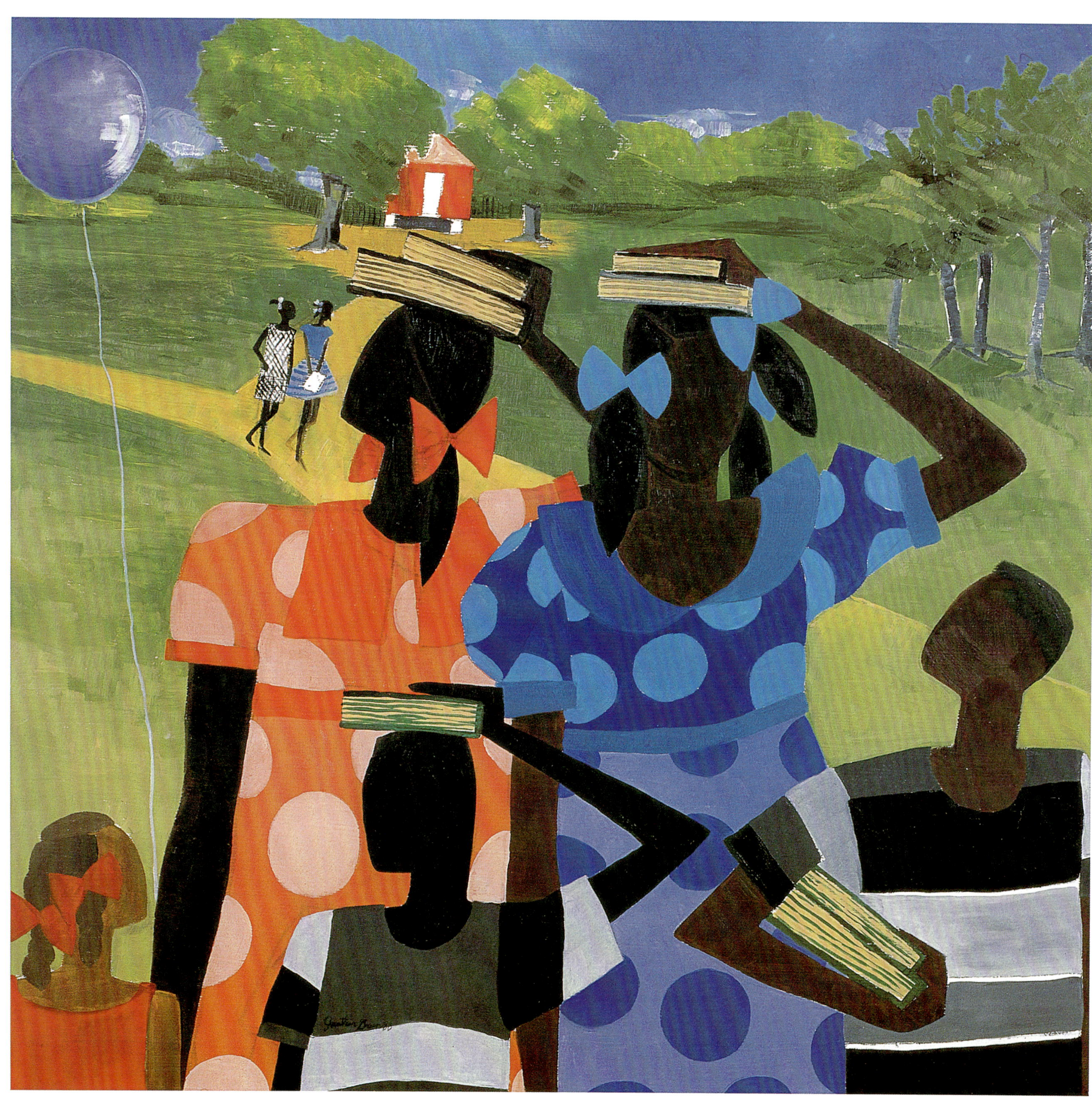

The Mather School, 1988. Oil on masonite, 23.5 x 23.5".
Courtesy of Ann E. Smith. Photograph by Tim Stamm.

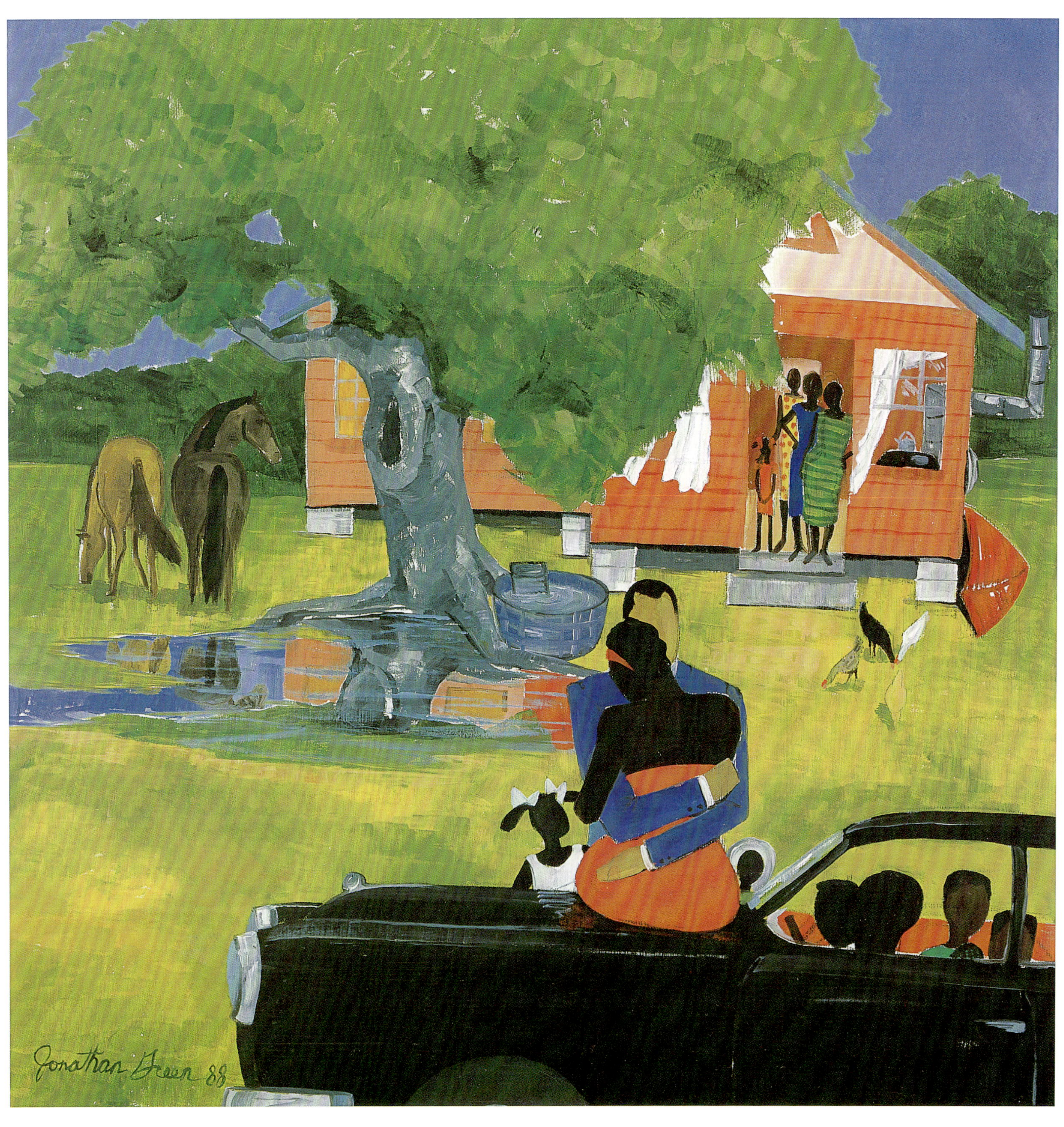

Bowes, 1988. Oil on masonite, 23 x 23".
Courtesy of Vanessa G. Niles. Photograph by Katherine Wetzel.

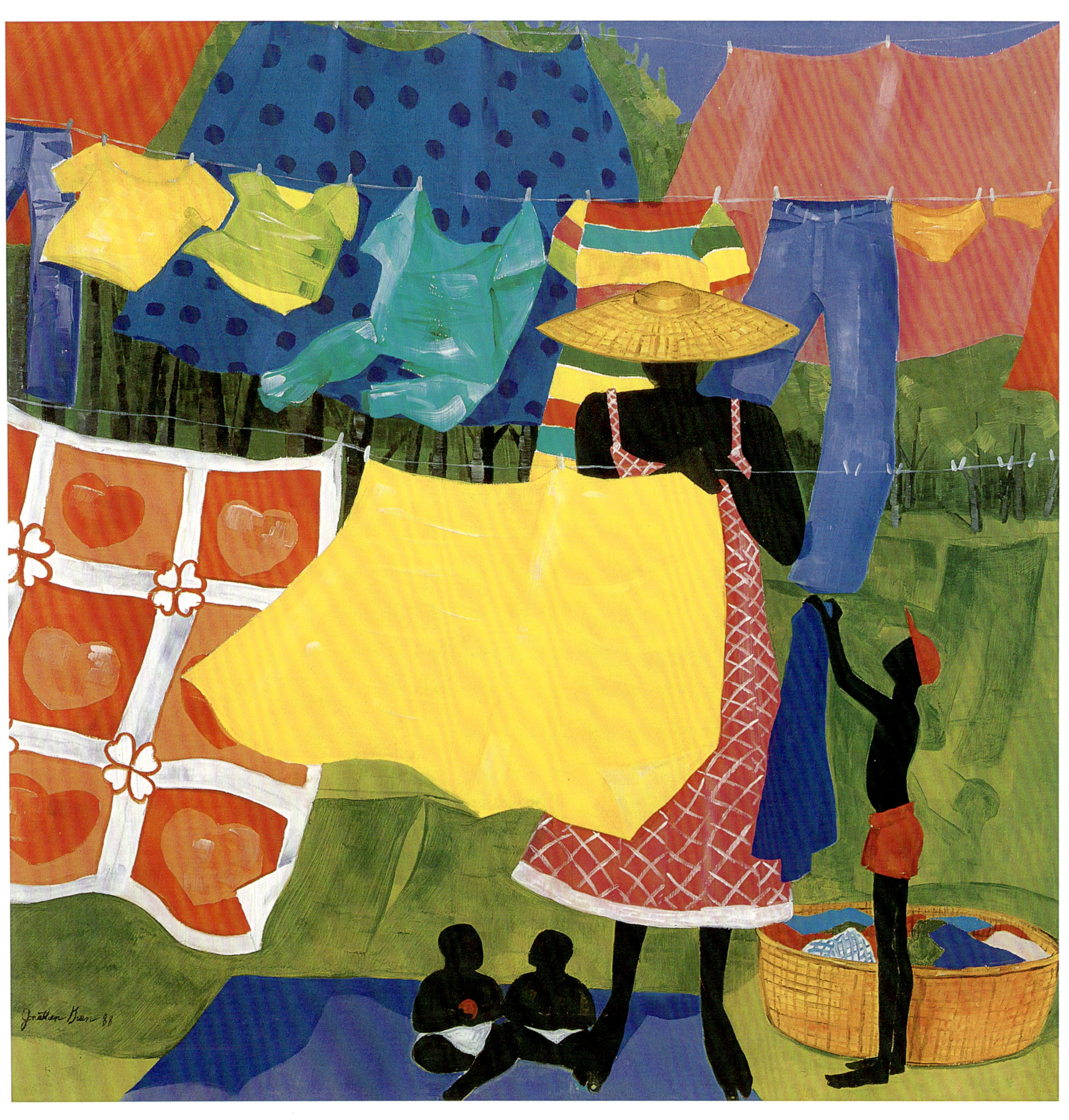

Colored Clothes, 1988. Oil on masonite, 23 x 23".
Courtesy of Carroll Greene, Jr. Photograph by Katherine Wetzel.

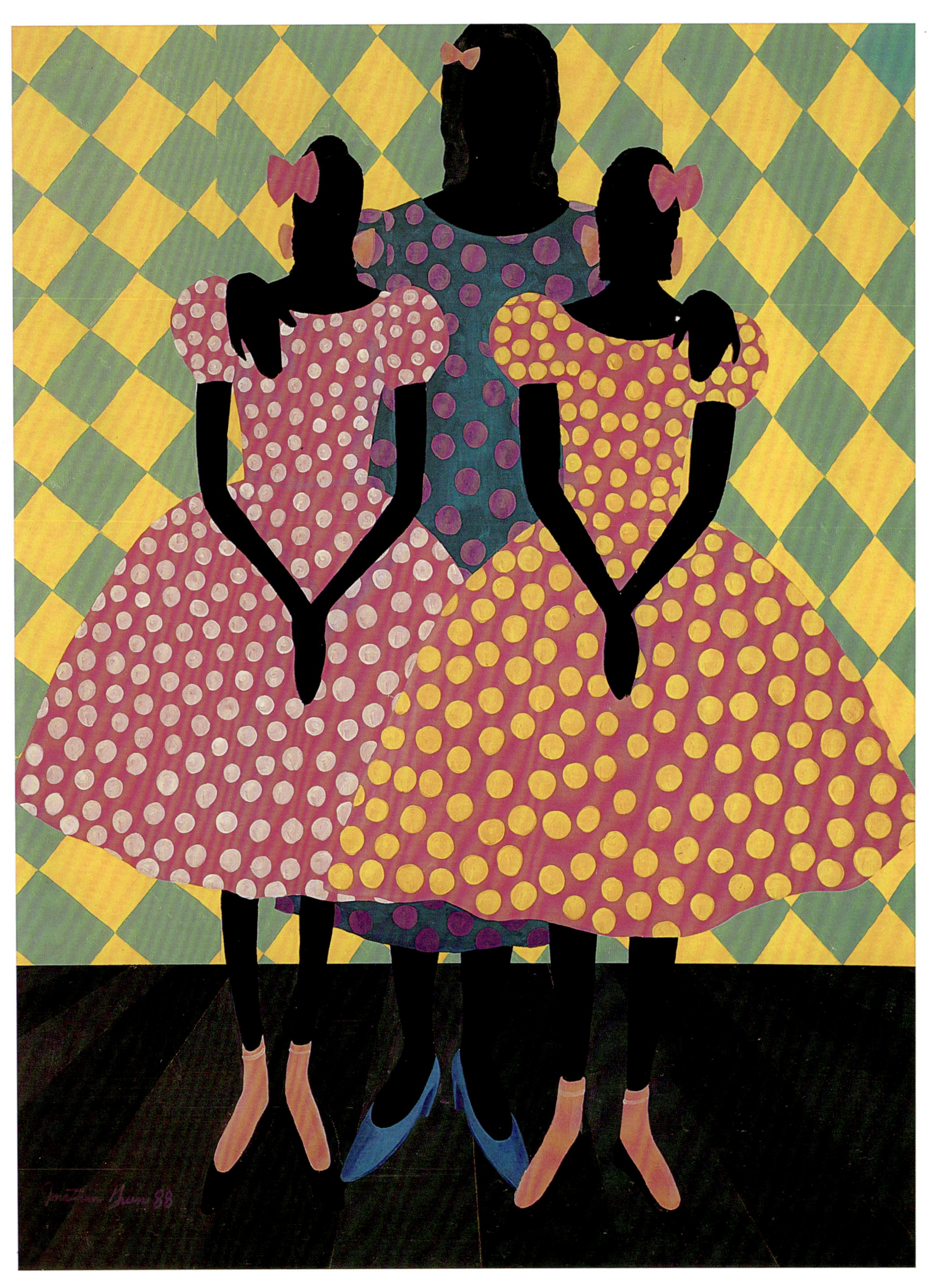

A Special Sunday, 1988. Acrylic on canvas, 48 x 36".
Courtesy of George and Dee Crawford. Photograph by Tim Stamm.

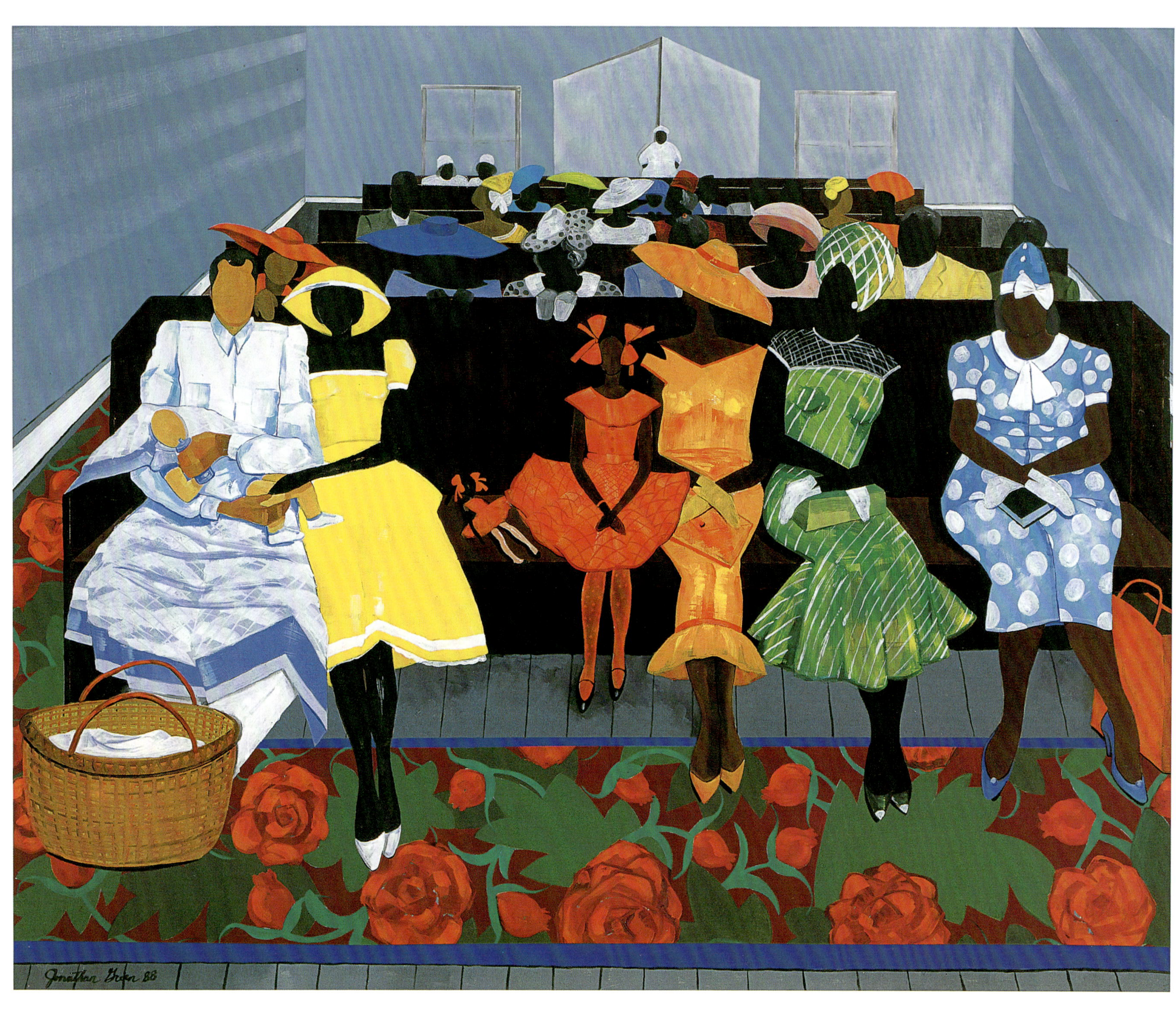

First Born, 1988. Oil on masonite, 38 x 48".
Courtesy of Arnold Rampersad. Photograph by Katherine Wetzel.

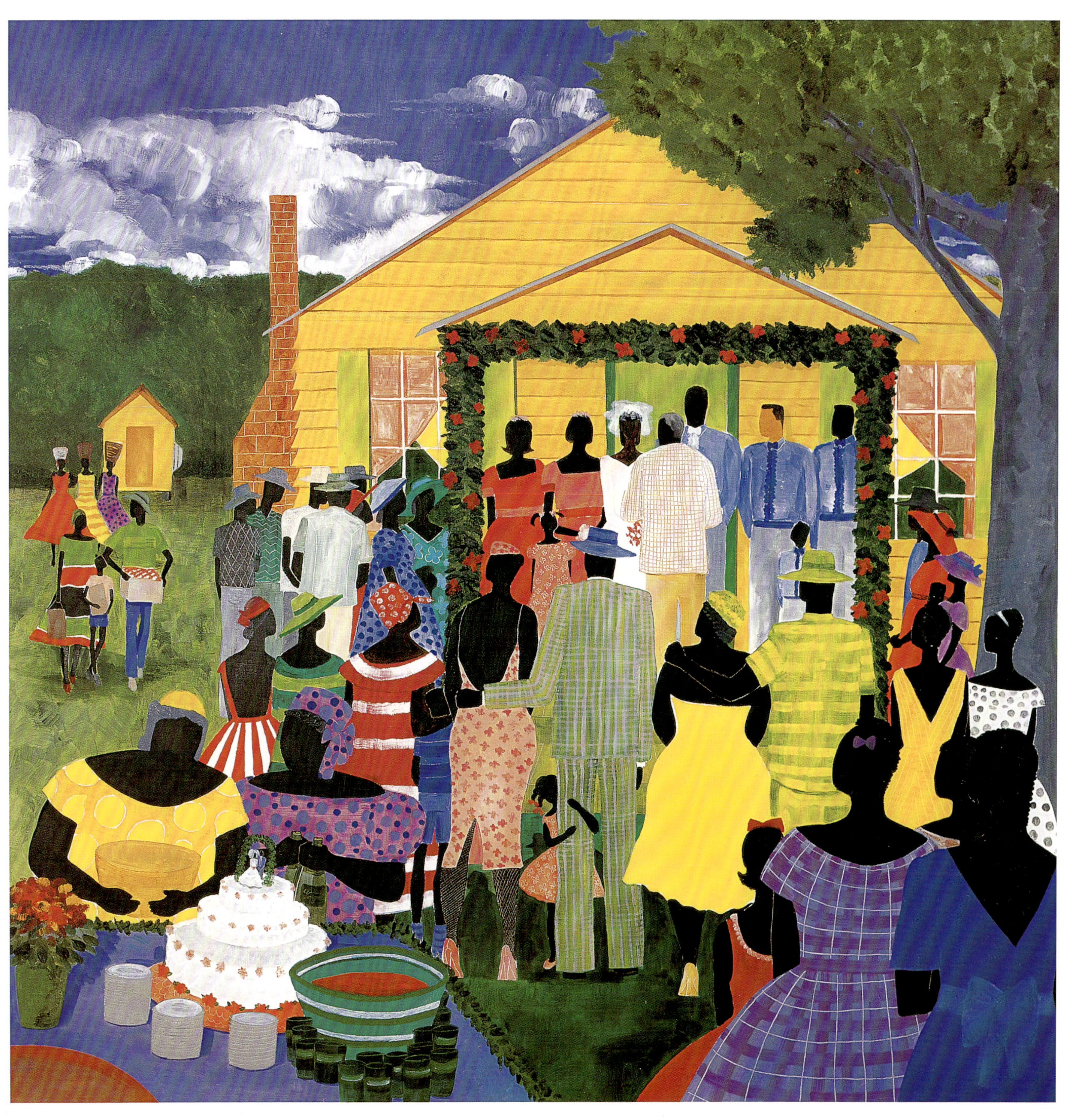

The Wedding, 1988. Oil on masonite, 48 x 48".
Private collection. Photograph by Tim Stamm.

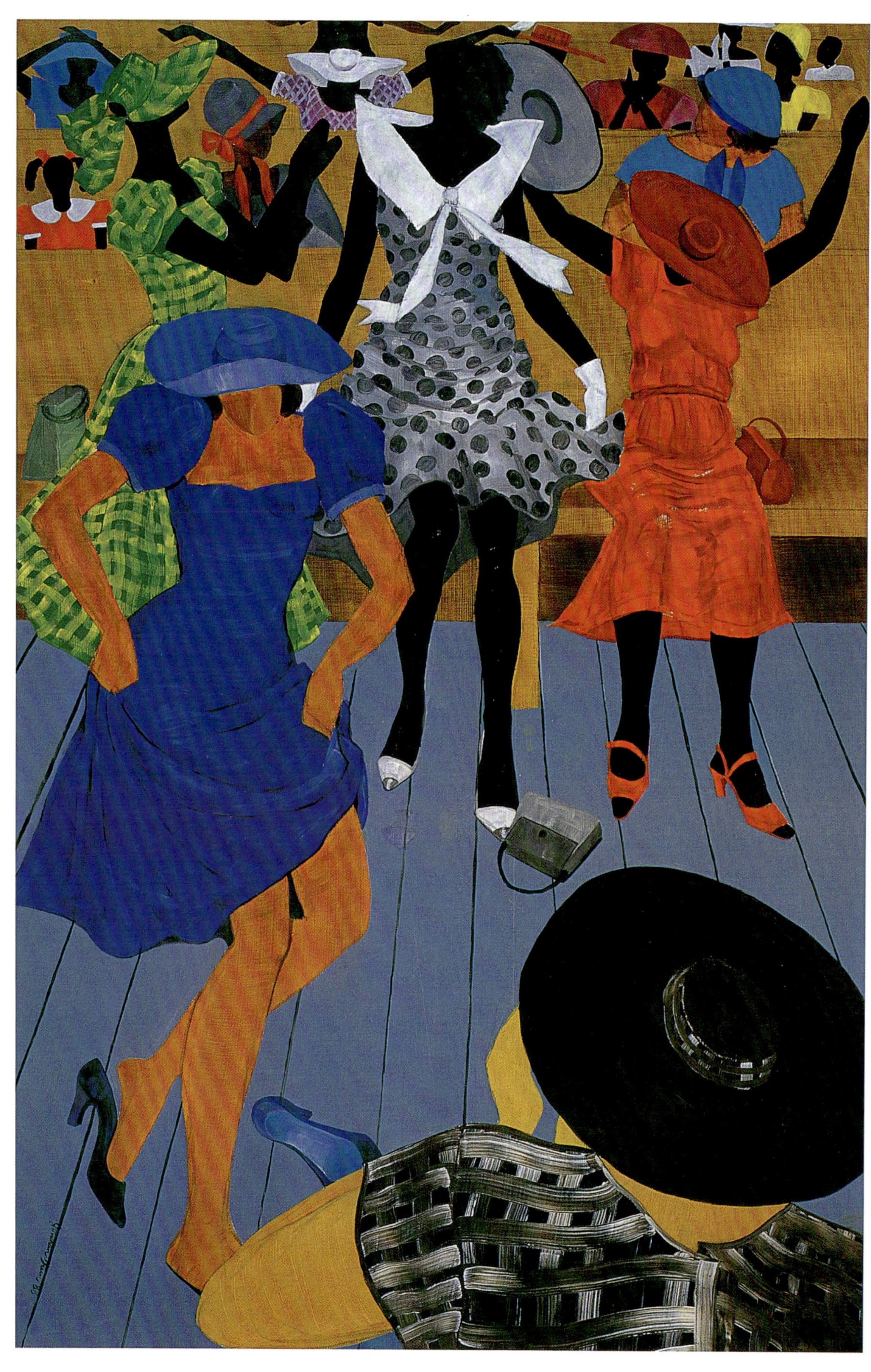

The Shout, 1988. Oil on masonite, 36 x 24".
Courtesy of Martin Luther Polite. Photograph by Tim Stamm.

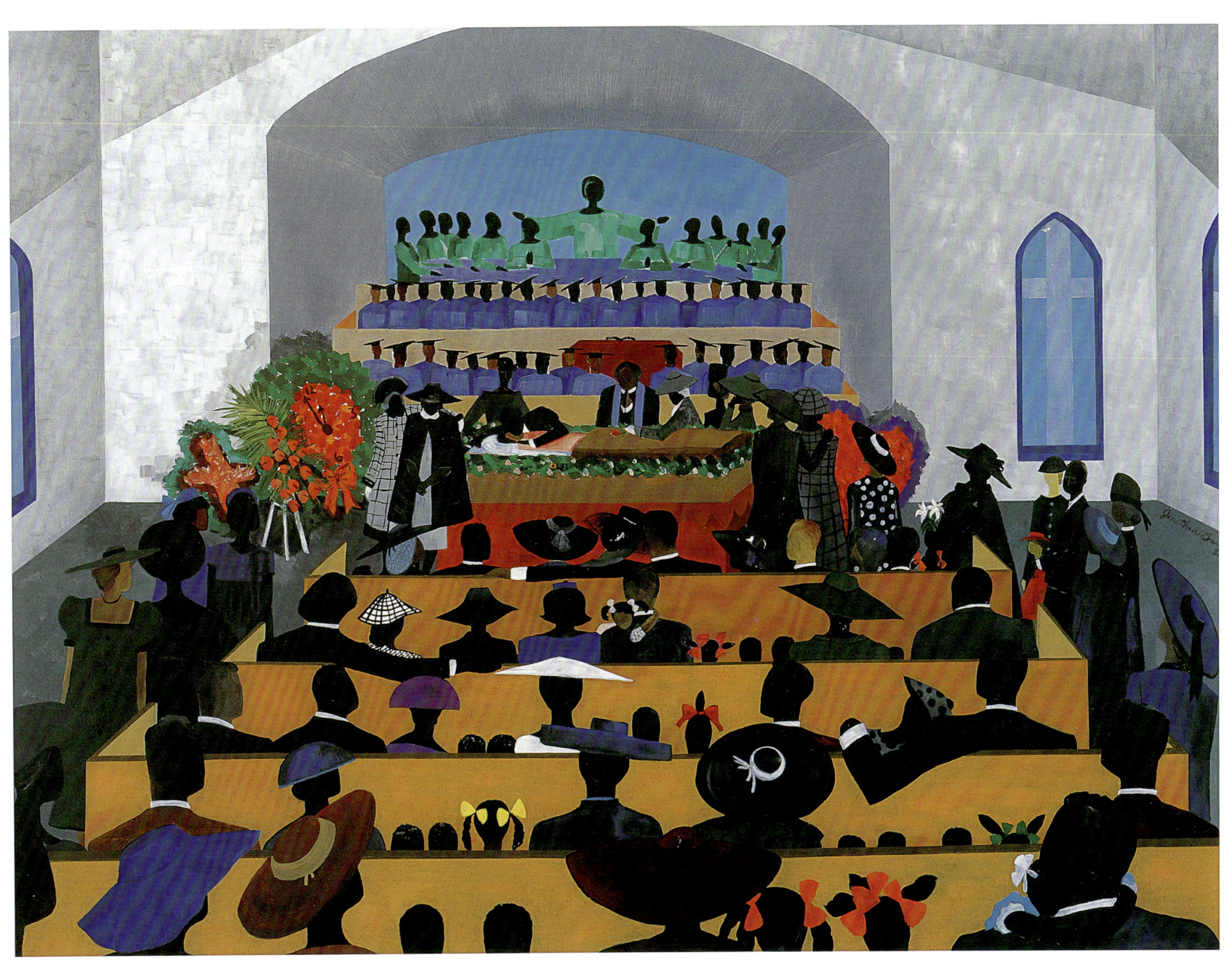

The Passing of Eloise, 1988. Oil on masonite, 36 x 48".
Courtesy of Julia J. Norrell. Photograph by Katherine Wetzel.

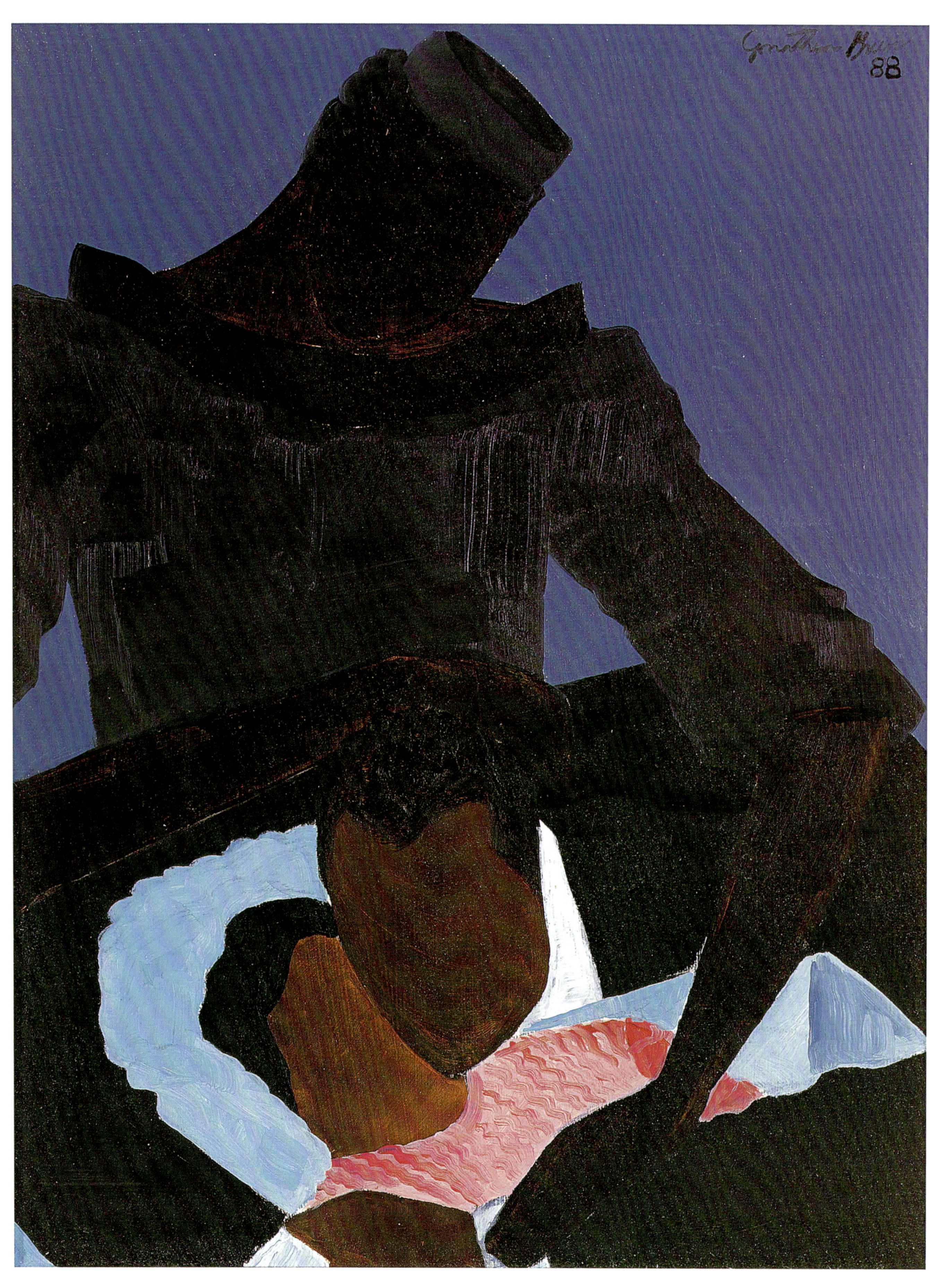

Eloise, 1988. Oil on masonite, 14 x 11".
Collection of the artist. Photograph by Tim Stamm.

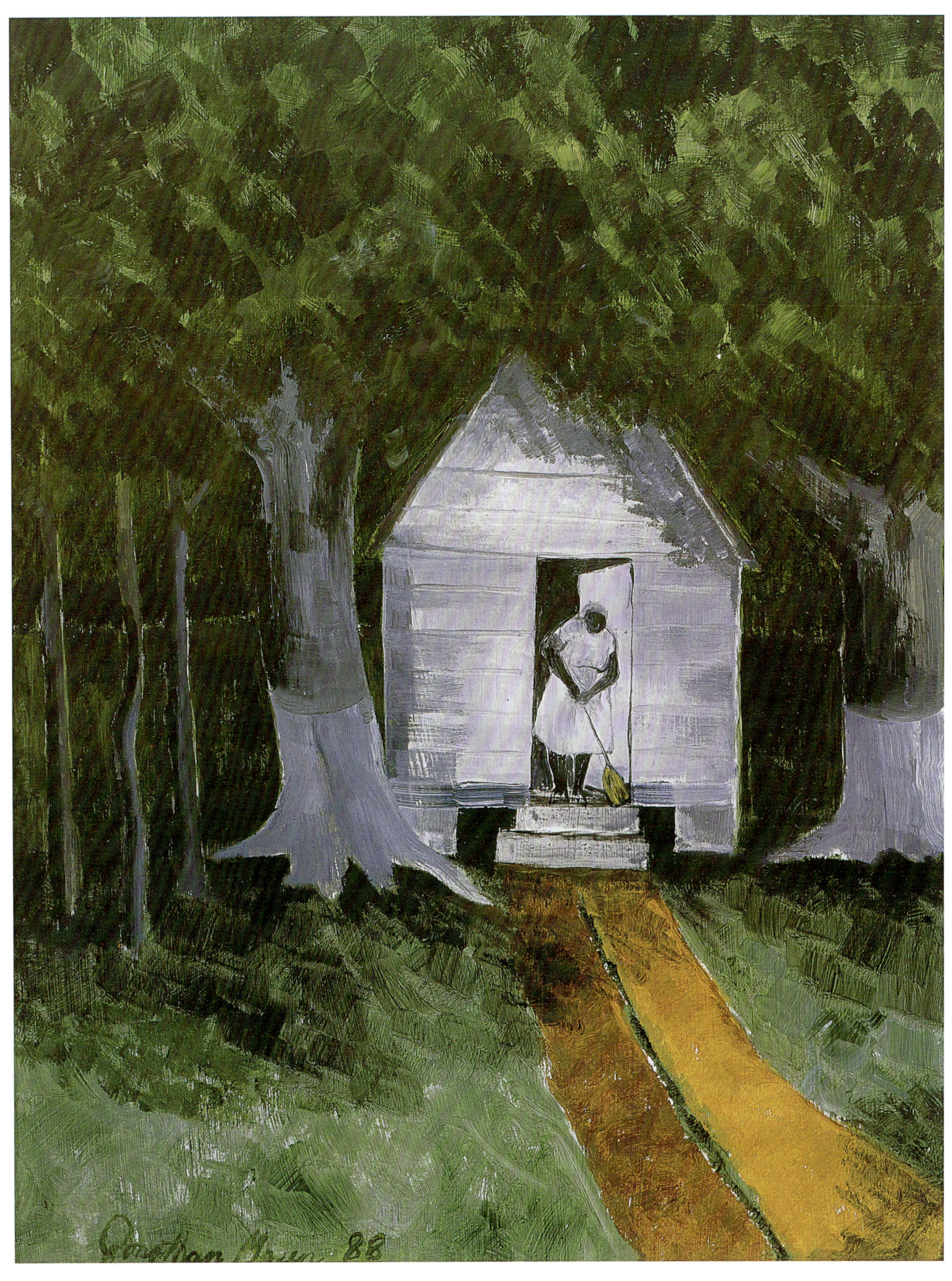

Praise House, 1988. Oil on masonite, 14 x 11".
Courtesy of Sam Reed. Photograph by Katherine Wetzel.

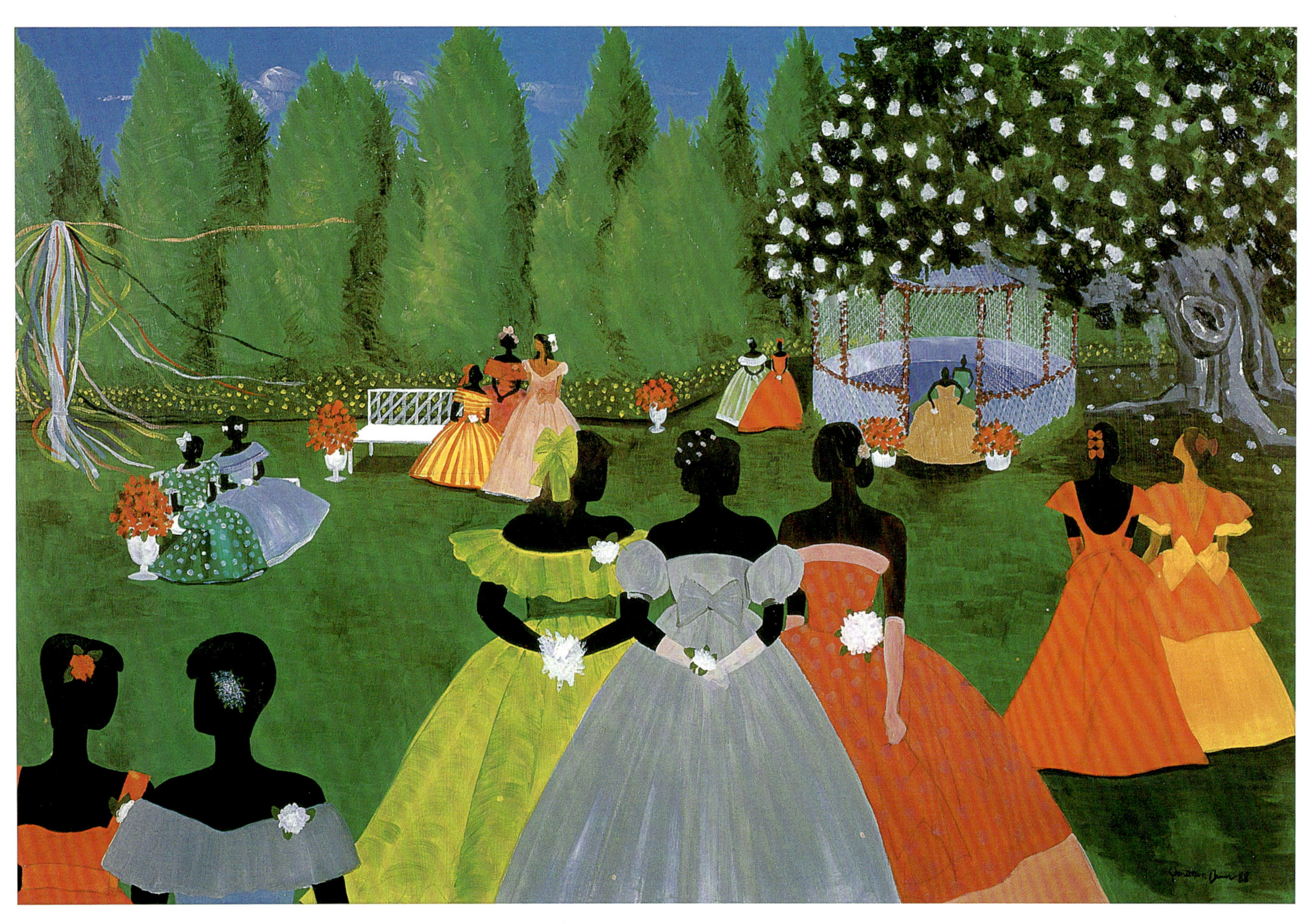

The Gazebo, 1988. Oil on masonite, 24 x 36".
Courtesy of Mary and Enoch Roberts. Photograph by Tim Stamm.

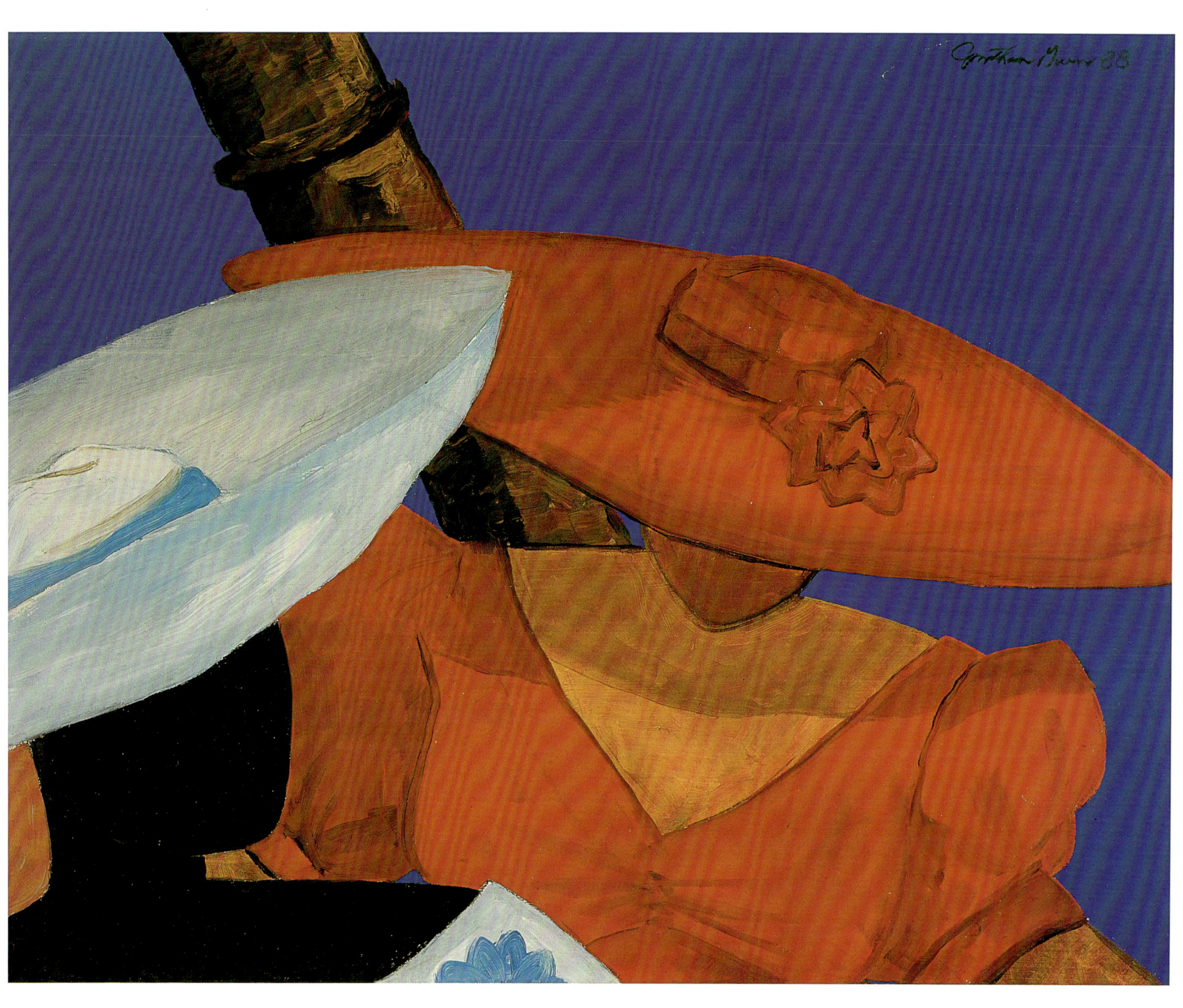

Ruth and Friend, 1988. Oil on masonite, 11 x 14".
Courtesy of Ernst and Christina Bruderer. Photograph by Tim Stamm.

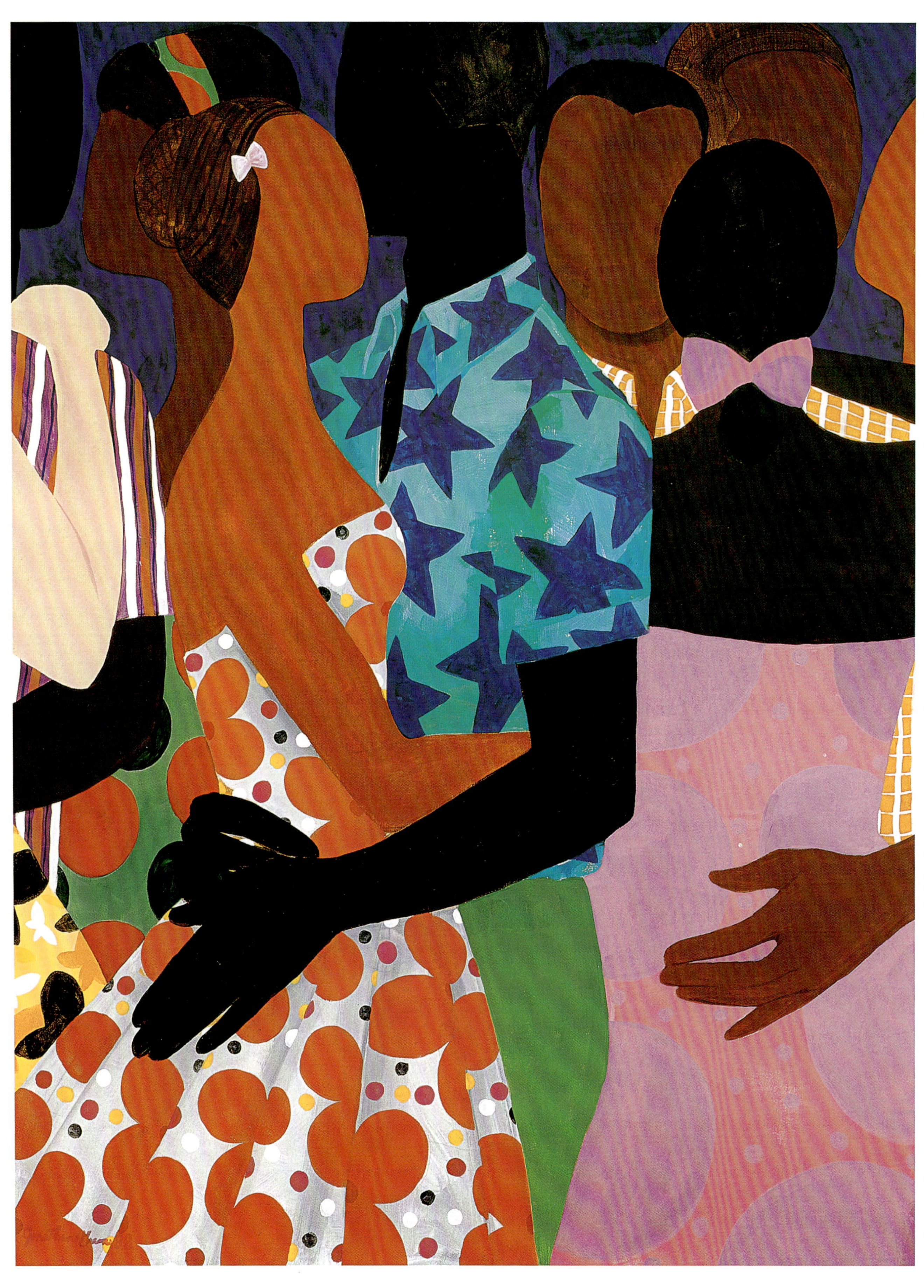

Dixie Crystal, 1988. Acrylic on canvas, 48 x 36".
Courtesy of Dr. and Mrs. Charles E. Freidman. Photograph by Rick Rhodes.

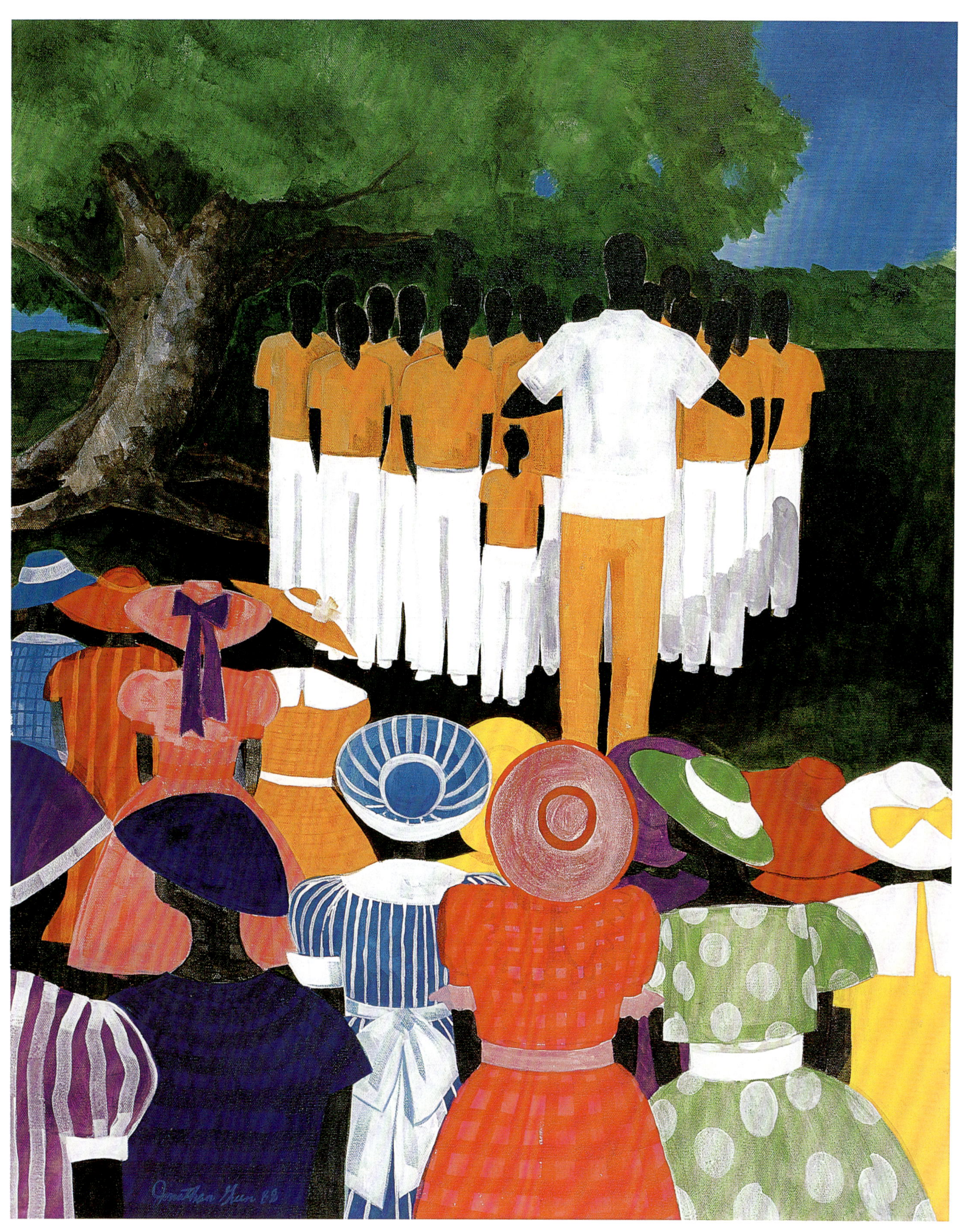

Yemassee Choir, 1988. Acrylic on canvas, 30 x 24".
Courtesy of Wayne King. Photograph by Tim Stamm.

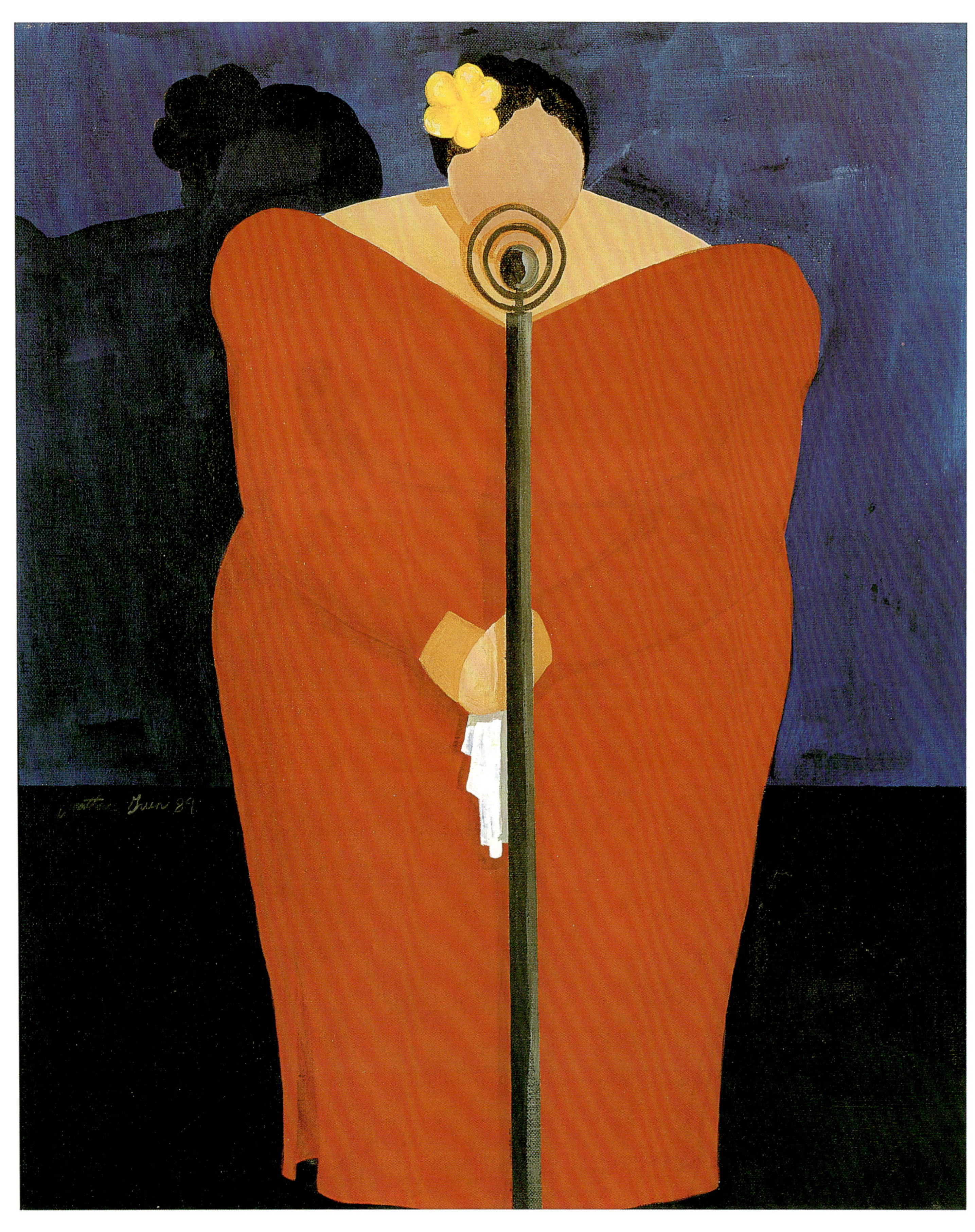

Bessie Mae, 1989. Acrylic on canvas, 24 x 20".
Courtesy of Louis and Marlene Osteen. Photograph by Tim Stamm.

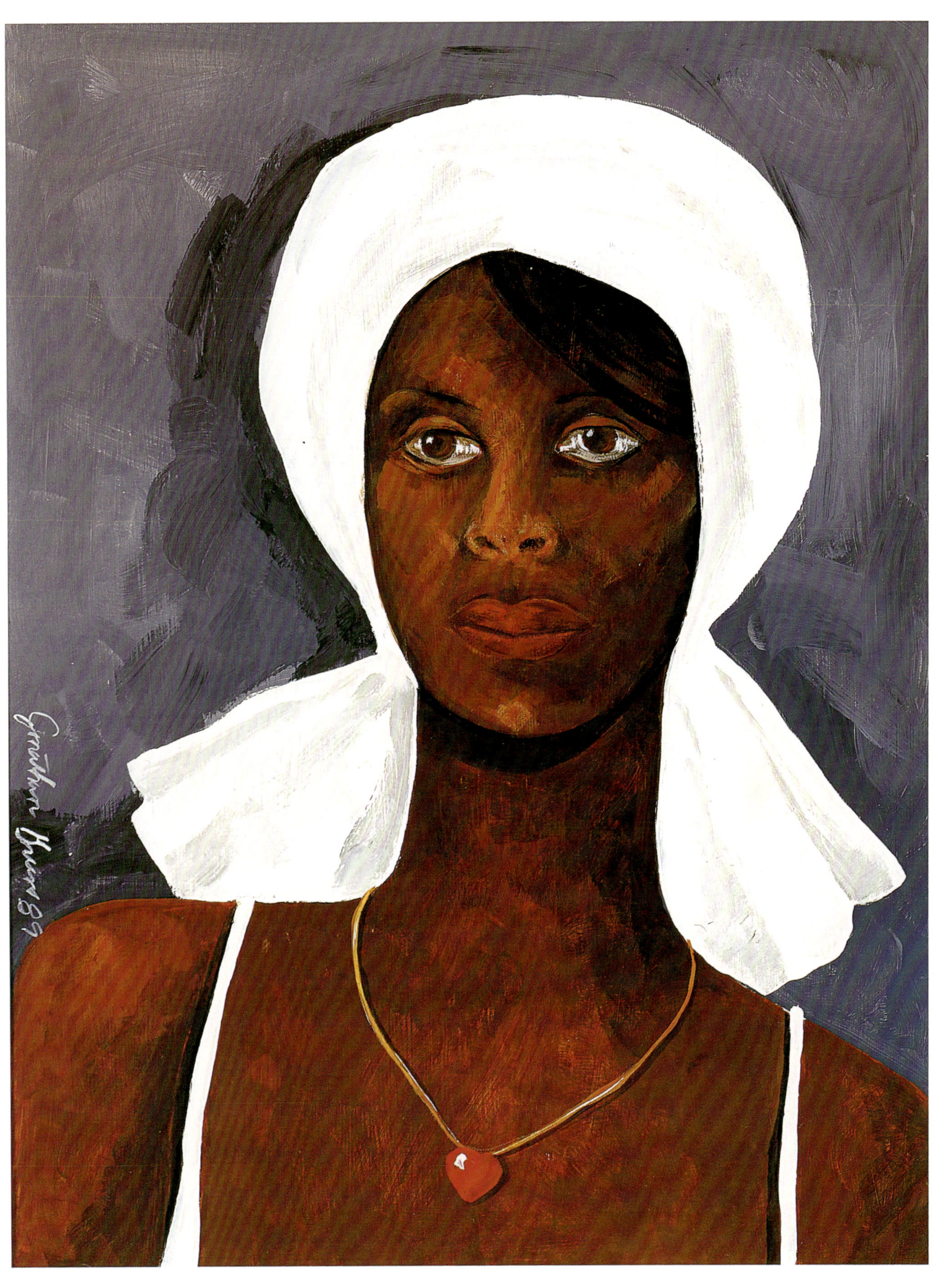

Nadene, 1989. Acrylic on masonite, 14 x 11".
Courtesy of Mary Mack. Photograph by Tim Stamm.

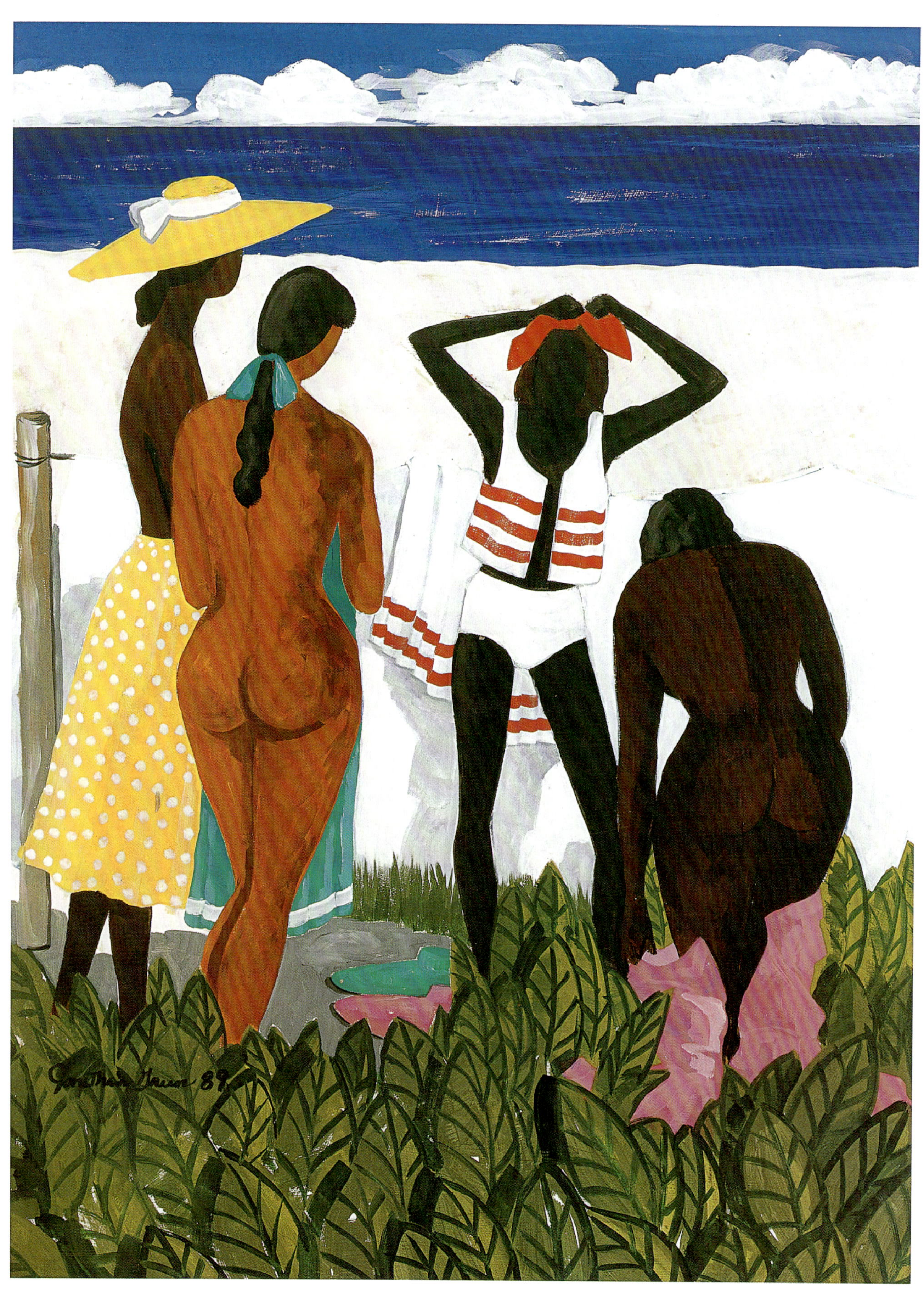

Lady Sun Bathers, 1989. Acrylic on masonite, 32 x 24".
Courtesy of Betty Lawrence. Photograph by Katherine Wetzel.

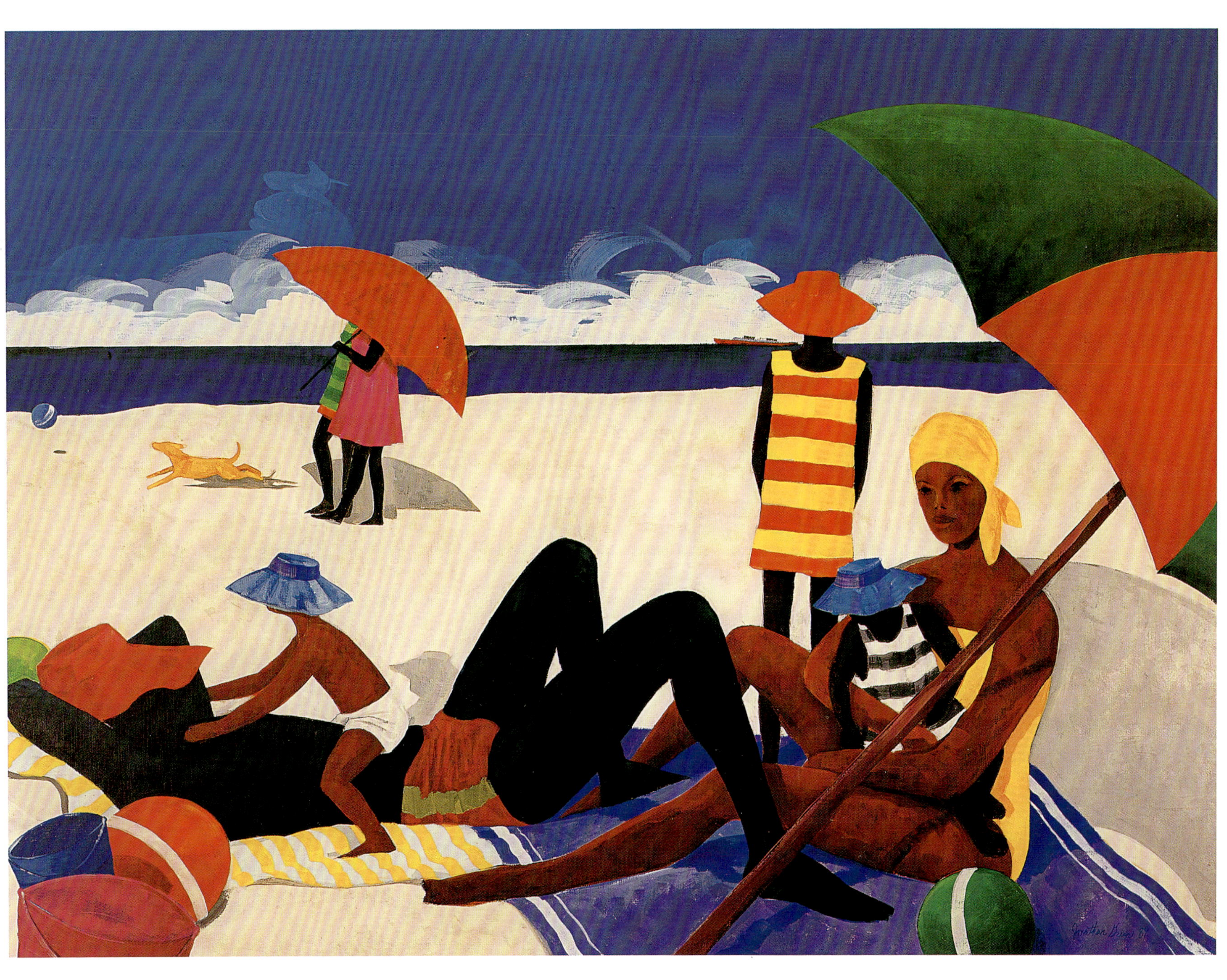

Family at the Beach, 1989. Acrylic on masonite, 24 x 32".
Courtesy of Lana E. Williams-Smith. Photograph by Tim Stamm.

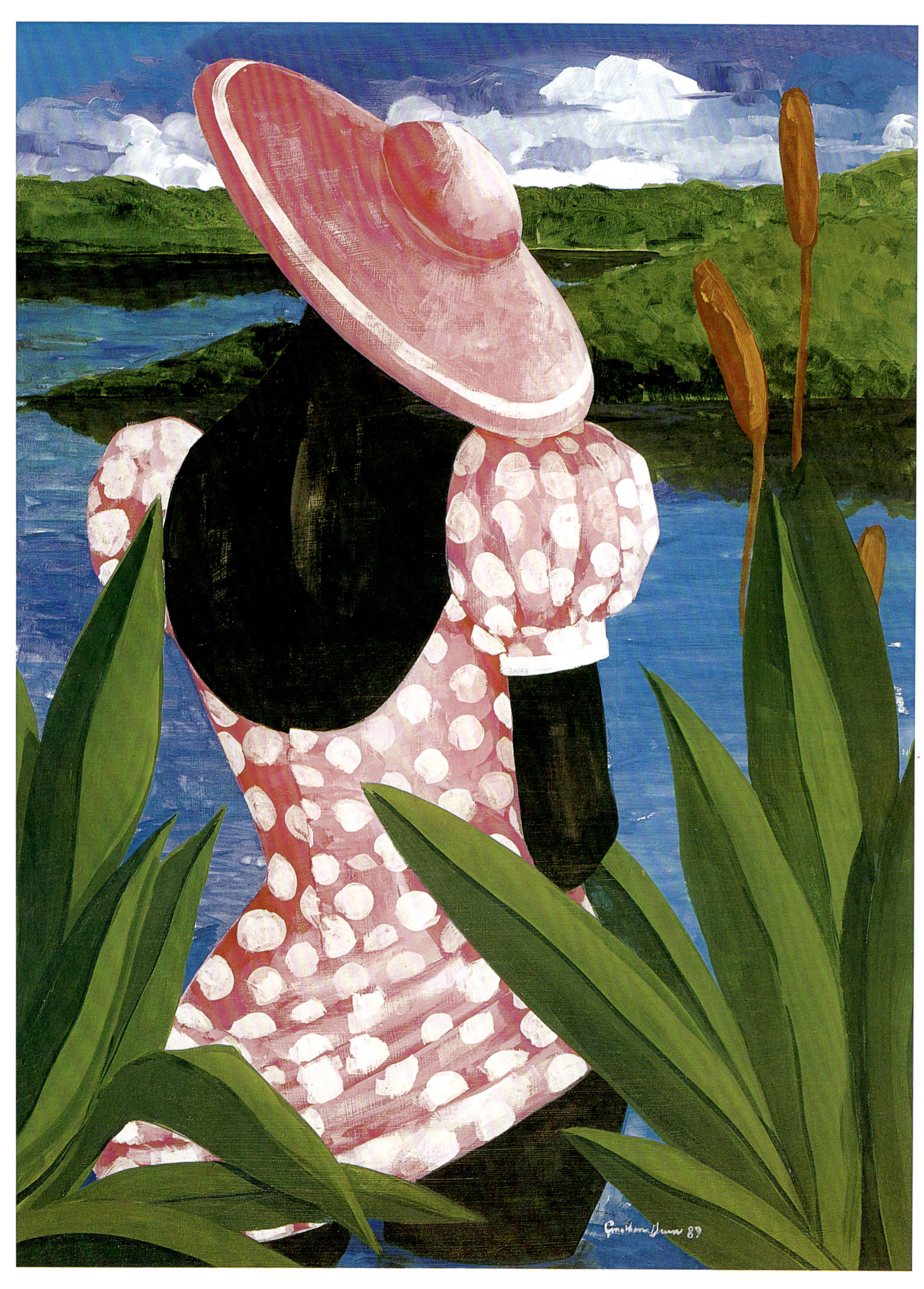

Innocent Flirtation, 1989. Acrylic on masonite, 32 x 24".
Courtesy of Terry and Thelma Harris. Photograph by Tim Stamm.

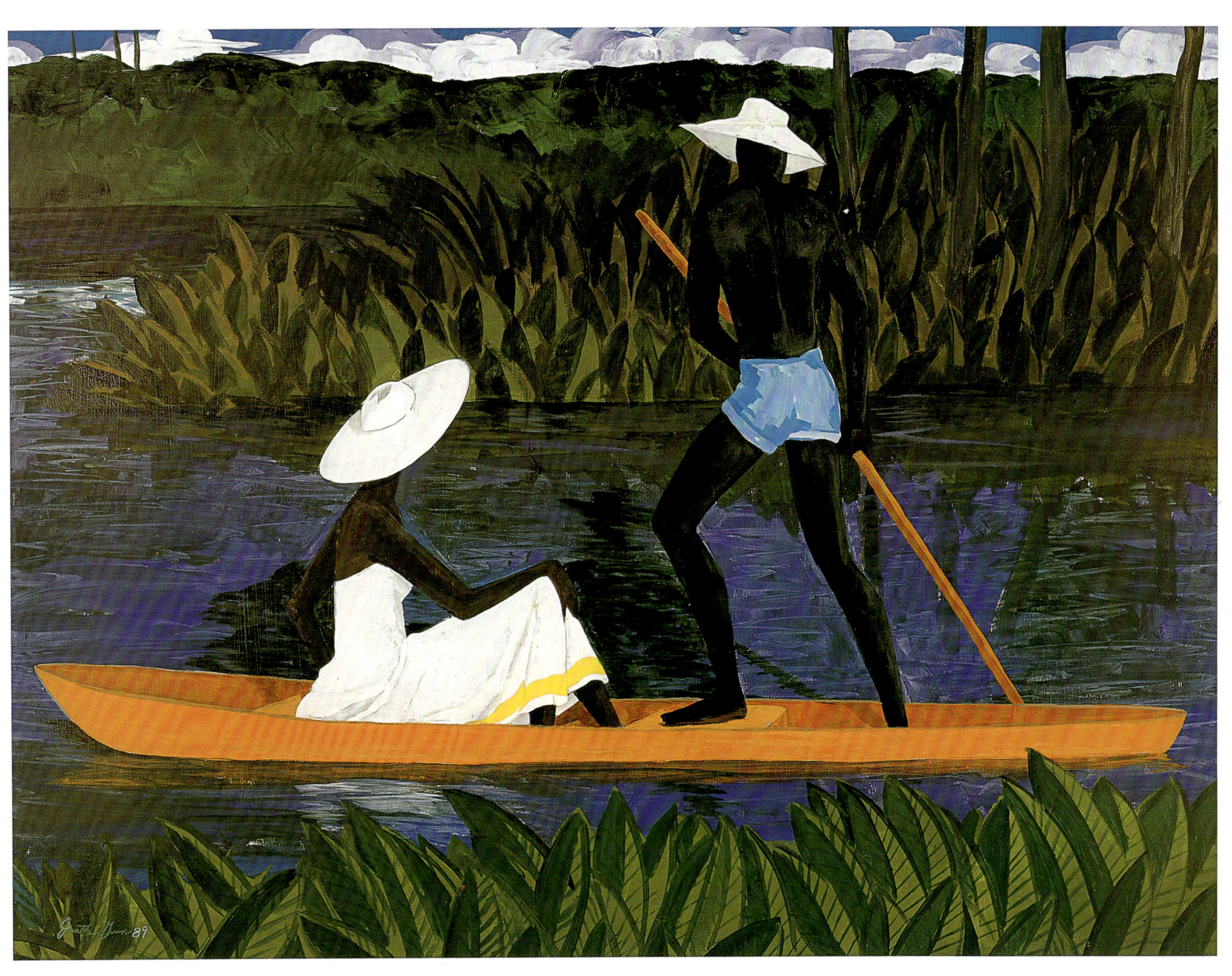

Boat Ride in the Marshland, 1989. Acrylic on canvas, 24 x 32".
Courtesy of Louis and Marlene Osteen. Photograph by Tim Stamm.

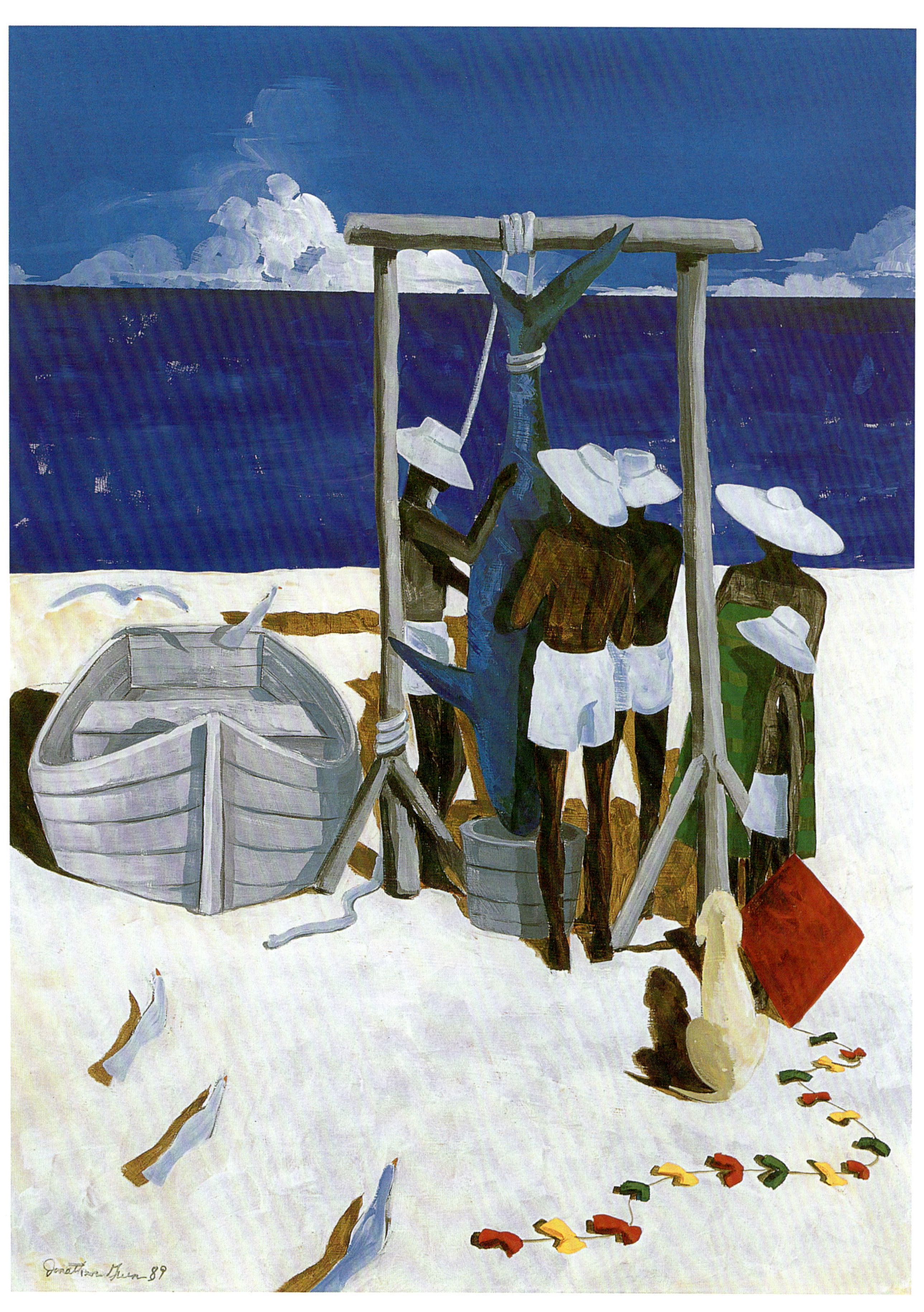

The Big Catch, 1989. Acrylic on masonite, 32 x 24".
Courtesy of Dwight and Camille Mosley. Photograph by Katherine Wetzel.

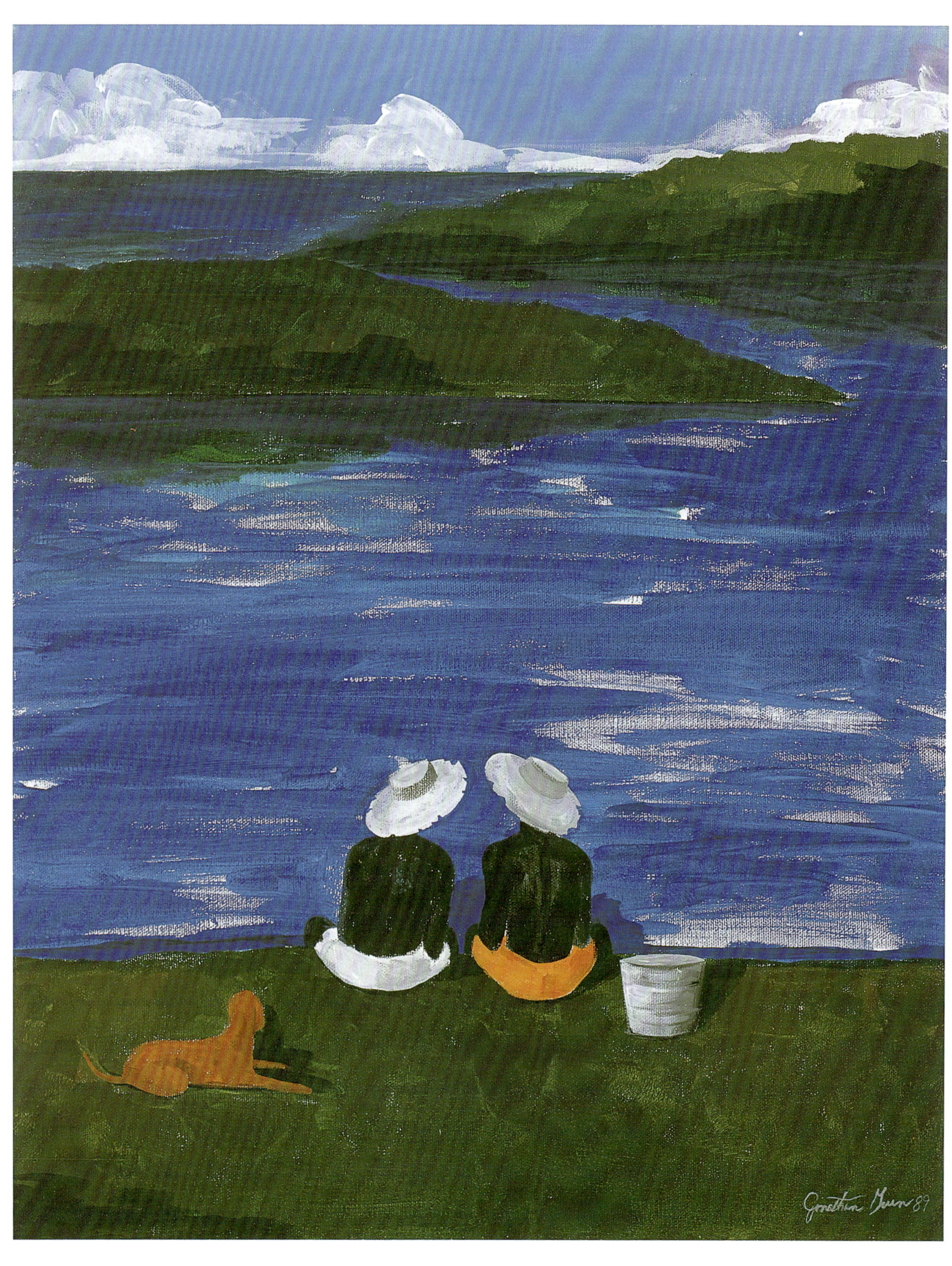

Sitting by the River, 1989. Acrylic on canvas, 20 x 16".
Courtesy of Julia J. Norrell. Photograph by Katherine Wetzel.

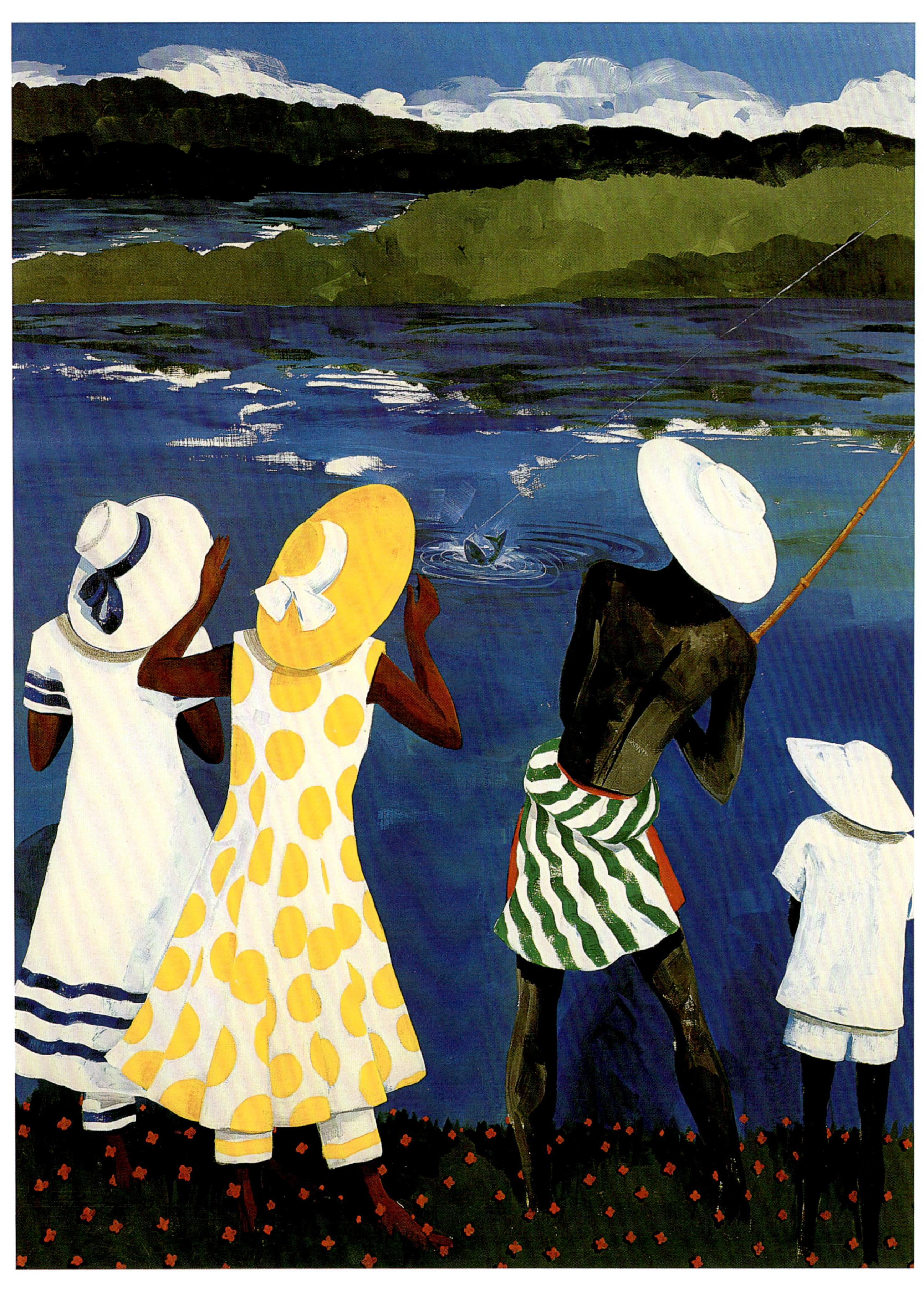

Fishing from the Shore, 1989. Acrylic on masonite, 32 x 24".
Courtesy of Tim and Tanya Stamm. Photograph by Tim Stamm.

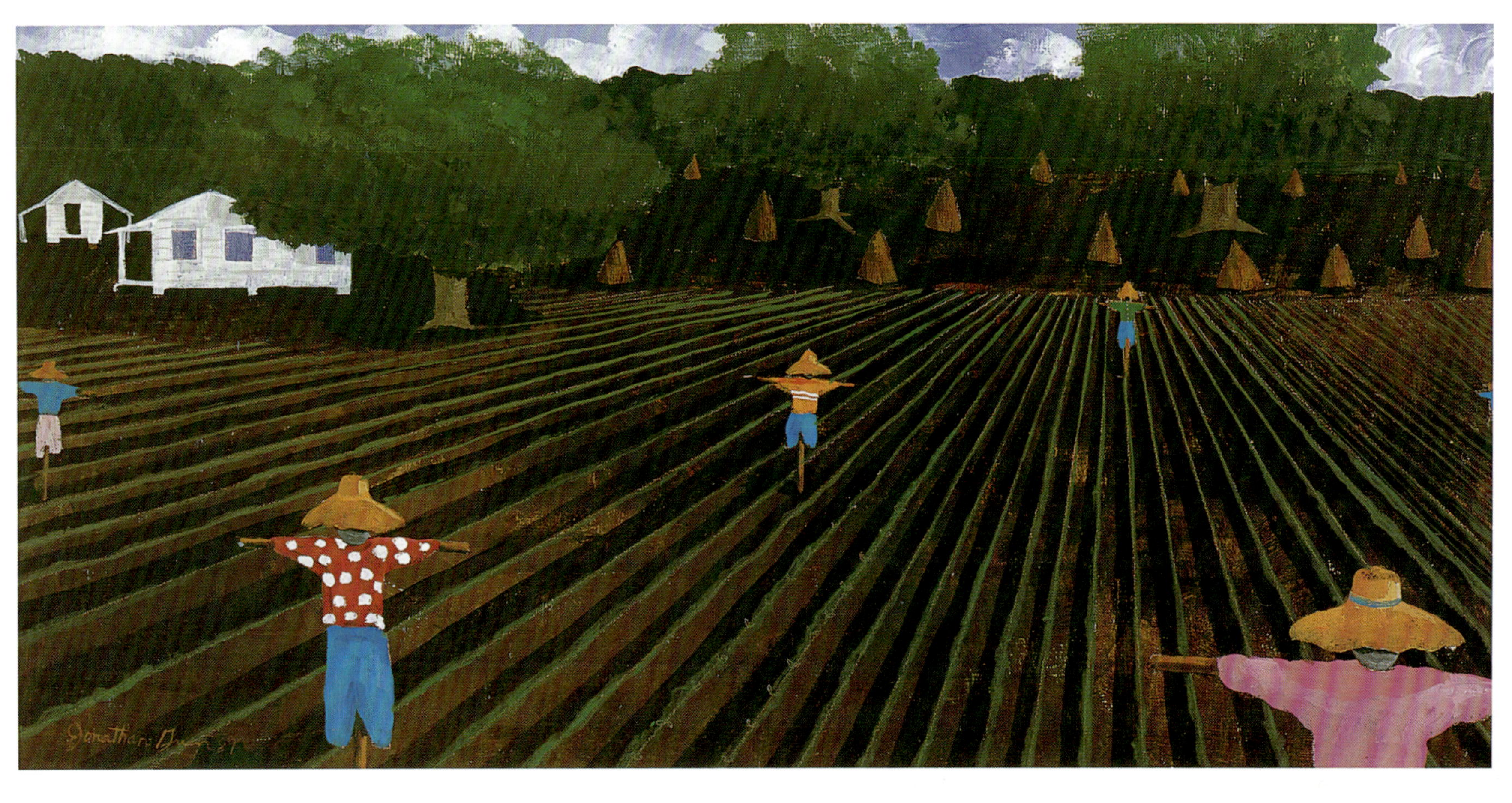

The Scarecrows, 1989. Acrylic on masonite, 12 x 24".
Courtesy of Richard Weedman. Photograph by Katherine Wetzel.

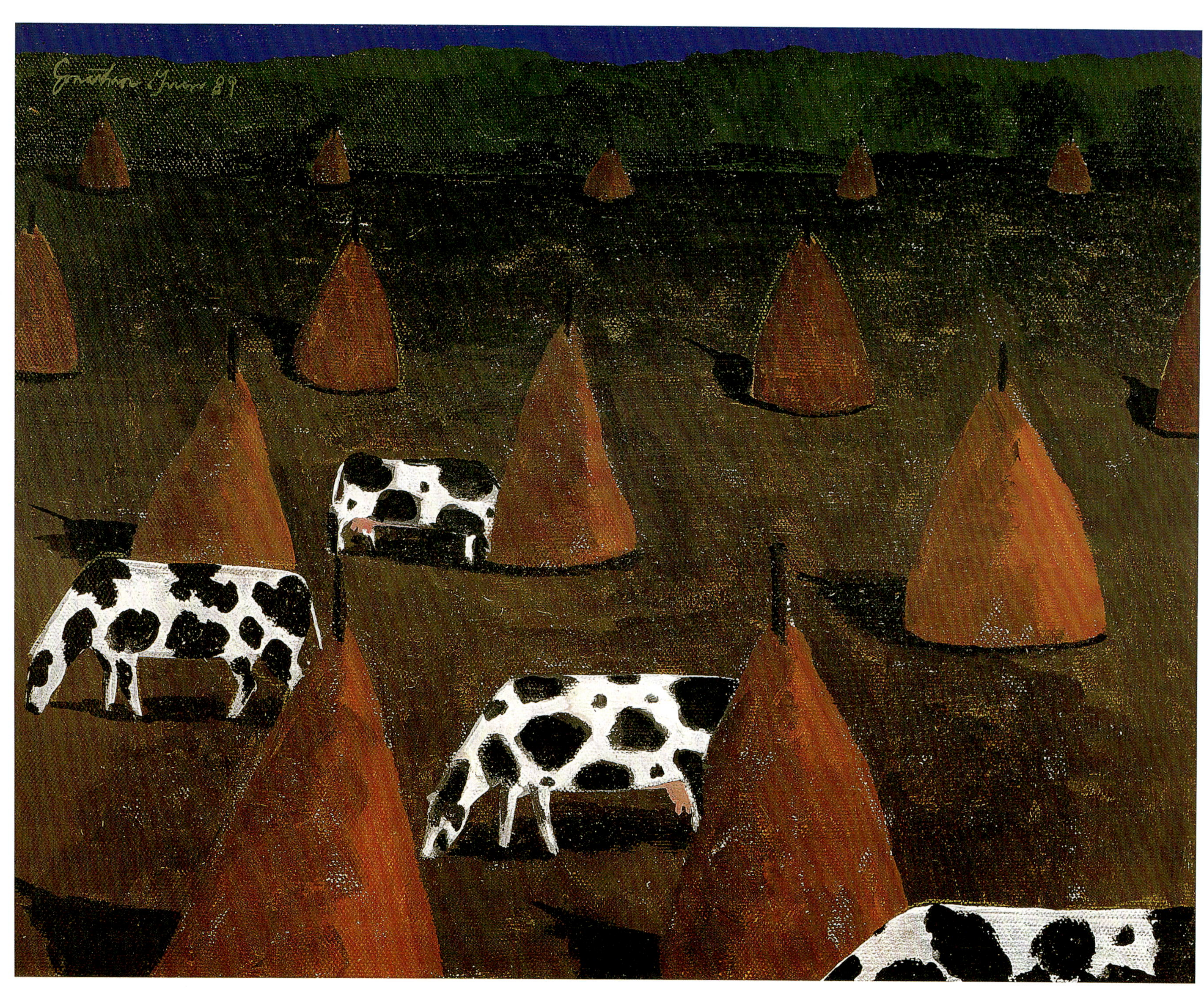

Grazing Cattle, 1989. Oil on canvas, 11 x 14".
Courtesy of Richard Weedman. Photograph by Tim Stamm.

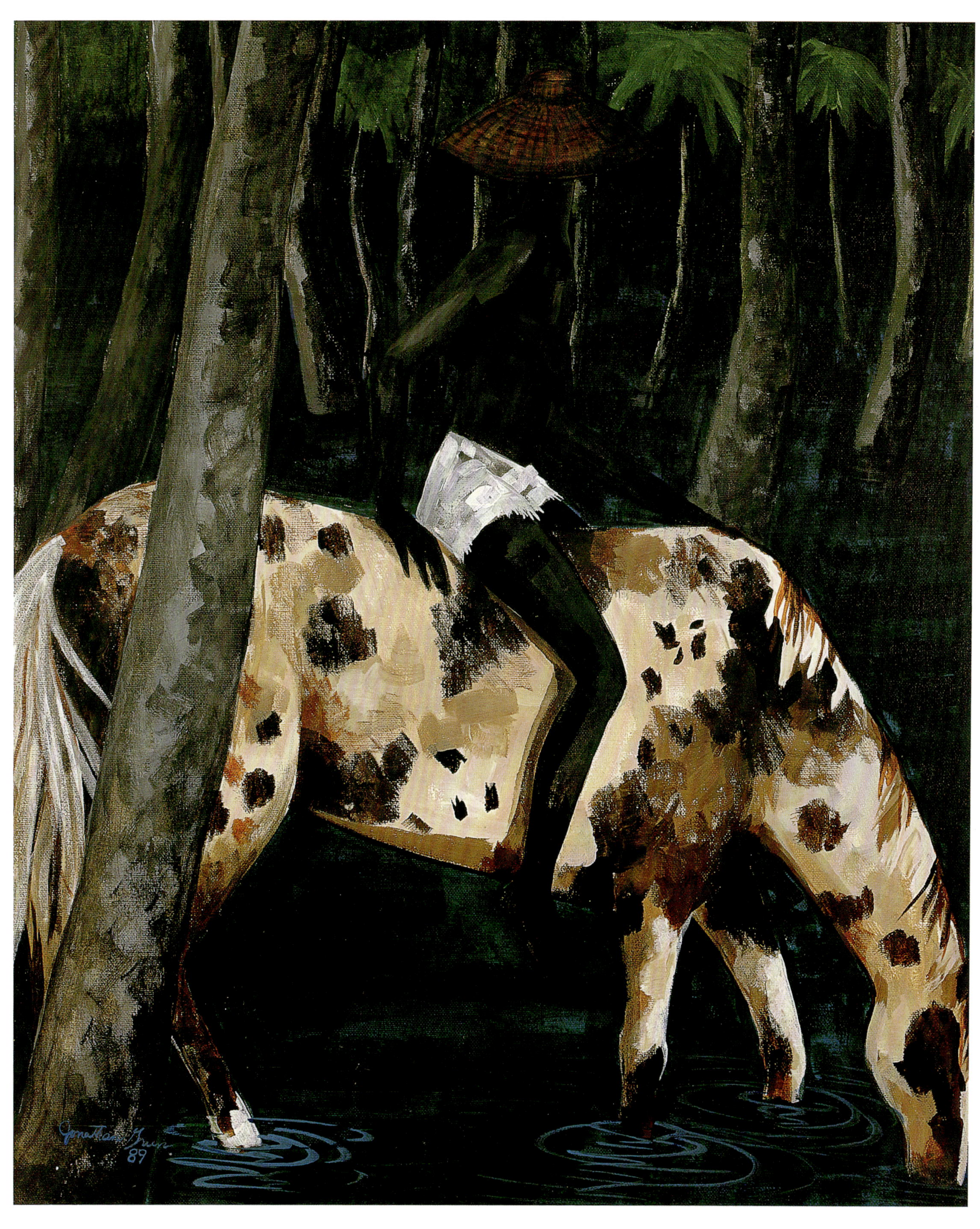

Noon Day Crossing, 1989. Acrylic on canvas, 24 x 20".
Courtesy of David and Judy White. Photograph by Tim Stamm.

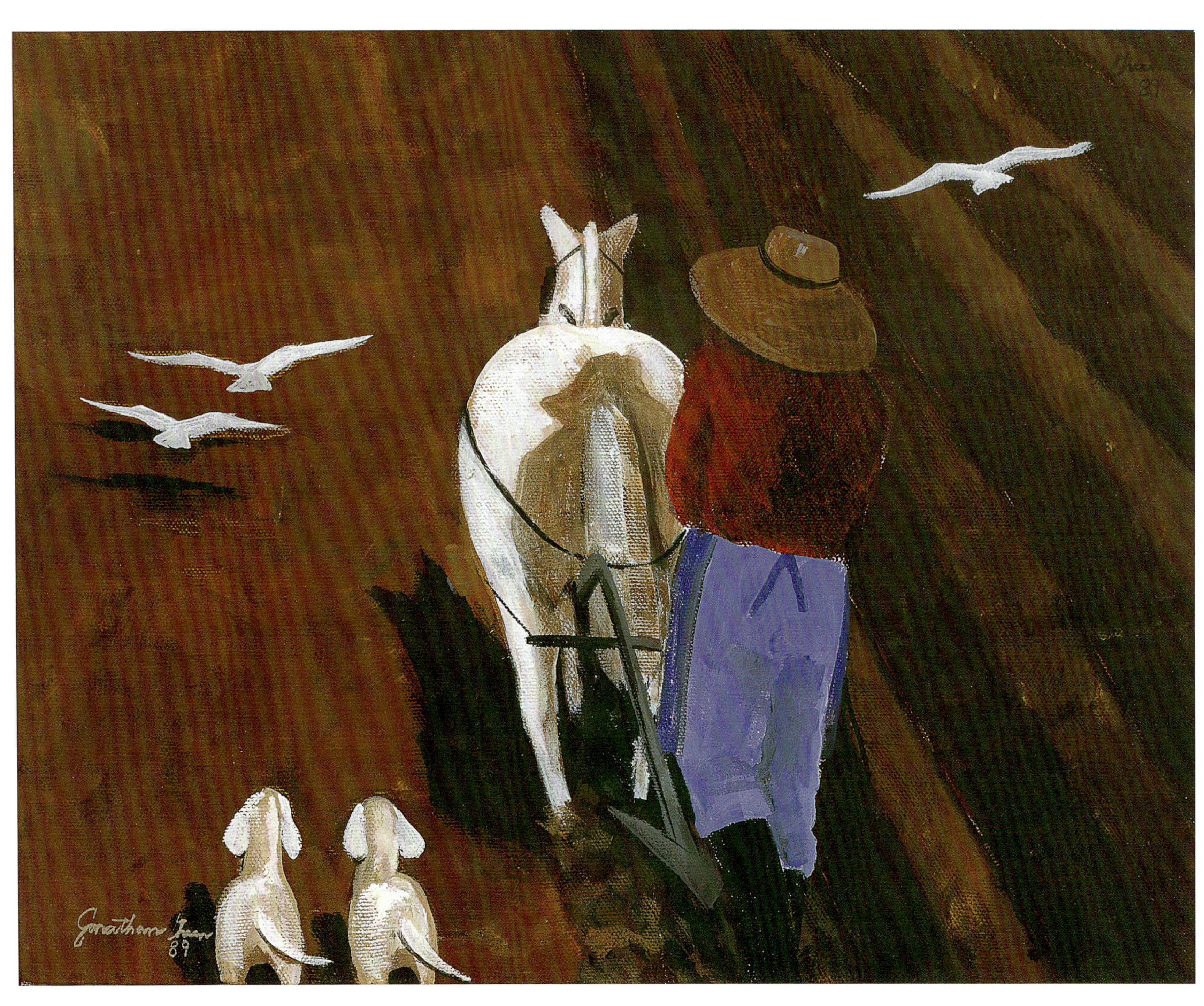

The Plowman, 1989. Oil on canvas, 11 x 14".
Courtesy of Richard Weedman. Photograph by Katherine Wetzel.

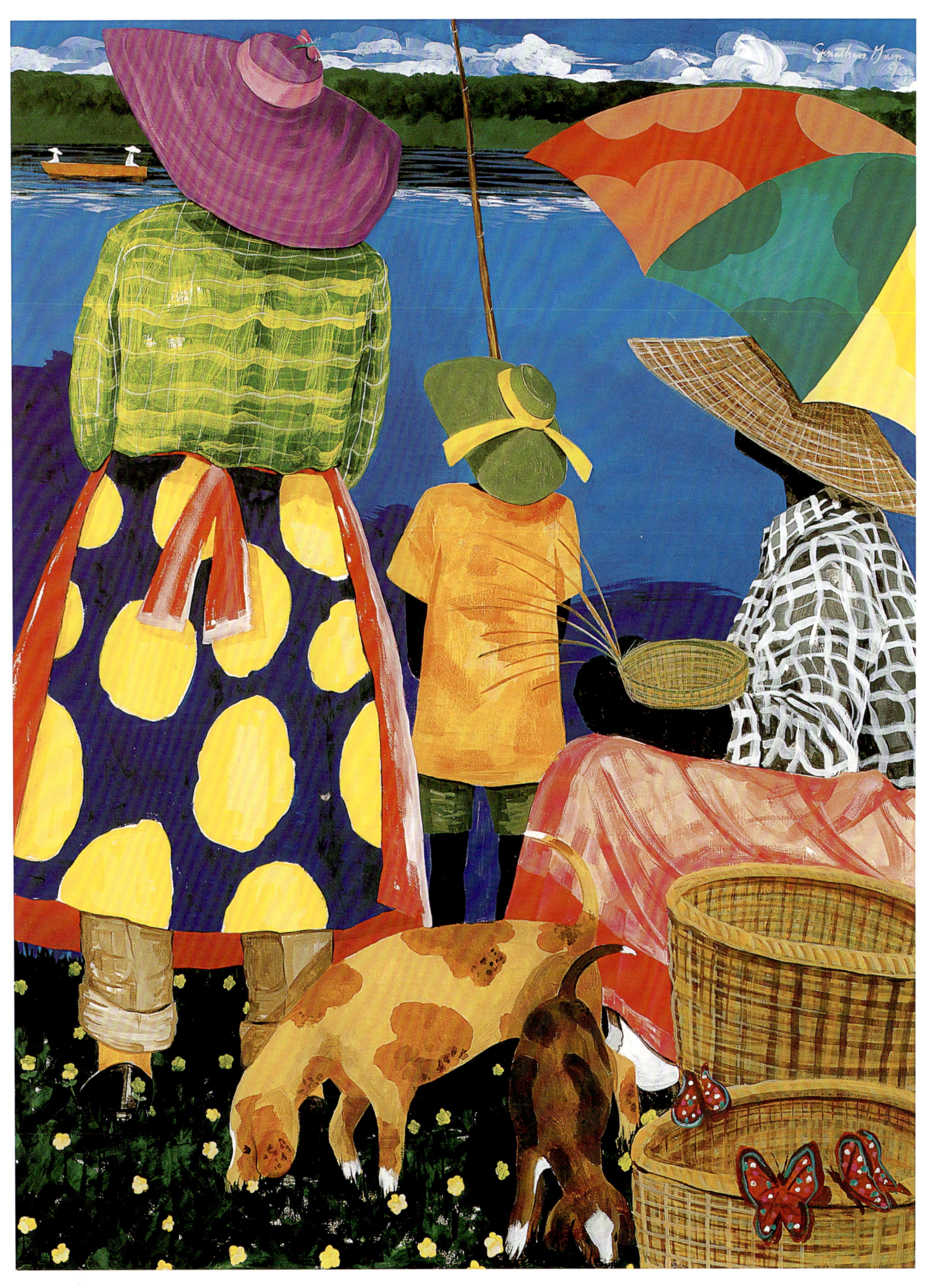

Family Fishing, 1990. Acrylic on canvas, 48 x 36".
Courtesy of John and Barbara Langston. Photograph by Rick Rhodes.

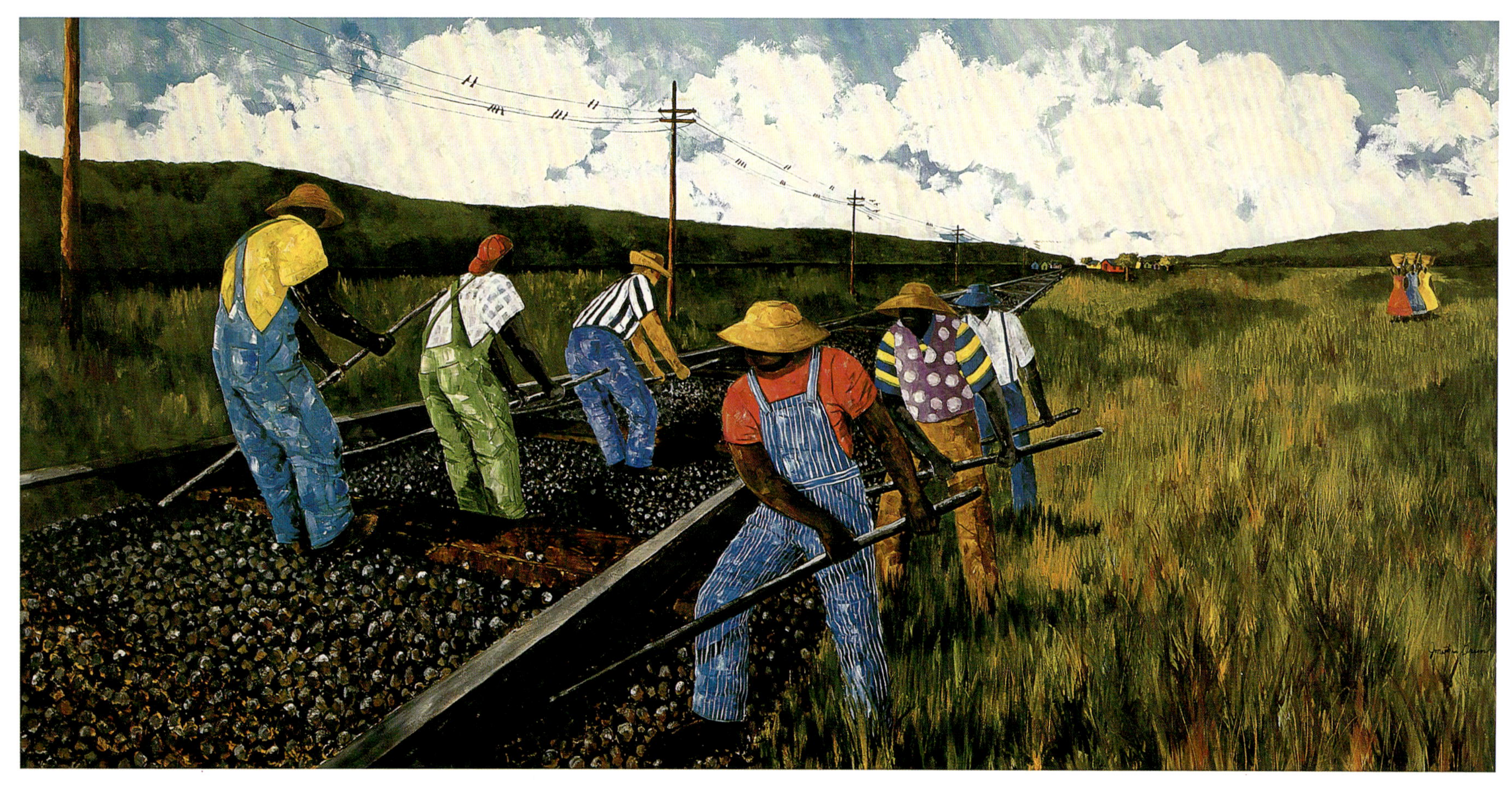

Gandy Men, 1990. Oil on canvas, 47 x 98".
Courtesy of William A. Boone. Photograph by Tim Stamm.

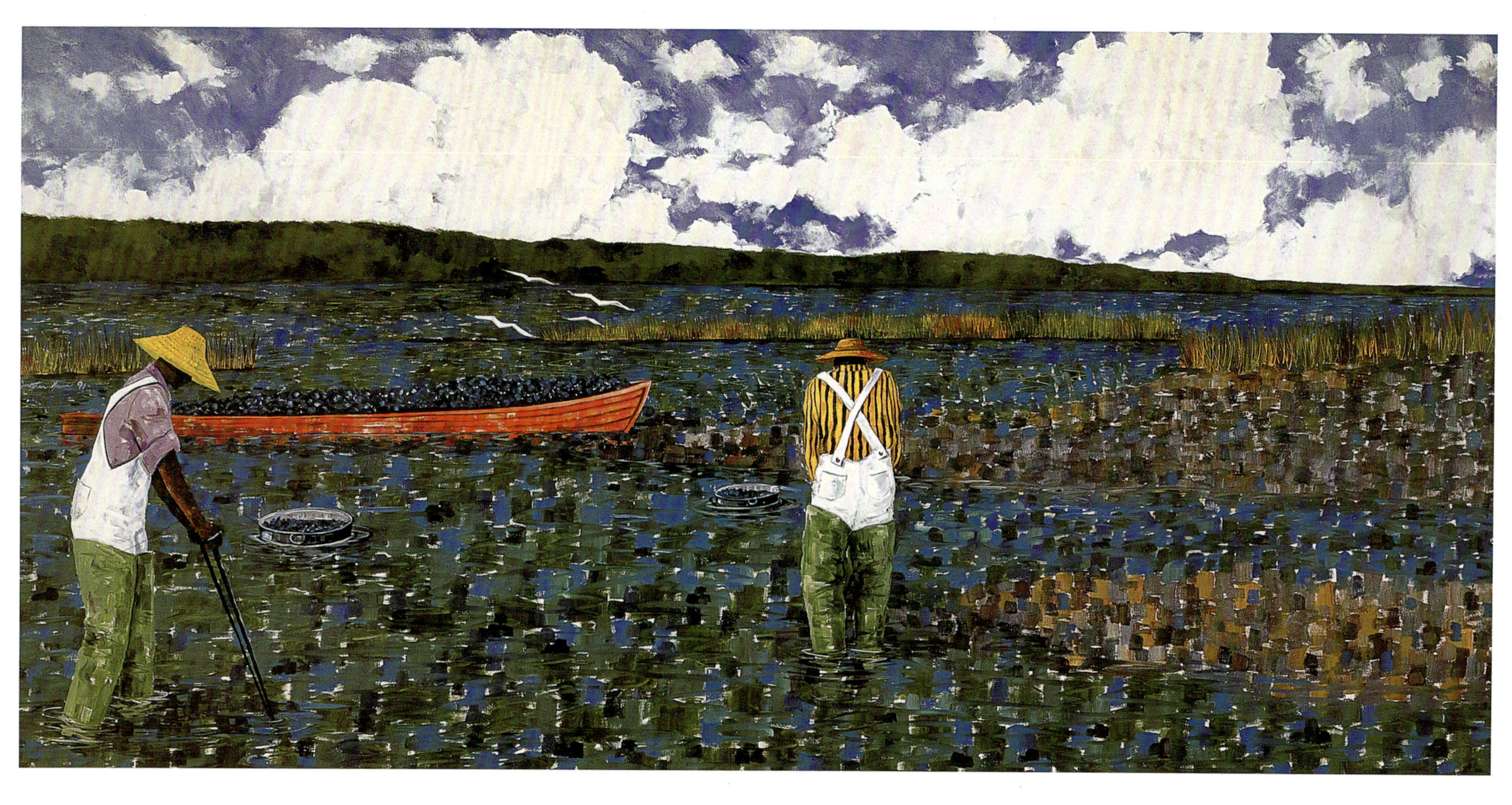

Oyster Pickers, 1990. Oil on canvas, 47 x 98".
Courtesy of Drs. Yele and Shirley Aluko. Photograph by Tim Stamm.

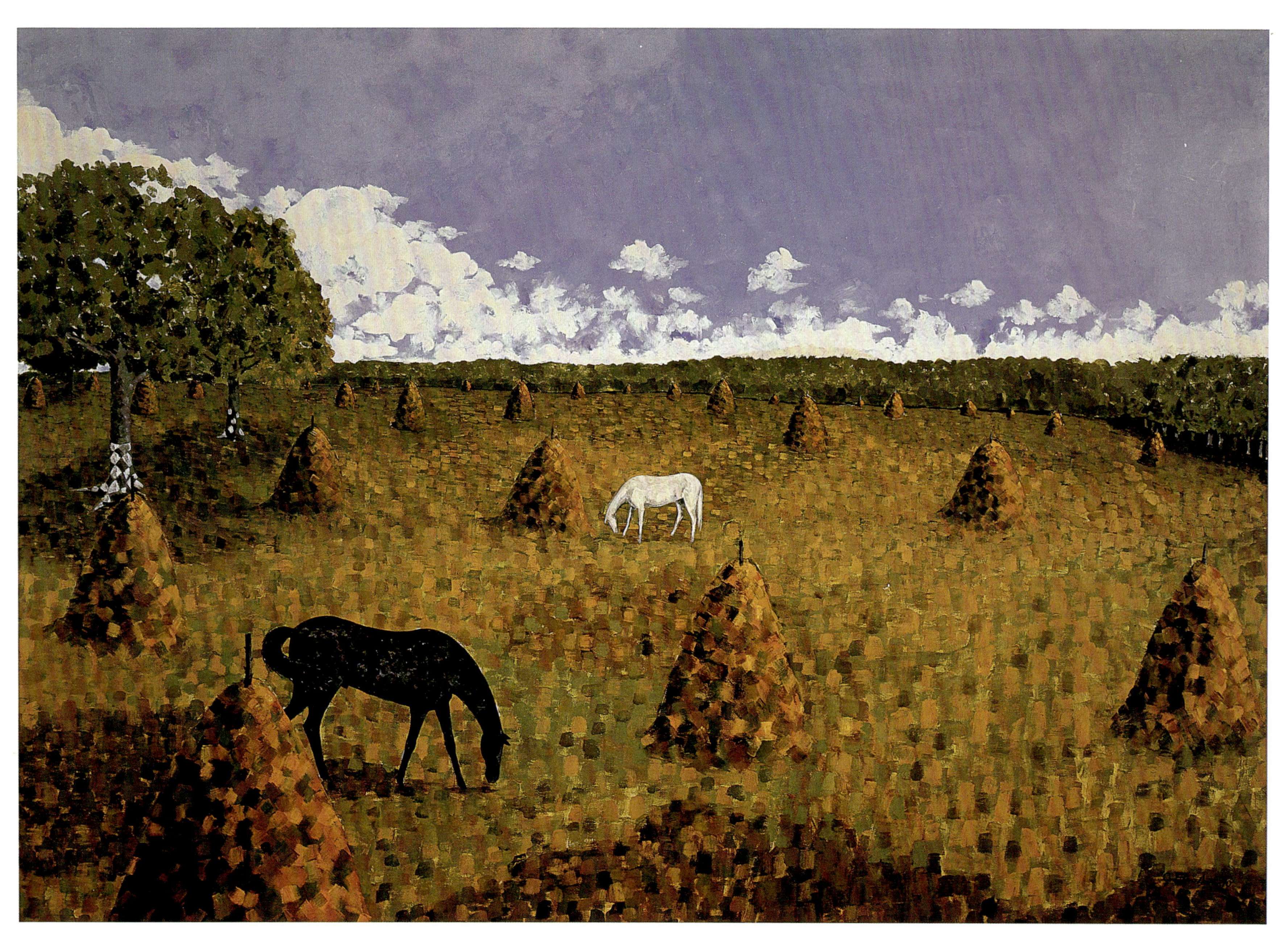

The Meadow, 1990. Oil on canvas, 66 x 110".
Courtesy of Richard Weedman. Photograph by Tim Stamm.

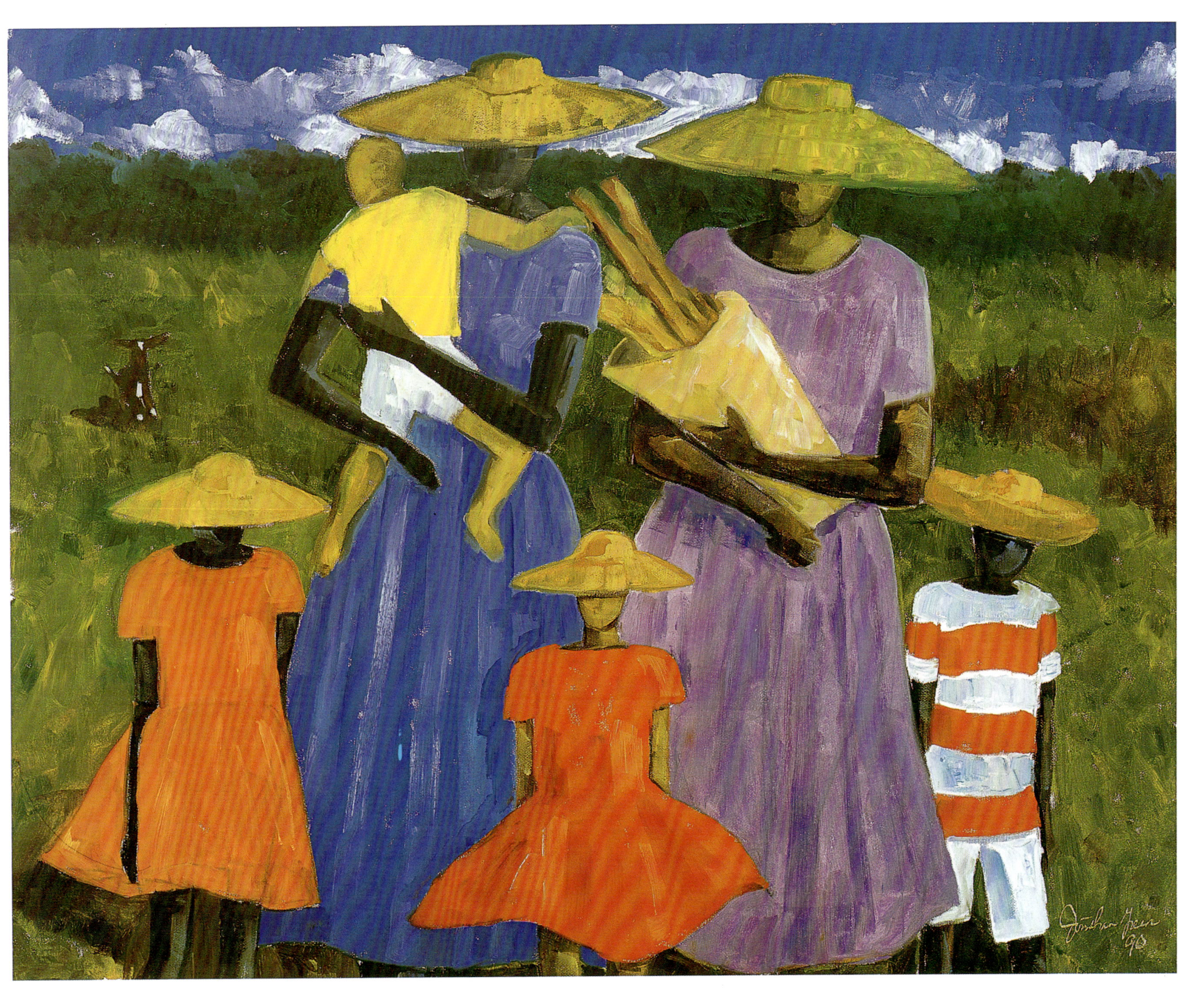

Family Strolling, 1990. Oil on canvas, 19 x 23".
Courtesy of J. Quitman Marshall. Photograph by Katherine Wetzel.

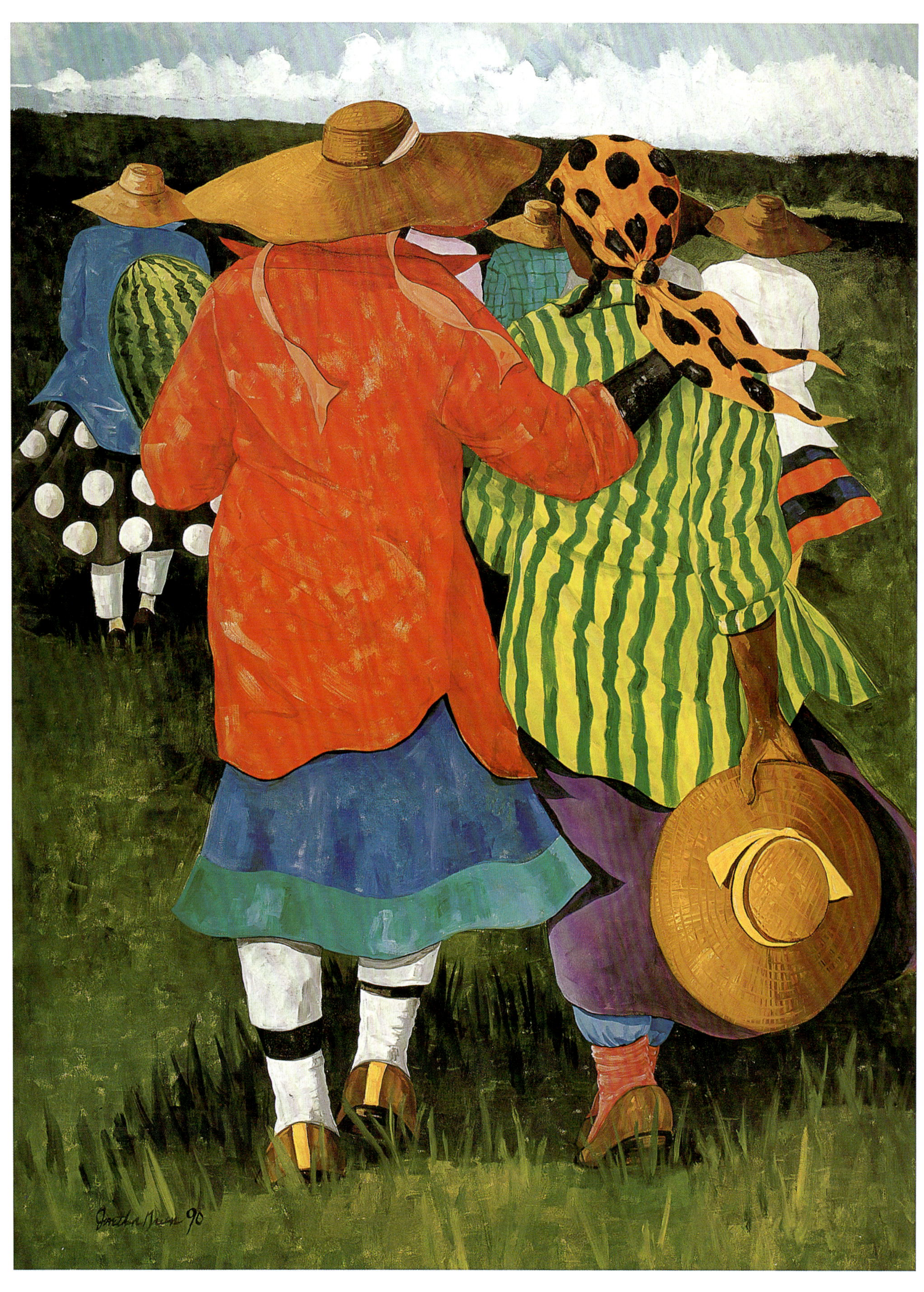

Quitting Time, 1990. Oil on canvas, 72 x 55".
Courtesy of Gary E. Gardner. Photograph by Tim Stamm.

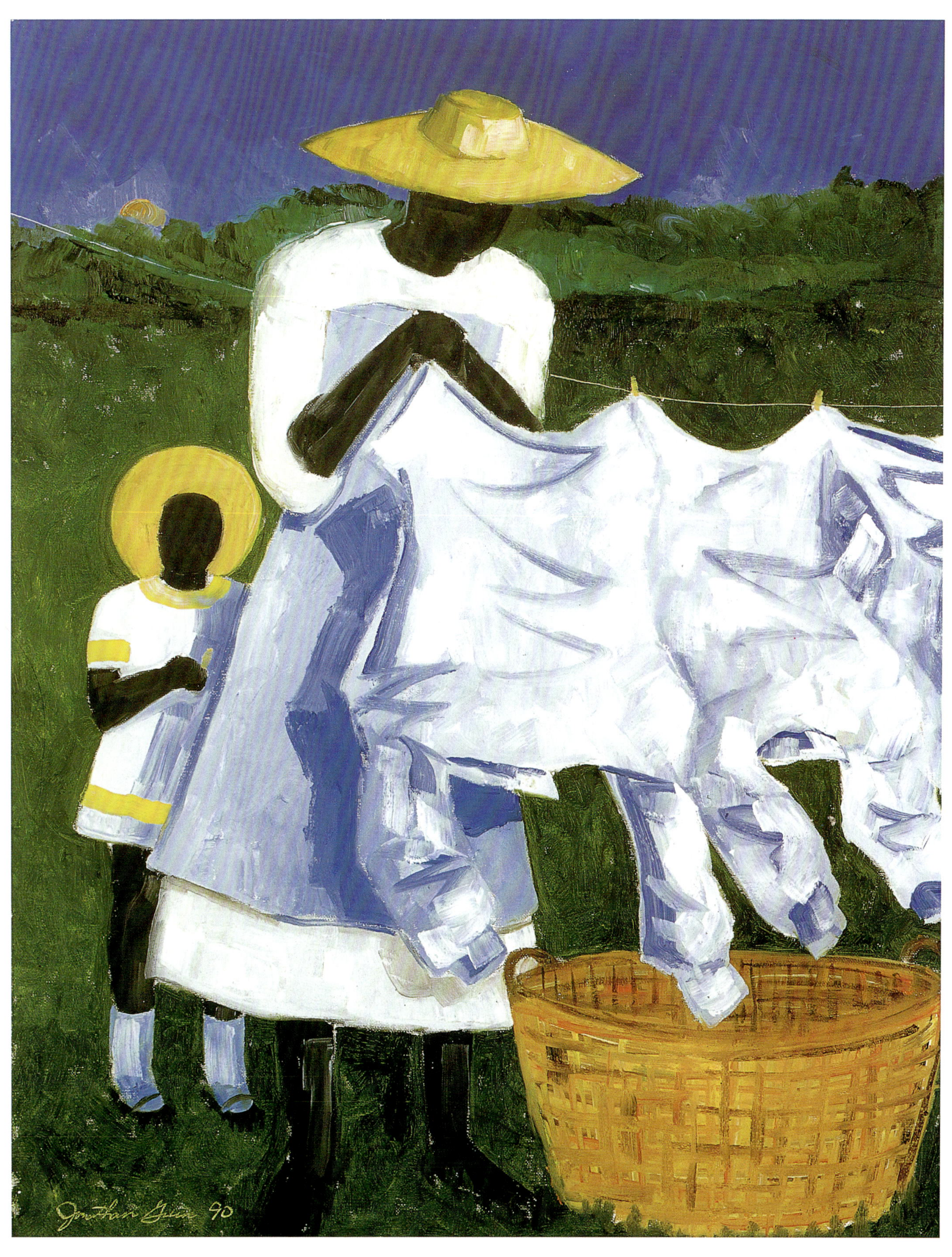

Starched White, 1990. Oil on canvas, 23 x 19".
Courtesy of John Elliott. Photograph by Tim Stamm.

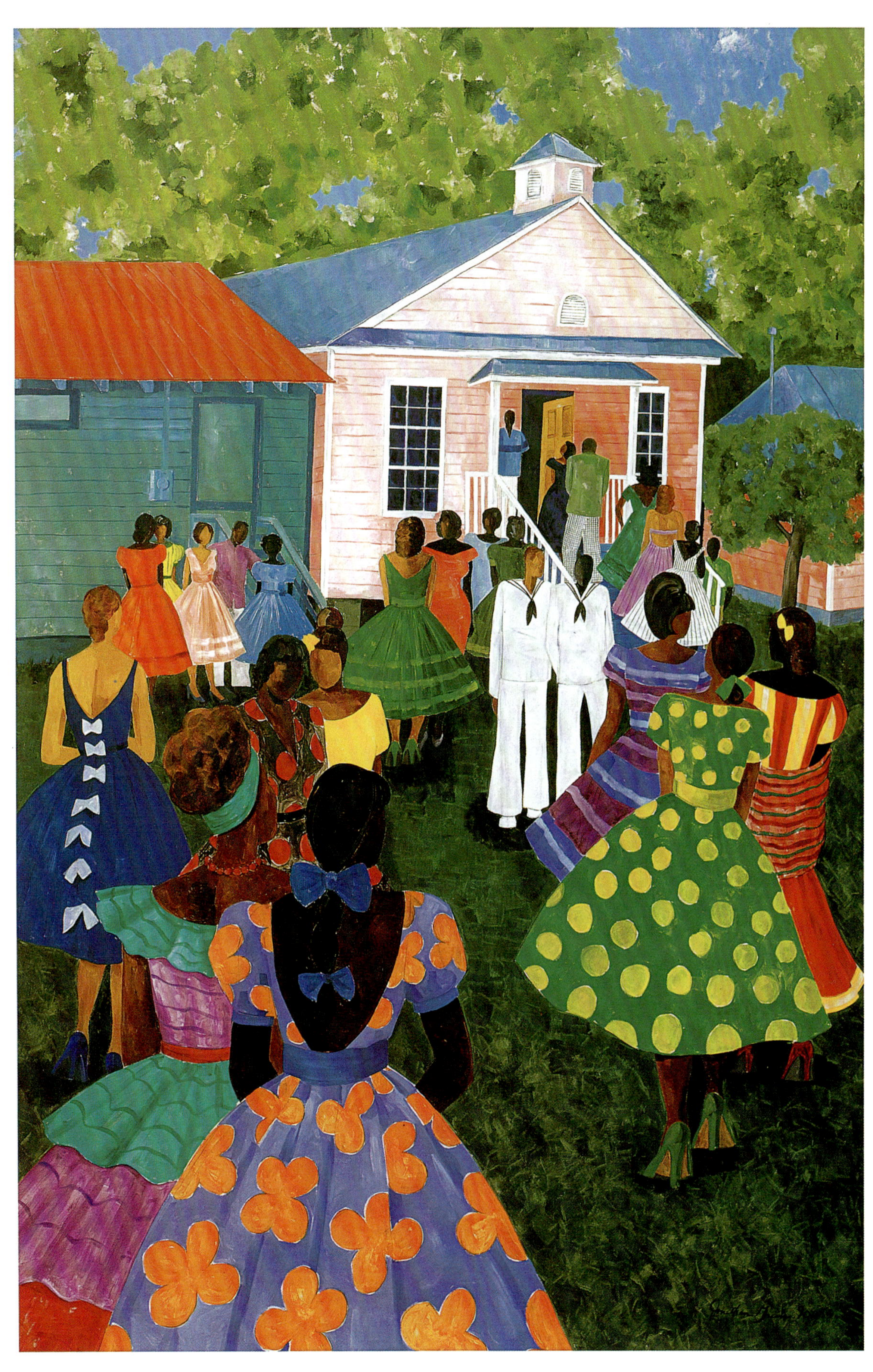

Silver Slipper Dance Hall, 1990. Oil on canvas, 99 x 67".
Courtesy of Ernst and Christina Bruderer. Photograph by Tim Stamm.

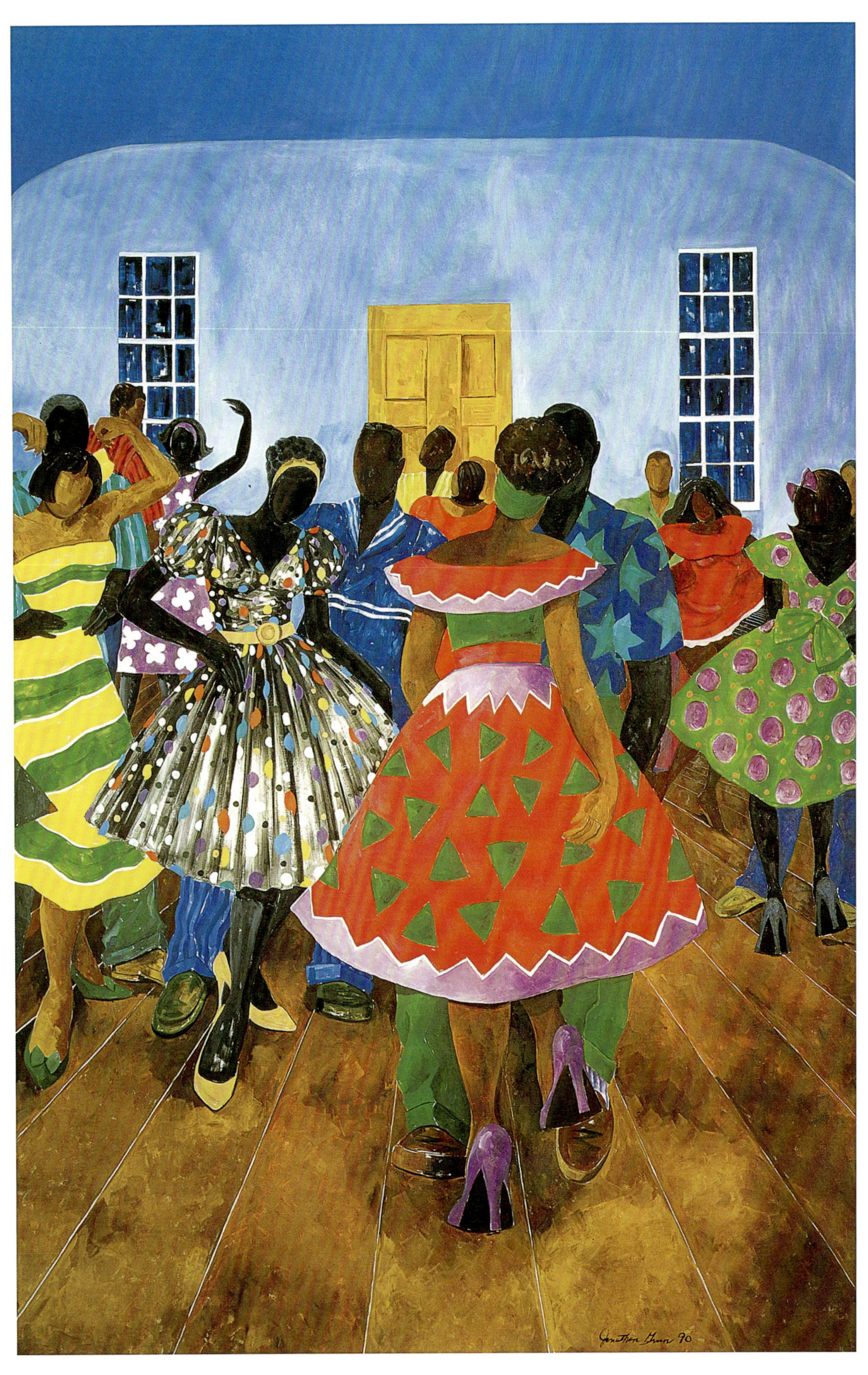

The Silver Slipper Club, 1990. Oil on canvas, 99 x 67".
Collection of Morris Museum of Art, Augusta, Ga. Photograph by Tim Stamm.

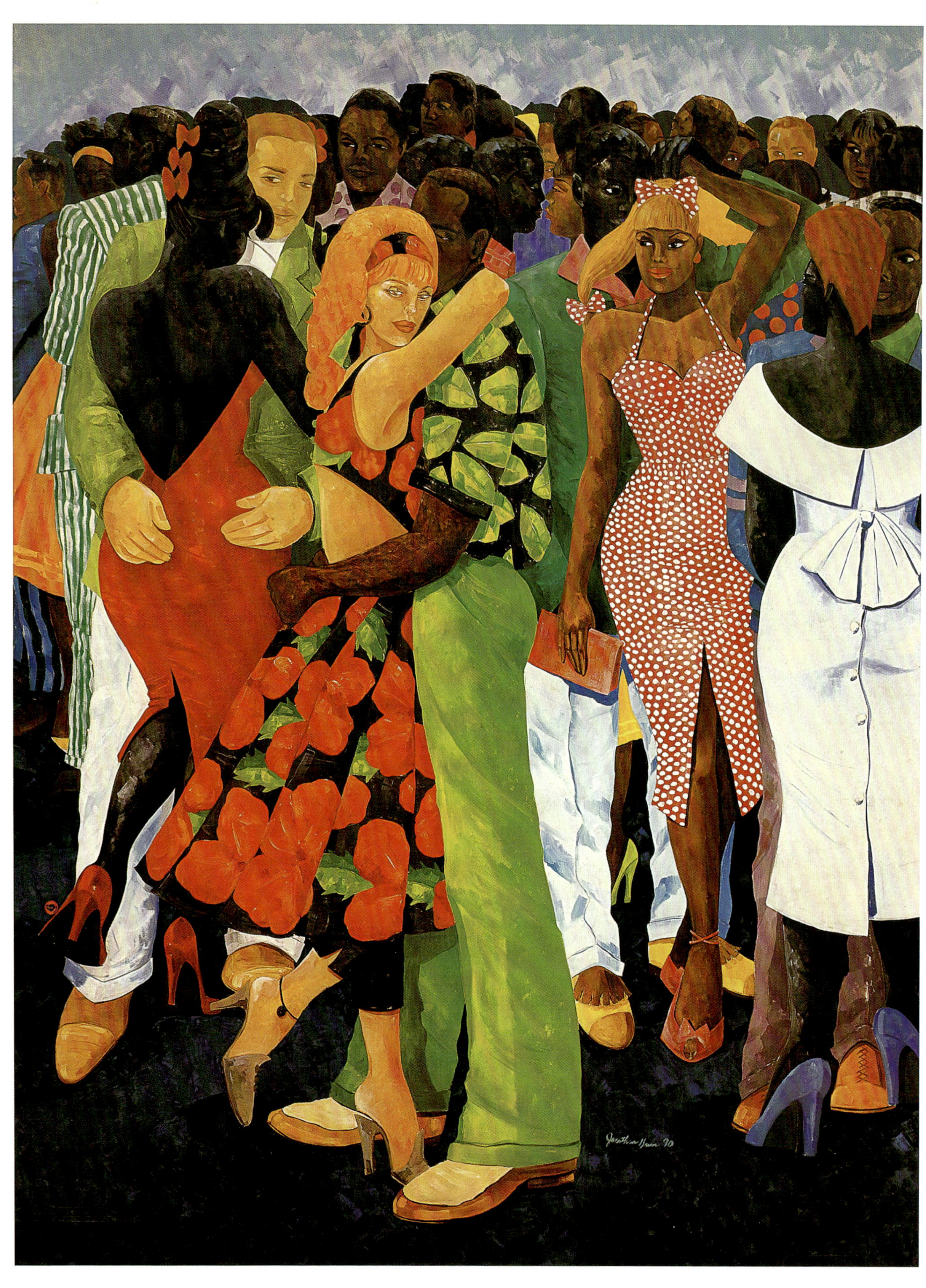

Yemassee Lounge, 1990. Oil on canvas, 99 x 67".
Courtesy of Vanessa G. Niles. Photograph by Tim Stamm.

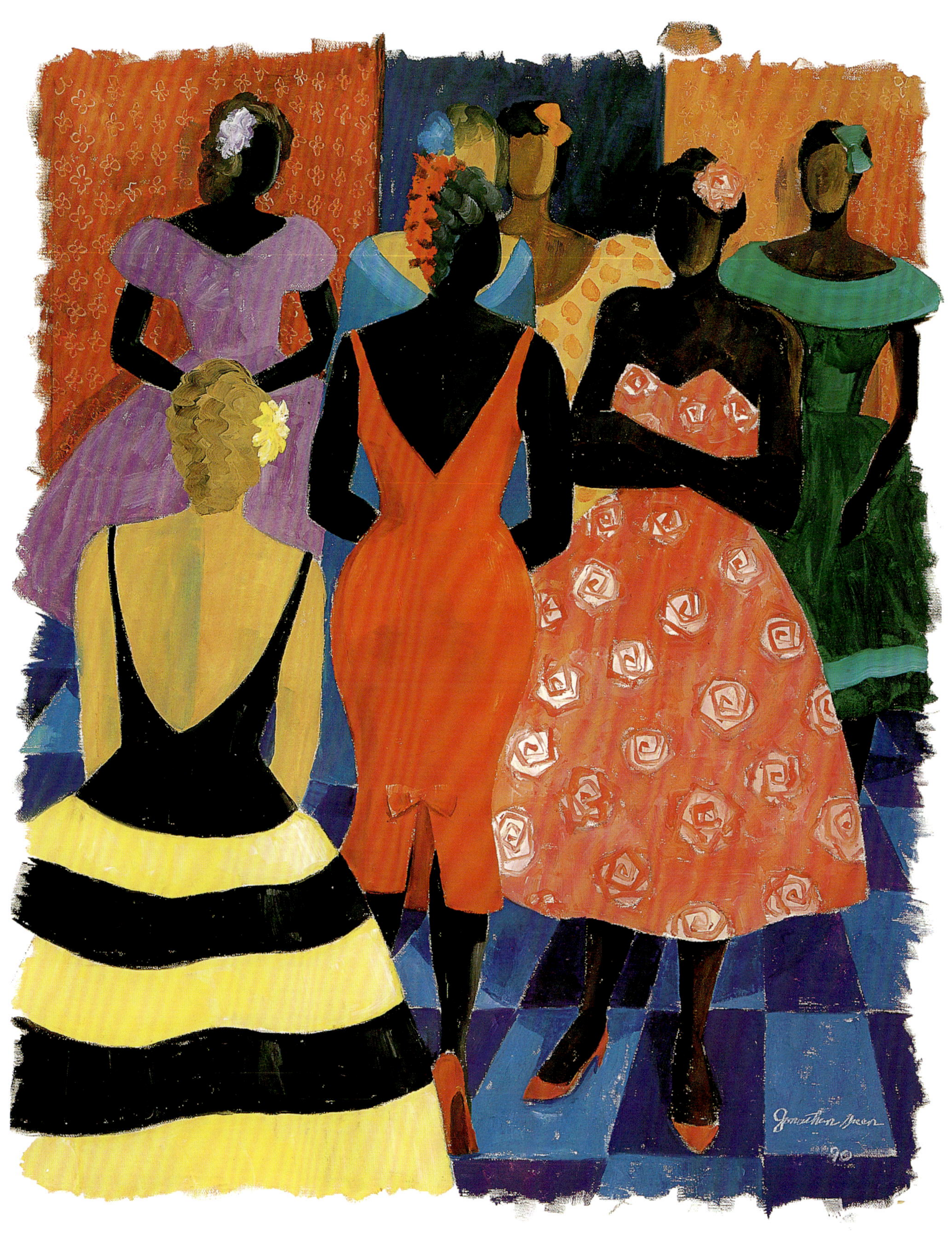

The Power Room, 1990. Oil on canvas, 24 x 19".
Courtesy of Metchthild Borries-Knopp. Photograph by Tim Stamm.

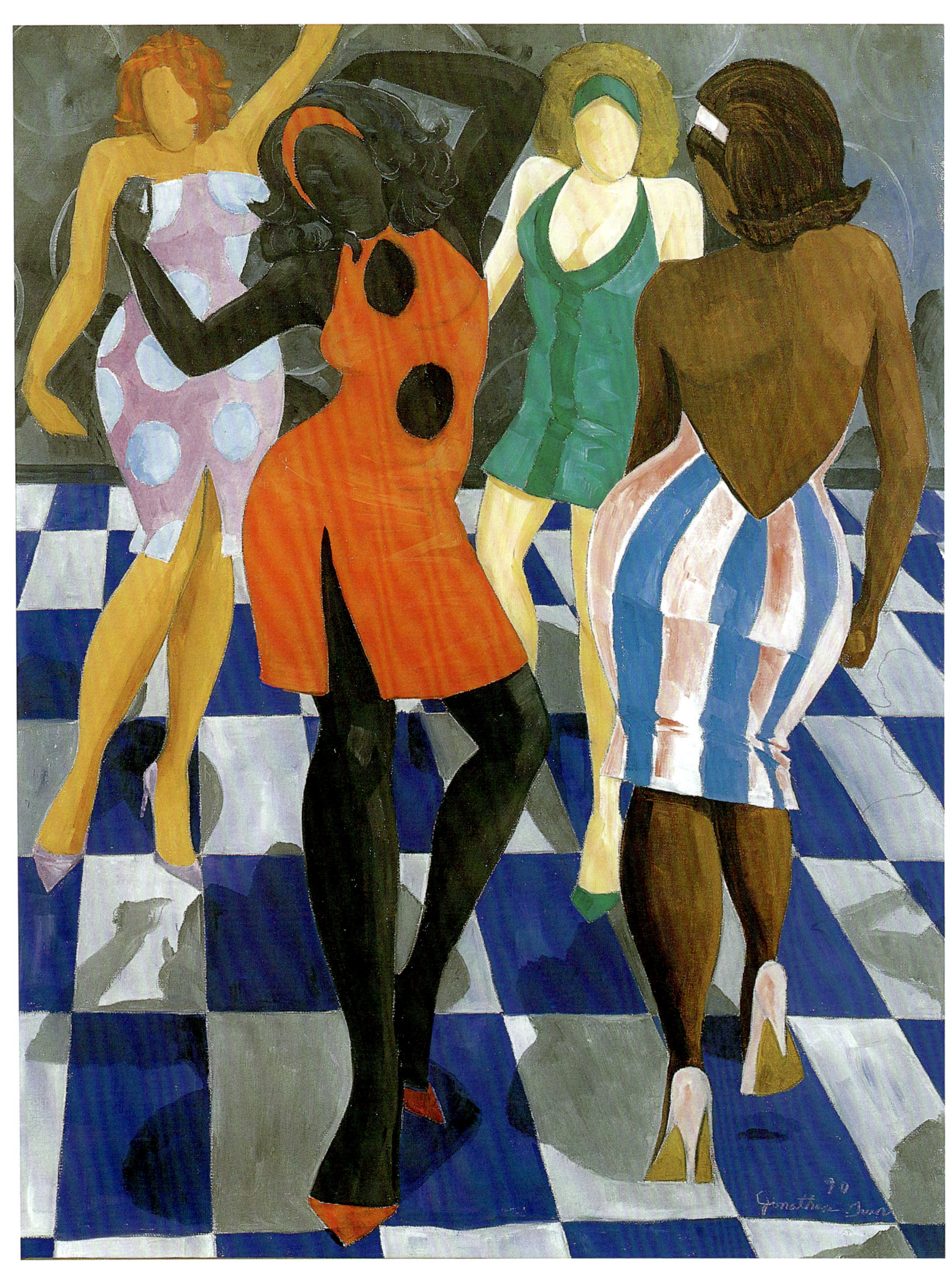

Lady Bug Lounge, 1990. Oil on canvas, 24 x 19".
Courtesy of Charles L. Shumway, Jr. Photograph by Katherine Wetzel.

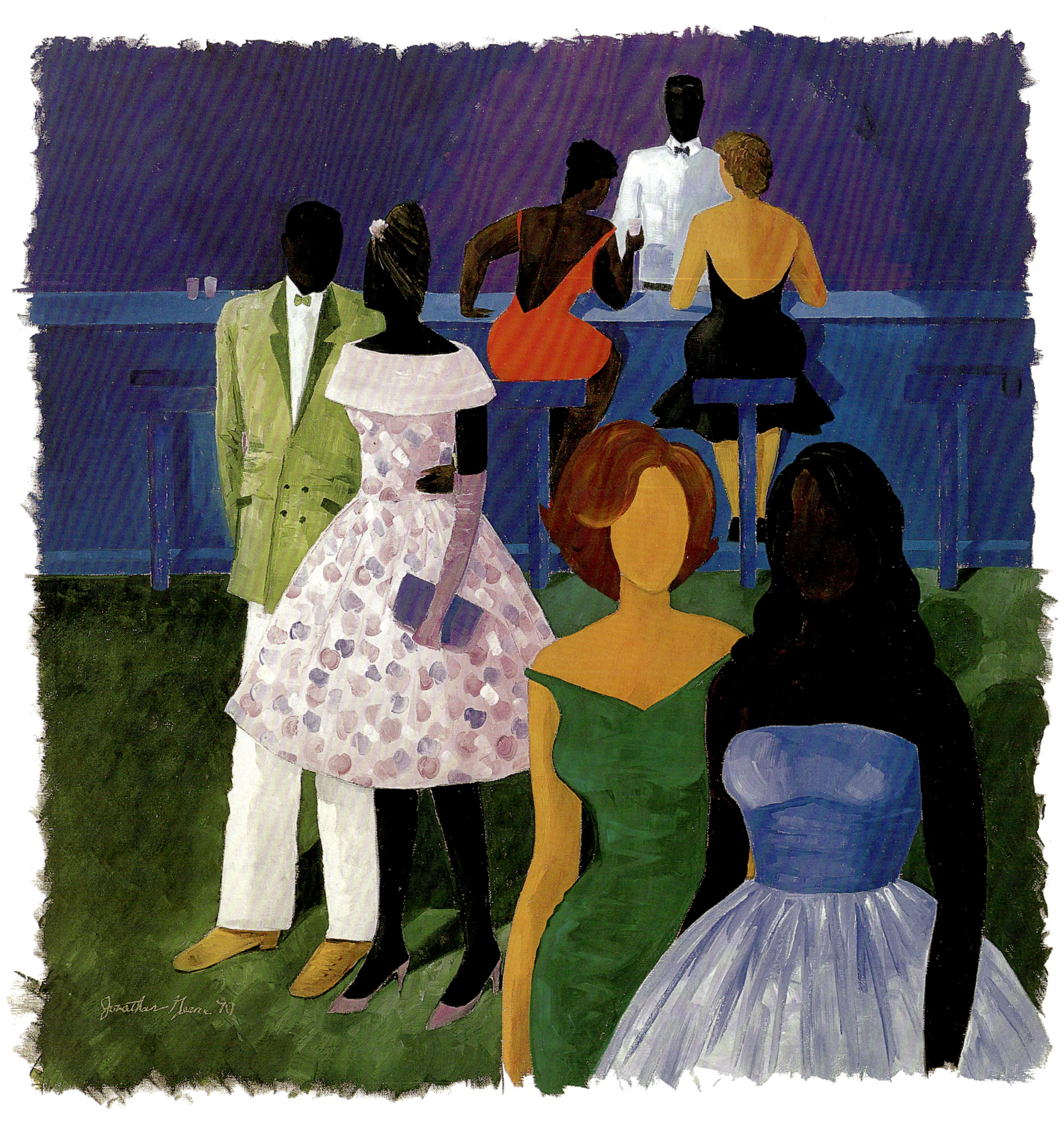

Seaside Lounge, 1990. Oil on canvas, 24 x 24".
Courtesy of Clarence J. Brooks. Photograph by Tim Stamm.

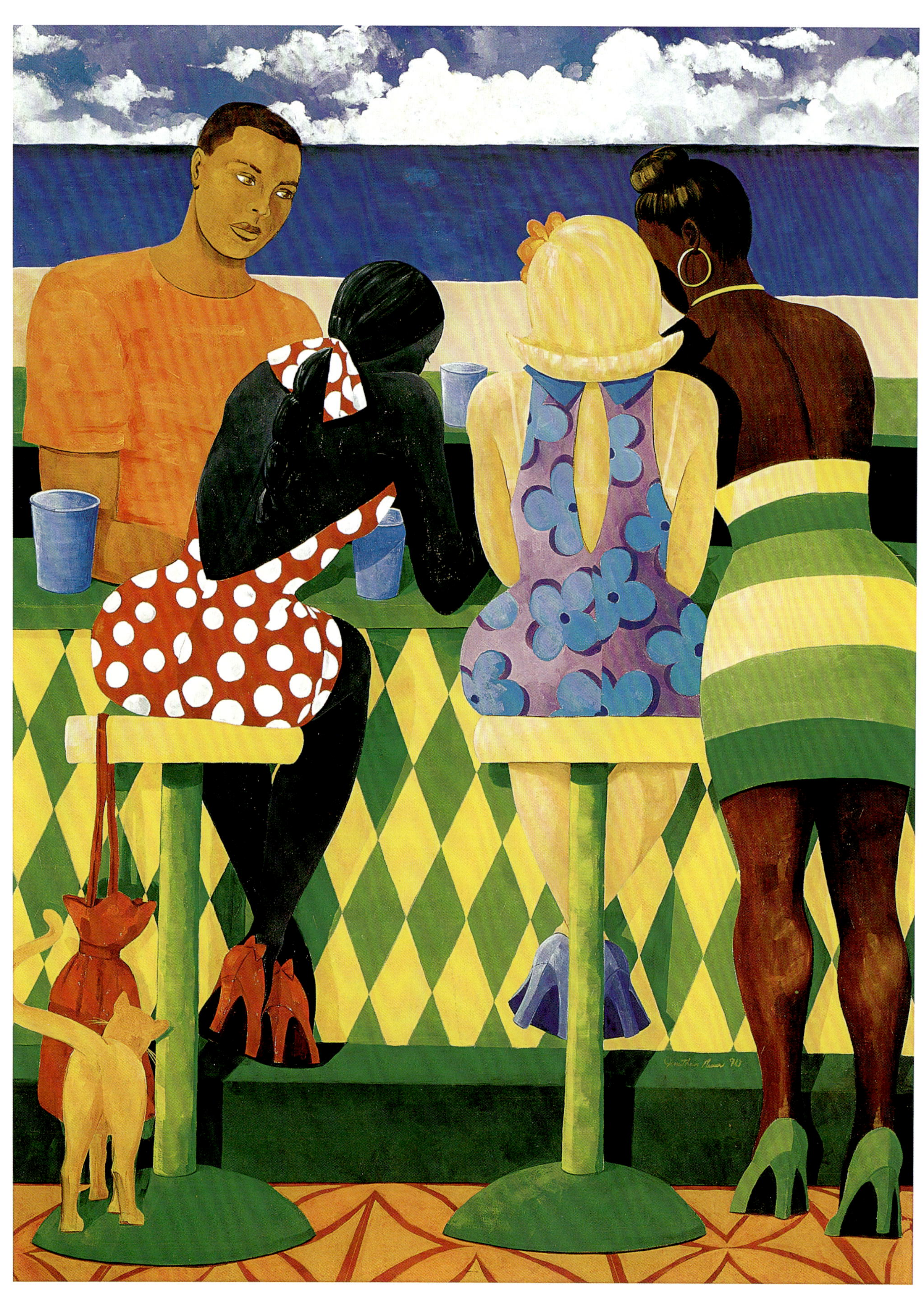

The Sand Bar, 1990. Oil on canvas, 72 x 55".
Courtesy of Olden and Carol Lee. Photograph by Tim Stamm.

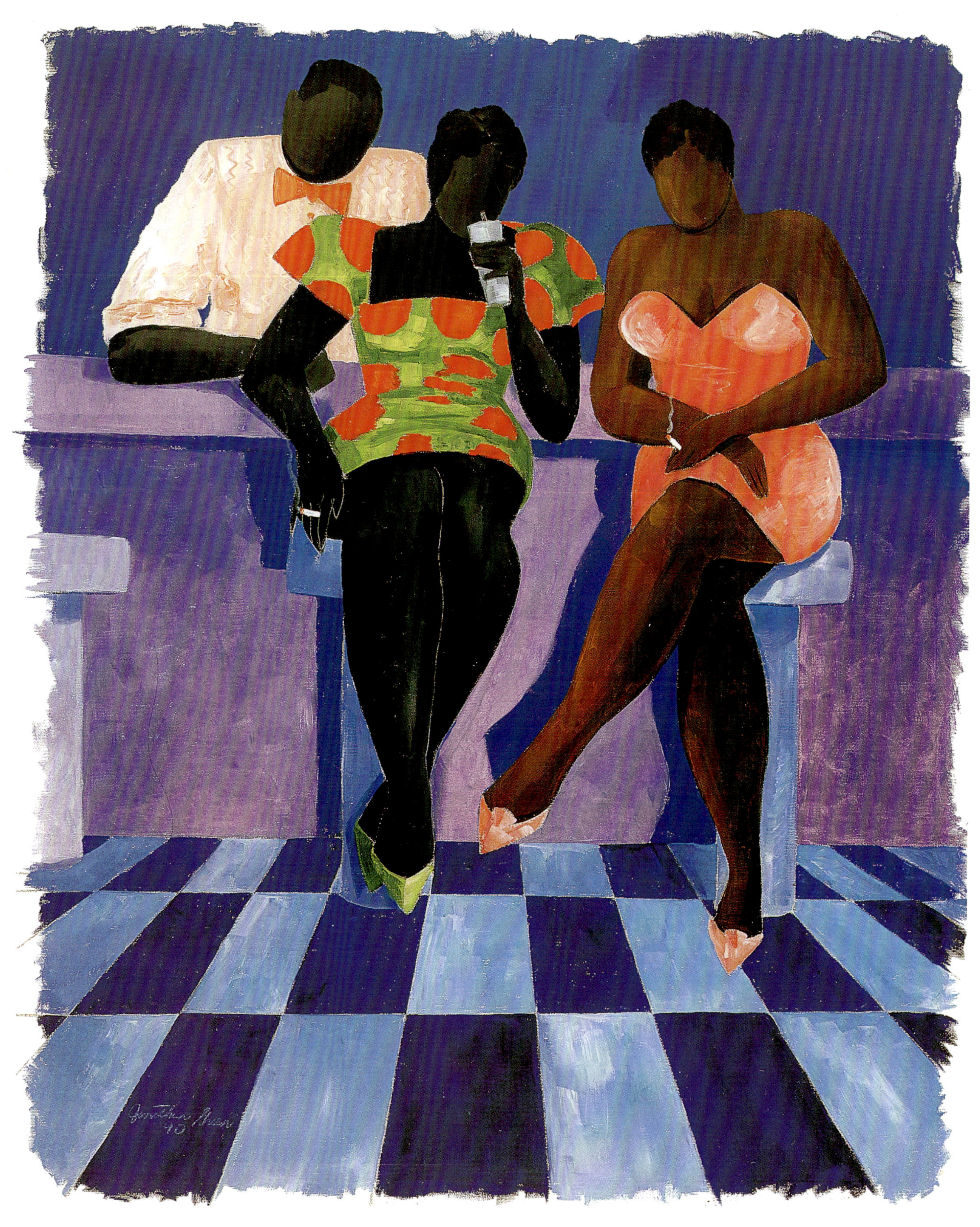

Folly Beach Lounge, 1990. Oil on canvas, 23 x 19".
Courtesy of Timothy J. Tomasi. Photograph by Tim Stamm.

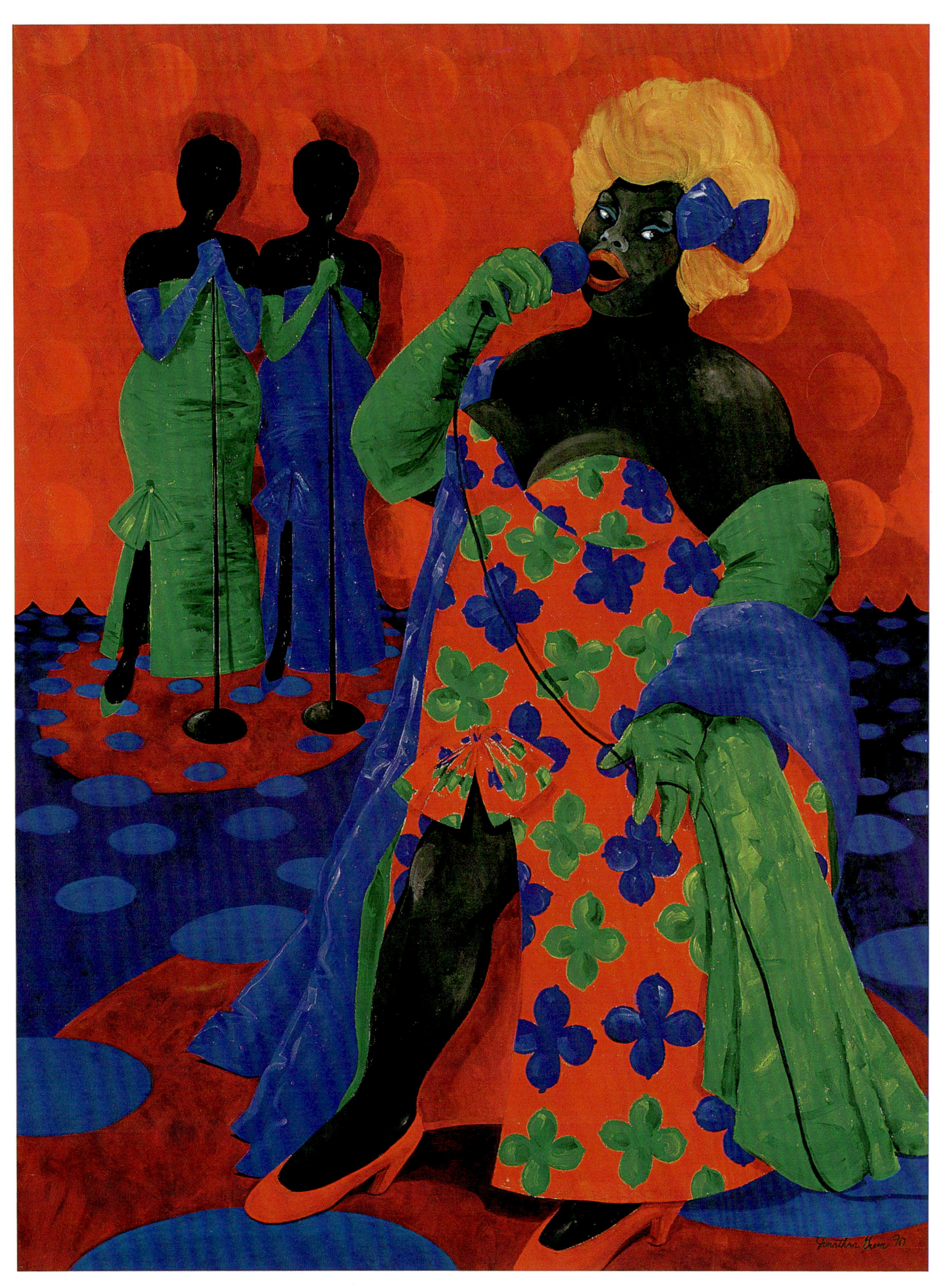

The Blues Singer, 1990. Oil on canvas, 72 x 55".
Collection of the artist. Photograph by Rick Rhodes.

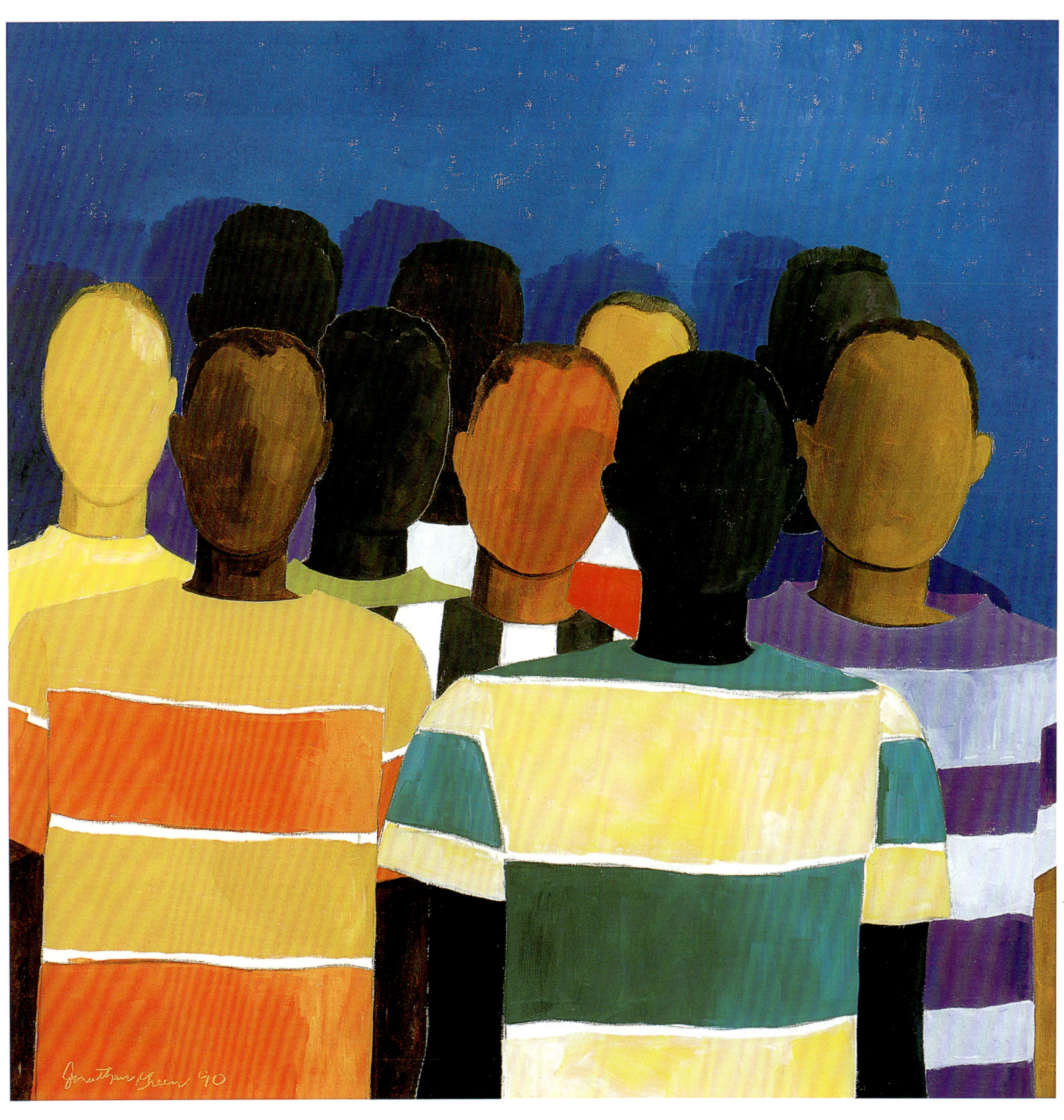

Sunday School Boys, 1990. Oil on canvas, 23 x 23".
Courtesy of Dr. and Mrs. William Mumby. Photograph by Katherine Wetzel.

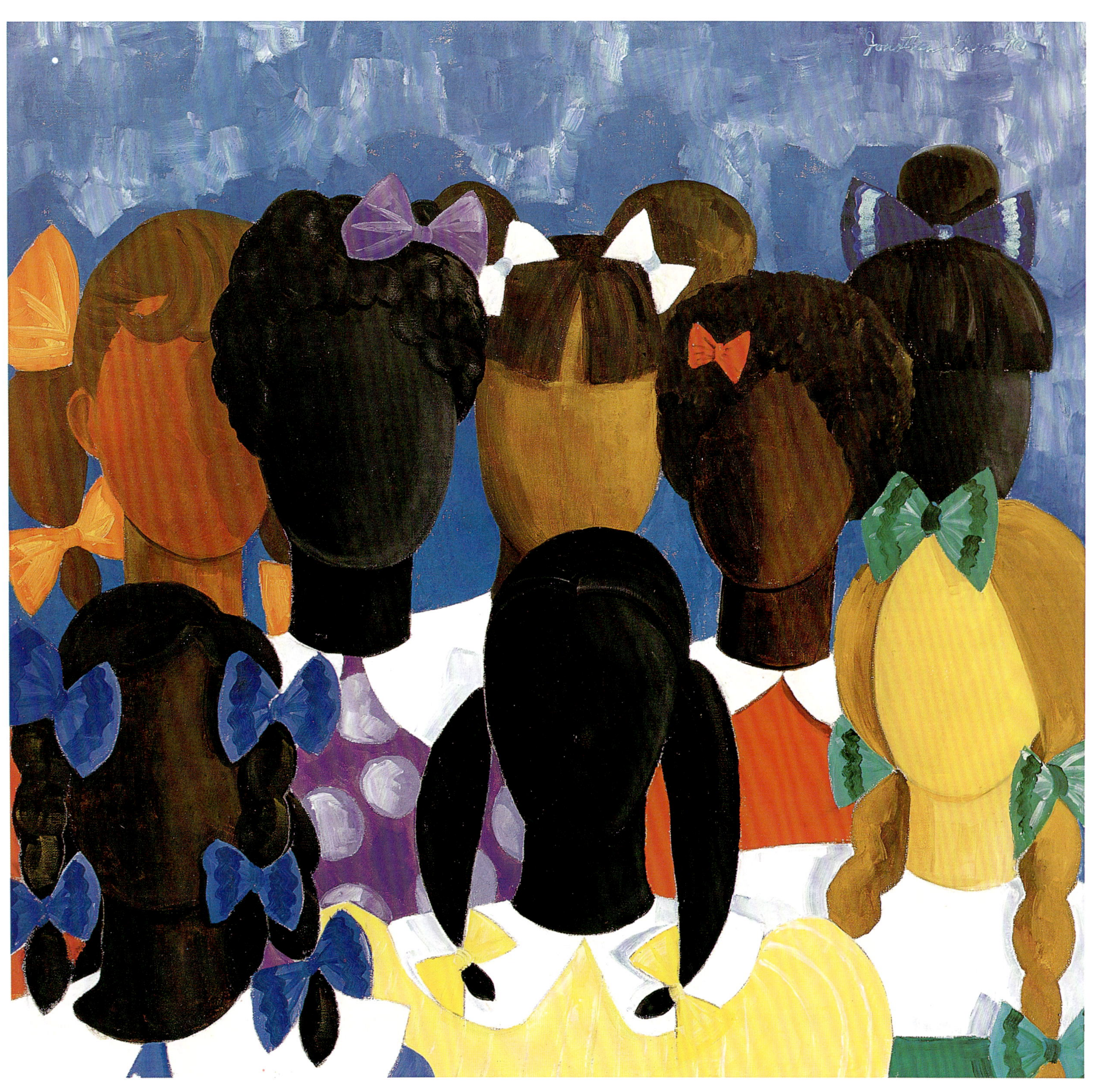

Sunday School Girls, 1990. Oil on canvas, 23 x 23".
Courtesy of Julia J. Norrell. Photograph by Tim Stamm.

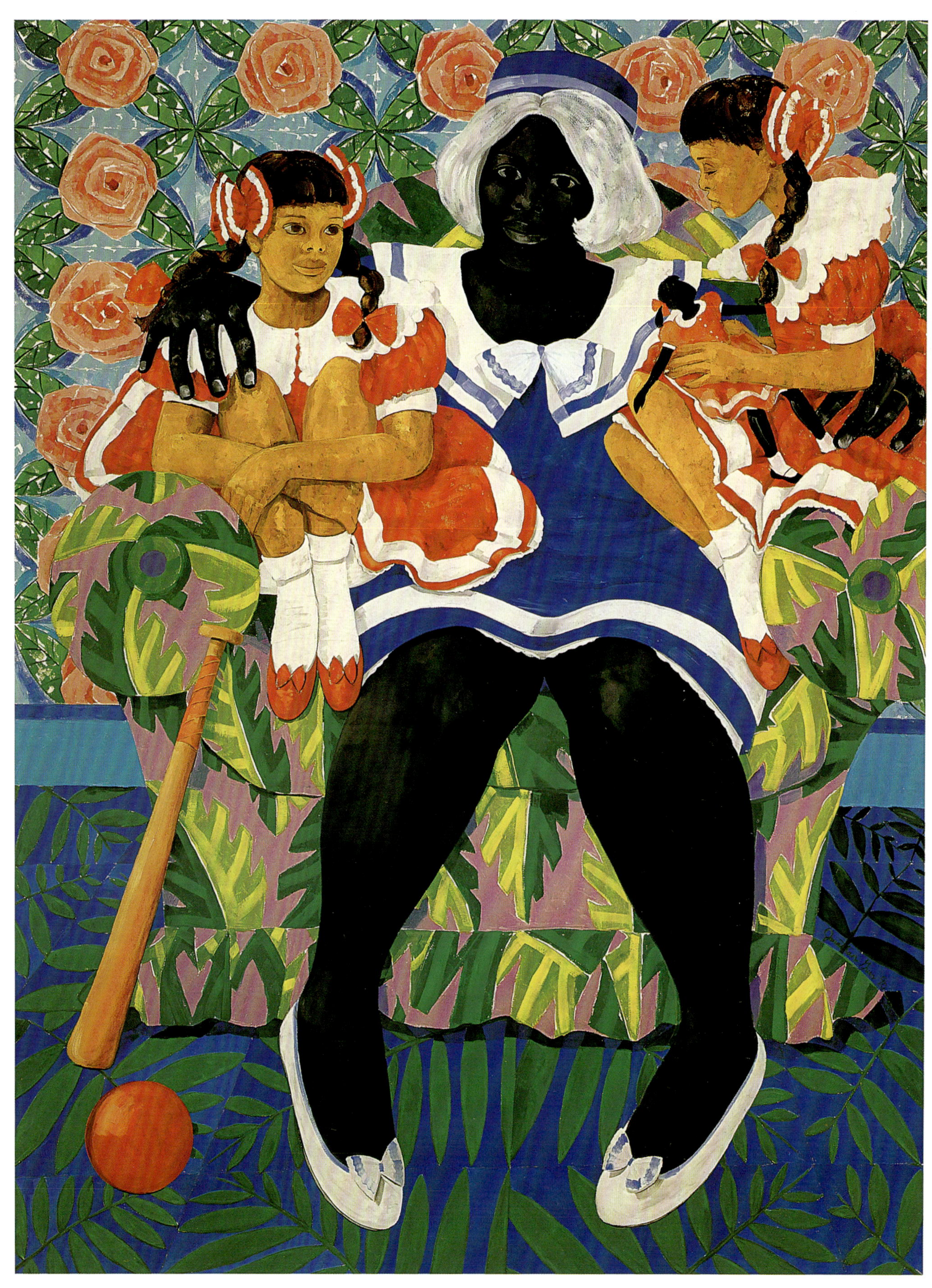

Pride, 1990. Oil on canvas, 72 x 55".
Collection of the artist. Photograph by Tim Stamm.

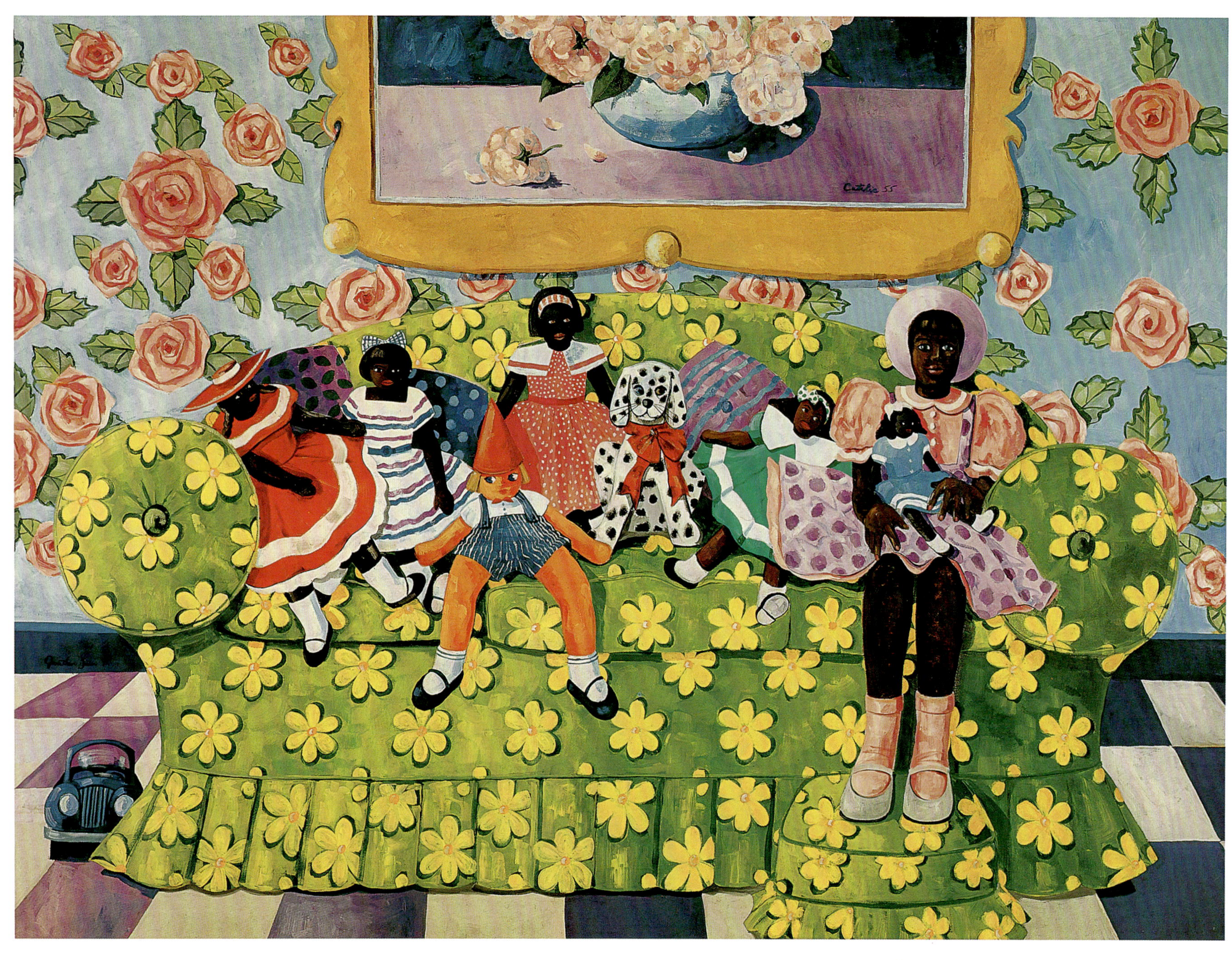

Annette's Dolls, 1990. Acrylic on canvas, 12 x 16".
Courtesy of Keven and Cheryll Stephens. Photograph by Tim Stamm.

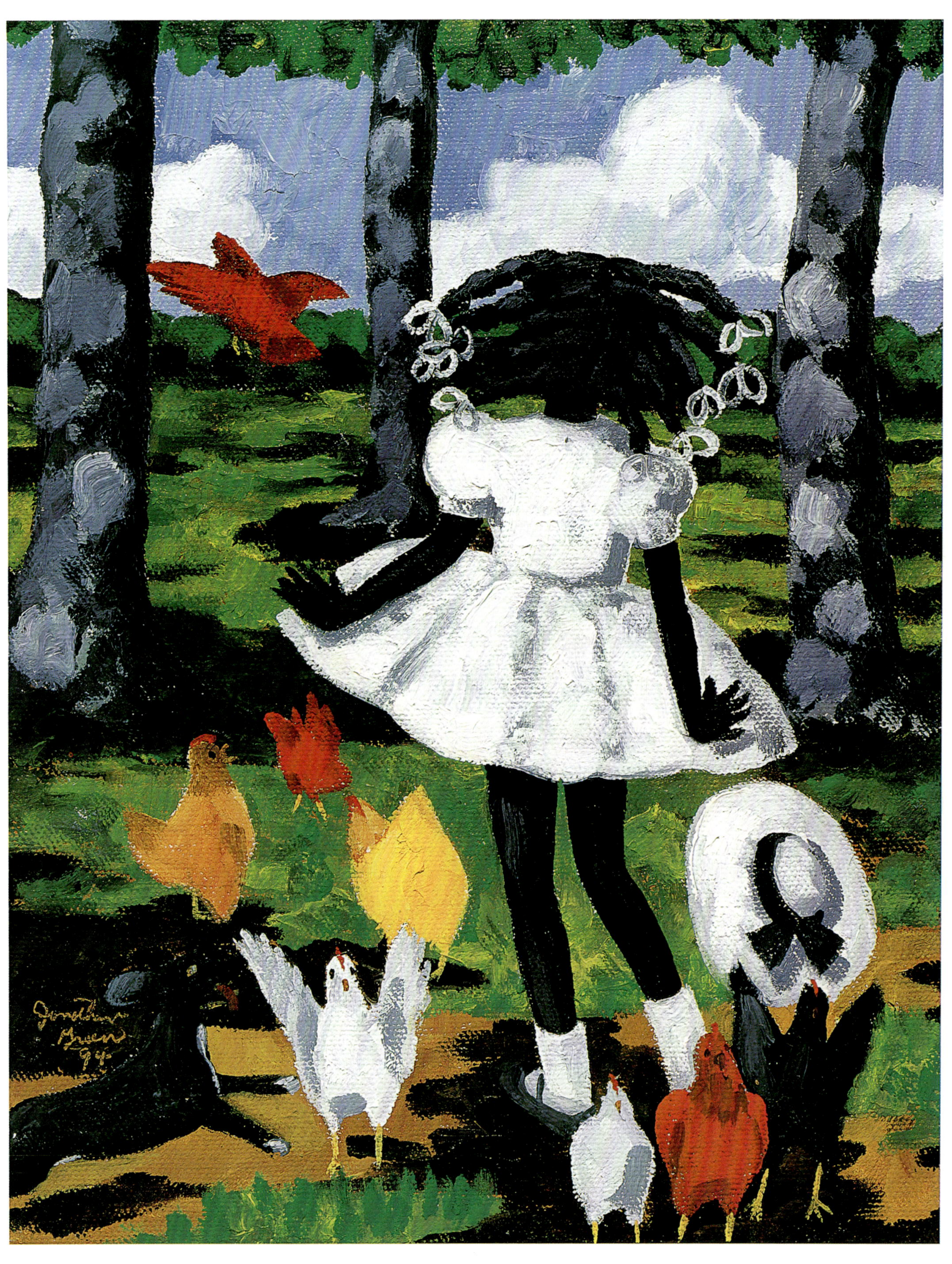

Before Sunday School, 1990. Oil on canvas, 10 x 8".
Courtesy of Paul G. Langston. Photograph by Tim Stamm.

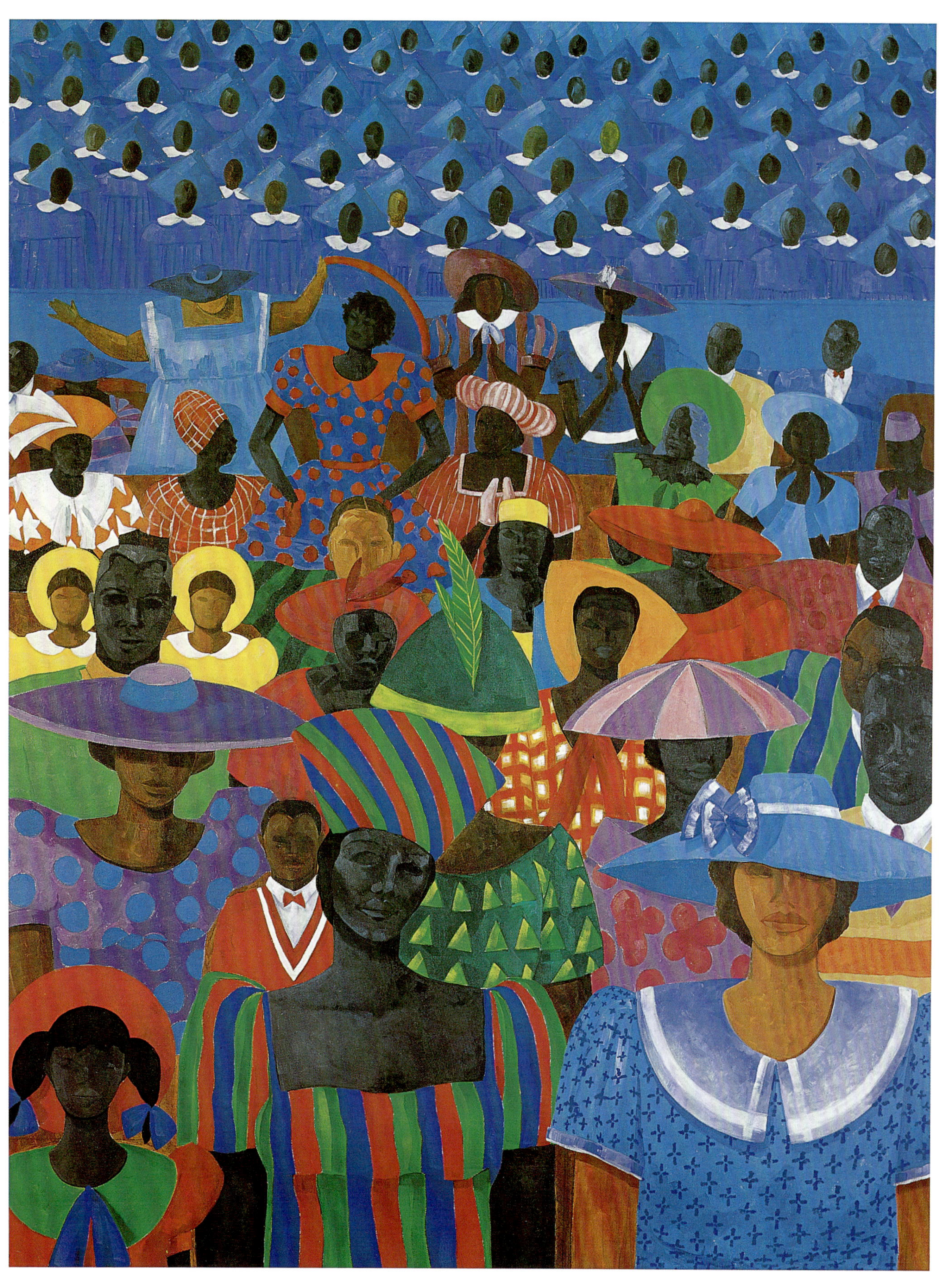

The Congregation, 1990. Oil on canvas, 72 x 55".
Courtesy of Julia J. Norrell. Photograph by Tim Stamm.

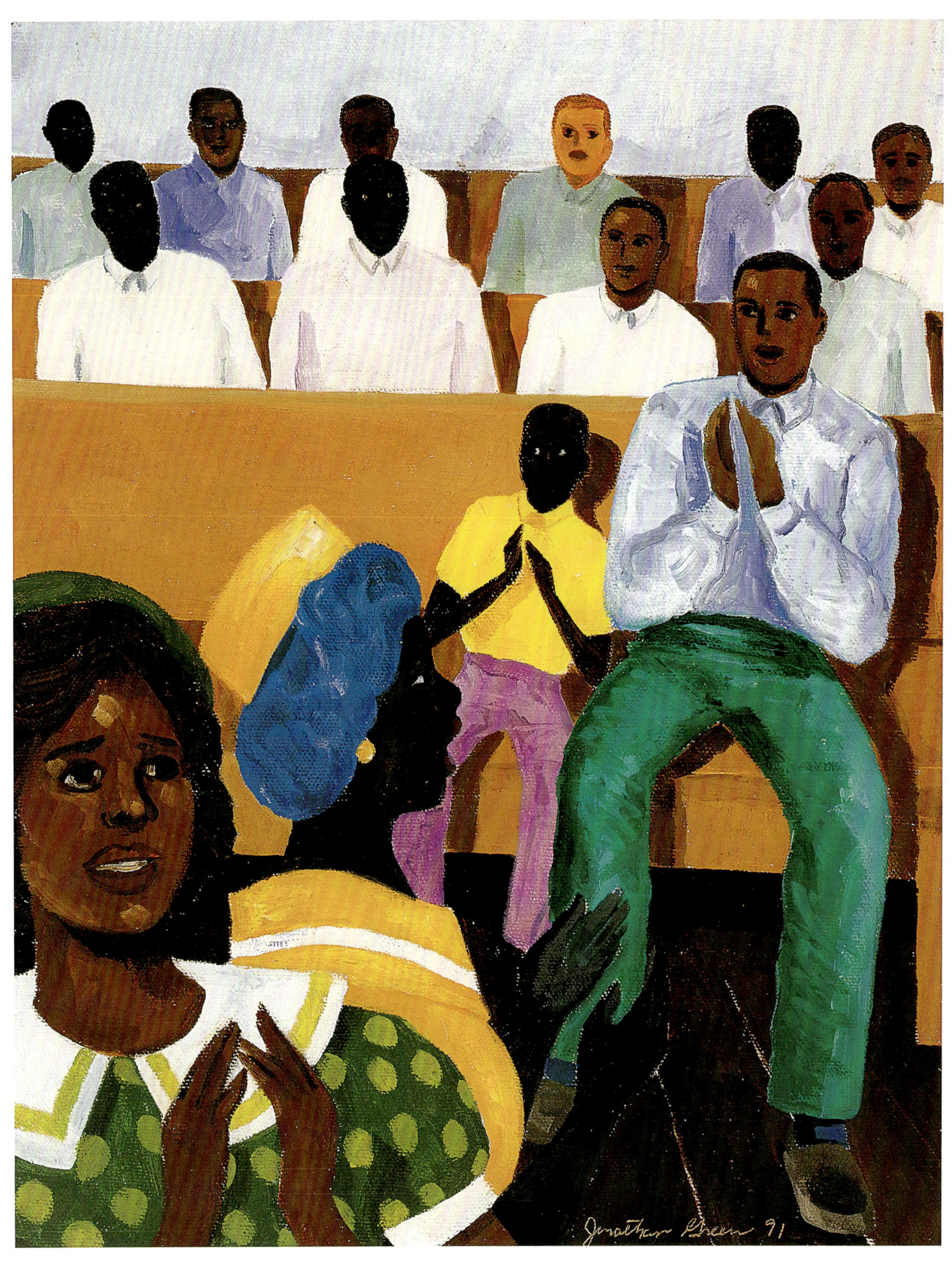

Deacon's Roost, 1991. Oil on canvas, 14 x 11".
Collection of the artist. Photograph by Tim Stamm.

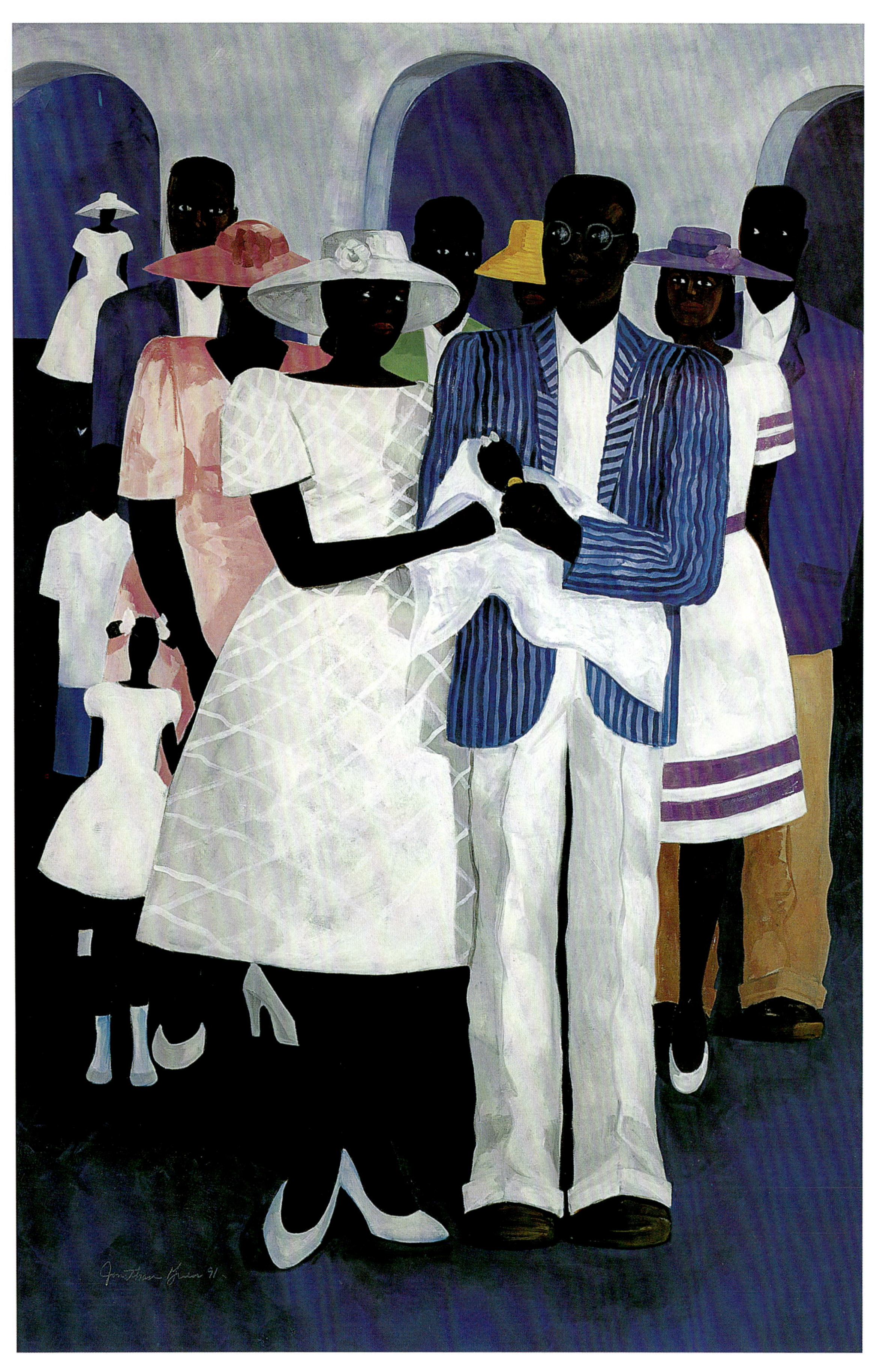

The Christening, 1991. Oil on canvas, 52 x 34".
Collection of the Greenville County Museum of Art, Greenville, S.C. Photograph by Tim Stamm.

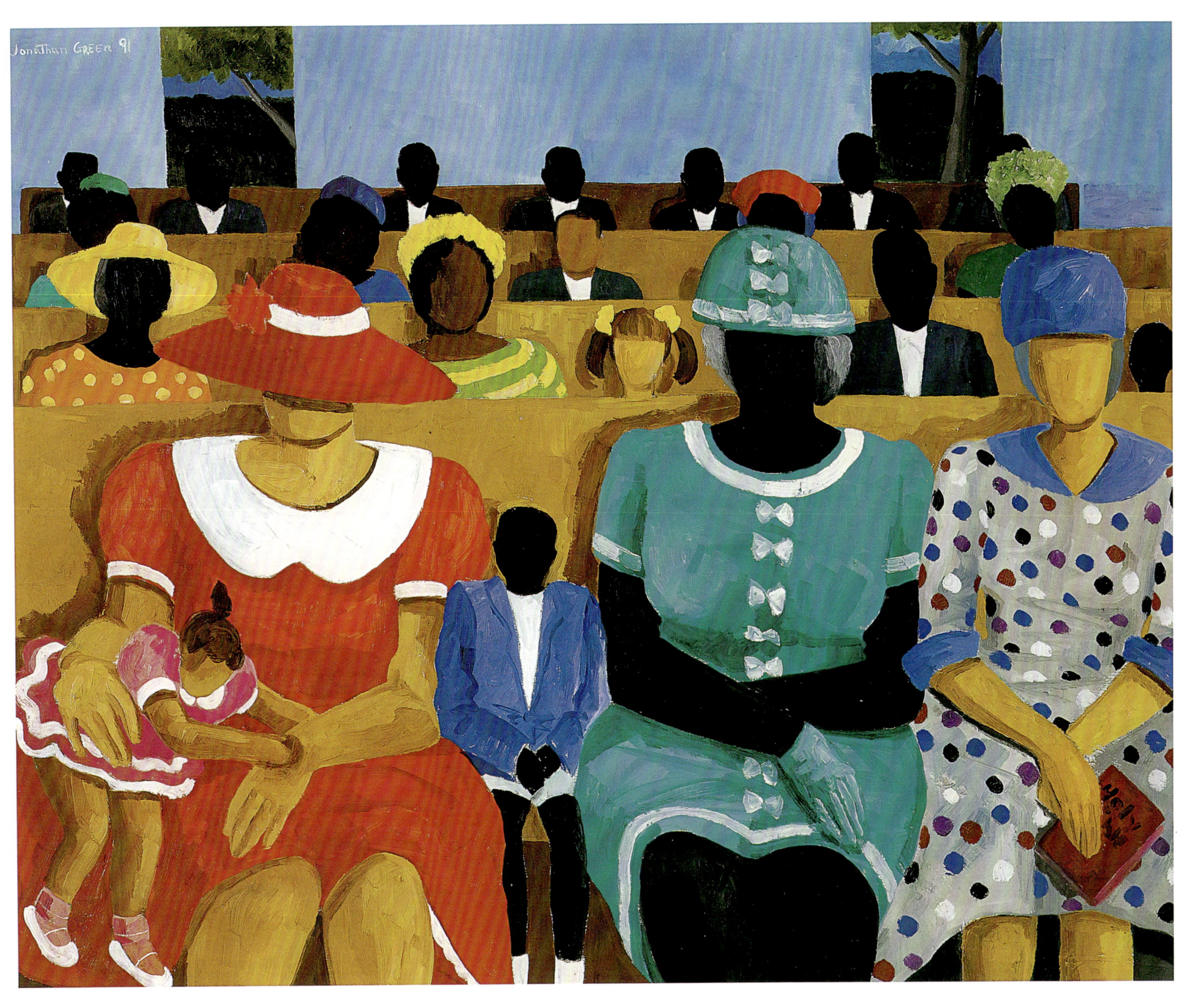

Sunday Morning, 1991. Oil on masonite, 16 x 20".
Courtesy of Clarence Brooks. Photograph by Tim Stamm.

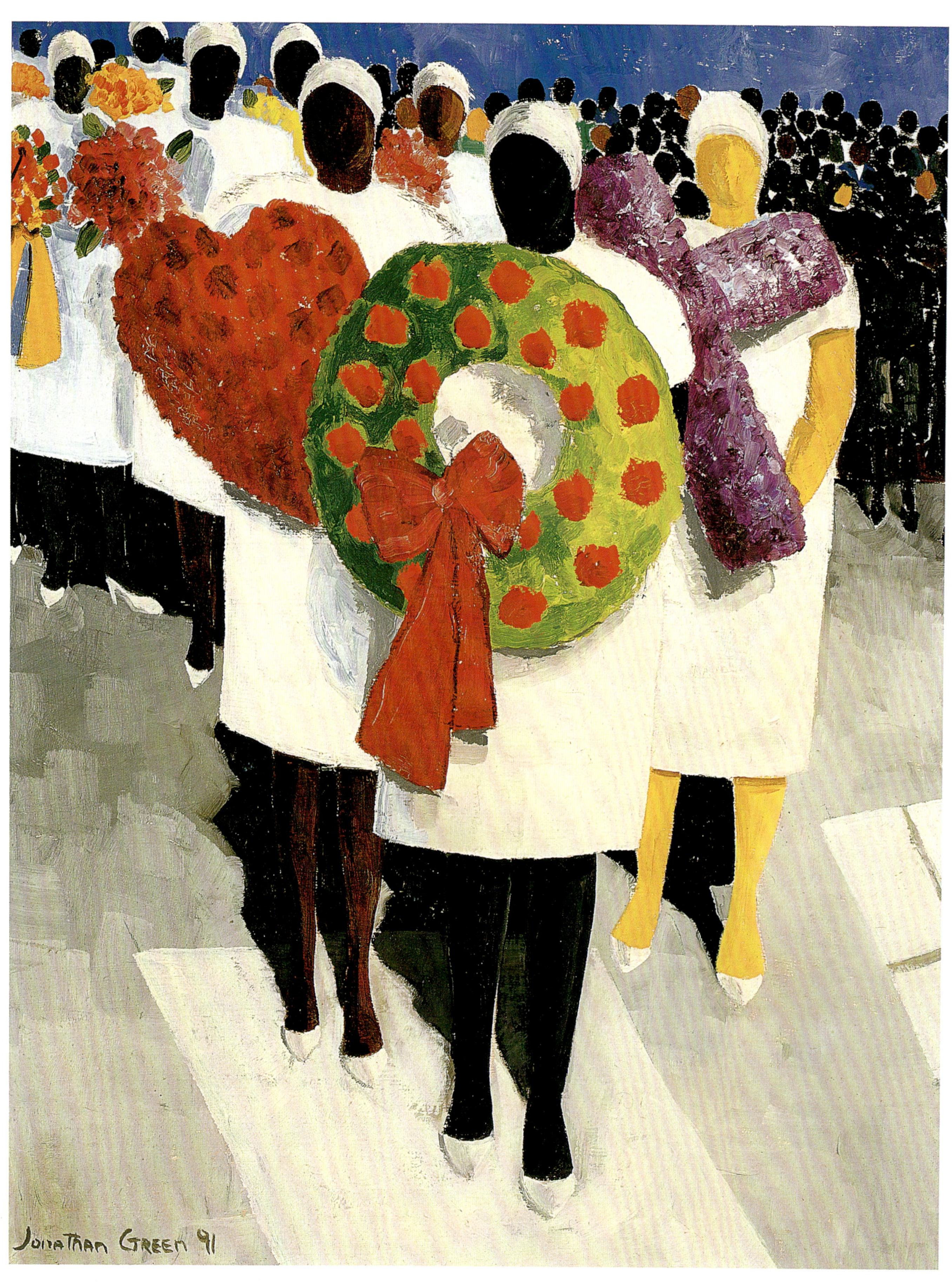

The Ushering, 1991. Oil on canvas, 14 x 11".
Collection of the artist. Photograph by Tim Stamm.

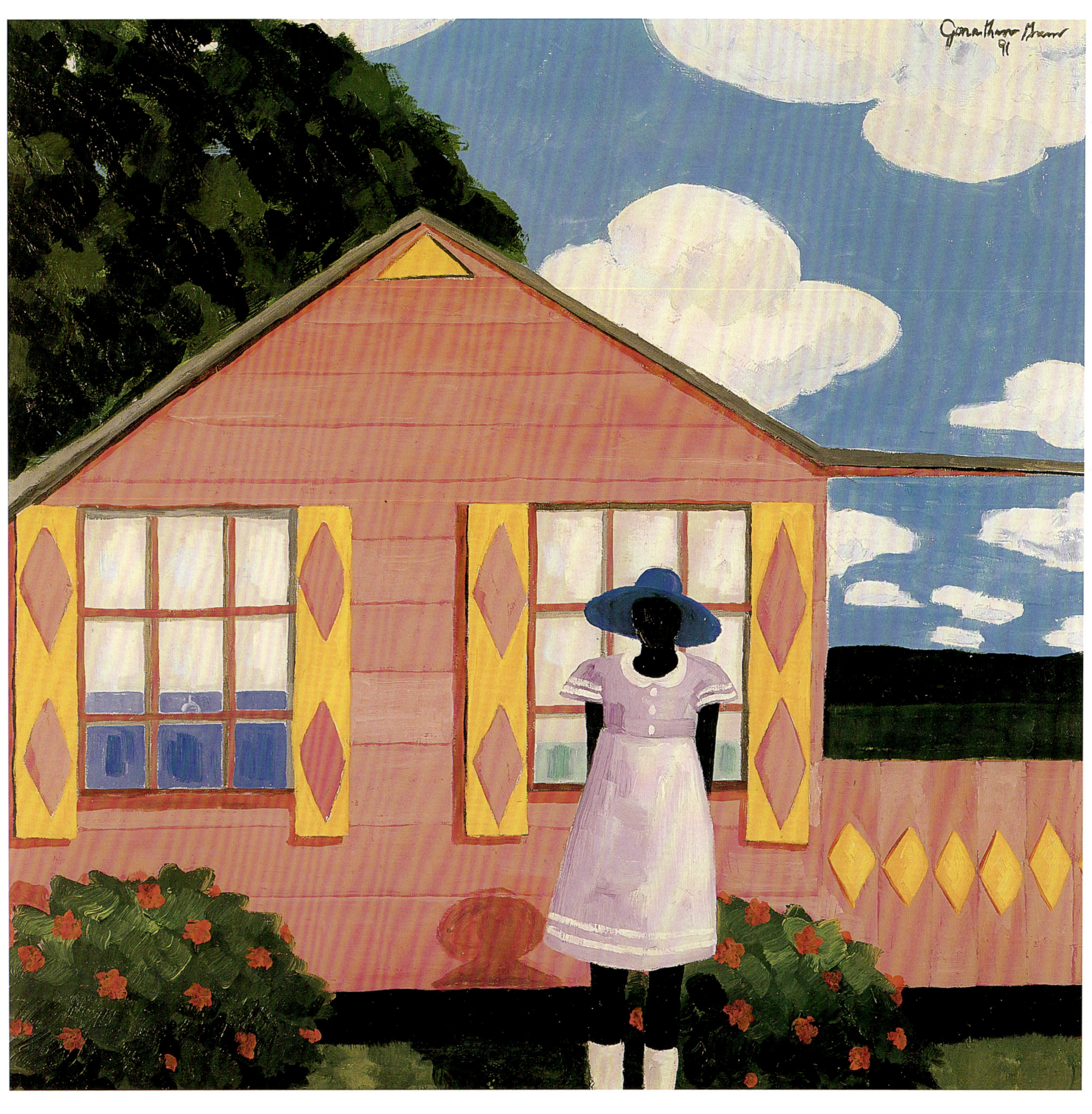

The Pink House, 1991. Oil on masonite, 16 x 16".
Courtesy of Kirk and Carolyn Woodson. Photograph by Tim Stamm.

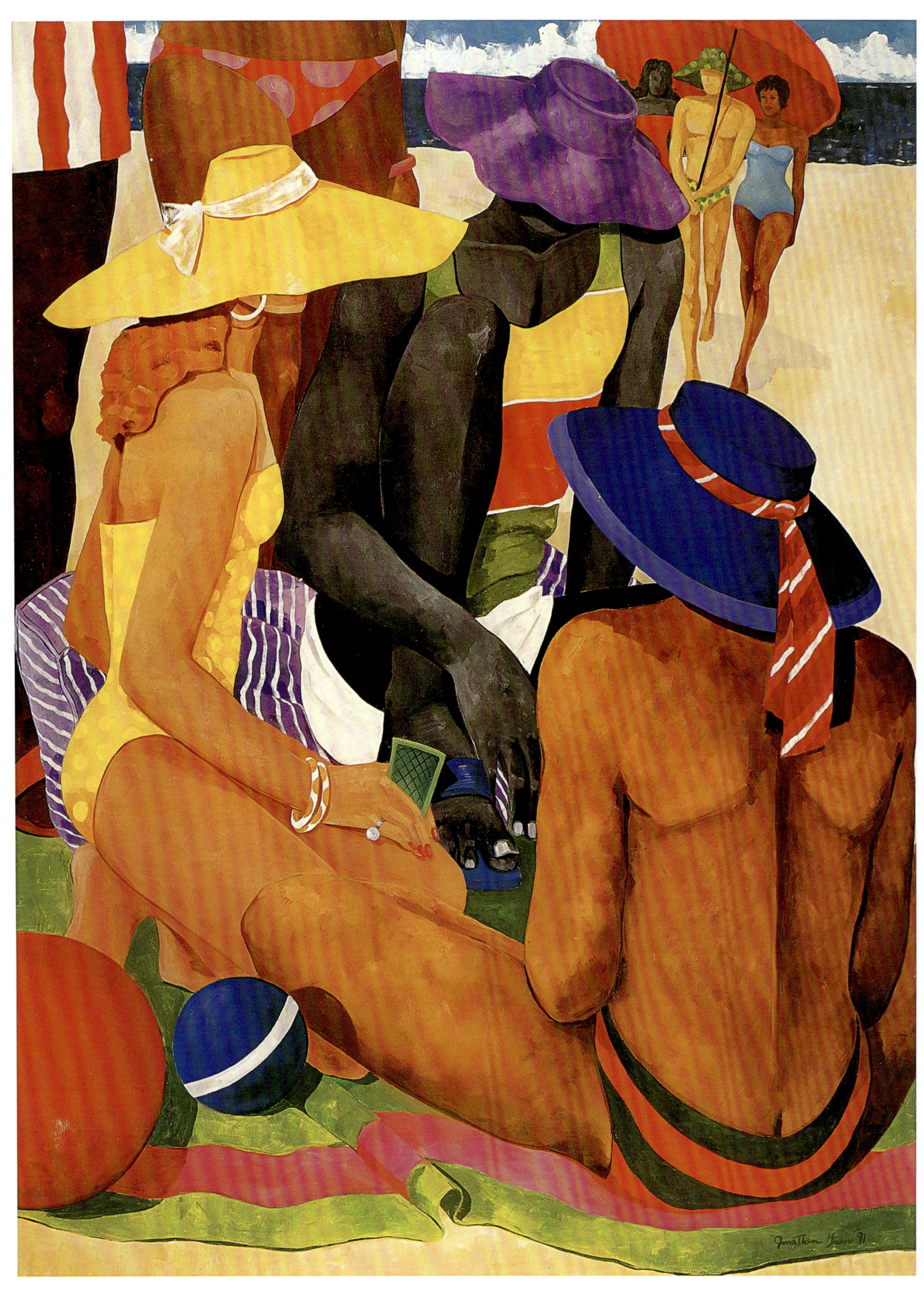

Beach Card Players, 1991. Oil on canvas, 70 x 52".
Private Collection. Photograph by Tim Stamm.

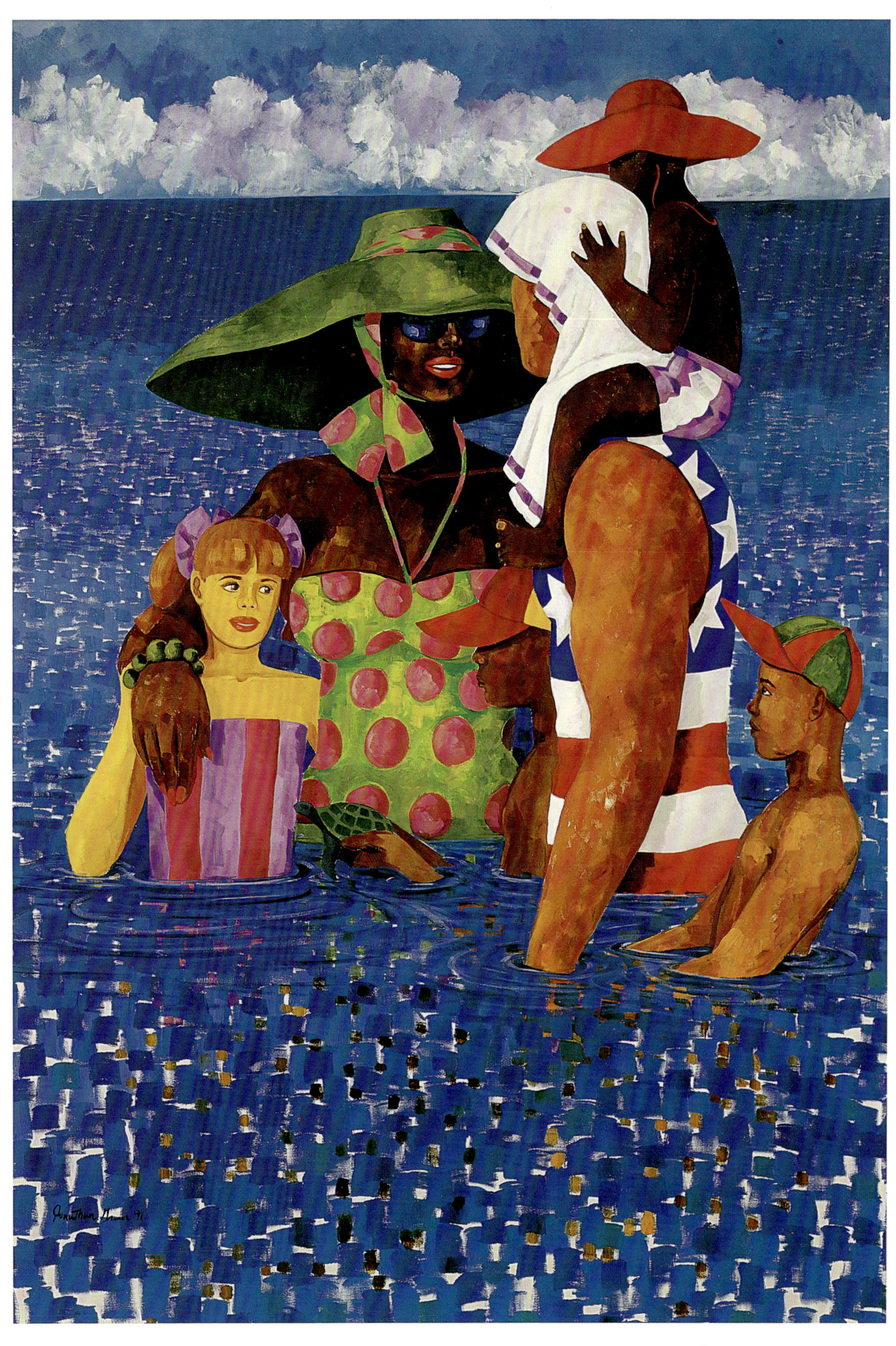

Family Wading, 1991. Oil on canvas, 70 x 52".
Collection of the artist. Photograph by Tim Stamm.

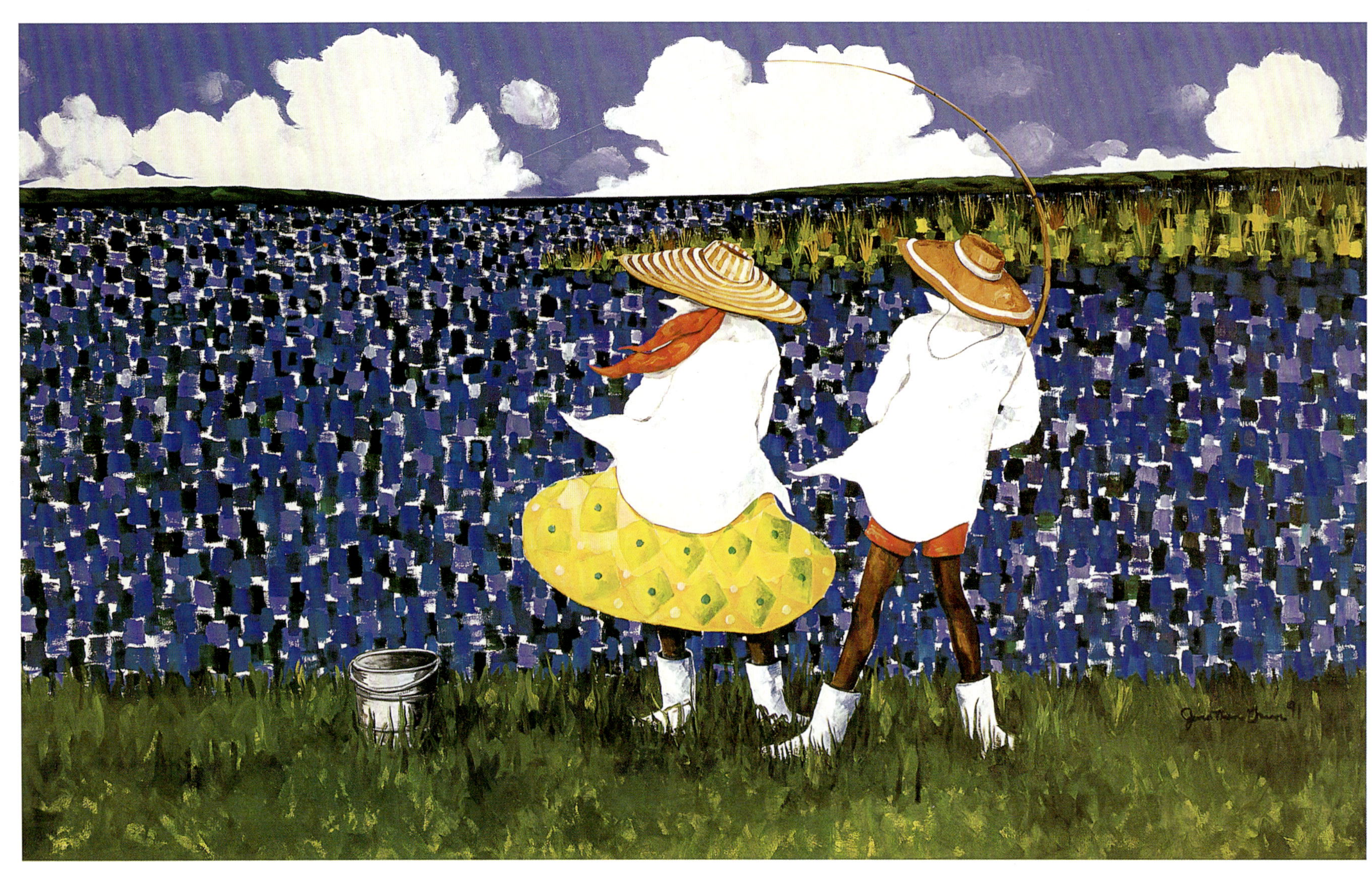

Fishing on the Trail, 1991. Oil on canvas, 74 x 98".
Courtesy of Tim and Tanya Stamm. Photograph by Tim Stamm.

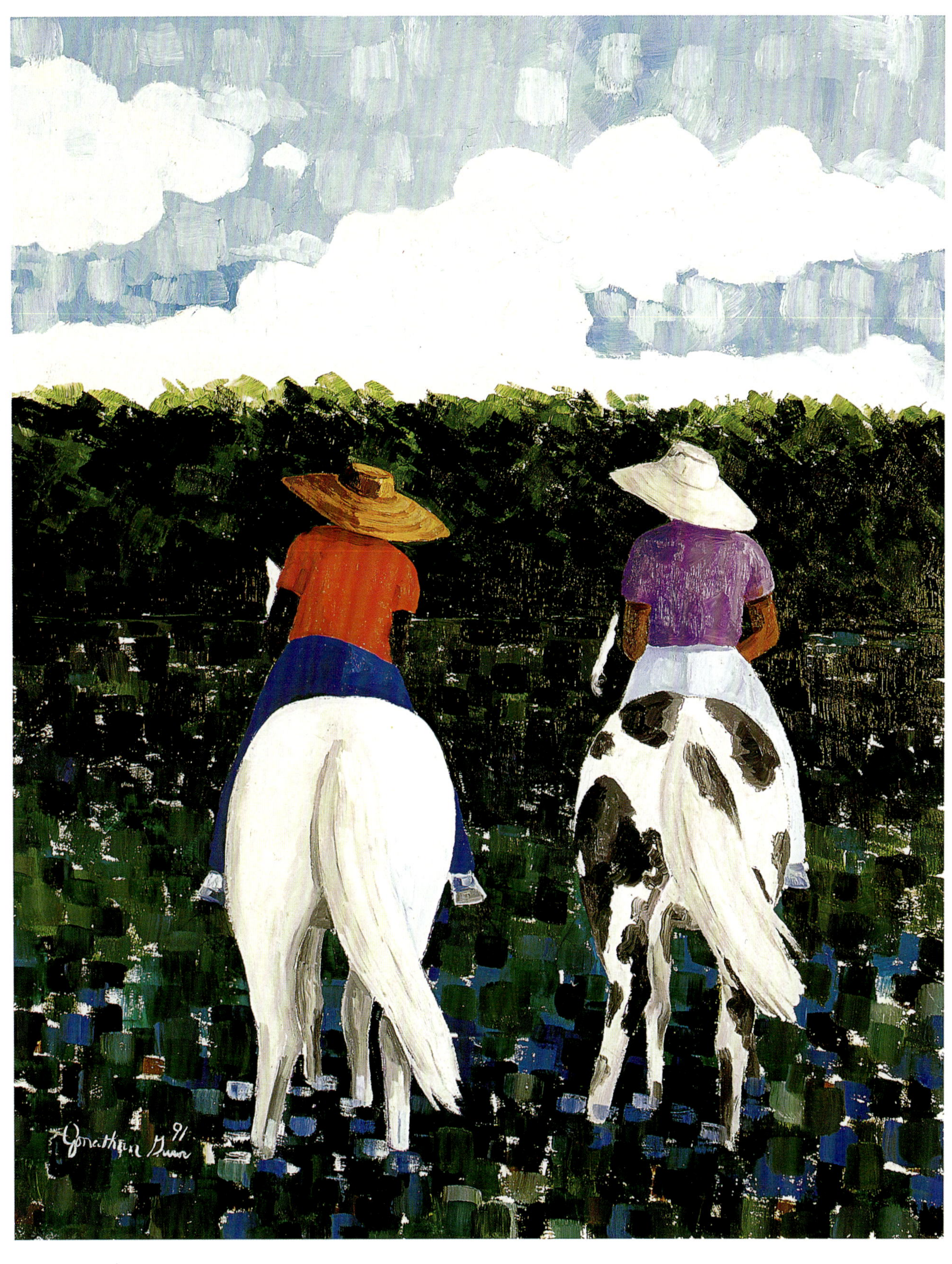

The Marshland Riders, 1991. Oil on masonite, 20 x 16".
Courtesy of James L. Davis. Photograph by Tim Stamm.

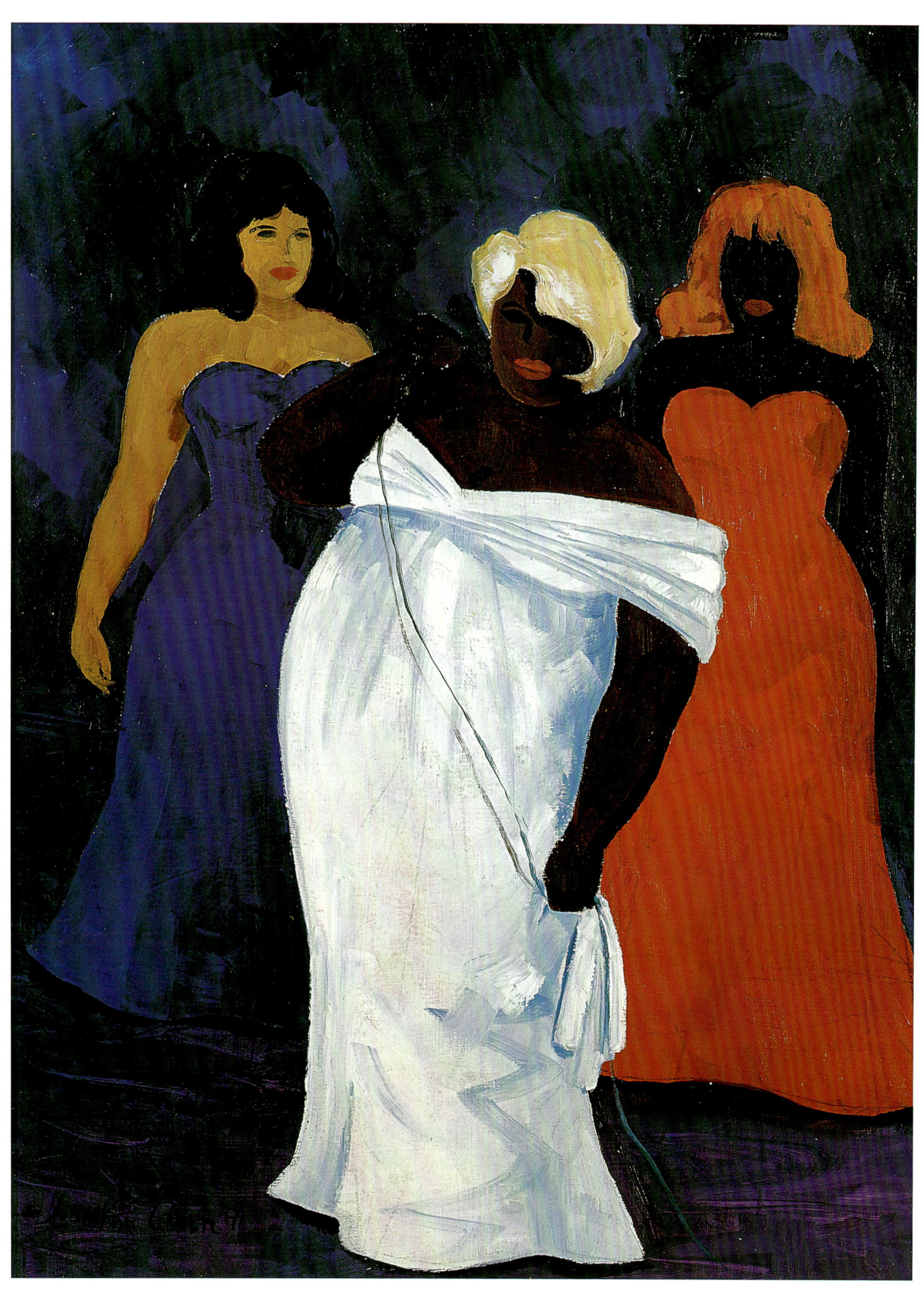

Ms. Etta James, 1991. Oil on masonite, 16 x 12".
Collection of Philharmonic Center for the Arts, Naples, Fla. Photograph by Tim Stamm.

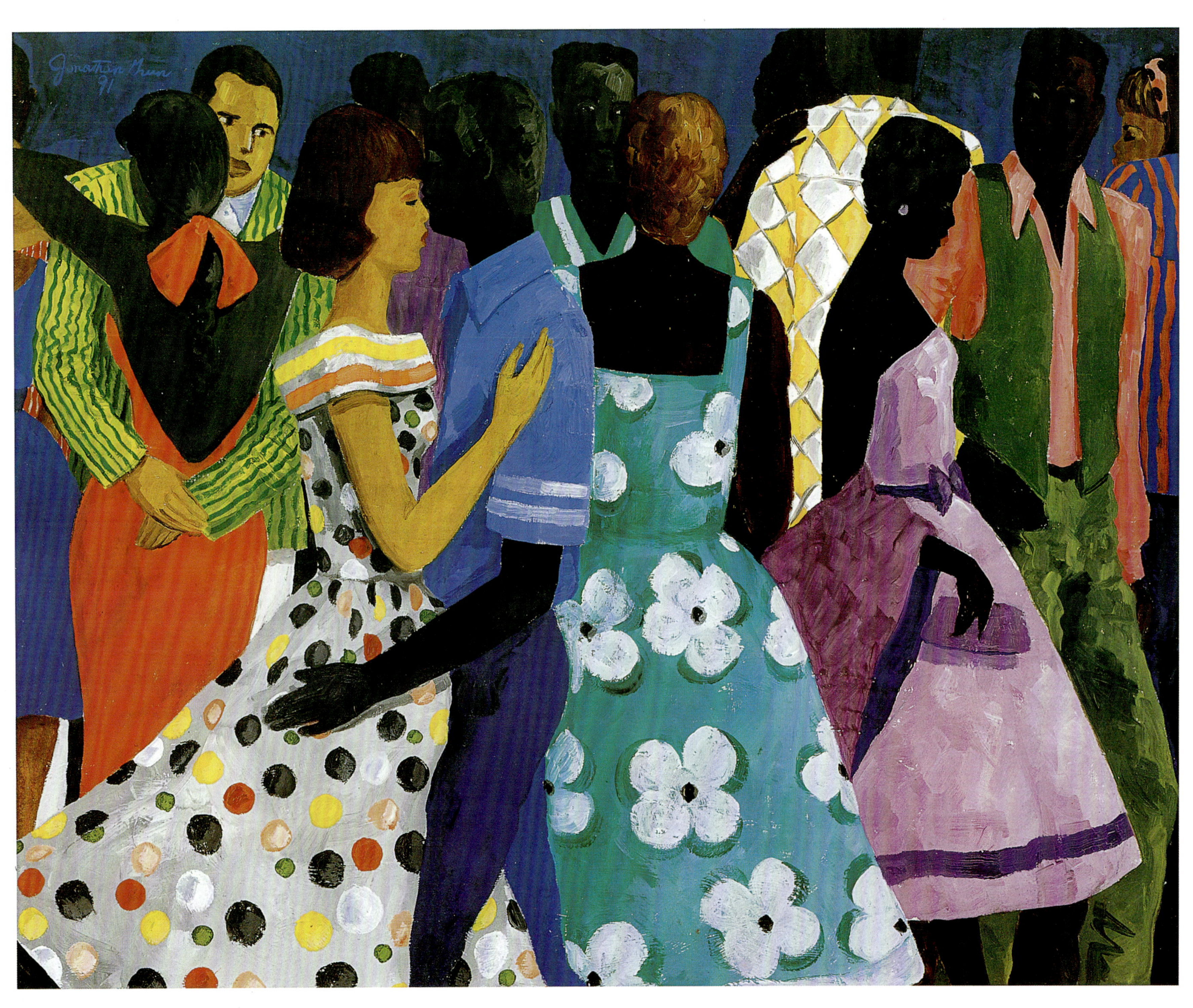

Mt. Pleasant Dance Hall, 1991. Oil on masonite, 16 x 20".
Courtesy of Edward and Carol Bleser. Photograph by Tim Stamm.

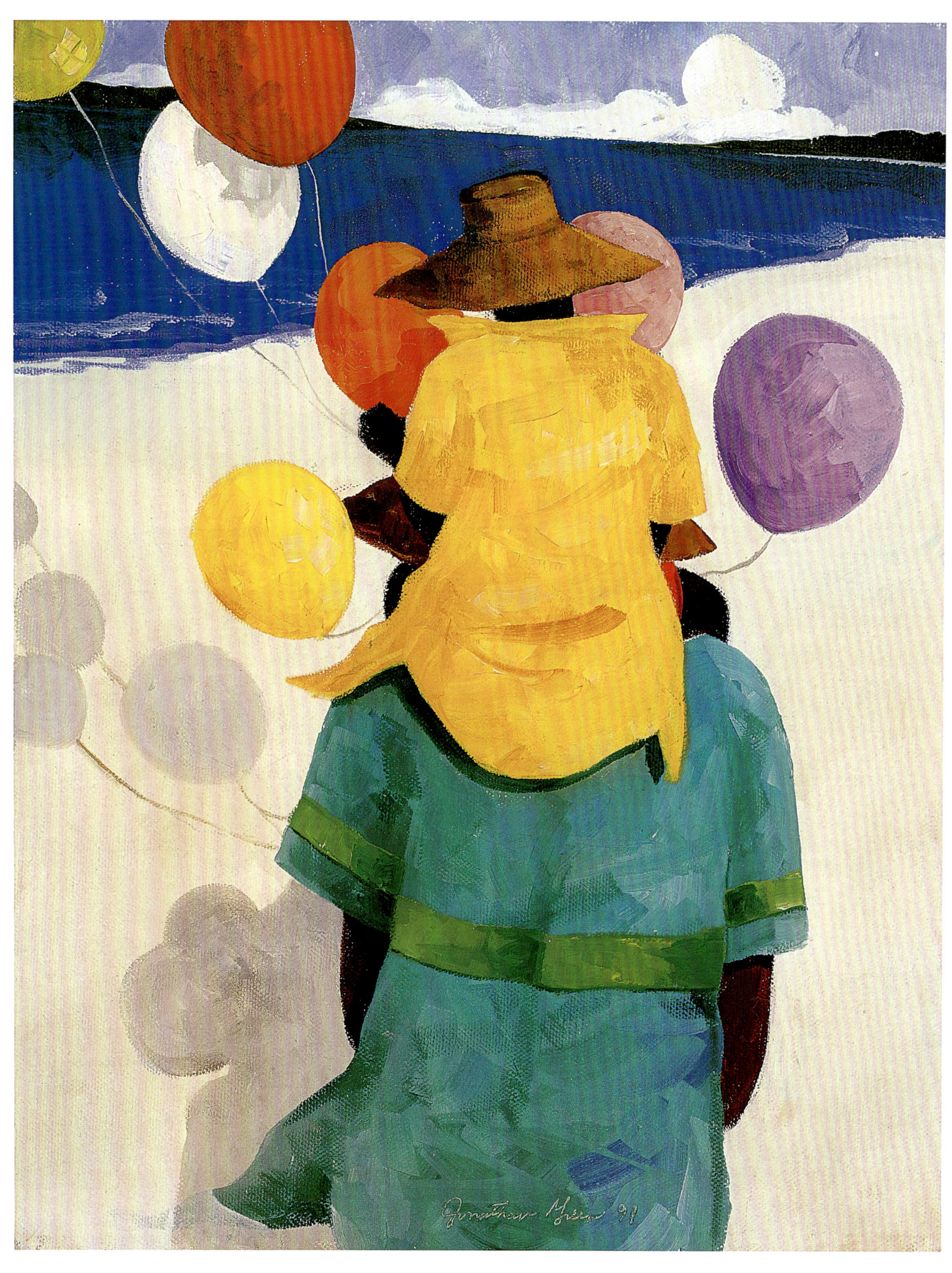

The Soul of One, 1991. Oil on canvas, 14 x 11".
Private collection. Photograph by Tim Stamm.

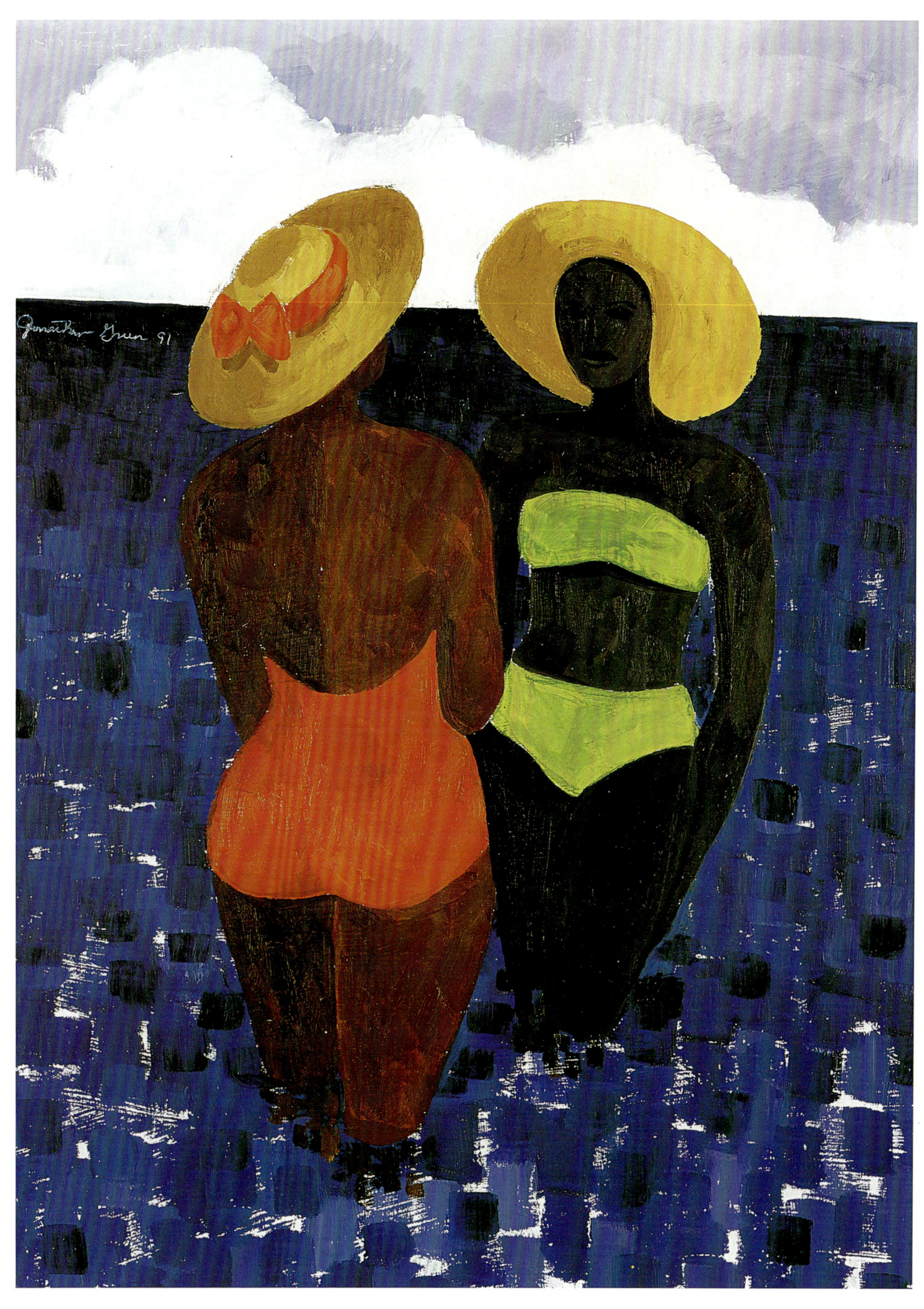

Charleston Beauties, 1991. Oil on masonite, 16 x 12".
Courtesy of Sandra L. Fowler. Photograph by Rick Rhodes.

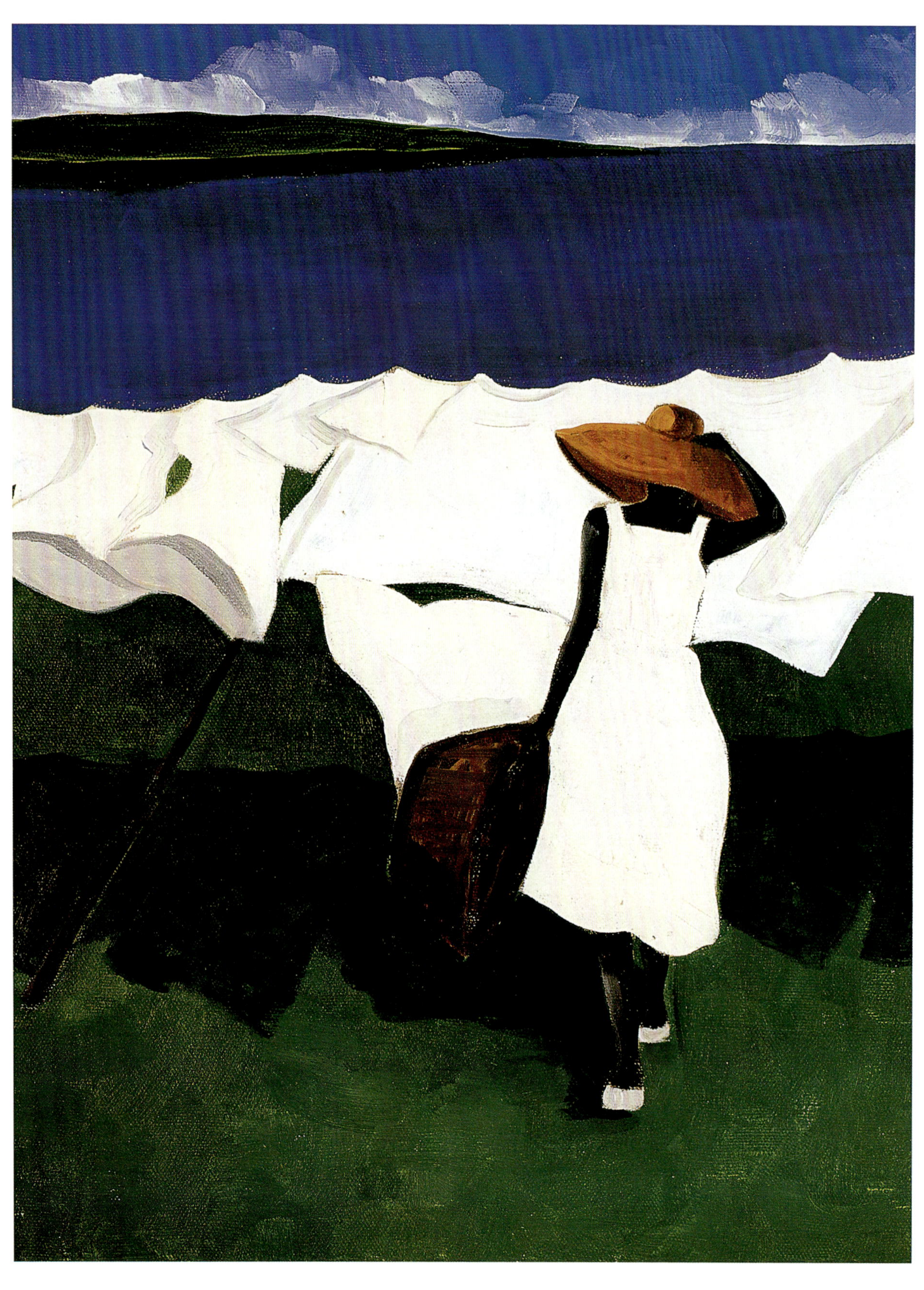

Noon Wash, 1991. Oil on canvas, 16 x 20".
Courtesy of Michael and Mary James. Photograph by Ron Breazeale.

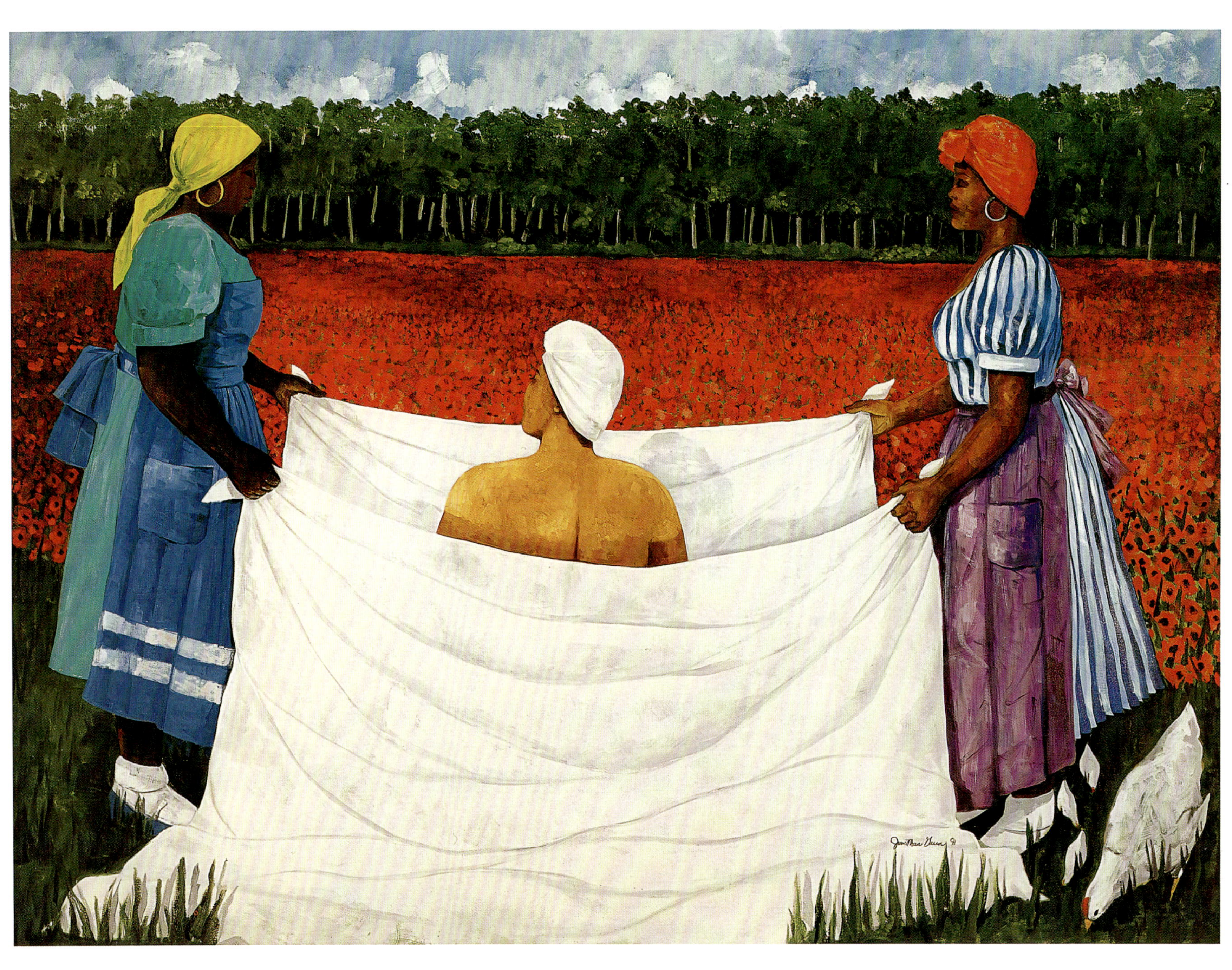

Bathing, 1991. Oil on canvas, 55 x 72".
Collection of the Norton Gallery, West Palm Beach, Fla. Photograph by Tim Stamm.

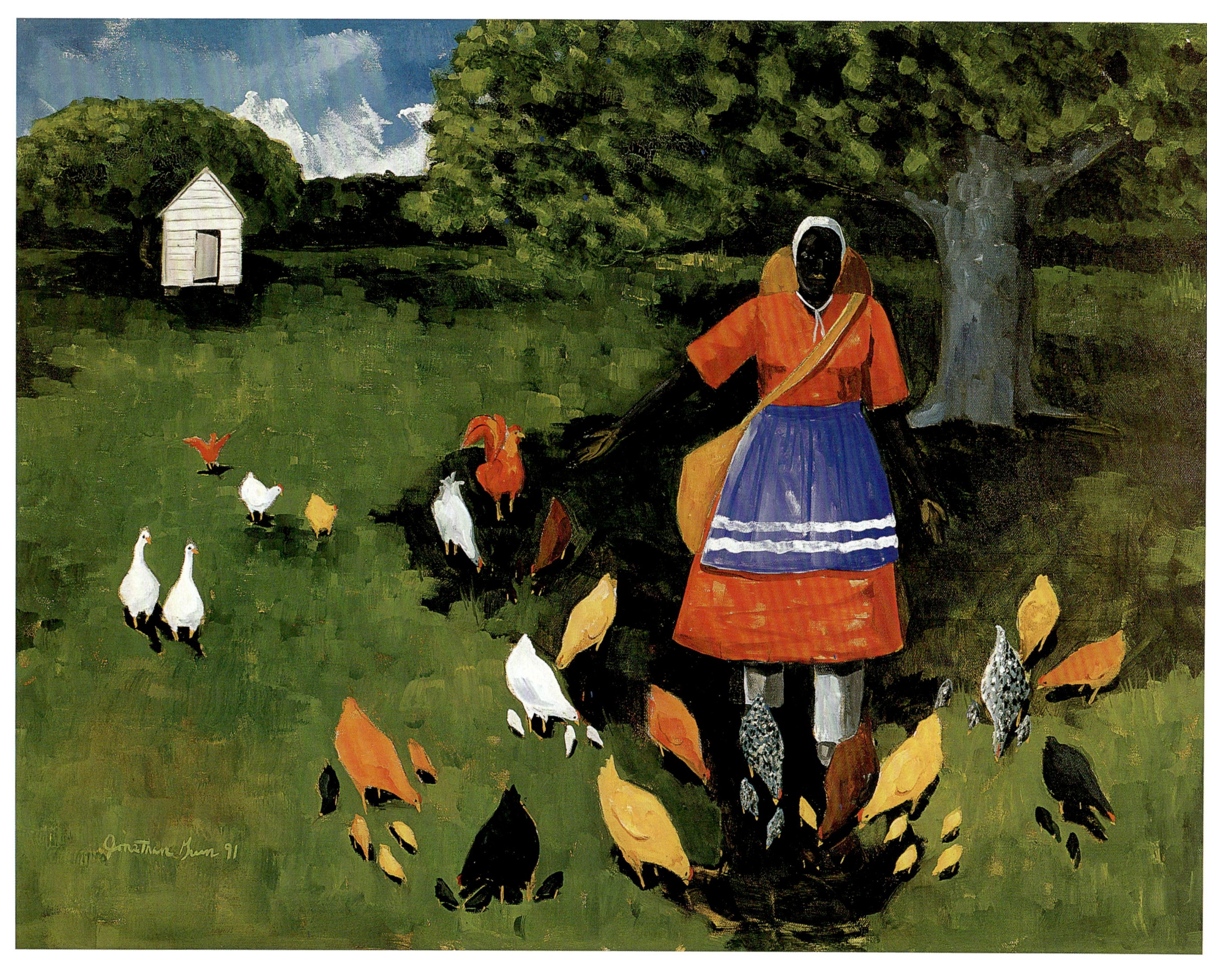

Chicken Yard, 1991. Oil on canvas, 25 x 34".
Courtesy of Anne Baruch. Photograph by Tim Stamm.

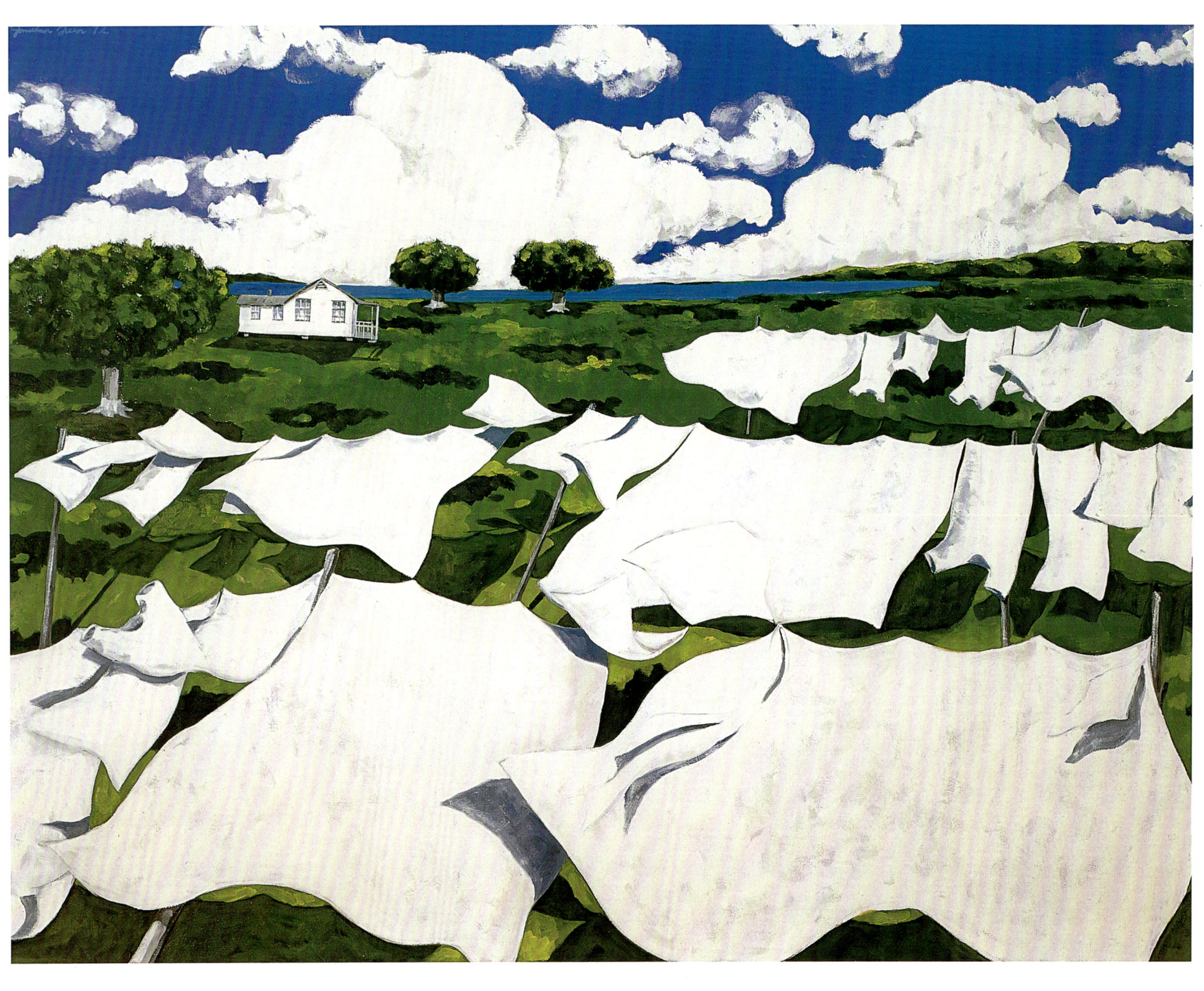

White Memories, 1992. Oil on canvas, 36 x 48".
Courtesy of Drs. Yele and Shirley Aluko. Photograph by Tim Stamm.

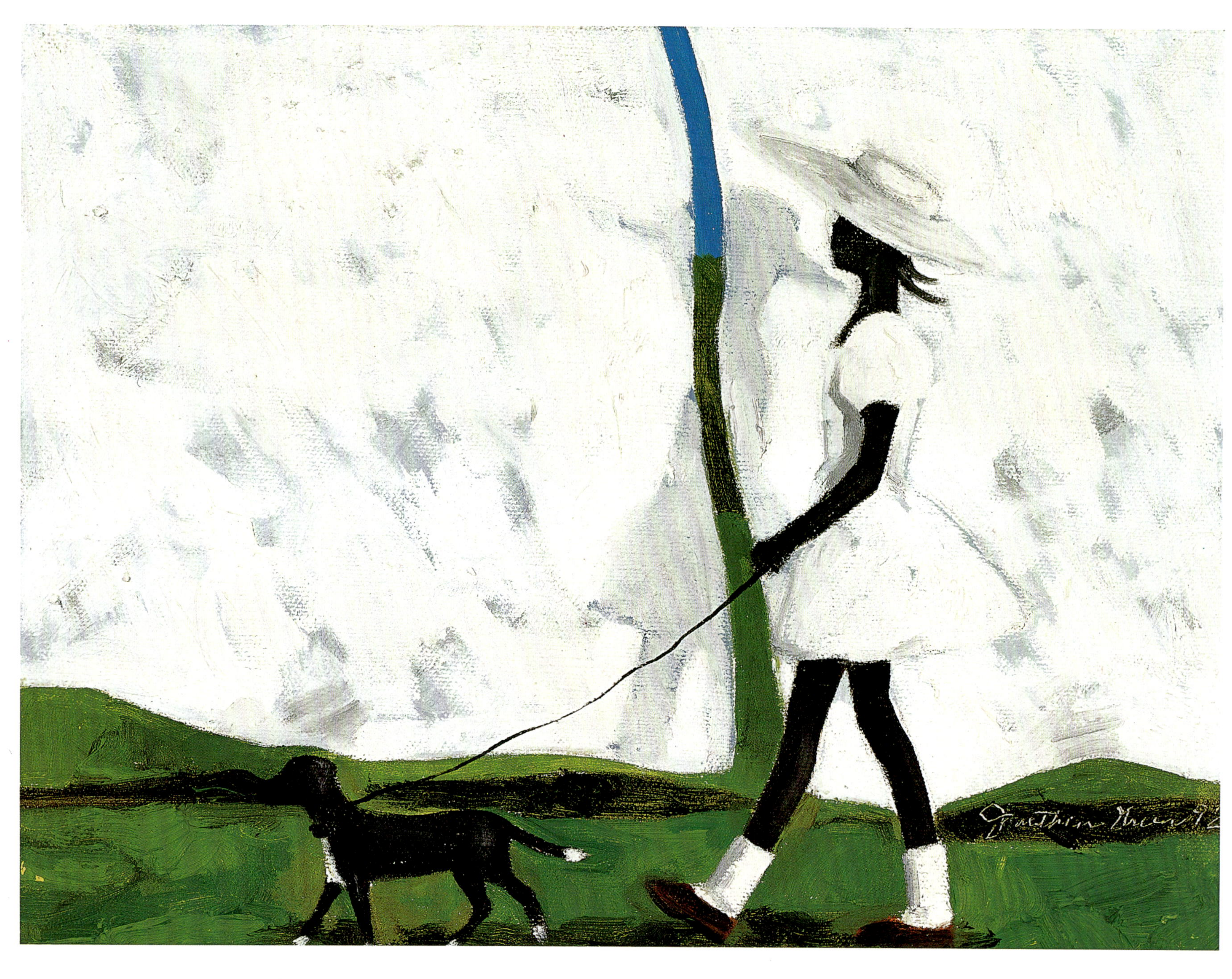

Sissy, 1992. Oil on canvas, 9 x 12".
Courtesy of Julia J. Norrell. Photograph by Tim Stamm.

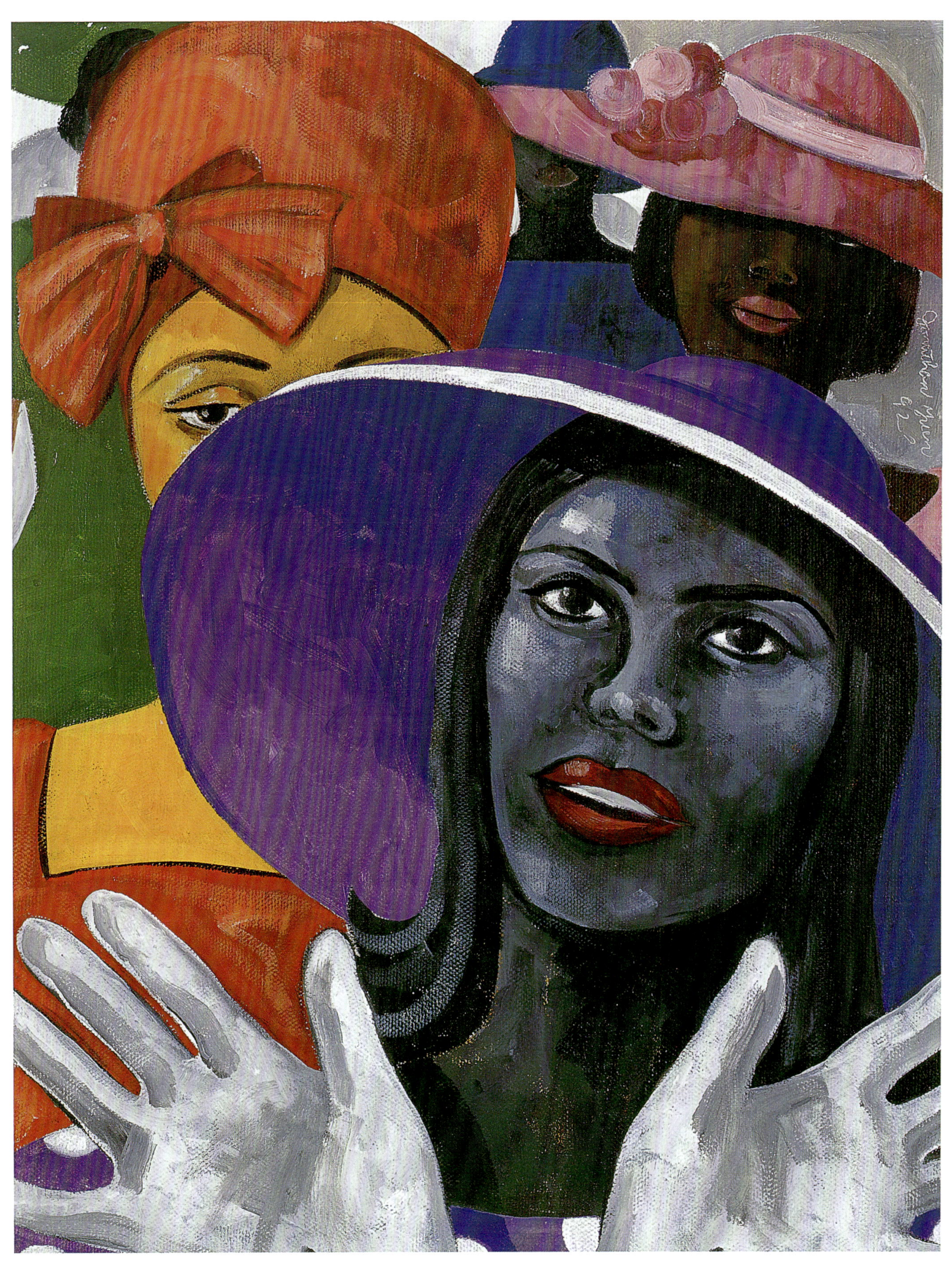

Spiritual Sighting, 1992. Oil on canvas, 14 x 11".
Courtesy of Shirley Robinson. Photograph by Tim Stamm.

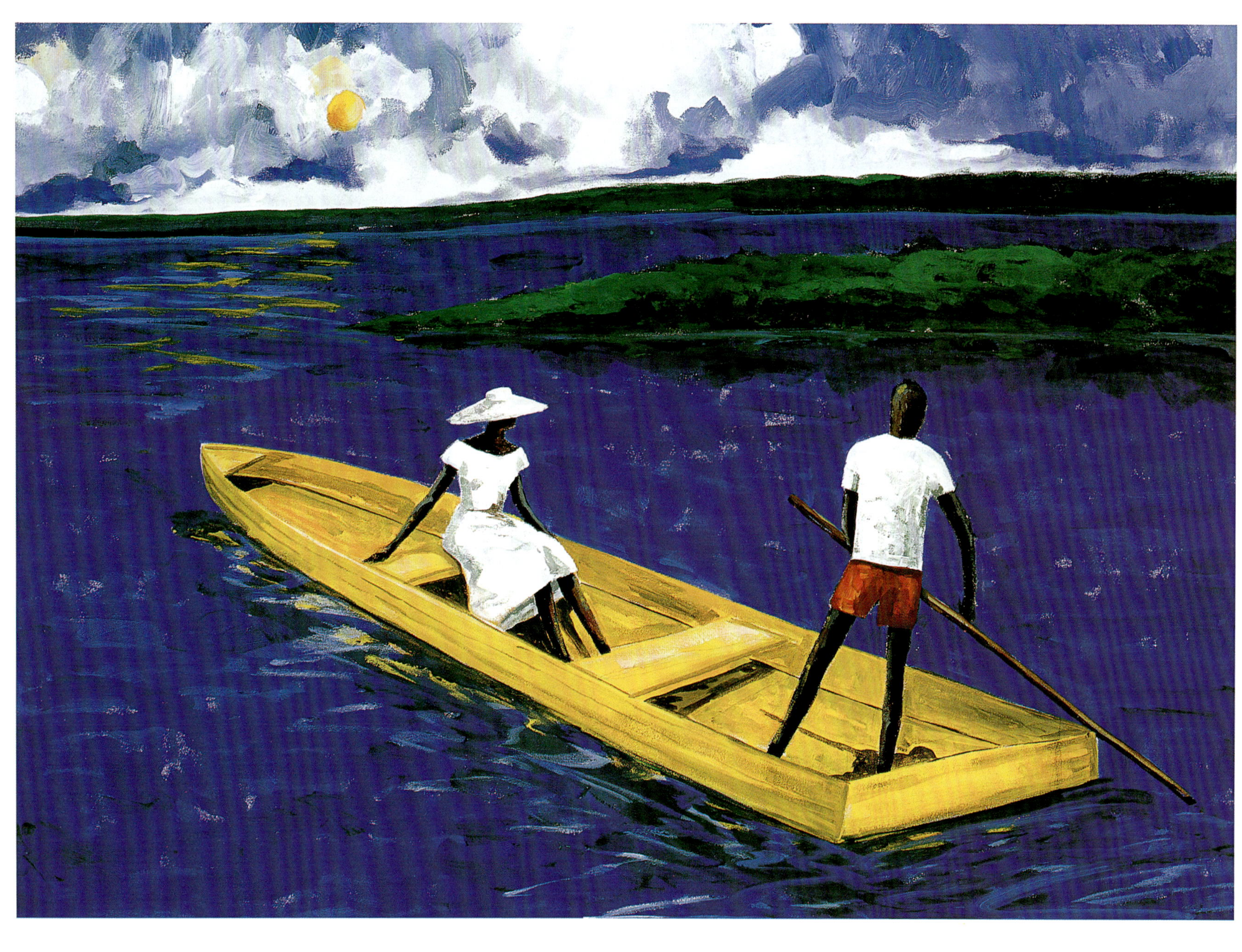

Yellow Boat Ride, 1992. Acrylic canvas, 24 x 32".
Courtesy of Timothy James Lyons. Photograph by Rick Rhodes.

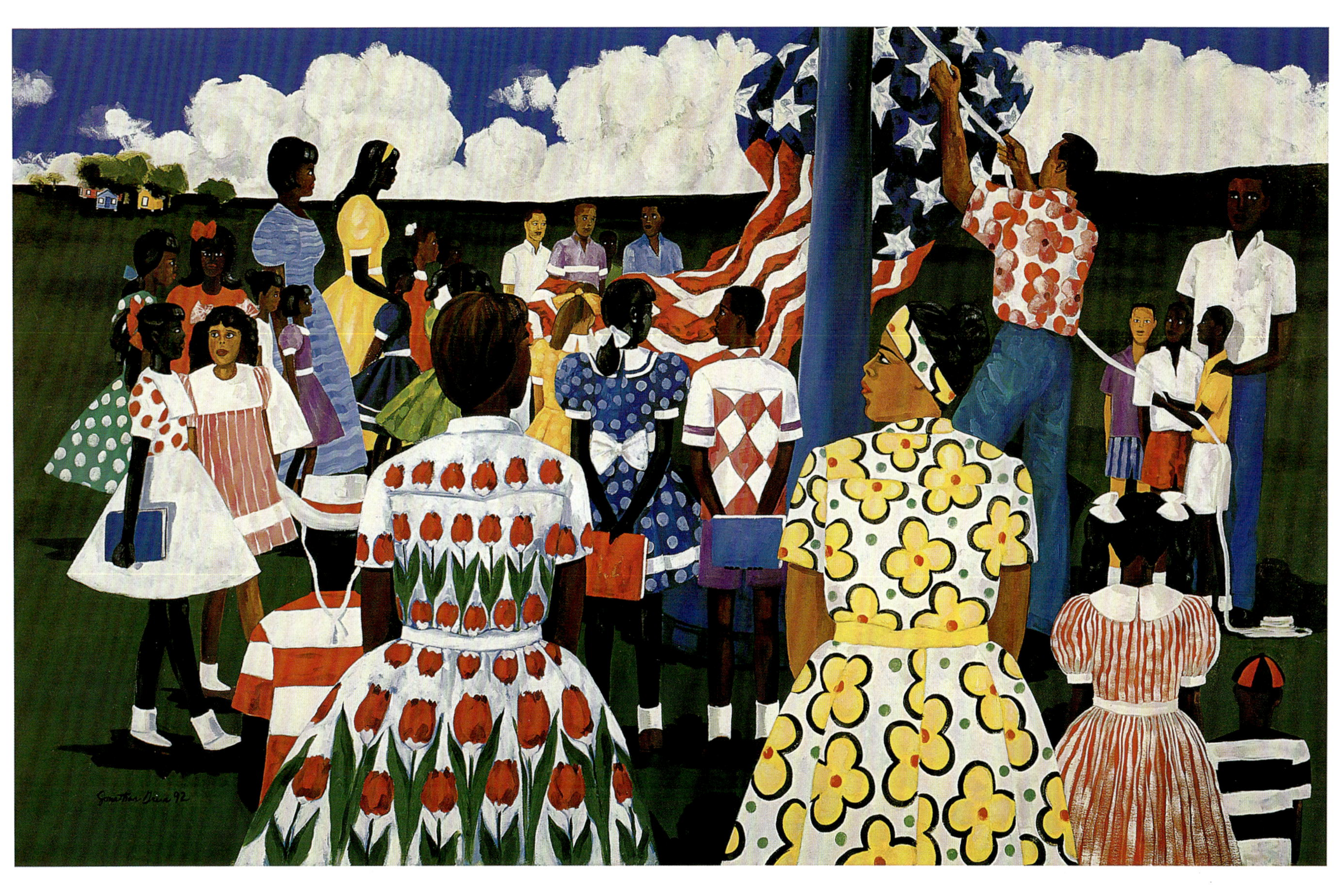

Decoration Day, 1992. Oil on canvas, 48 x 72".
Collection of the artist. Photograph by Tim Stamm.

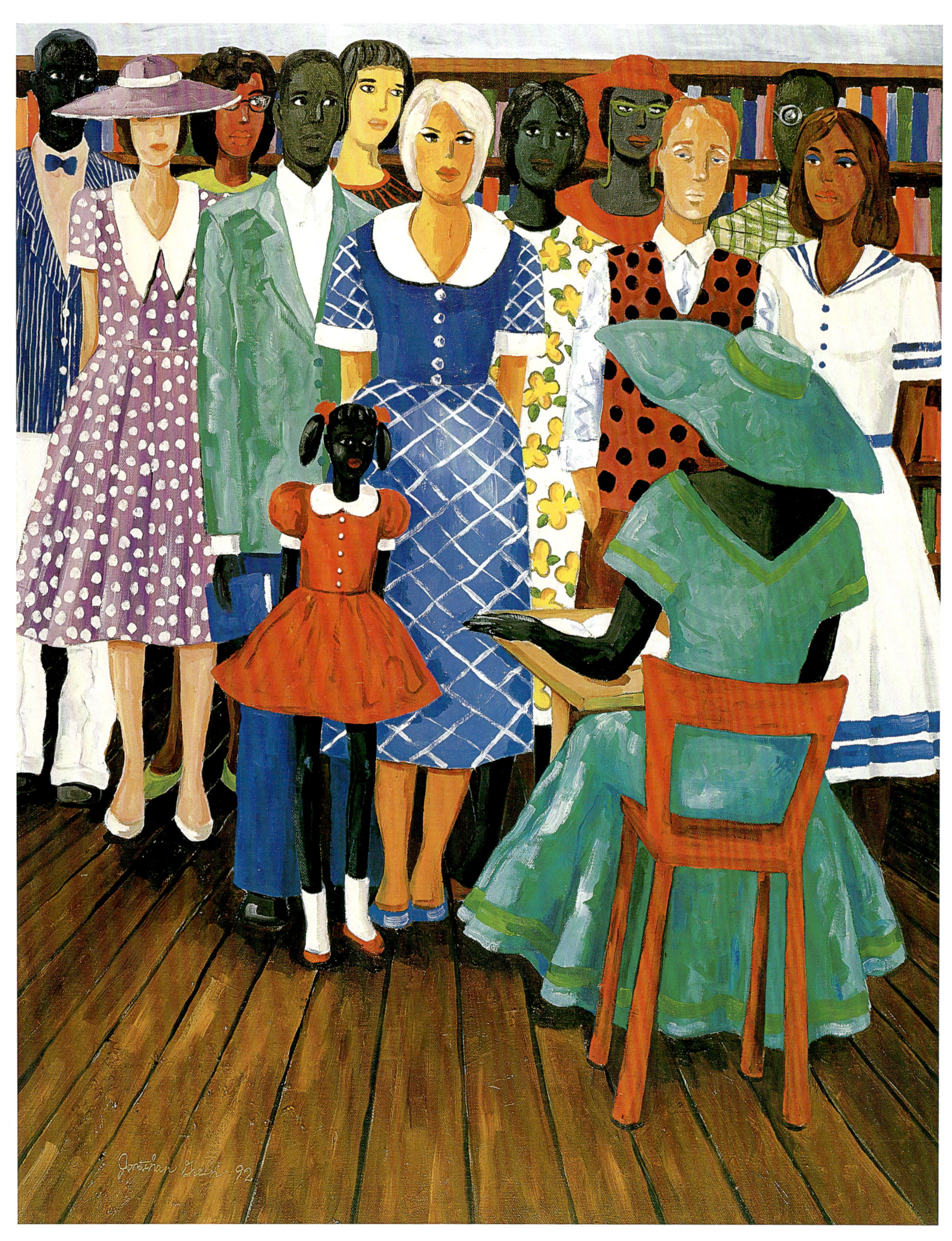

Literary Circle, 1992. Oil on canvas, 32 x 24".
Courtesy of Dianne McCall. Photograph by Tim Stamm.

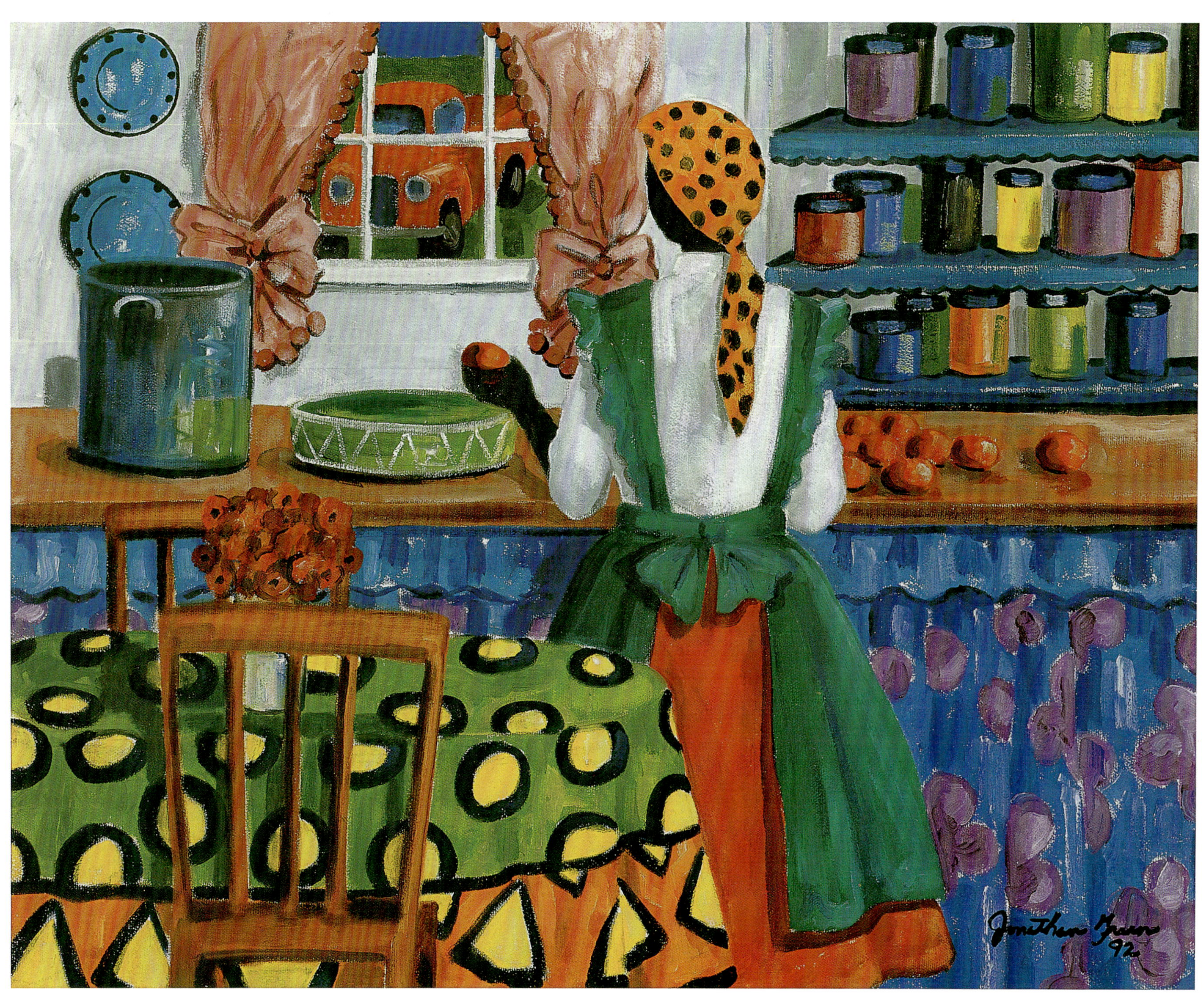

Red Tomatoes, 1992. Oil on canvas, 16 x 20".
Private collection. Photograph by Tim Stamm.

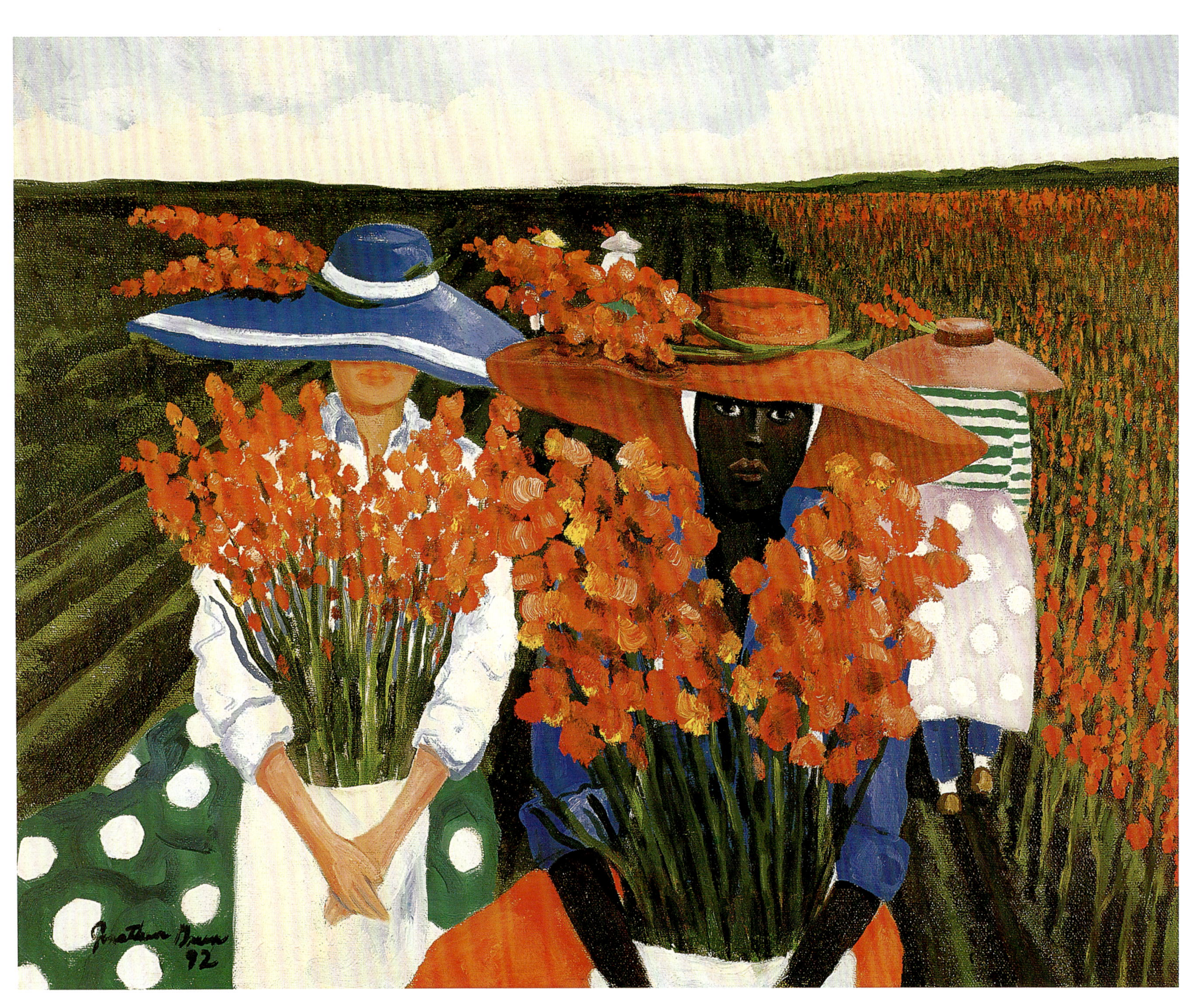

Gladiolus Harvest, 1992. Oil on canvas, 16 x 20".
Courtesy of William A. and Elizabeth W. Campbell. Photograph by Tim Stamm.

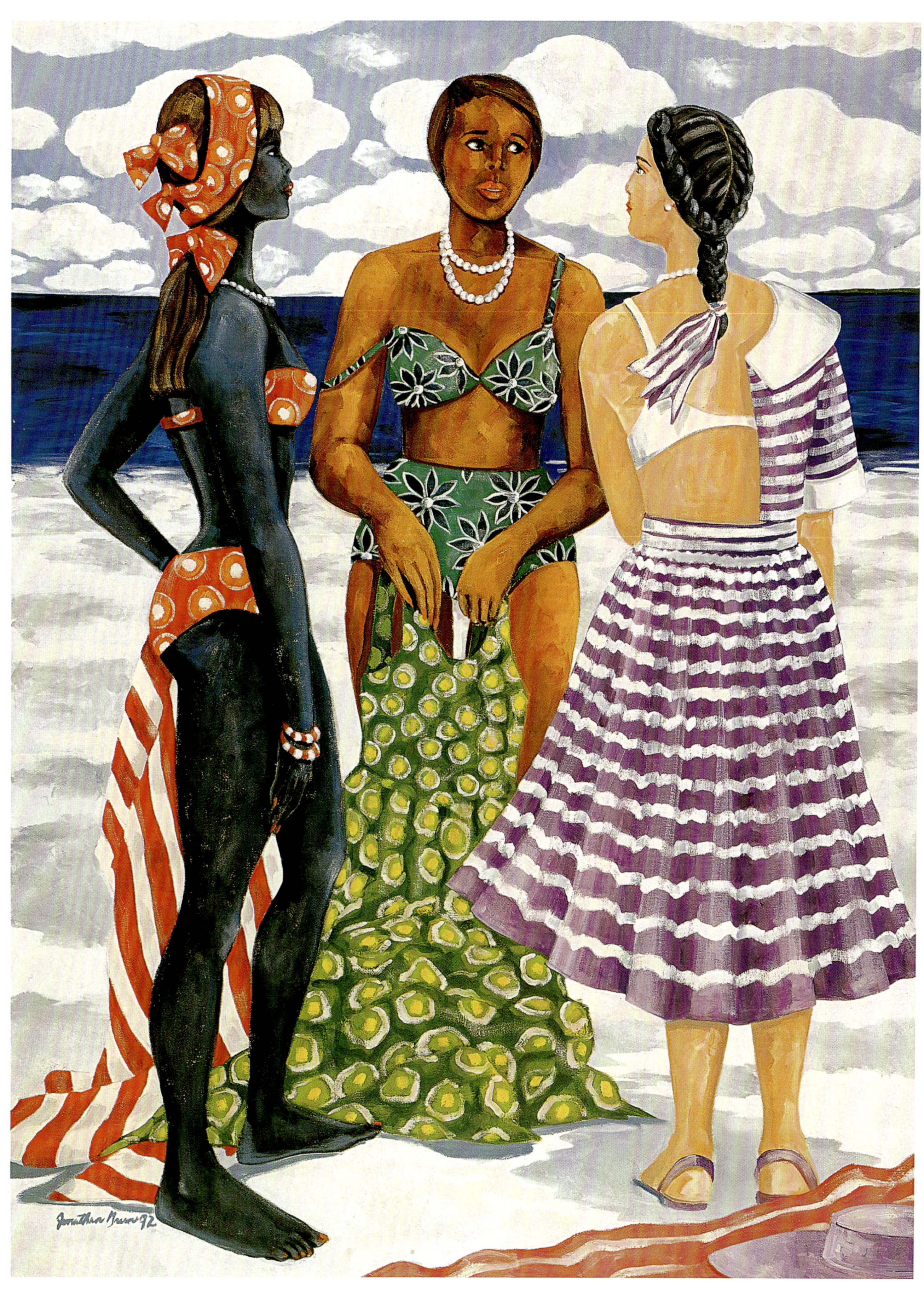

Noon Swim, 1992. Oil on canvas, 36 x 24".
Courtesy of Roy and Margaret Hull. Photograph by Tim Stamm.

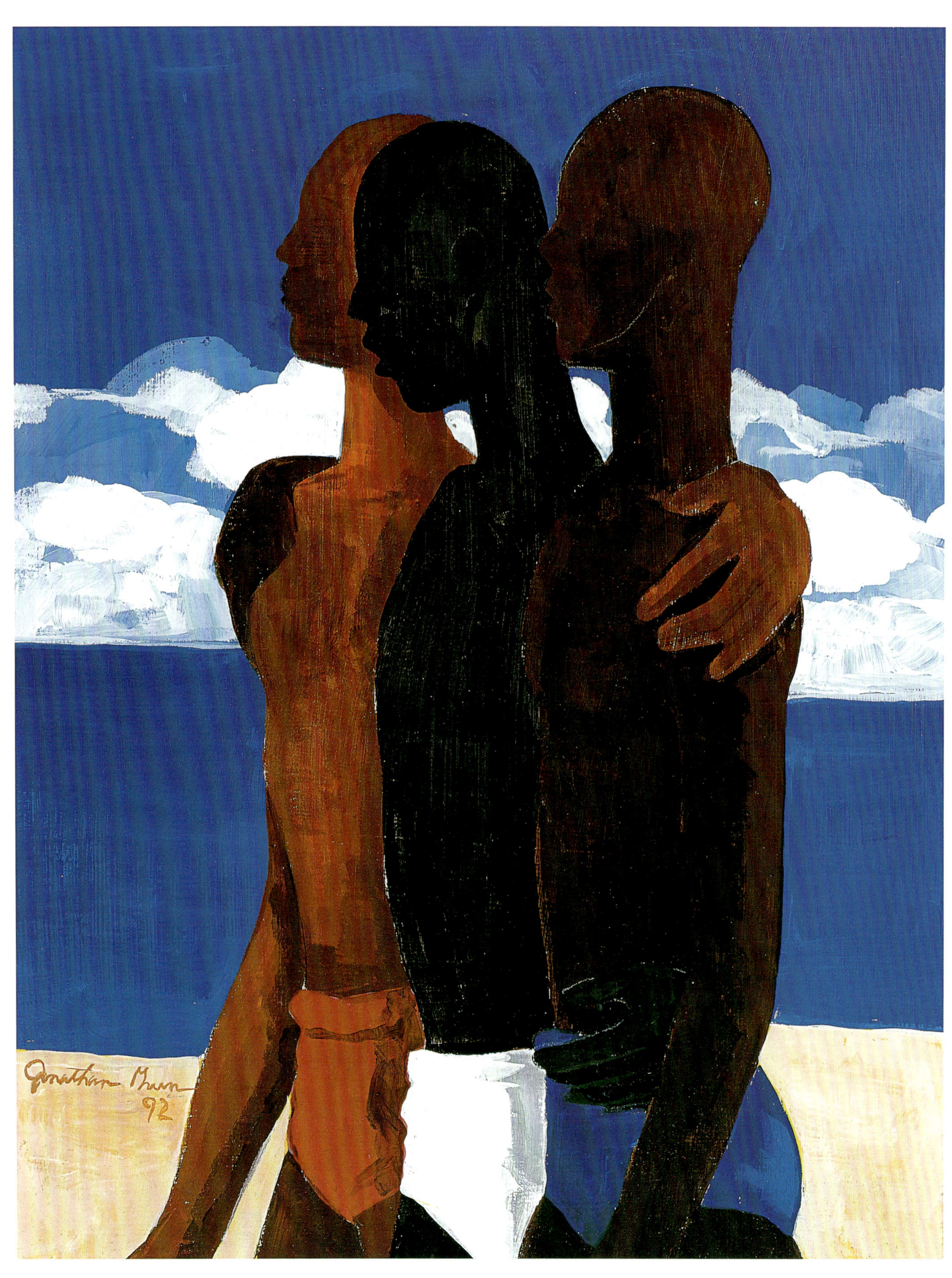

Friends, 1992. Acrylic on masonite, 14 x 11".
Courtesy of Patric McCoy. Photograph by Tim Stamm.

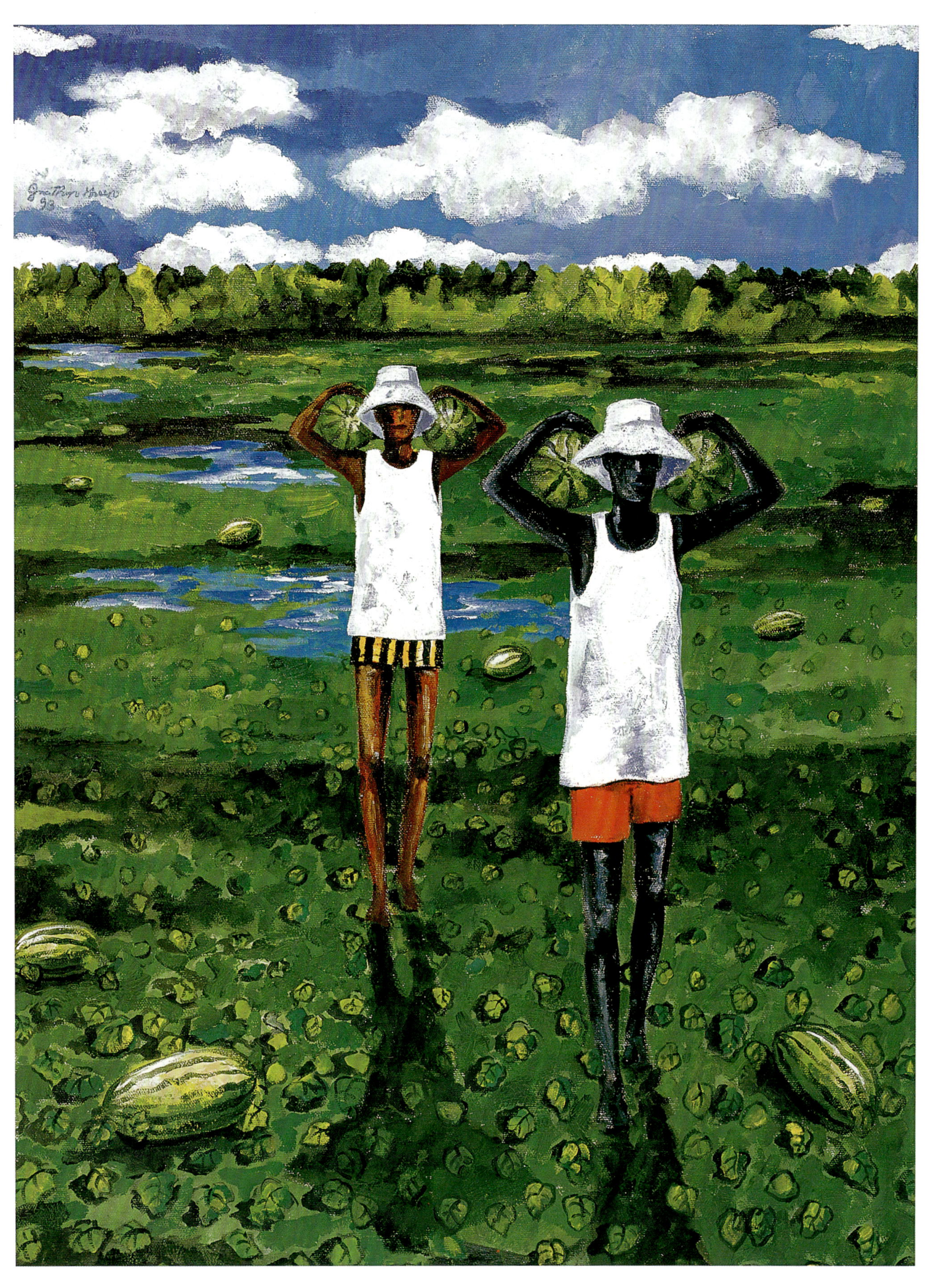

Melon Patch, 1993. Oil on canvas, 24 x 18".
Courtesy of Charles and Claudina Wells. Photograph by Tim Stamm.

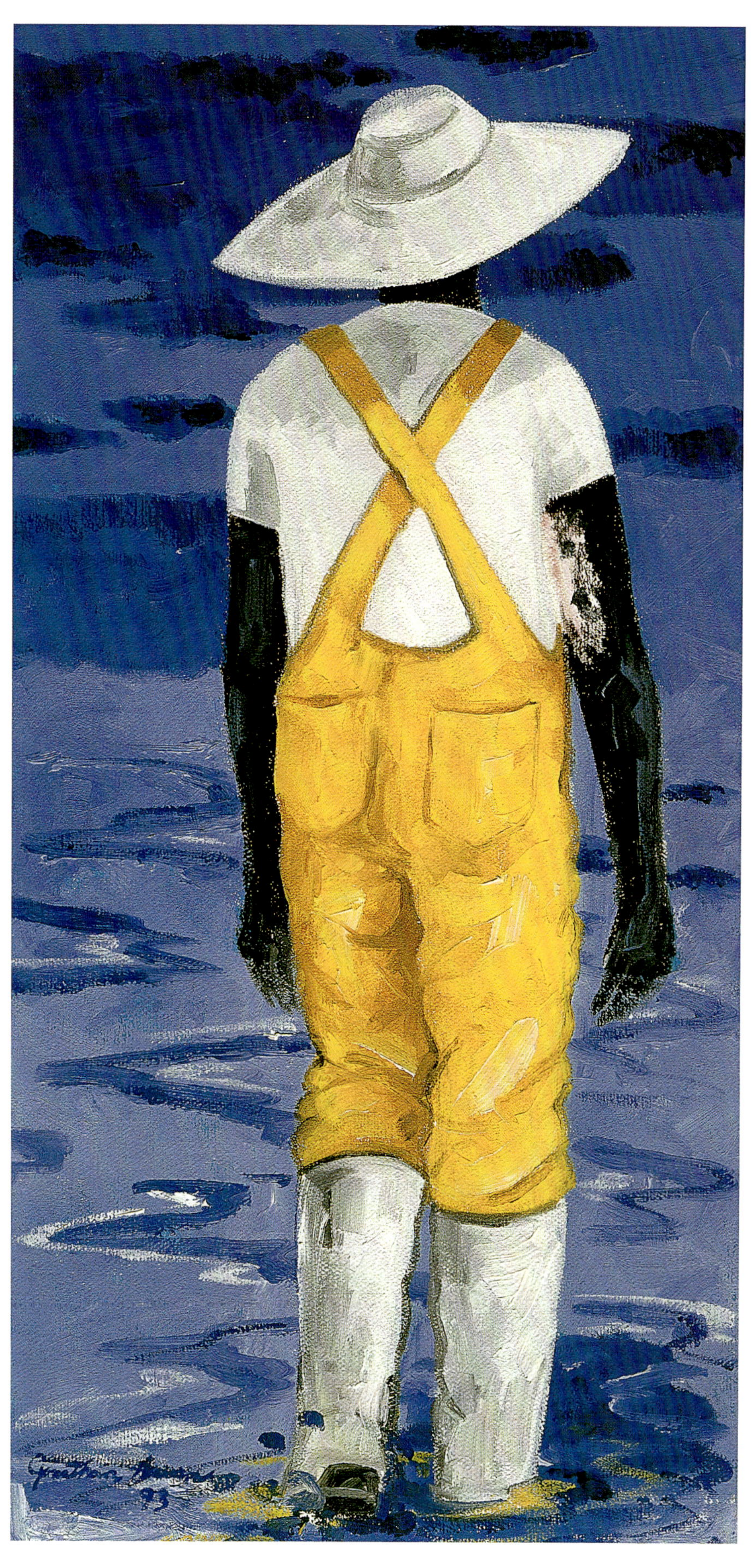

The Oyster Worker, 1993. Oil on canvas, 16 x 8".
Courtesy of Brant and Judy Bynum. Photograph by Tim Stamm.

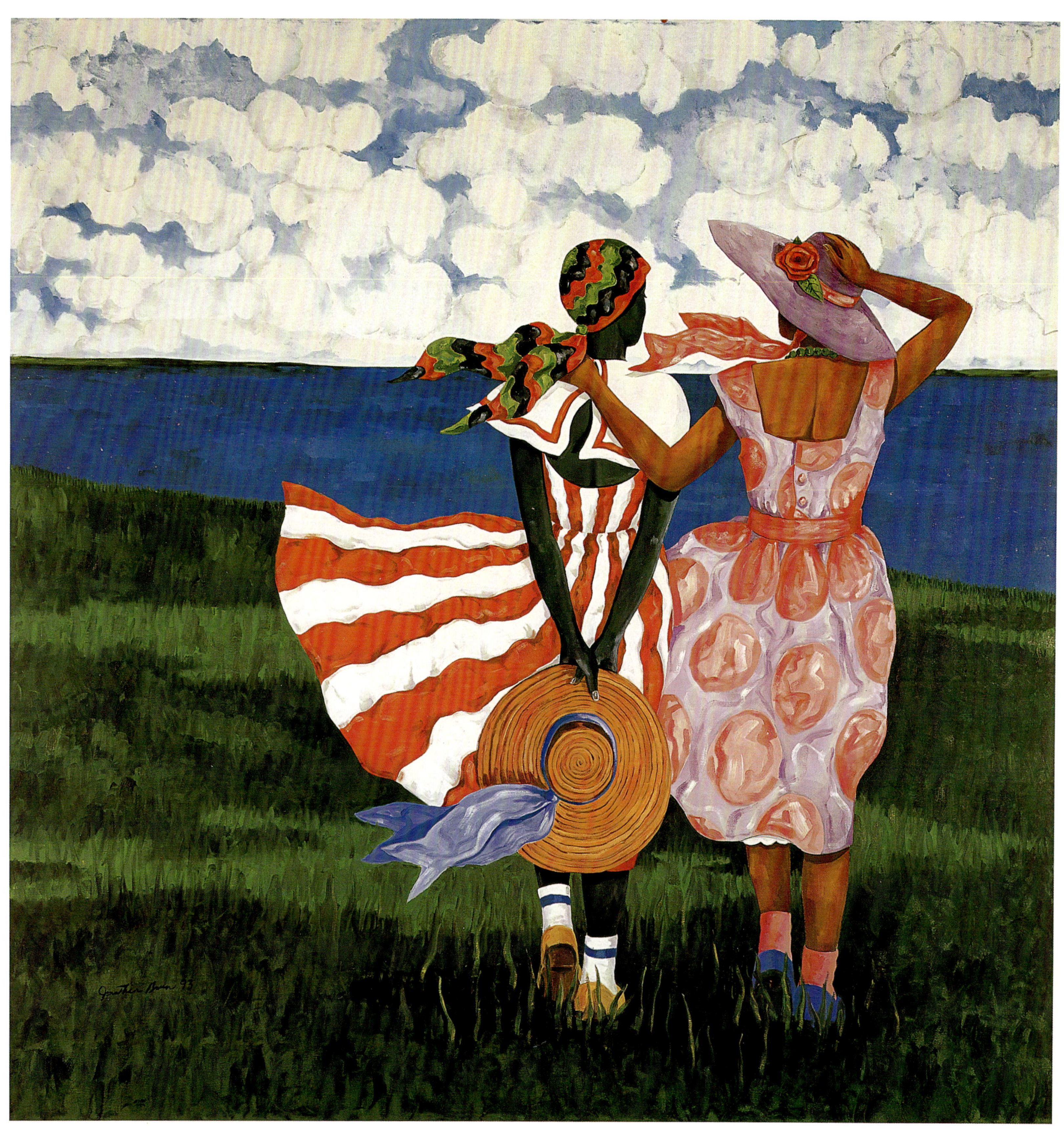

Daughters of the South, 1993. Oil on canvas, 72 x 72".
Courtesy of Julia J. Norrell. Photograph by Tim Stamm.

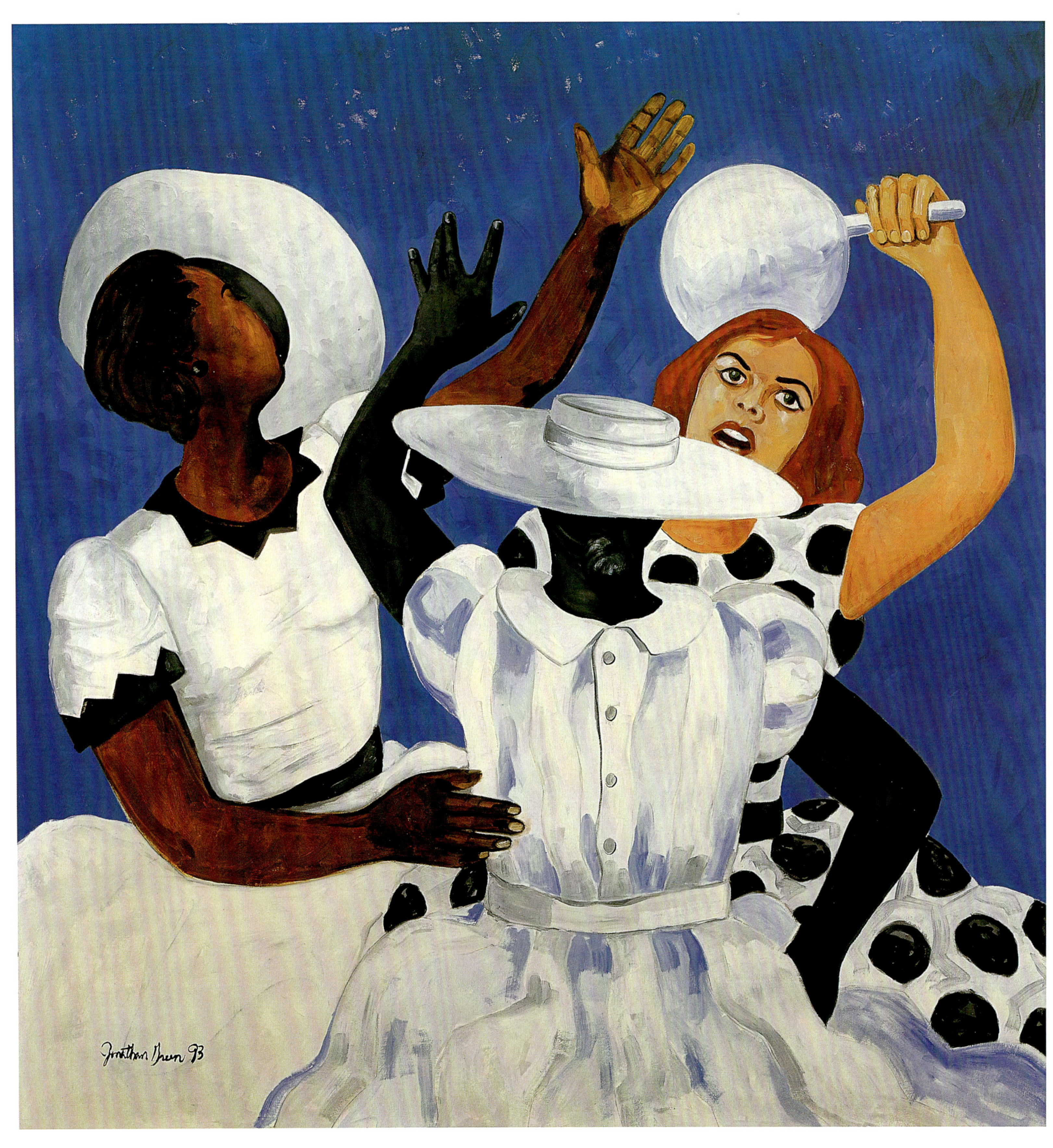

Praise Him, 1993. Oil on canvas, 54 x 54".
Courtesy of Wayne and Elaine Jones. Photograph by Tim Stamm.

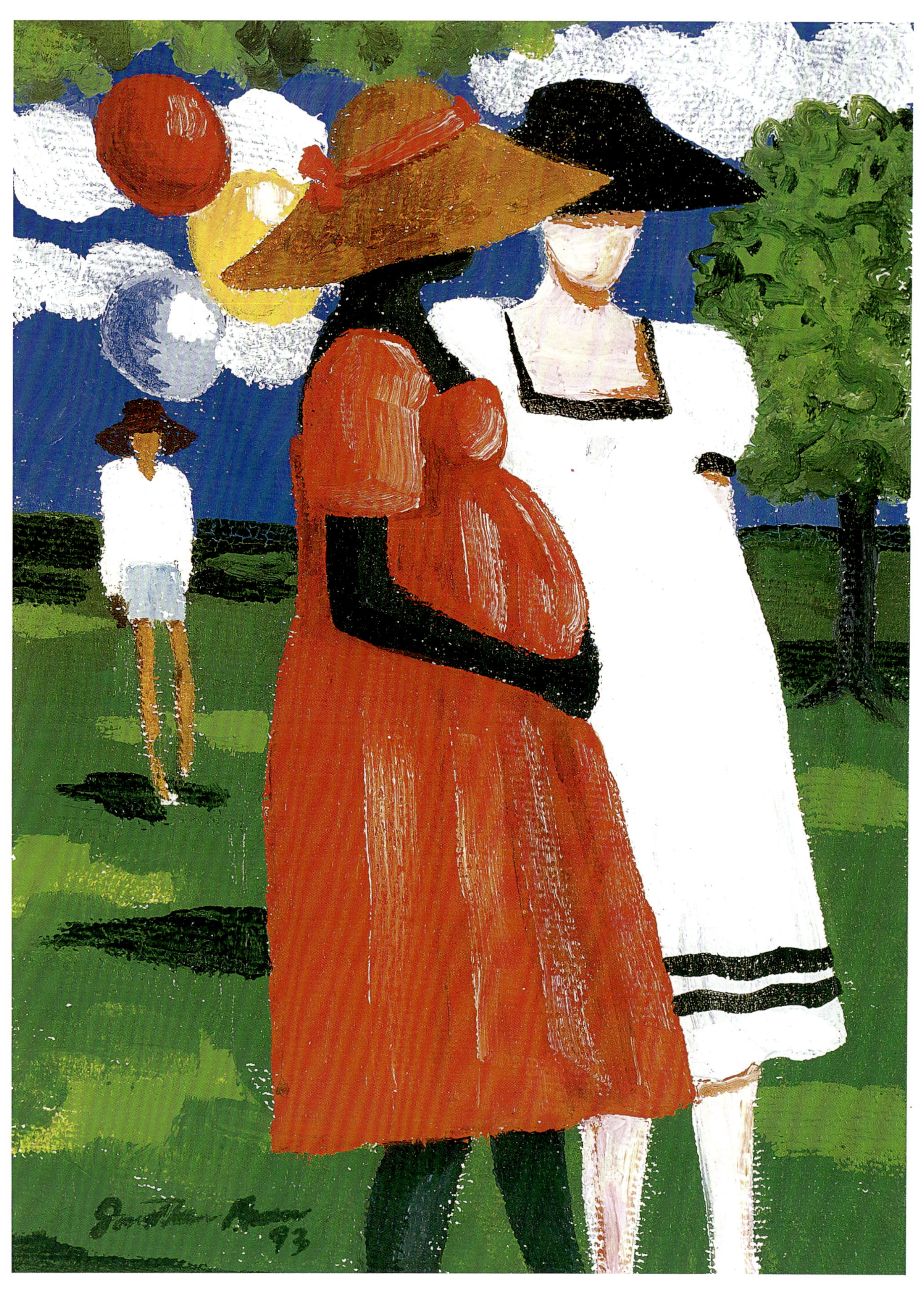

Ladies in Waiting, 1993. Oil on canvas, 7 x 5".
Courtesy of Terry and Thelma Harris. Photograph by Tim Stamm.

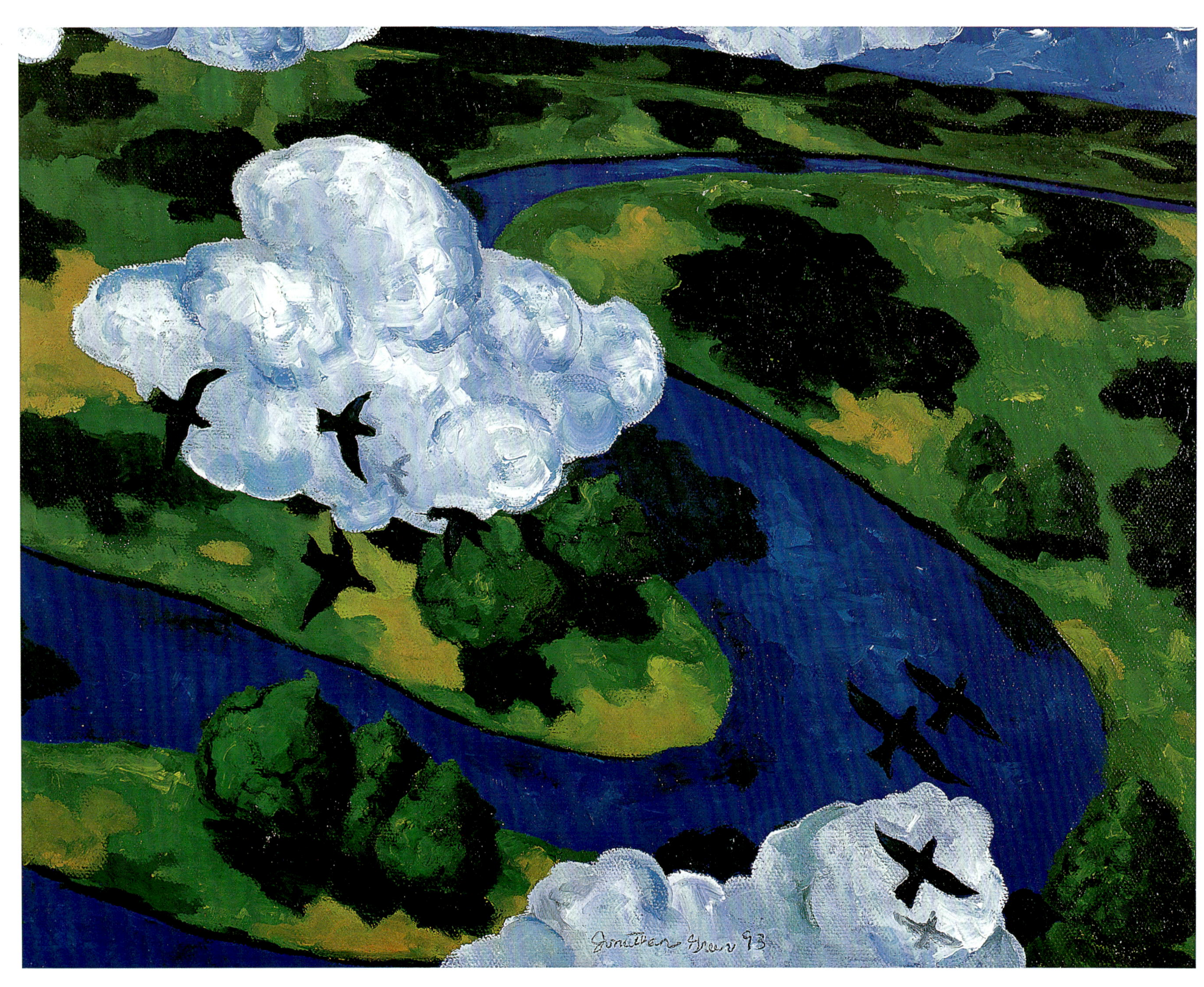

Snake River, 1993. Oil on canvas, 11 x 14".
Courtesy of Joan Albright. Photograph by Tim Stamm.

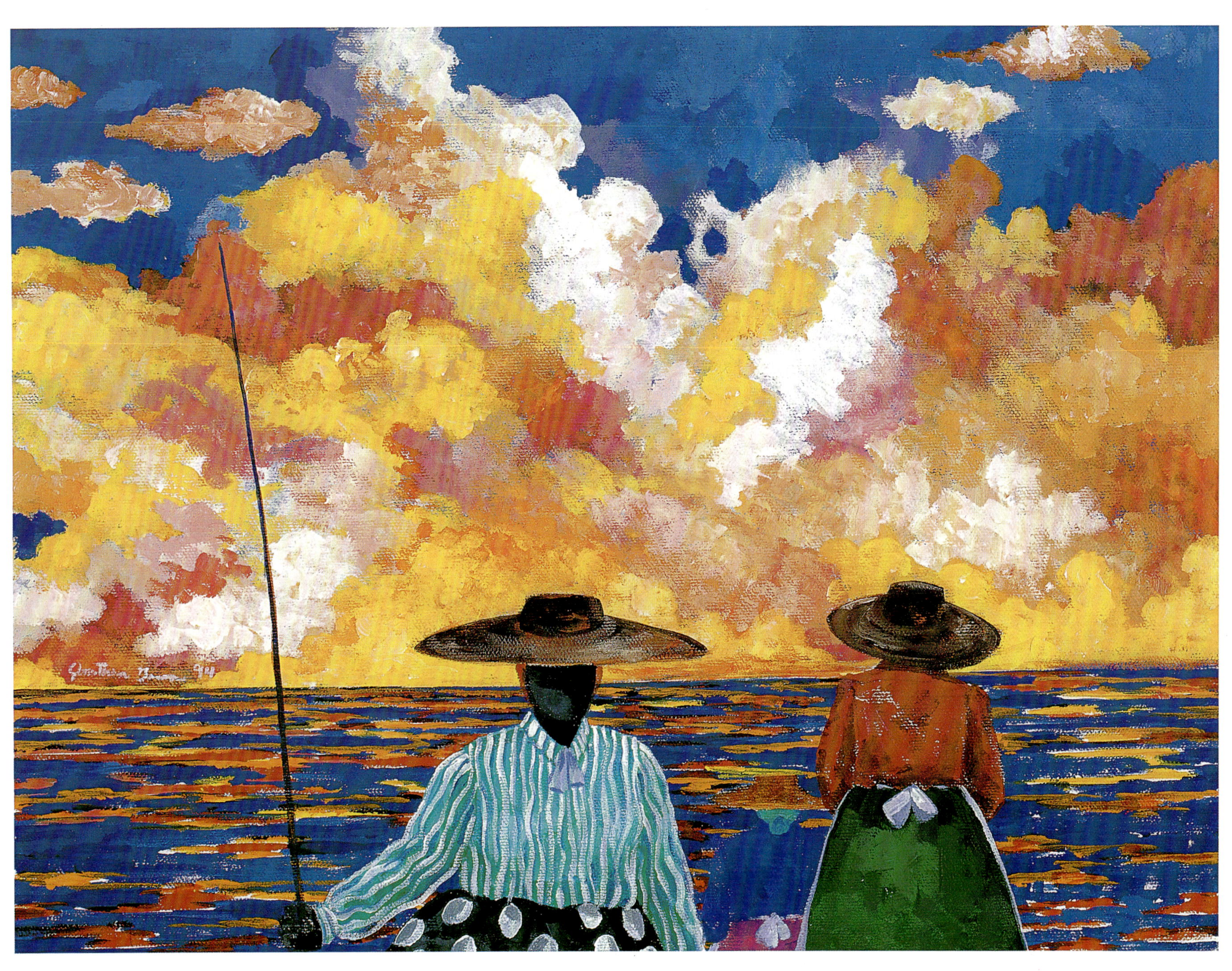

Autumn Sunrise, 1994. Oil on canvas, 12 x 16".
Courtesy of Jeffrey A.Weisbeng. Photograph by Tim Stamm.

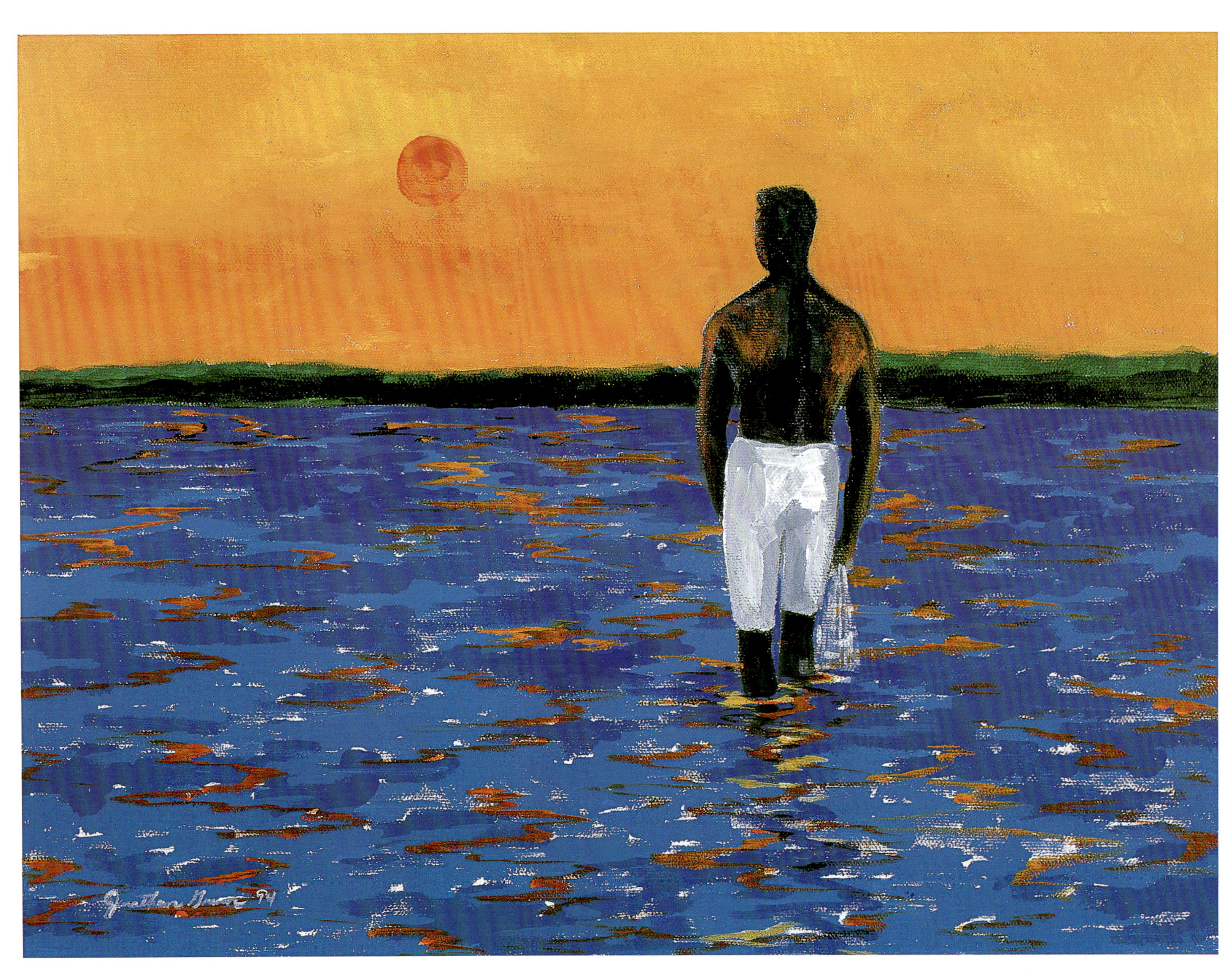

Dusk Catch, 1994. Acrylic on canvas, 12 x 16".
Courtesy of Gregg Kerr. Photograph by Tim Stamm.

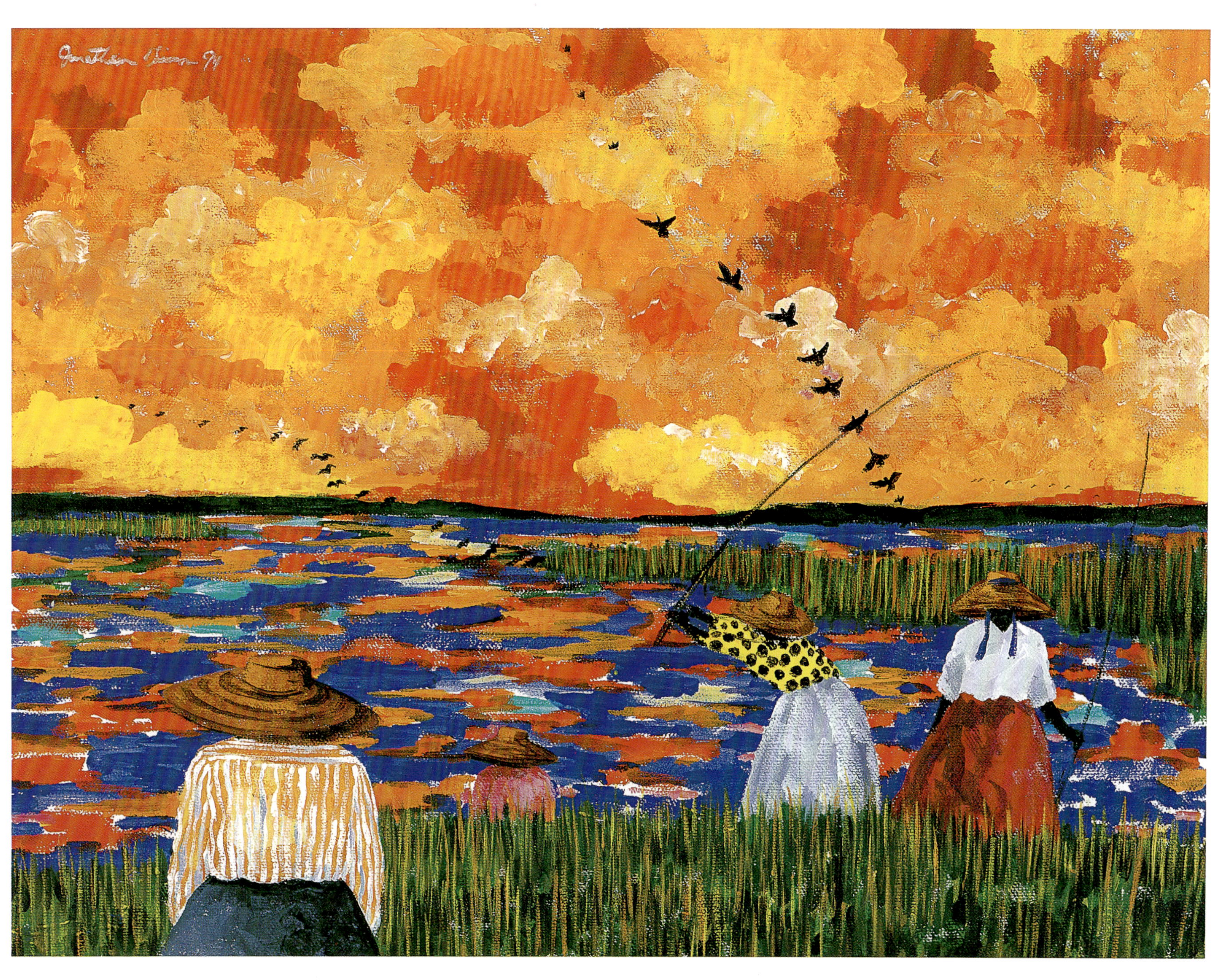

Marshland Sunrise, 1994. Acrylic on canvas, 12 x 16".
Collection of the artist. Photograph by Tim Stamm.

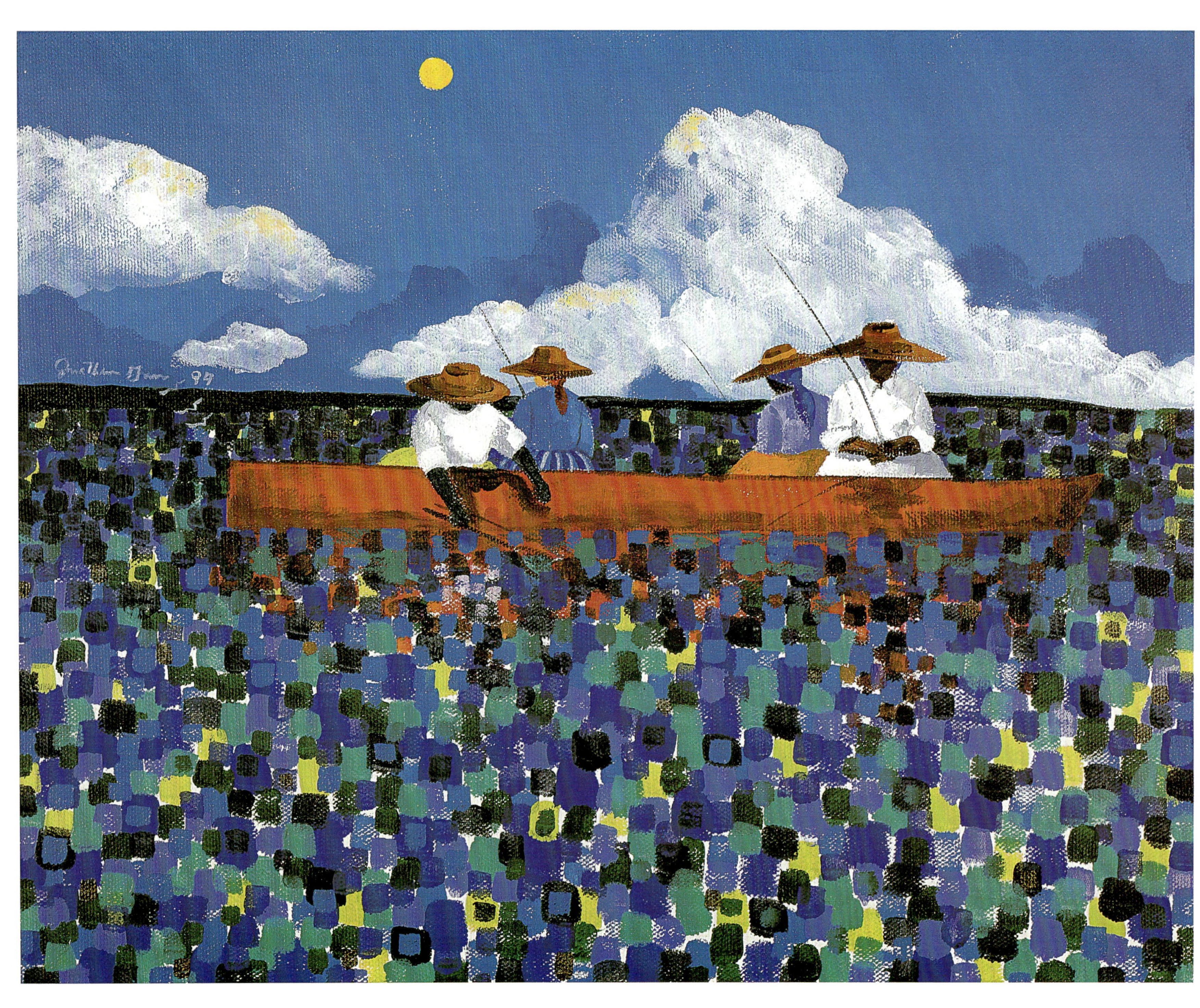

Fishing Women from Lobeco, 1994. Acrylic on canvas, 11 x 14".
Courtesy of Mac and Doris Williams. Photograph by Tim Stamm.

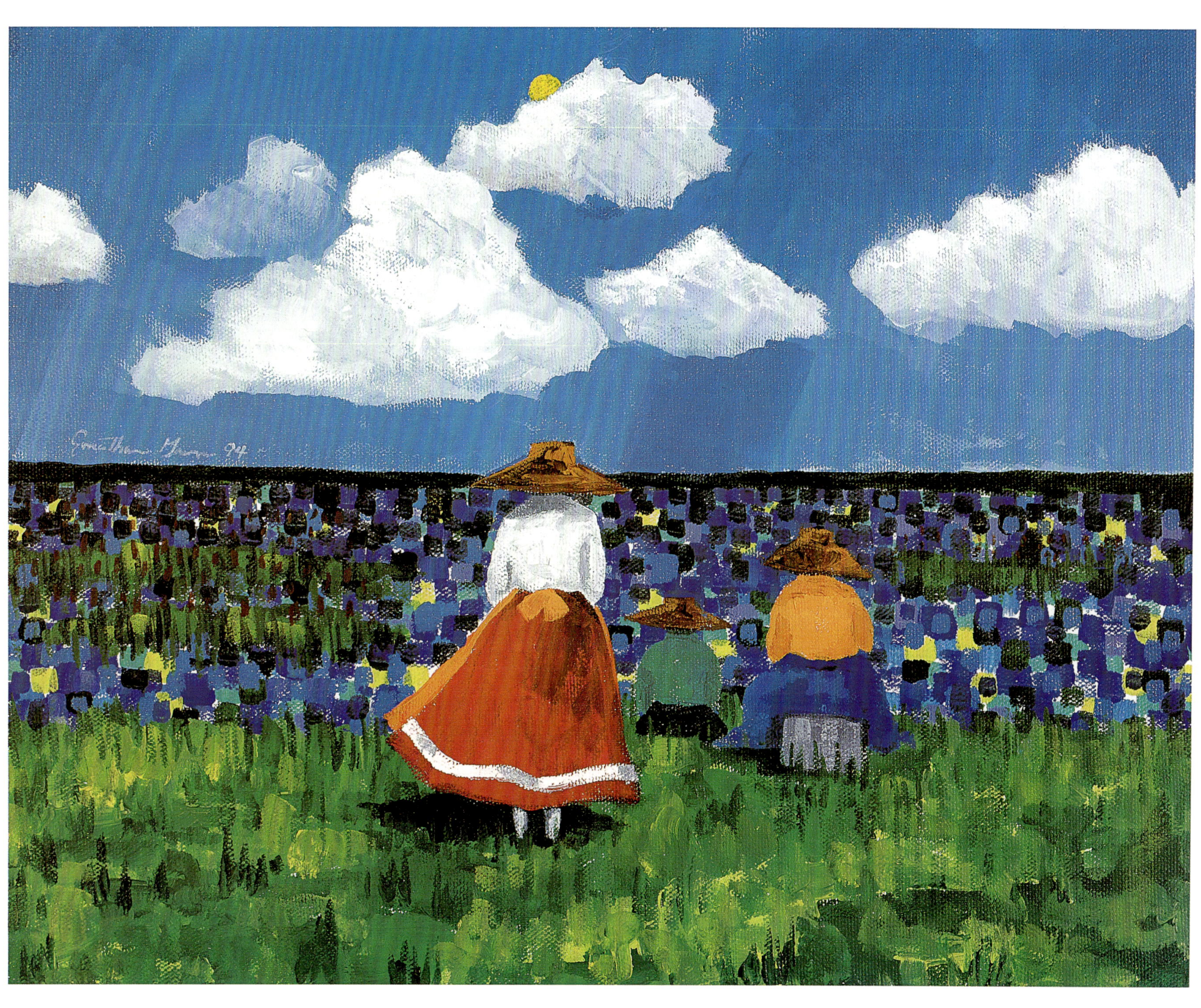

Waiting for the Tide, 1994. Acrylic on canvas, 11 x 14".
Courtesy of Peter and Pauline Milius. Photograph by Tim Stamm.

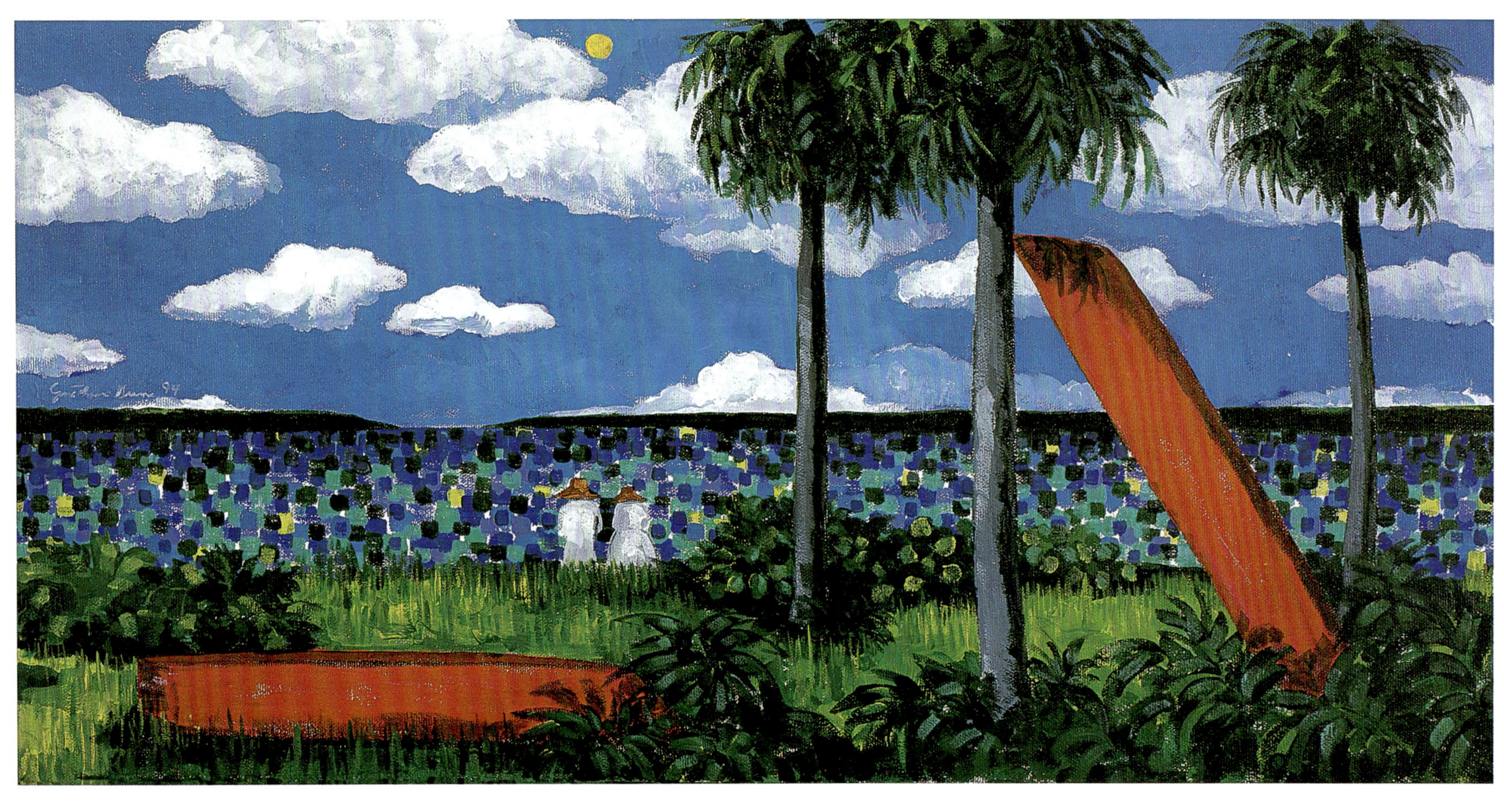

Two Red Boats, 1994. Acrylic on canvas, 12 x 24".
Courtesy of Julia Roberts. Photograph by Tim Stamm.

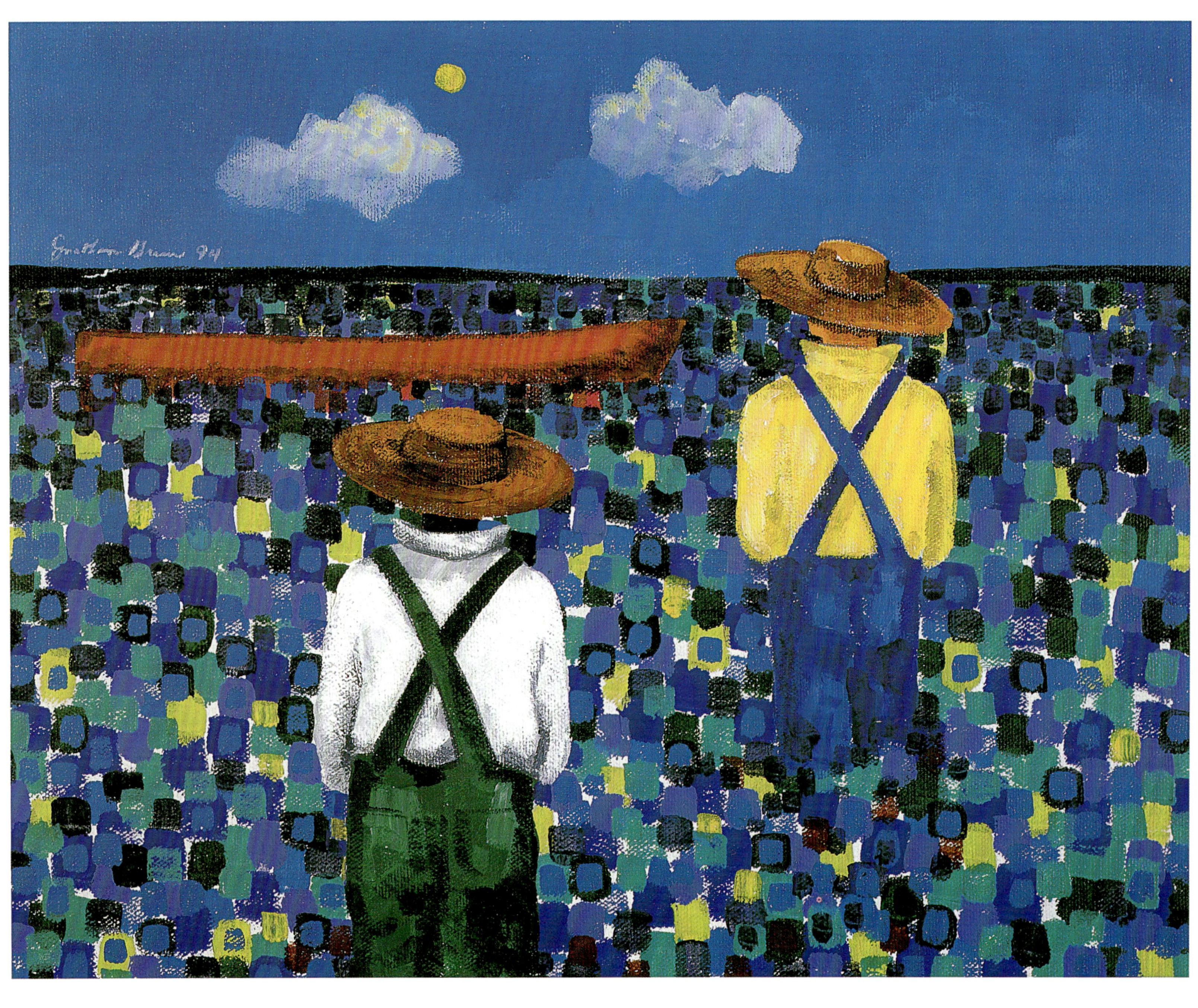

Two Oyster Men, 1994. Acrylic on canvas, 11 x 14".
Courtesy of Mac and Doris Williams. Photograph by Tim Stamm.

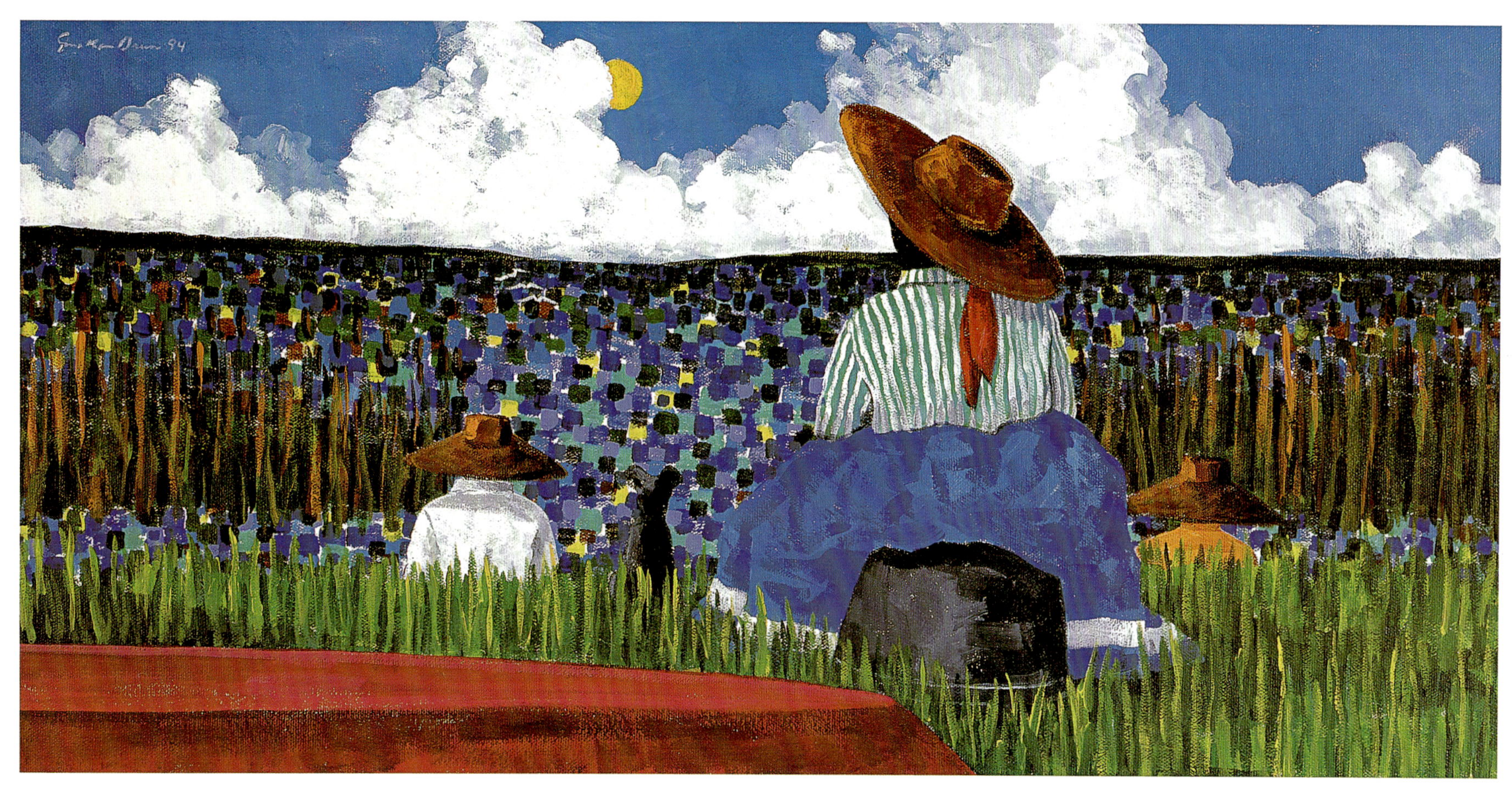

Watching the Tide, 1994. Acrylic on canvas, 12 x 24".
Courtesy of Jady Wade. Photograph by Tim Stamm.

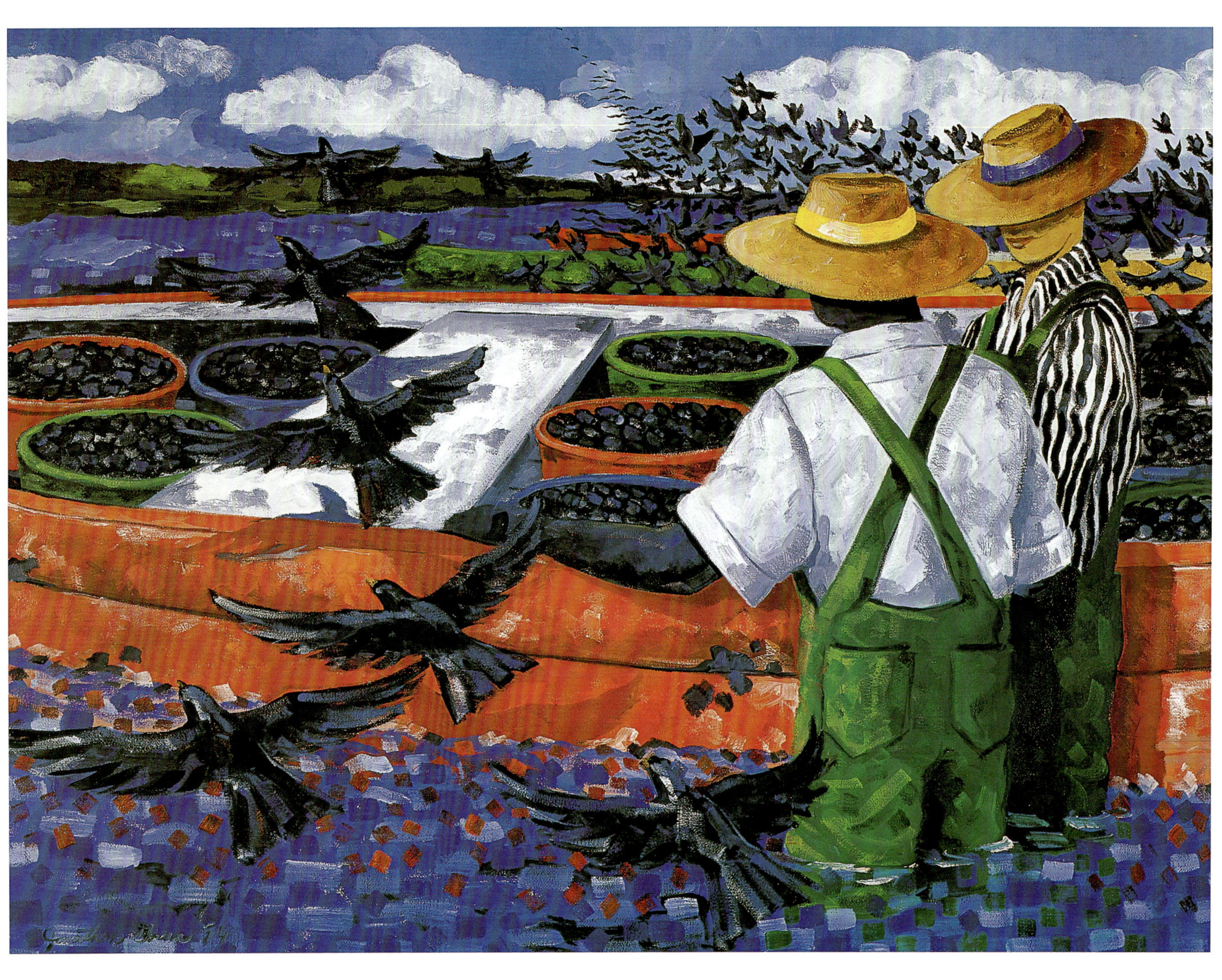

Red Shadows, 1994. Oil on canvas, 18 x 24".
Courtesy of Howard and Miriam Warshaw. Photograph by Tim Stamm.

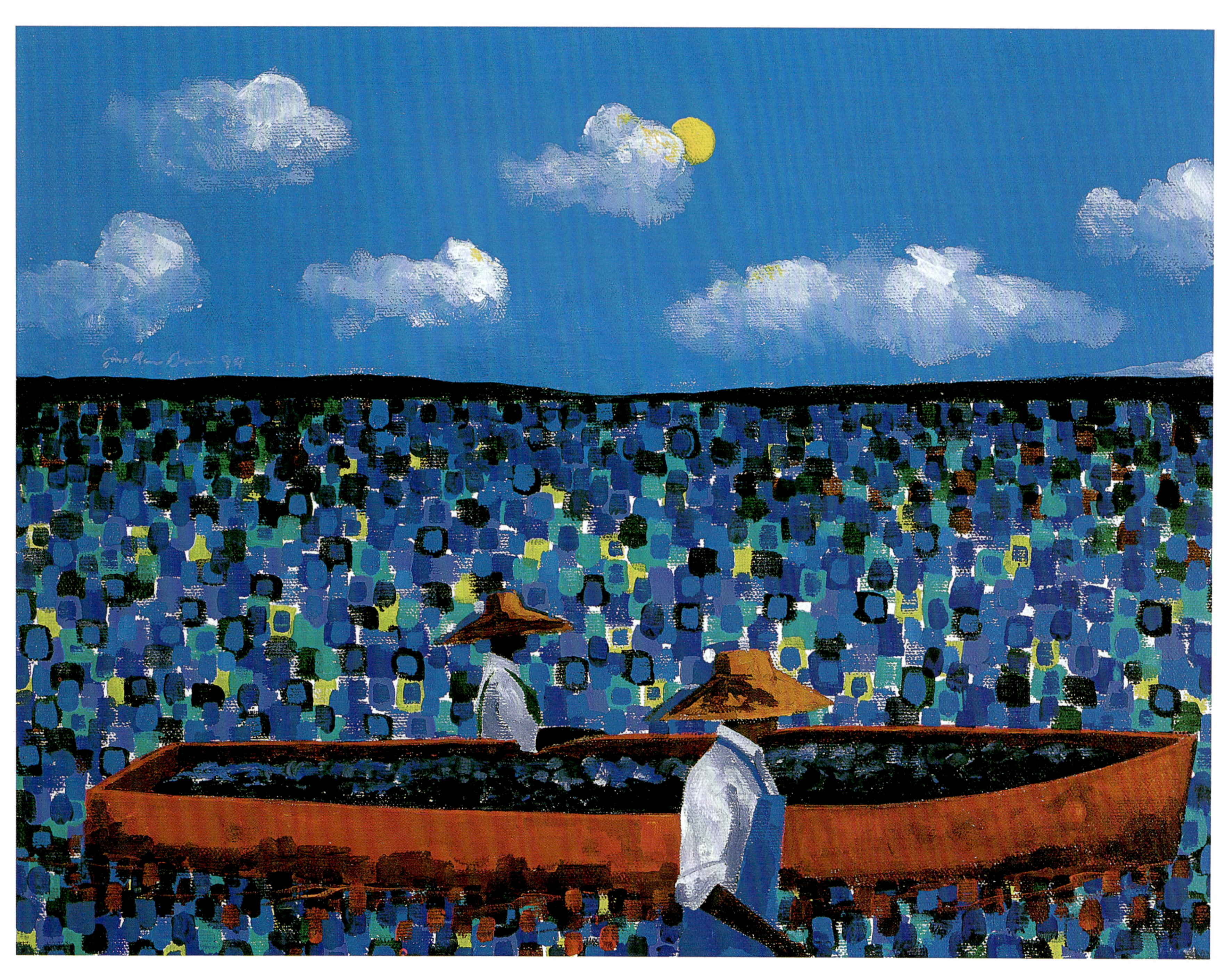

Oyster Boat, 1994. Acrylic on canvas, 12 x 16".
Courtesy of Dr. and Mrs. David M. Lombardo. Photograph by Tim Stamm.

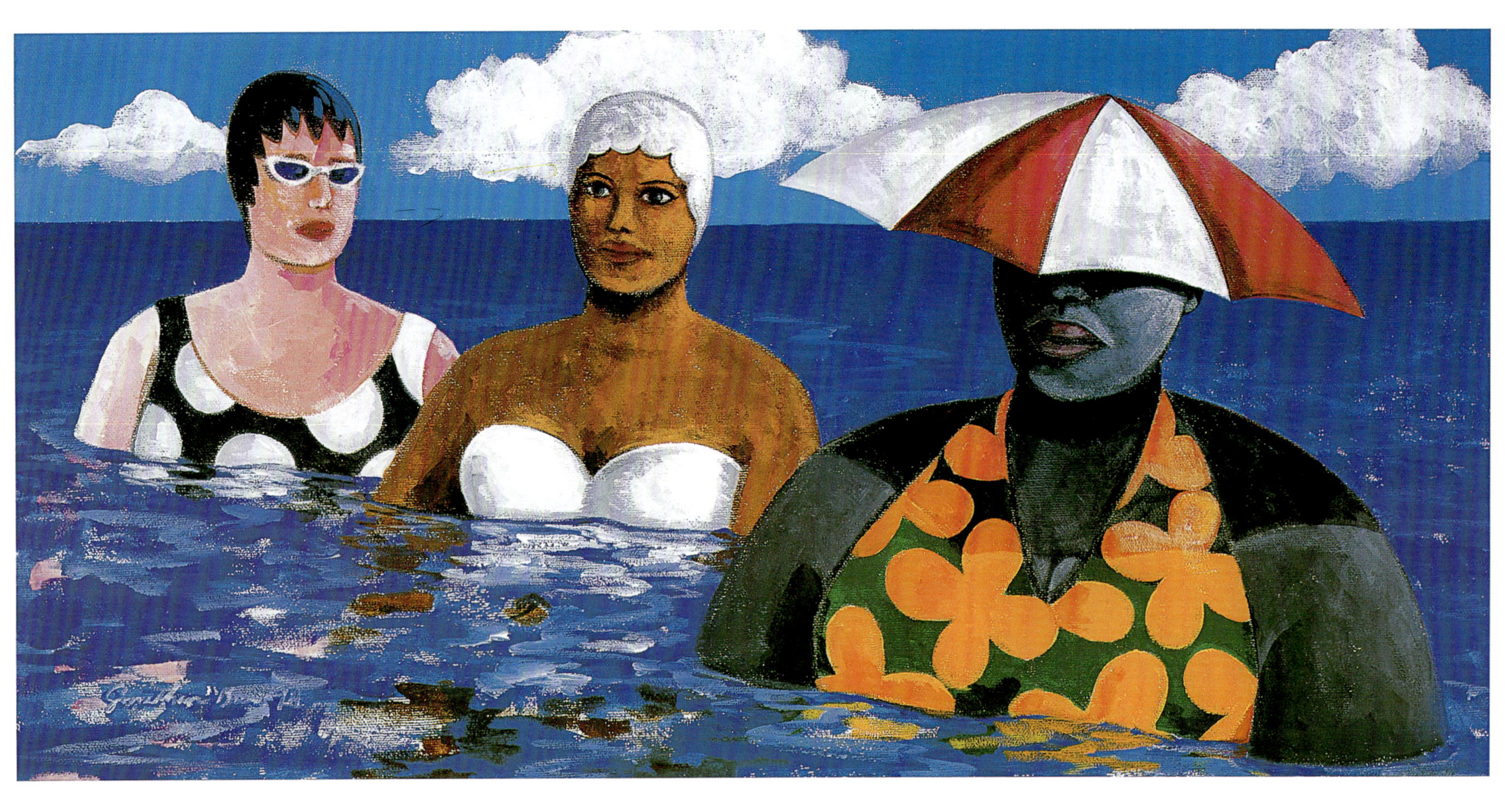

Ocean Beauties, 1994. Acrylic on canvas, 12 x 24".
Courtesy of Nancy Weingarten. Photograph by Tim Stamm.

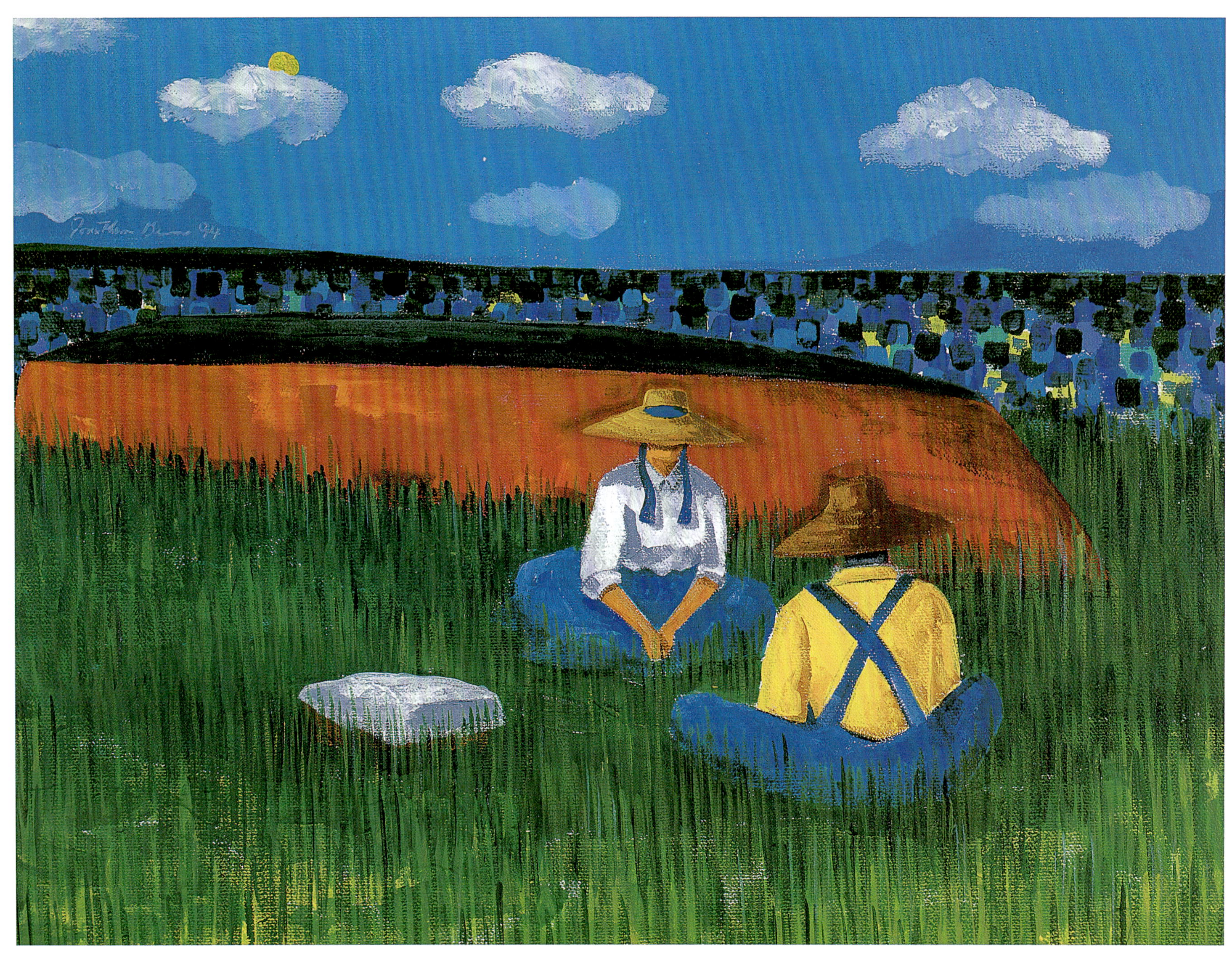

Sharing the Silence, 1994. Acrylic on canvas, 12 x 16".
Courtesy of John and Barbara Langston. Photograph by Tim Stamm.

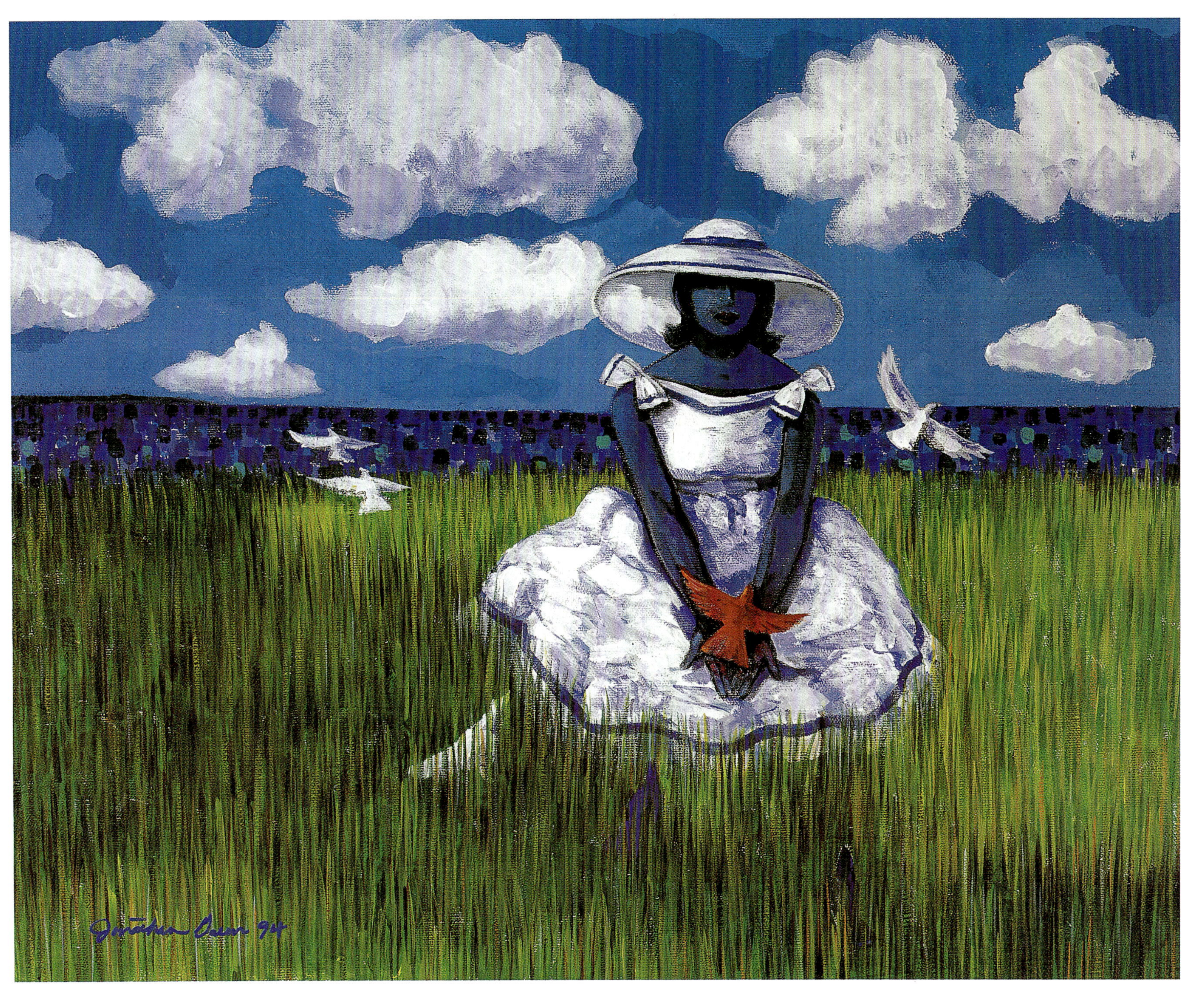

Silence with the Birds, 1994. Acrylic on canvas, 16 x 20".
Courtesy of Mr. and Mrs. Allen Jakes. Photograph by Tim Stamm.

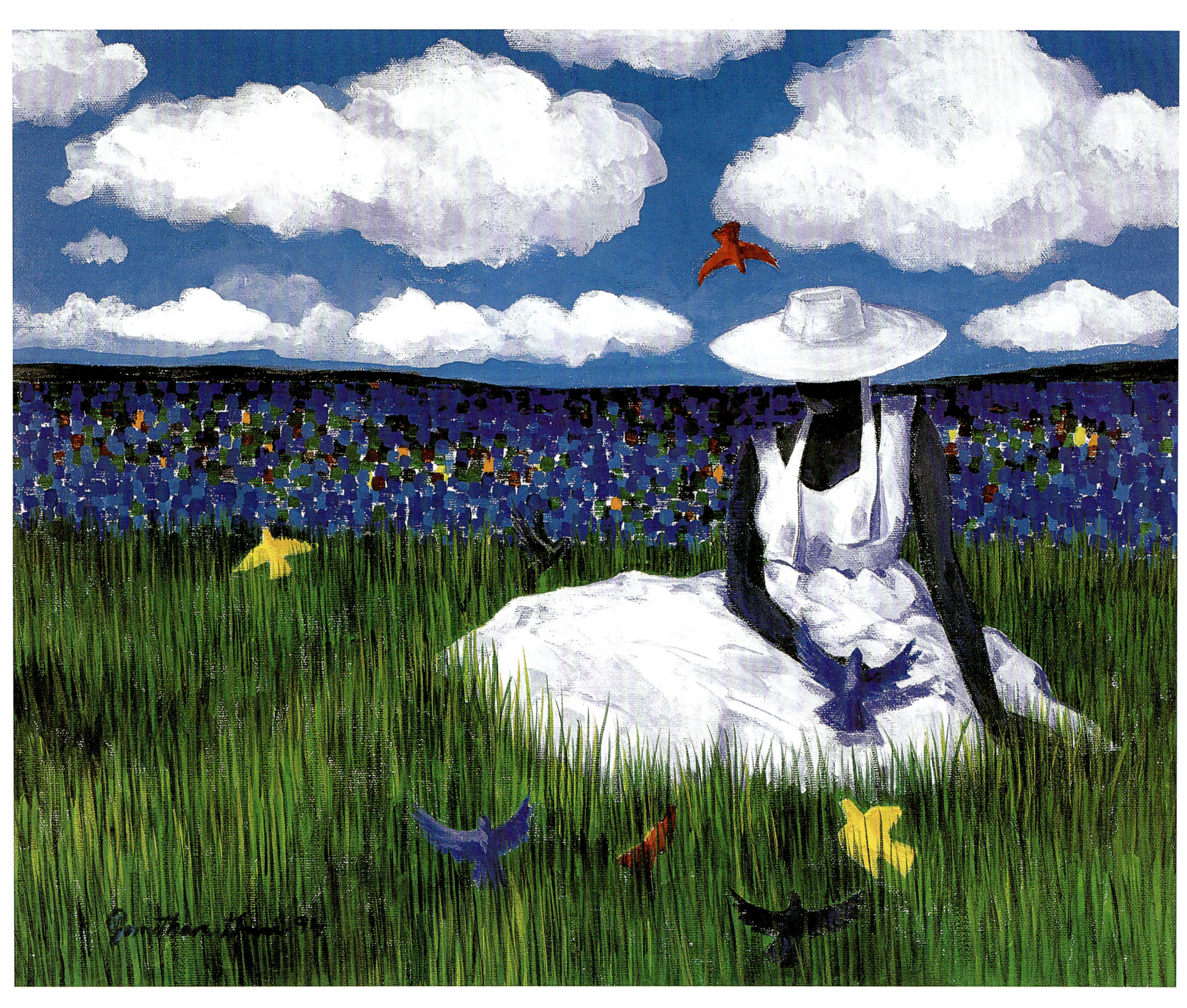

Quiet Time, 1994. Acrylic on canvas, 16 x 20".
Courtesy of Terry Flannery. Photograph by Tim Stamm.

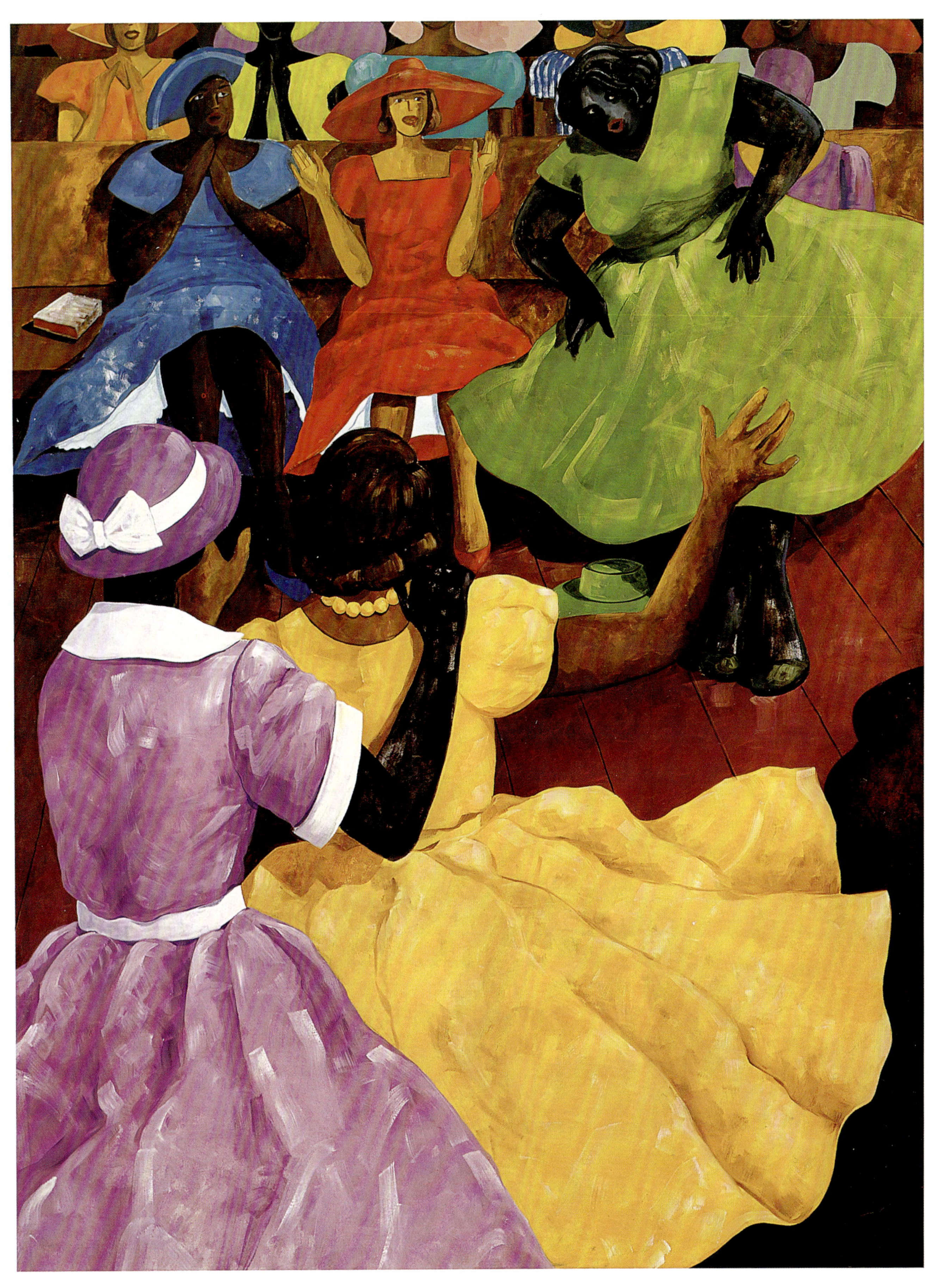

The Spirit, 1994. Oil on canvas, 72 x 55".
Courtesy of Jill Farwell. Photograph by Tim Stamm.

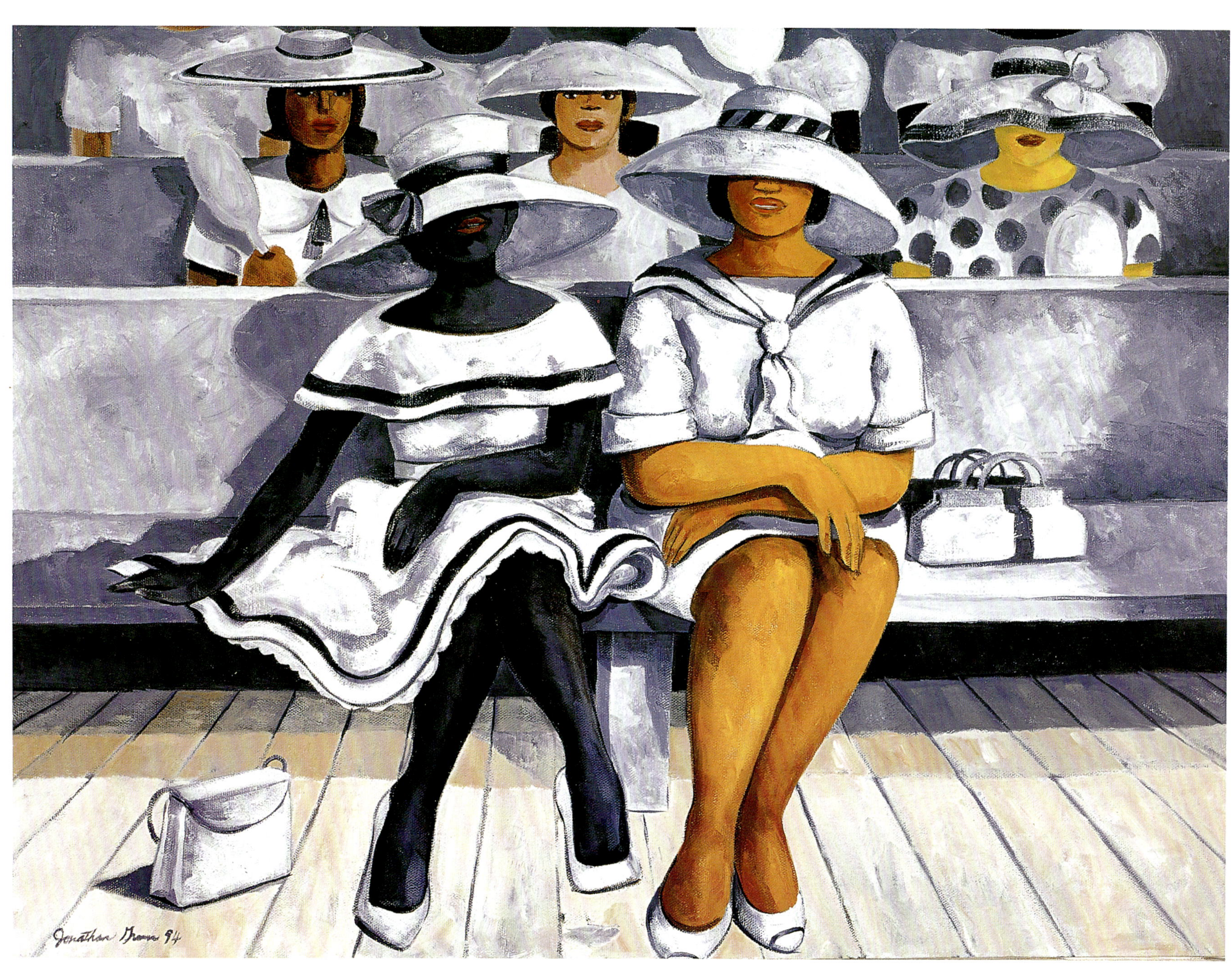

Huspah Congregation, 1994. Oil on canvas, 18 x 24".
Courtesy of Dr. and Mrs. Abraham Warshaw. Photograph by Tim Stamm.

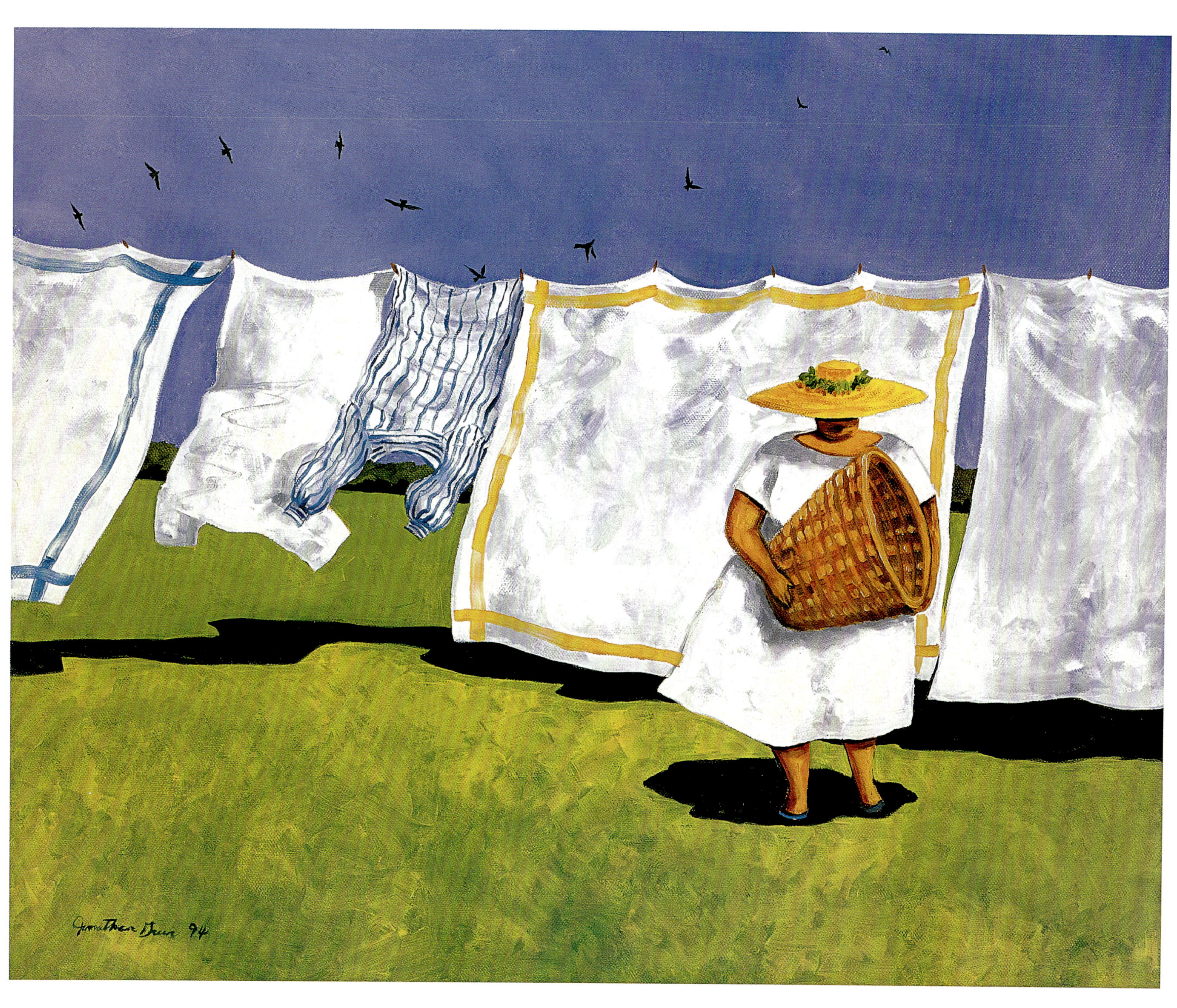

Grandma's Wash, 1994. Oil on canvas, 16 x 20".
Courtesy of William Grace. Photograph by Tim Stamm.

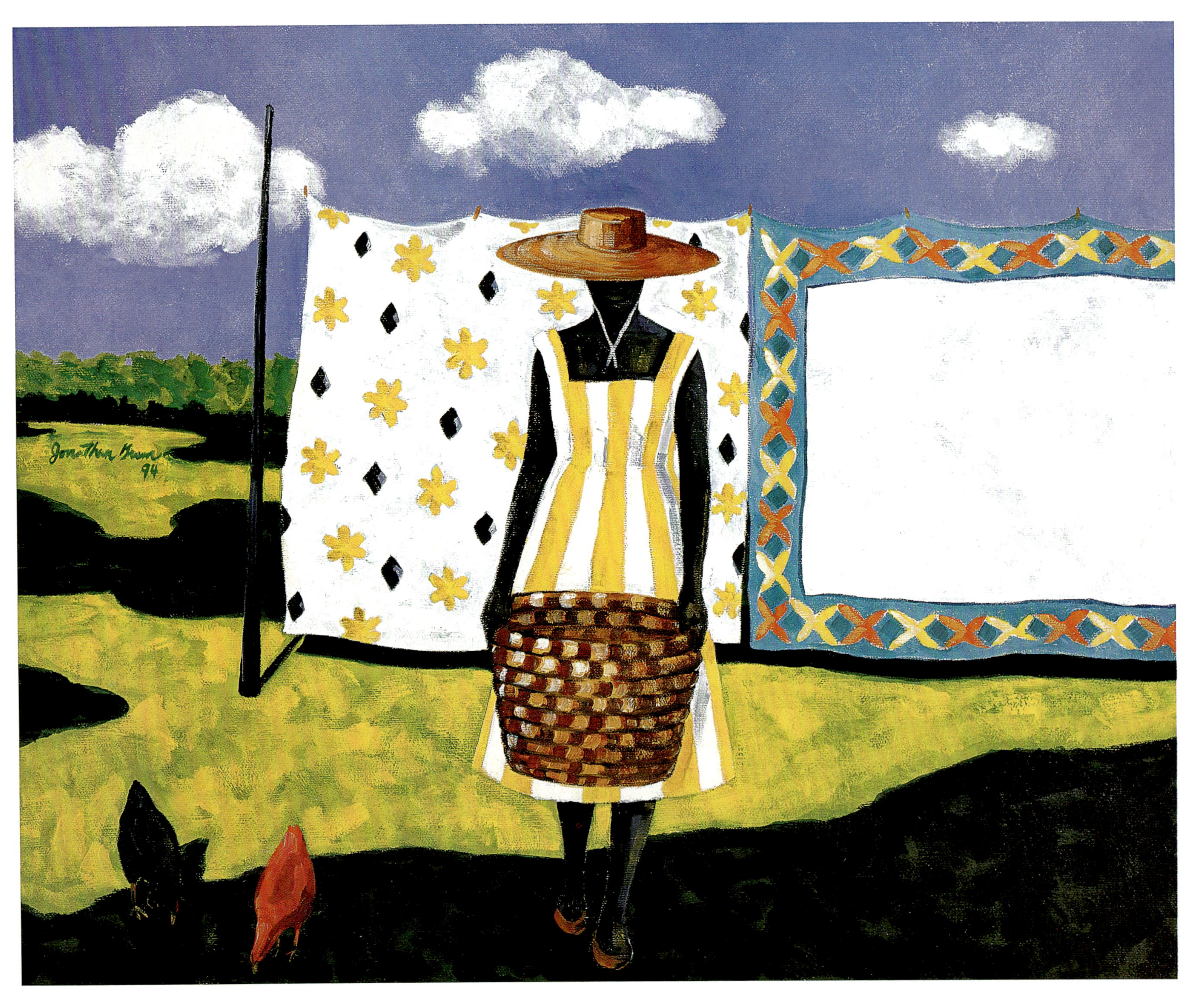

Washed Quilts, 1994. Oil on canvas, 16 x 20".
Courtesy of George and Dee Crawford. Photograph by Tim Stamm.

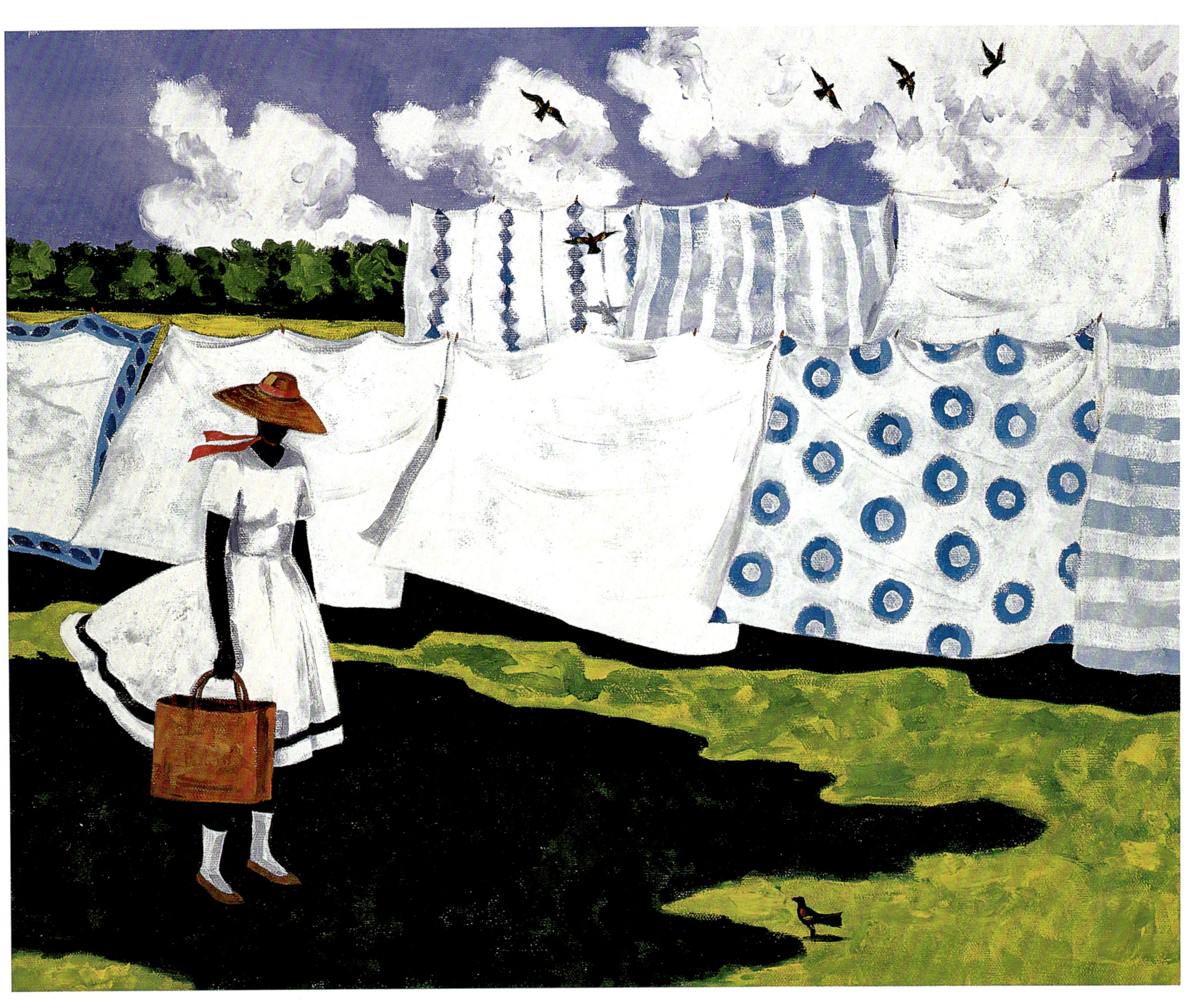

Red Wing Black Bird, 1994. Oil on canvas, 16 x 20".
Courtesy of Dr. and Mrs. David M. Lombardo. Photograph by Tim Stamm.

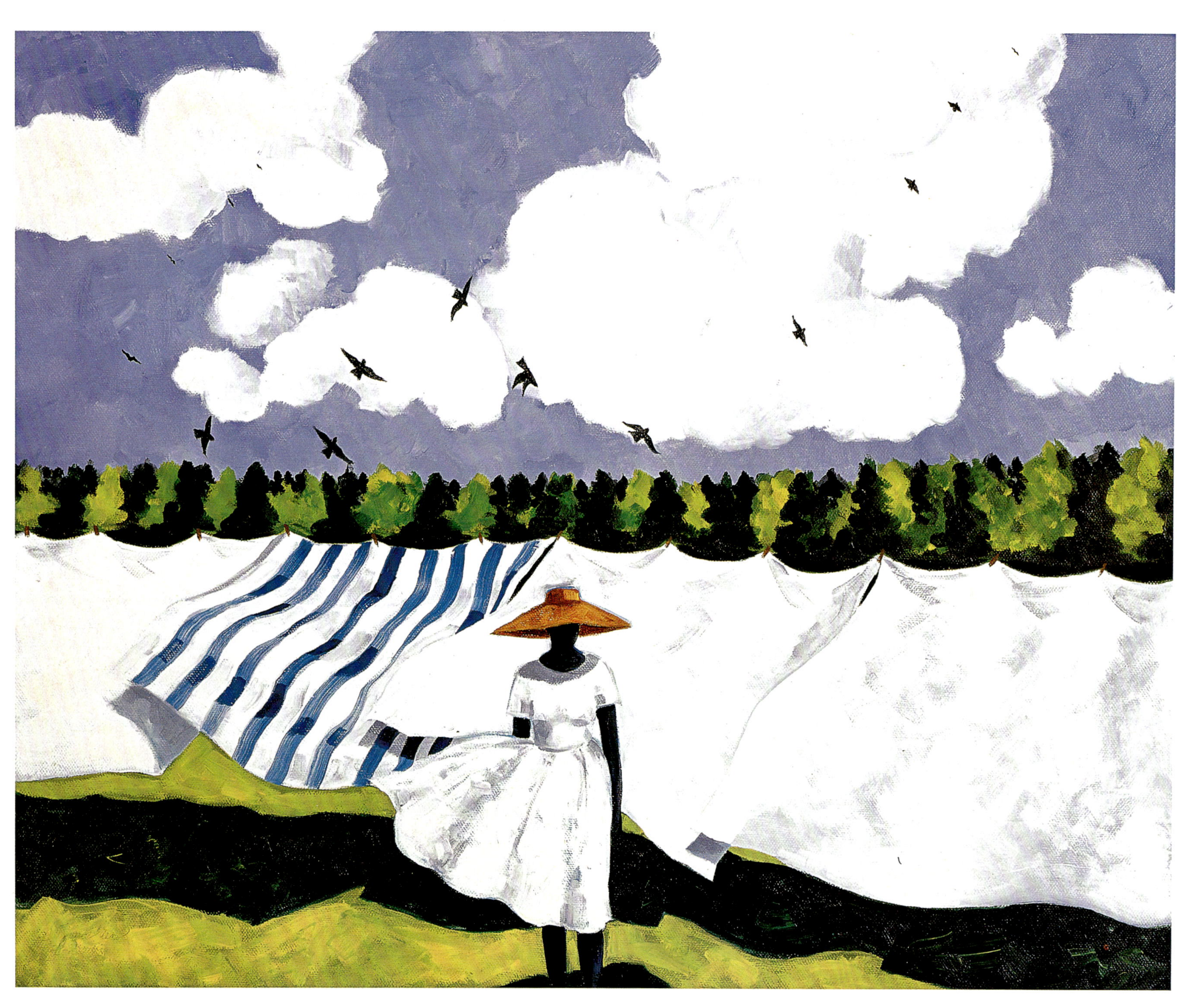

Striped Sheet, 1994. Oil on canvas, 16 x 20".
Courtesy of Gary and Kimberly Bean. Photograph by Tim Stamm.

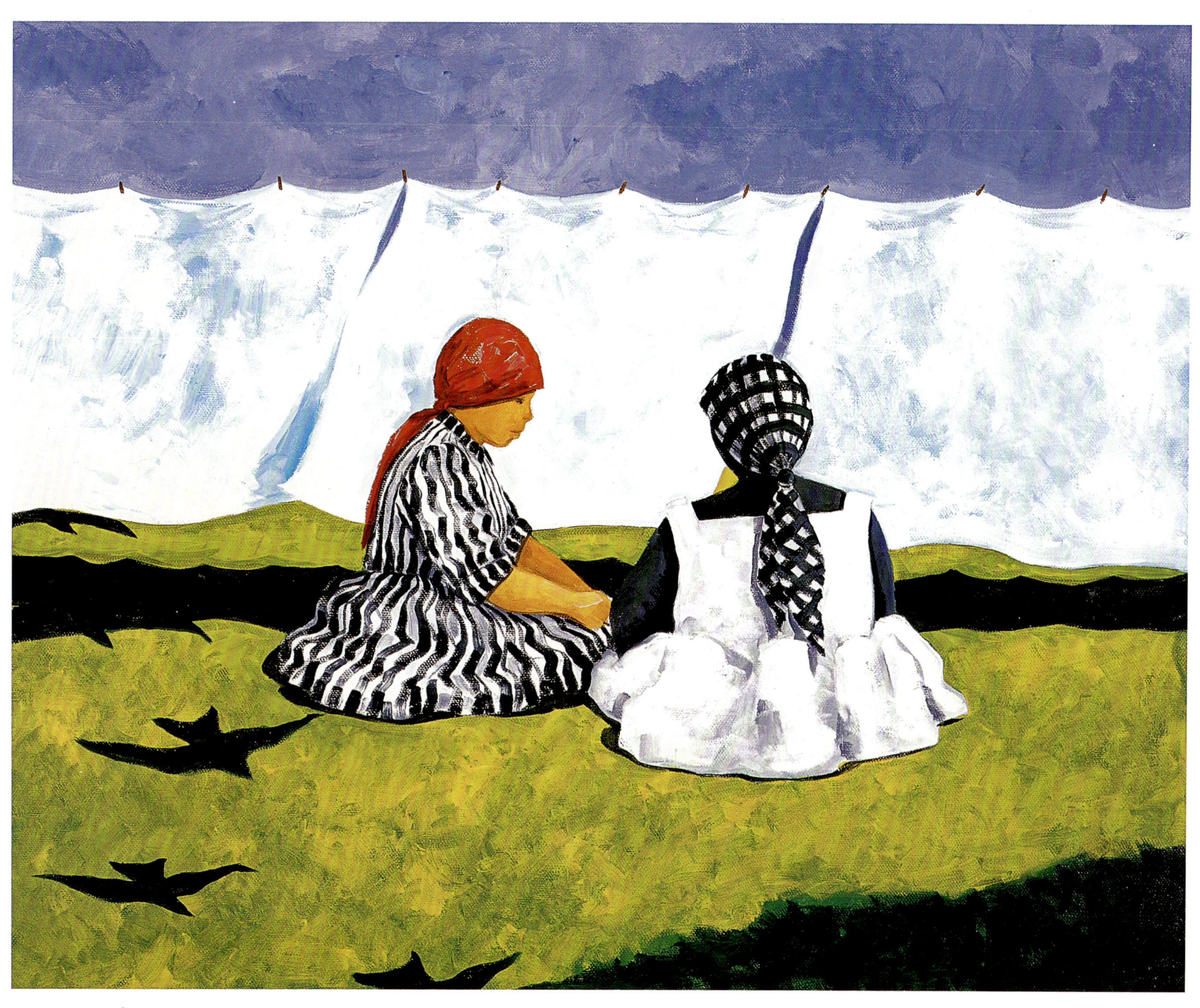

Green Shadows, 1994. Oil on canvas, 16 x 20".
Courtesy of Lucy Kuhne. Photograph by Tim Stamm.

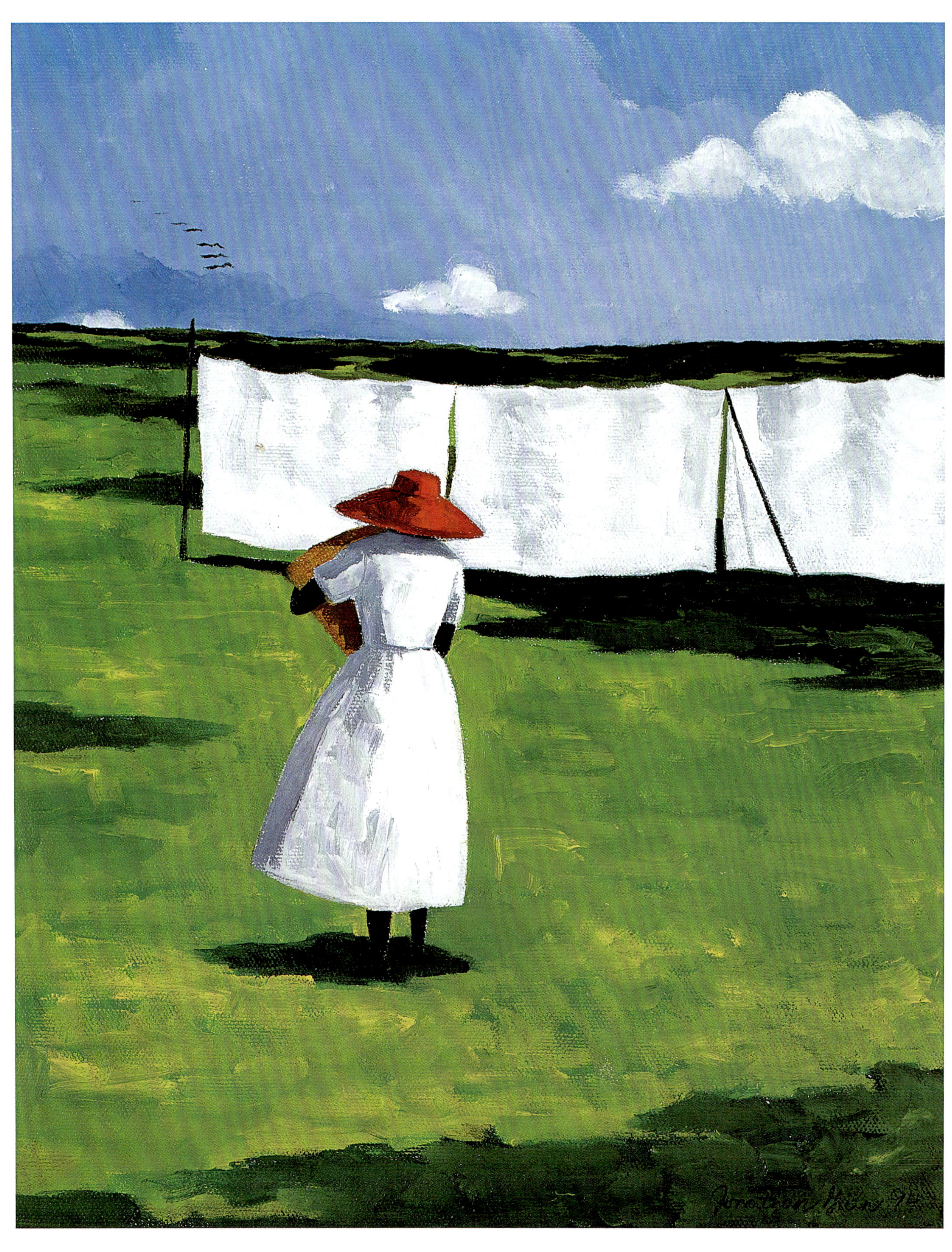

Red Hat Laundry Series #1, 1994. Oil on canvas, 14 x 11".
Courtesy of Charles and Claudena Wells. Photograph by Tim Stamm.

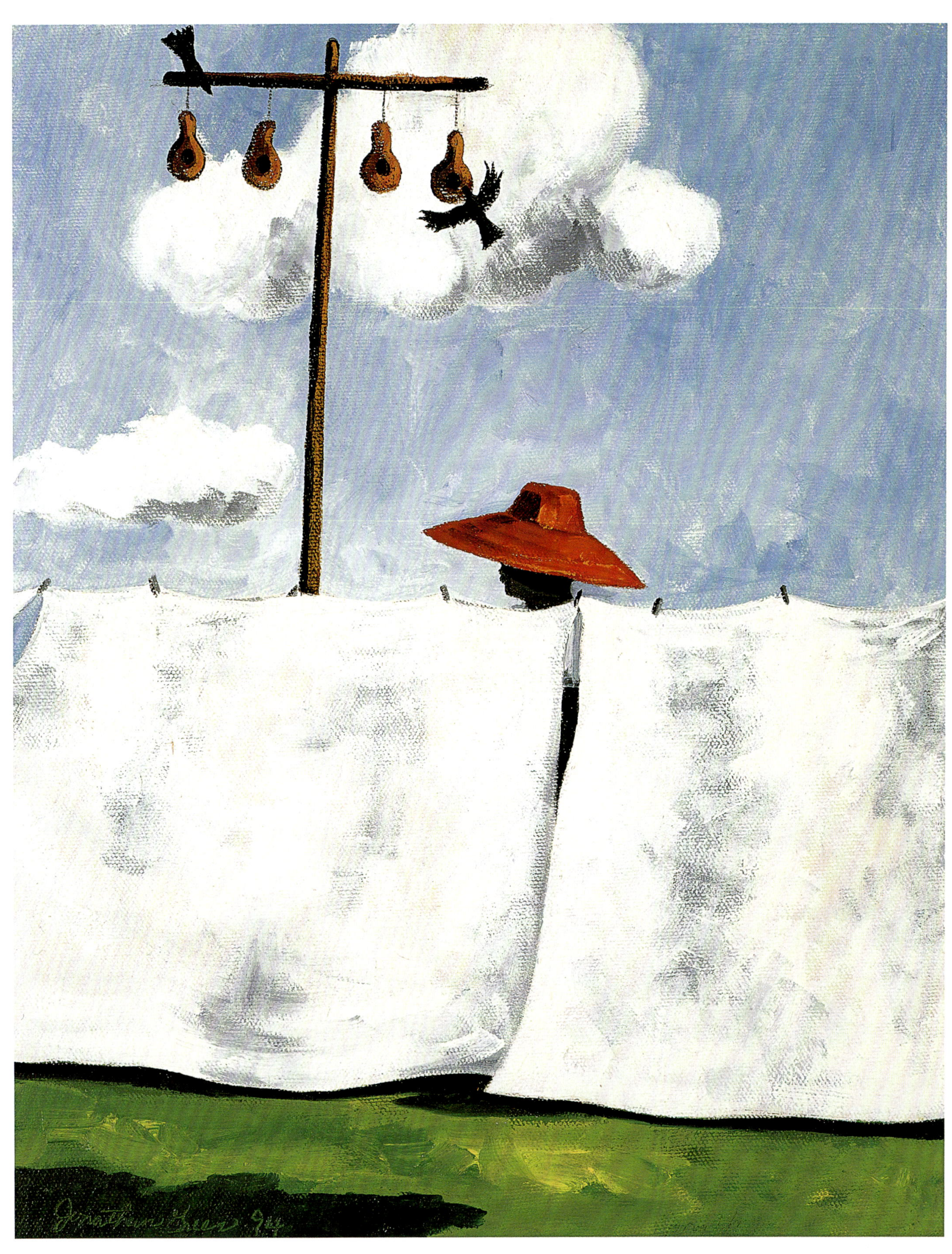

Red Hat Laundry Series #3, 1994. Oil on canvas, 14 x 11".
Courtesy of Carl and JoAnne M. Kuehner. Photograph by Tim Stamm.

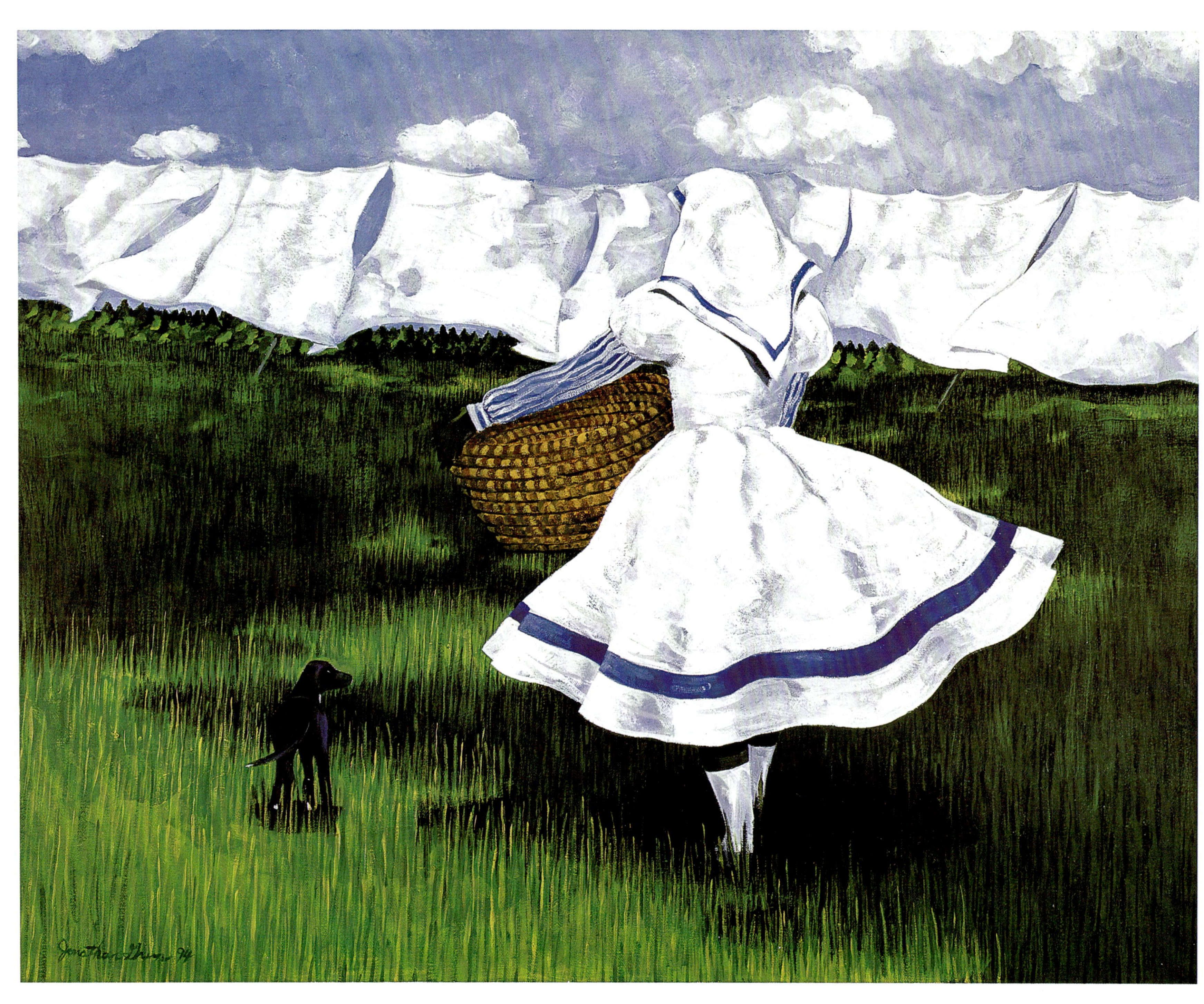

Spring Wash, 1994. Oil on canvas, 18 x 22".
Courtesy of Robyn Shallenberger. Photograph by Tim Stamm.

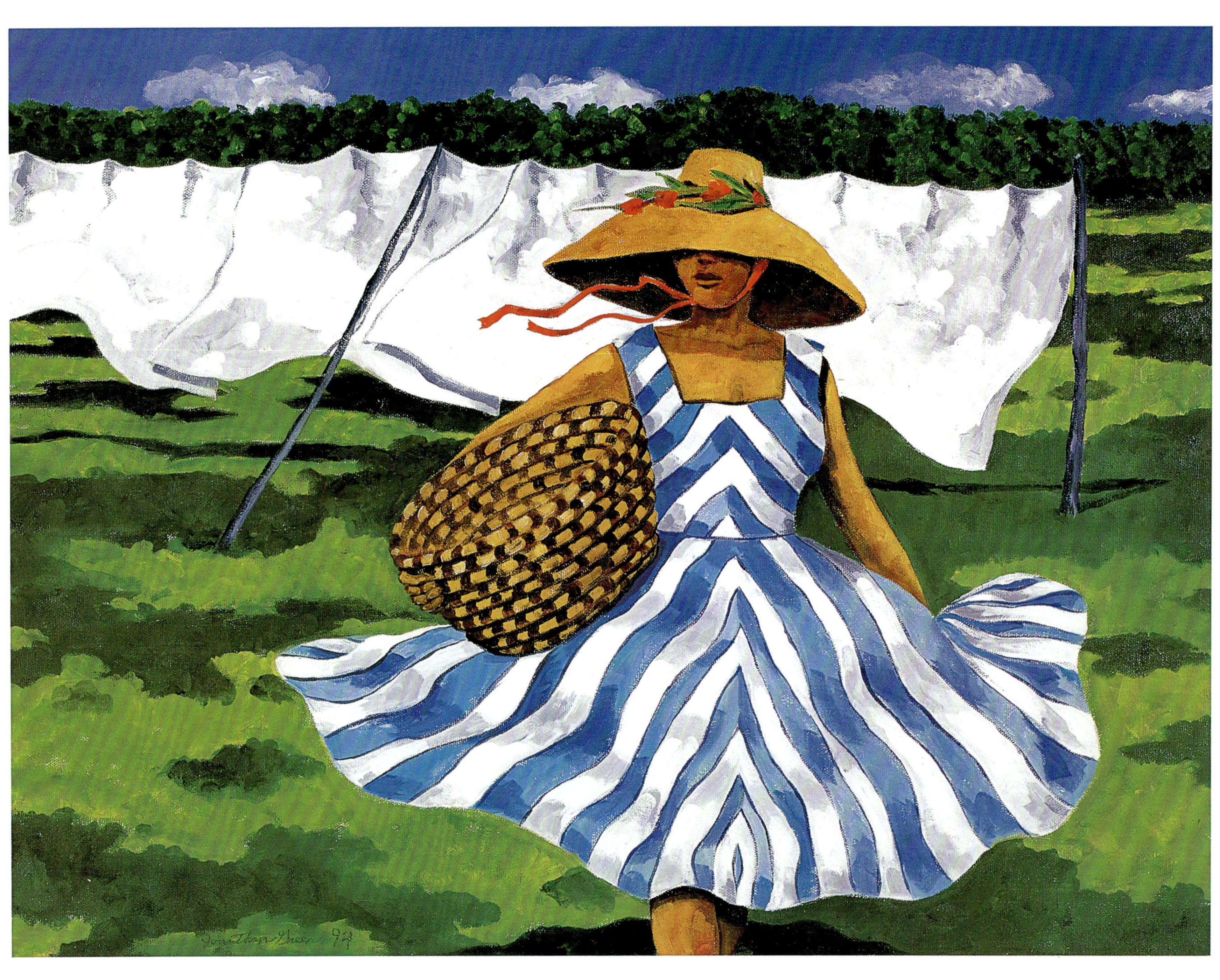

Monday Wash, 1994. Oil on canvas, 18 x 24".
Courtesy of Battery Creek High School, Burton, S.C. Photograph by Tim Stamm.

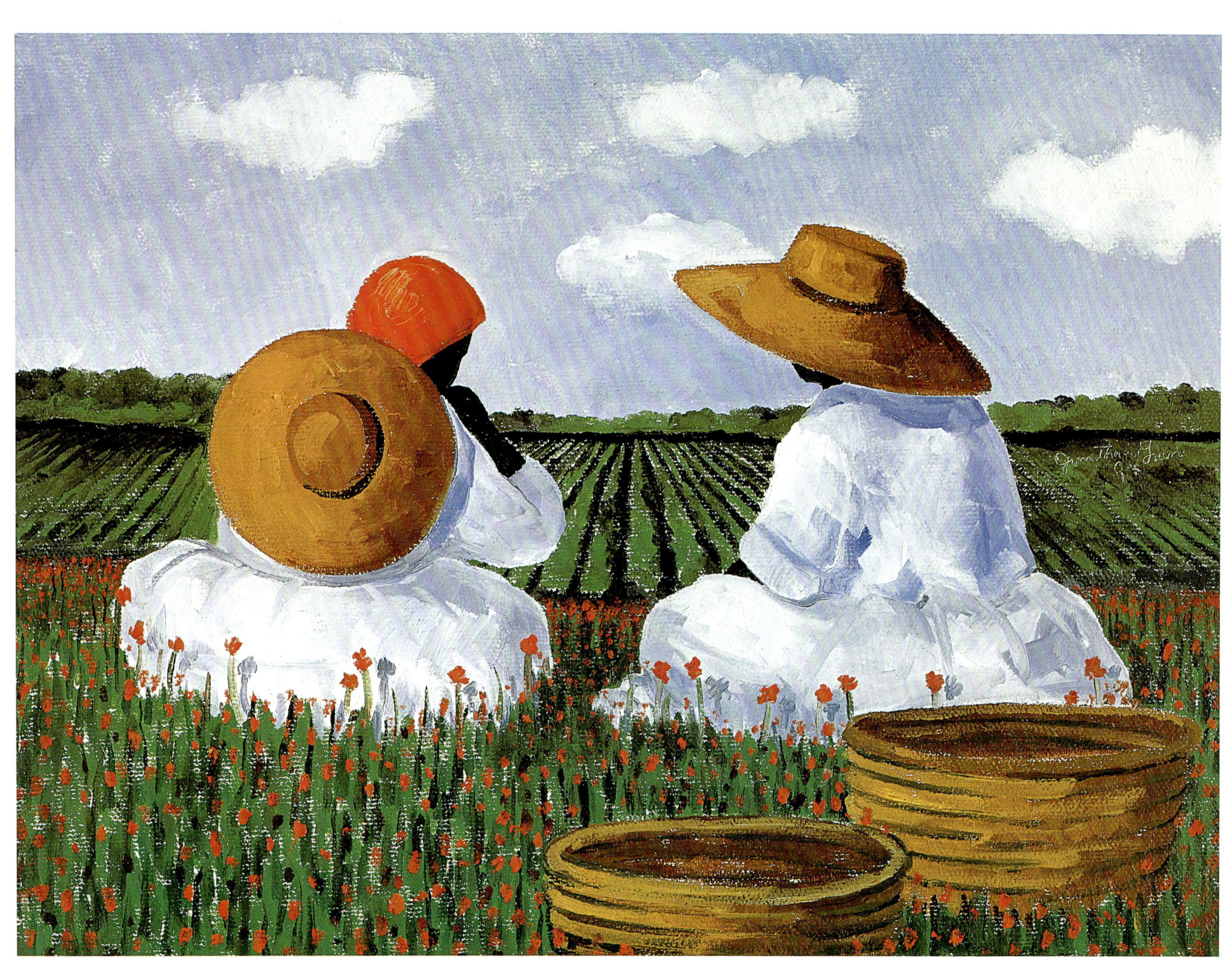

Dora and Friend, 1994. Oil on canvas, 9 x 12".
Courtesy of Dora D. Ohemeng. Photograph by Tim Stamm.

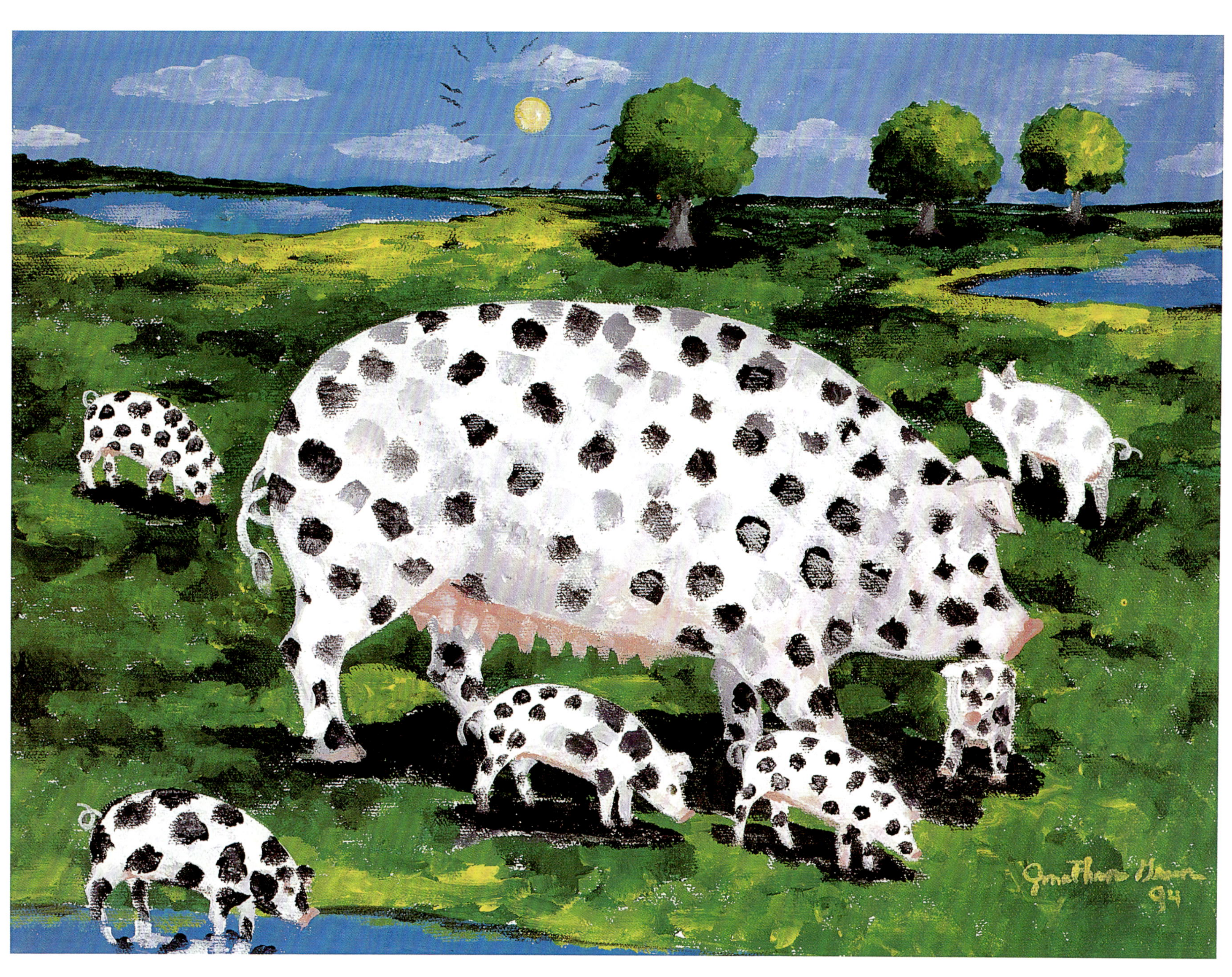

The Prescott Farm, 1994. Oil on canvas, 12 x 16".
Courtesy of Solomon and Mary Johnson. Photograph by Tim Stamm.

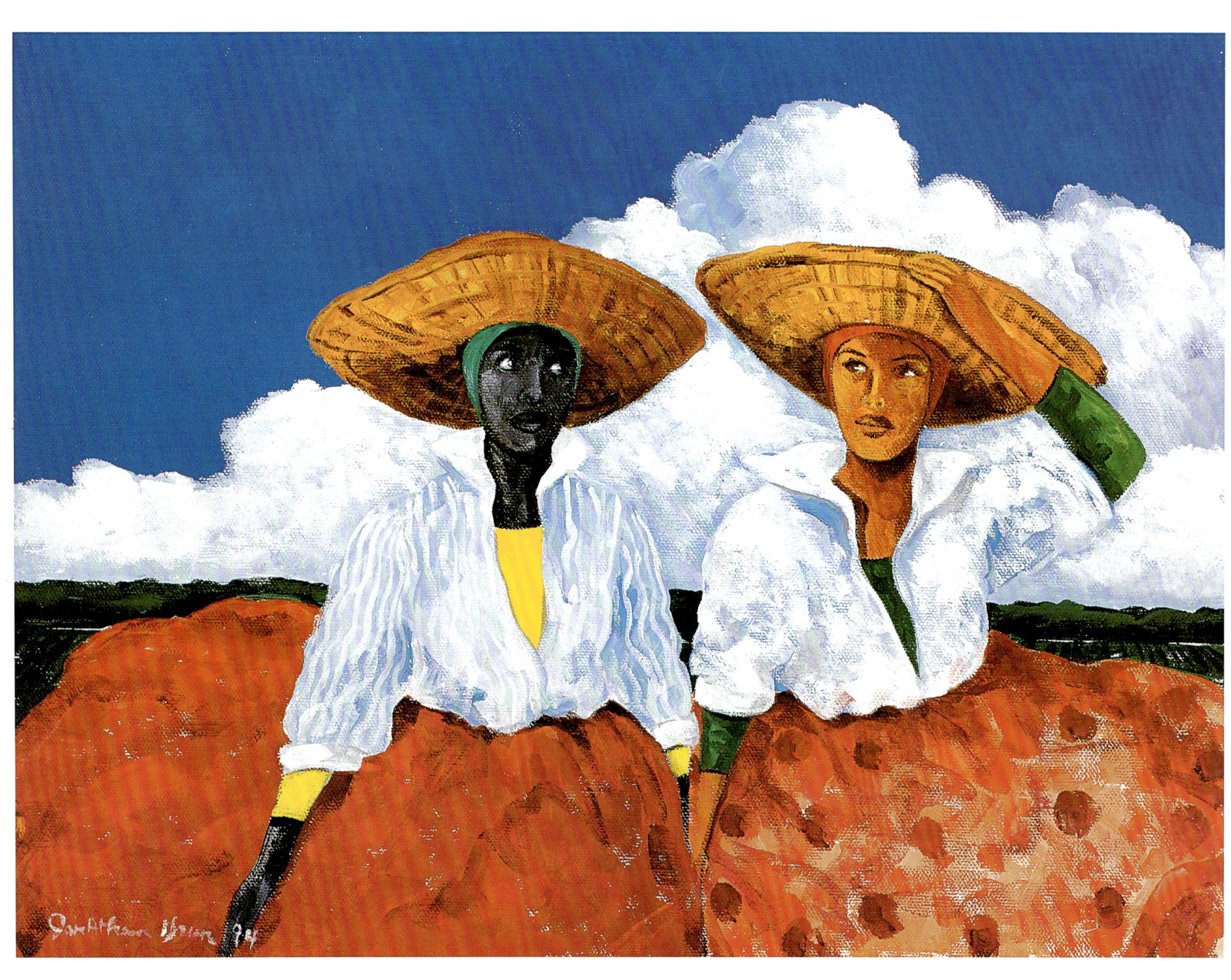

Before the Harvest, 1994. Acrylic on canvas, 11 x 14".
Courtesy of Paul G. Langston. Photograph by Tim Stamm.

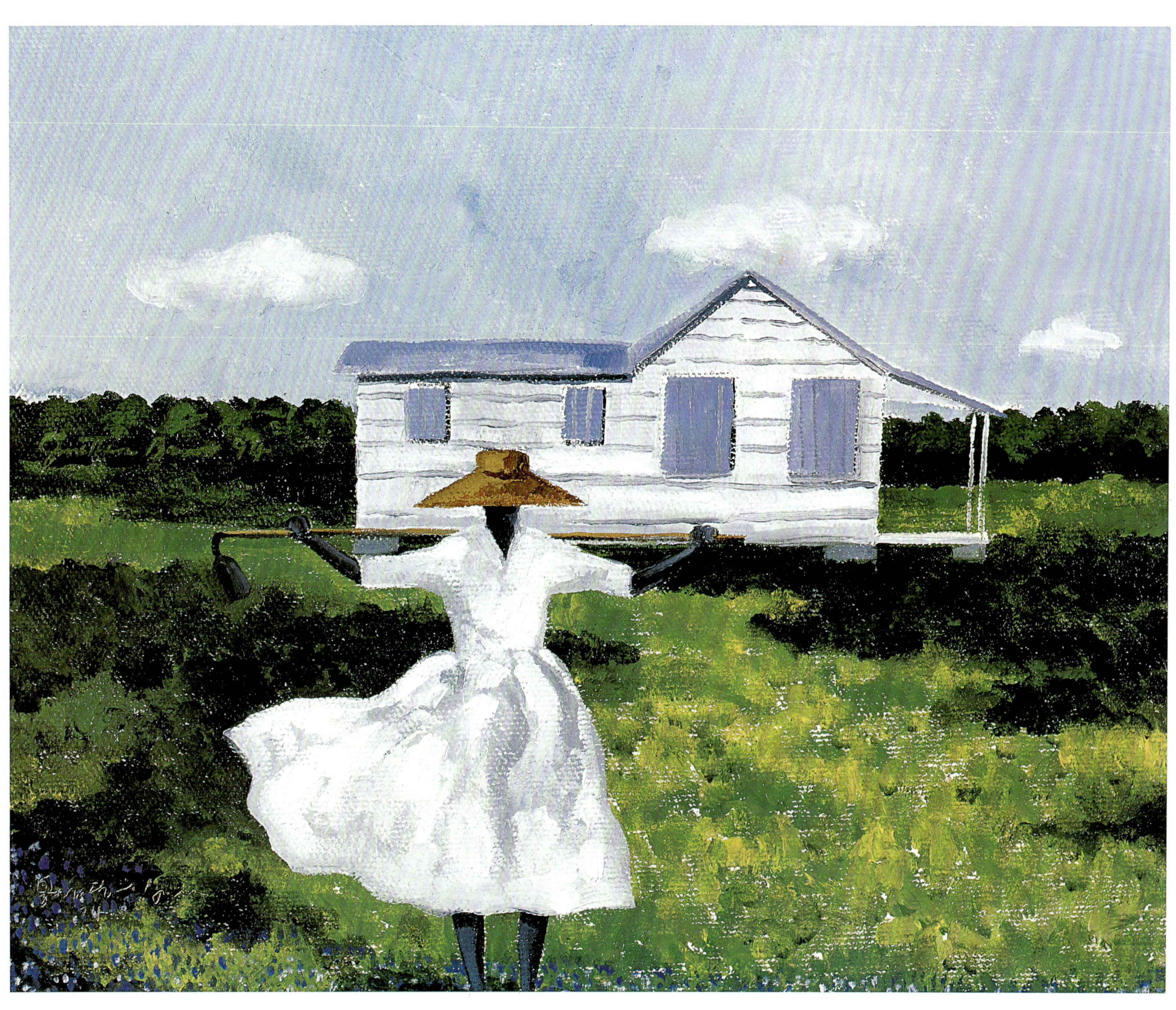

Woman with Hoe, 1994. Oil on canvas, 8 x 10".
Collection of the artist. Photograph by Tim Stamm.

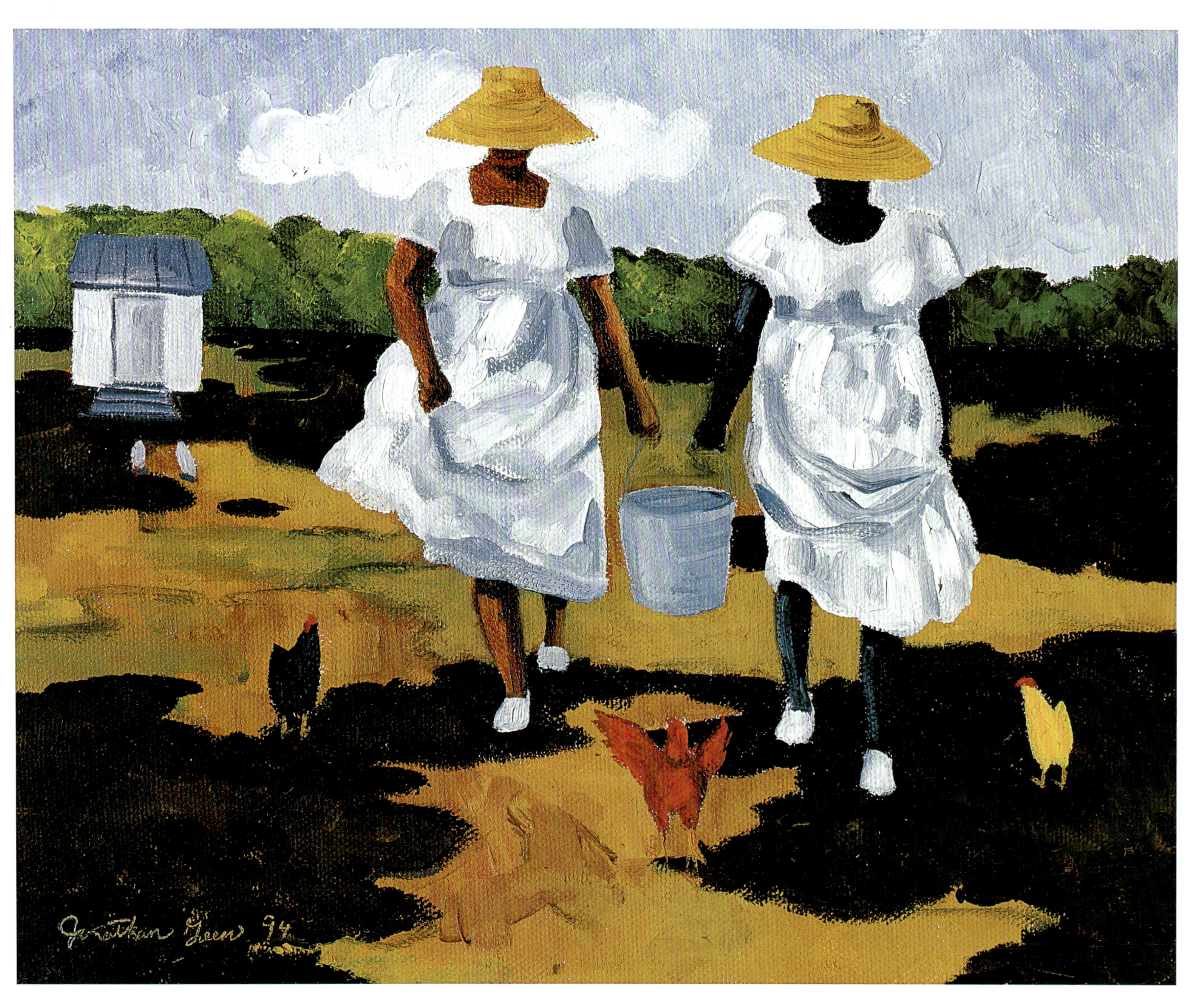

Sharing the Chores, 1994. Oil on canvas, 8 x 10".
Courtesy of Loris Crawford. Photograph by Tim Stamm.

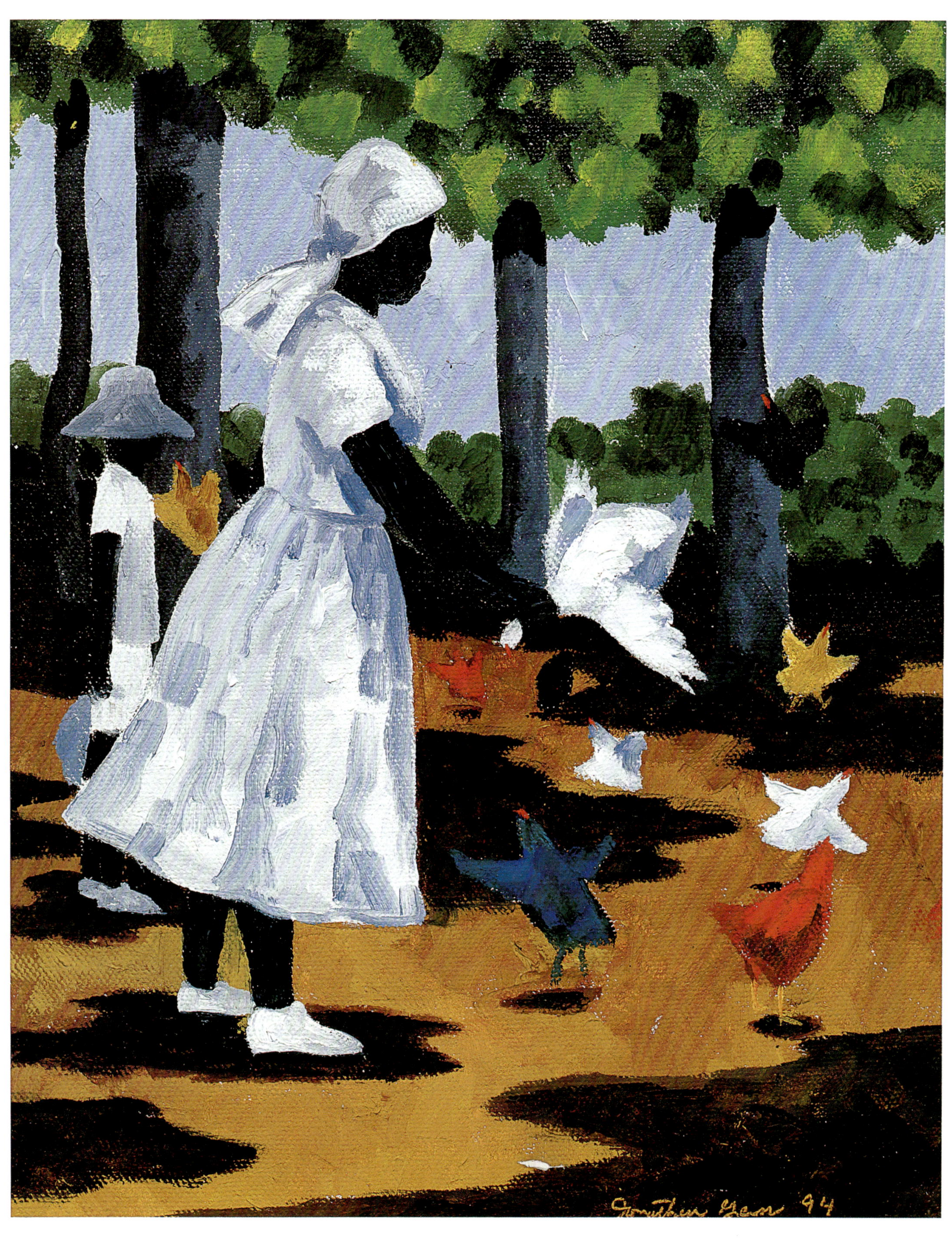

Dinner Preparation, 1994. Oil on canvas, 10 x 8".
Courtesy of John Casey. Photograph by Tim Stamm.

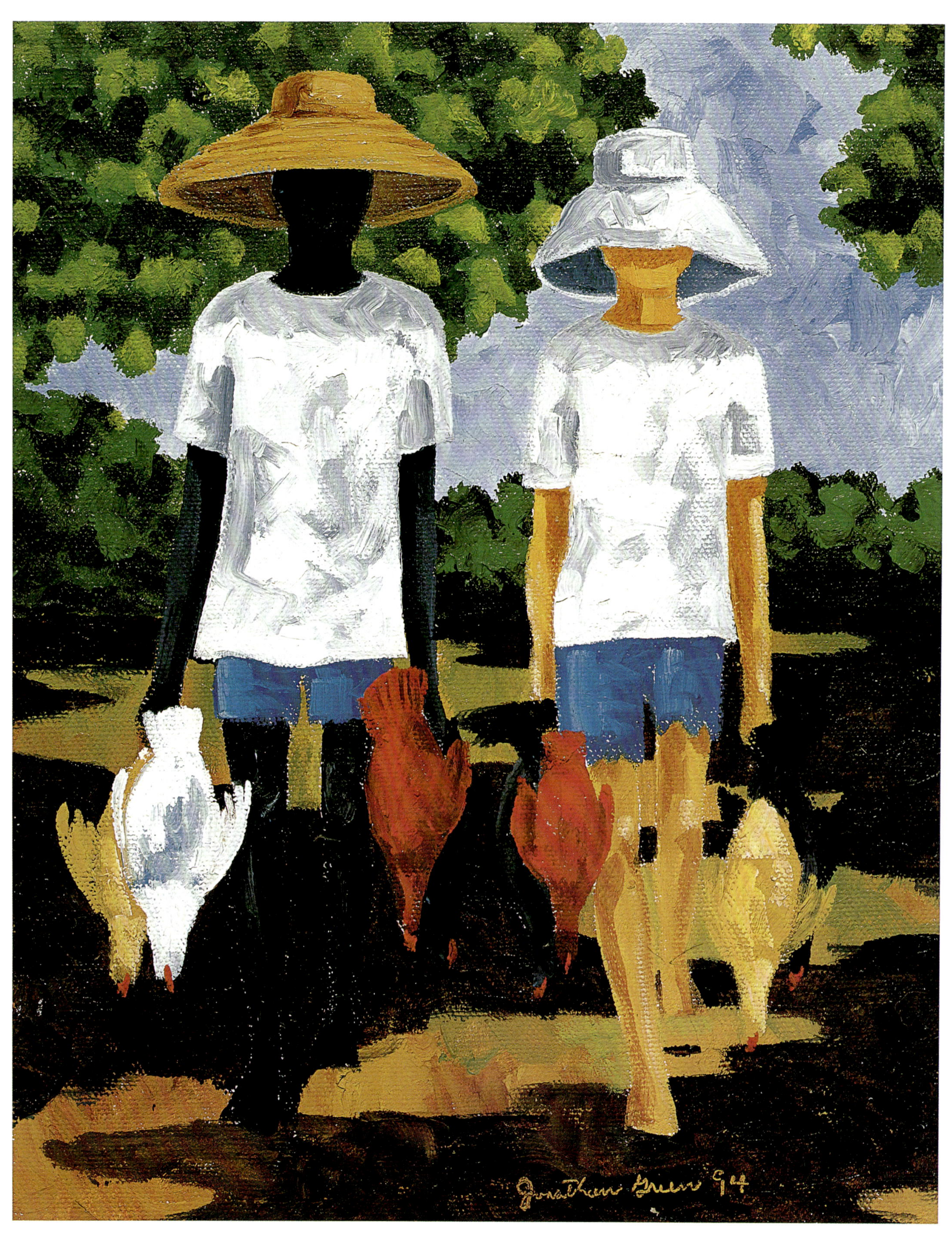

Carrying Dinner, 1994. Oil on canvas, 10 x 8".
Courtesy of Mr. and Mrs. John Sikes Johnston. Photograph by Tim Stamm.

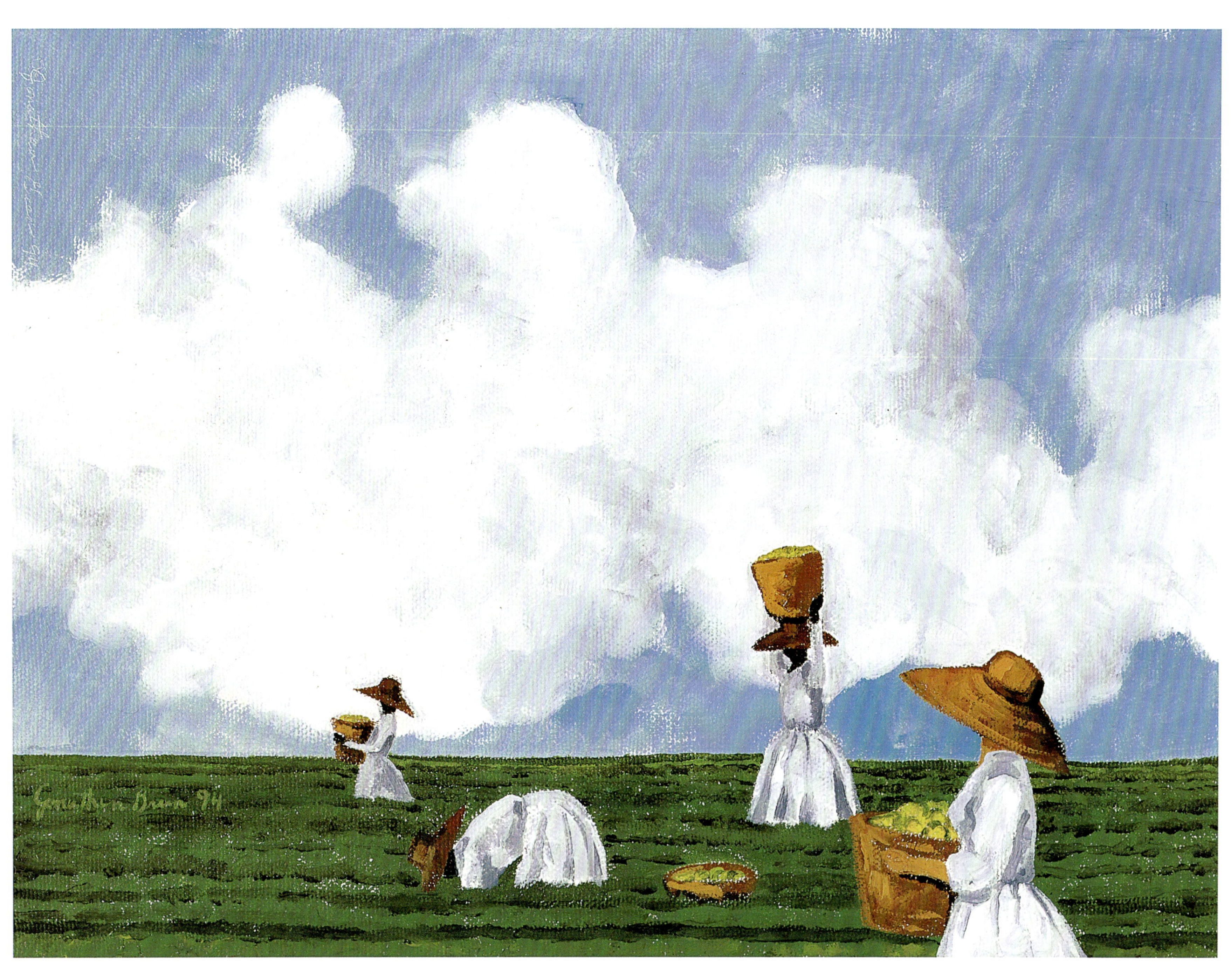

Green Tomatoes, 1994. Oil on canvas, 9 x 12".
Courtesy of Henry Louis Gates, Jr. Photograph by Tim Stamm.

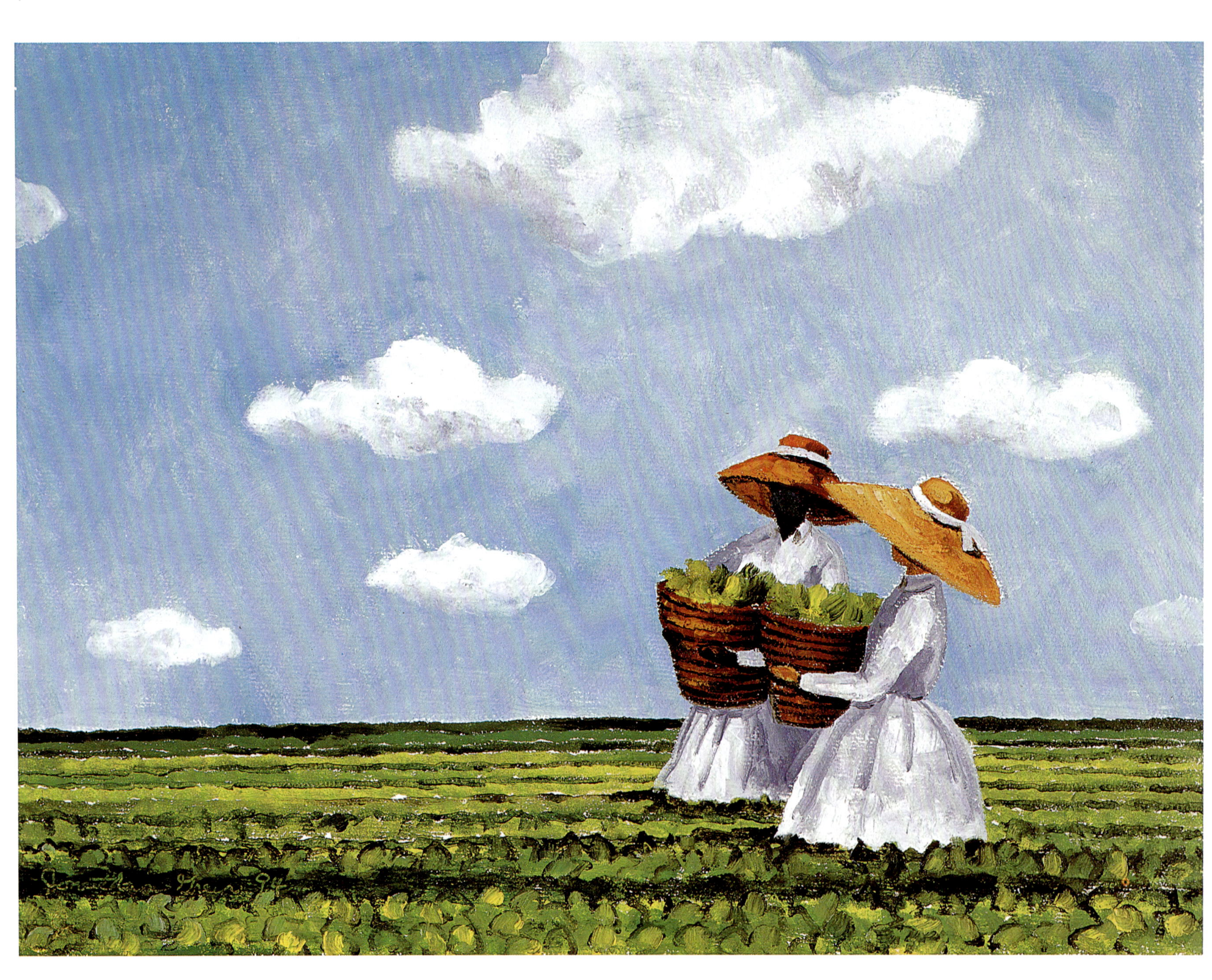

Mustard Greens, 1994. Oil on canvas, 9 x 12".
Private Collection. Photograph by Tim Stamm.

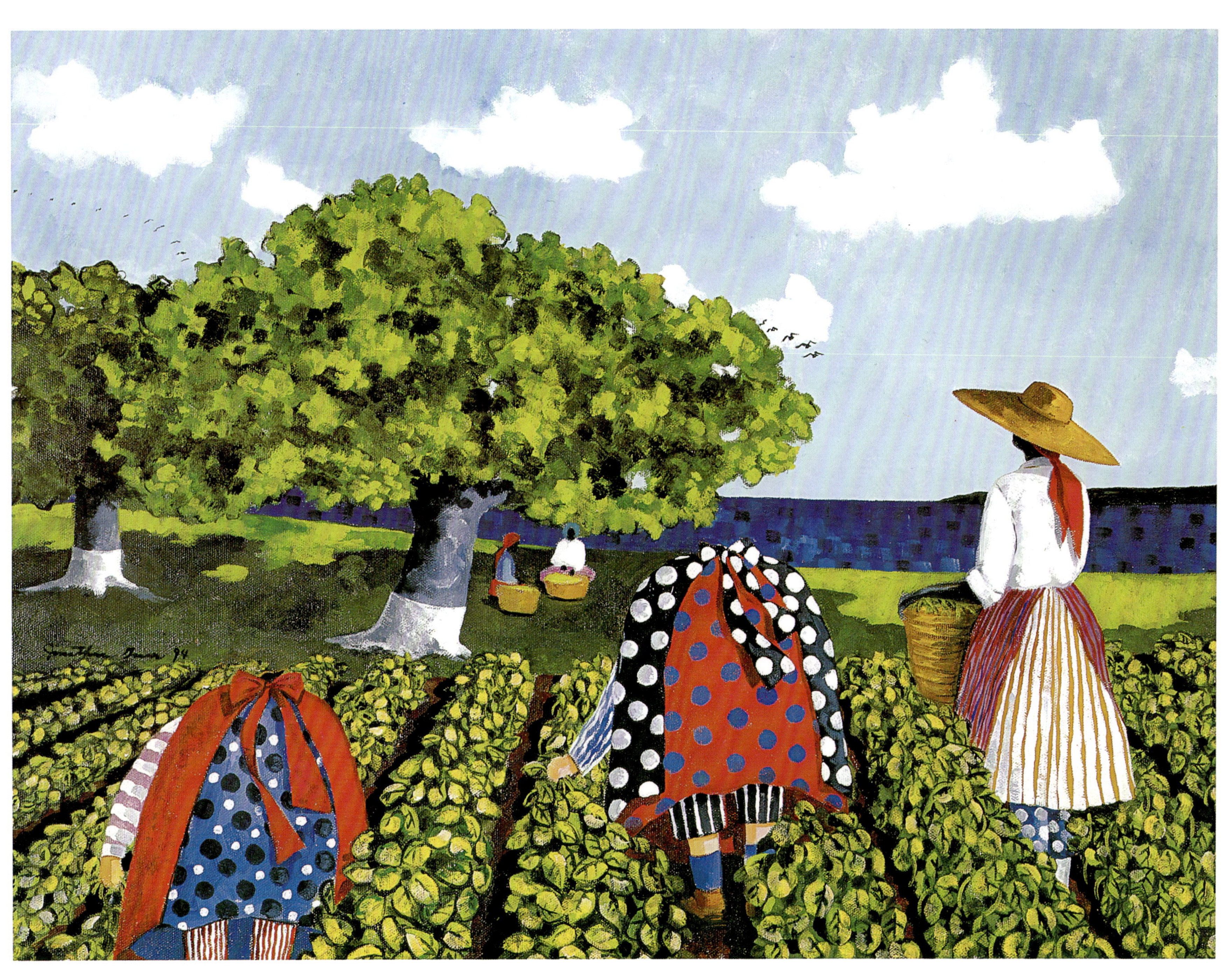

String Bean Harvest, 1994. Oil on canvas, 24 x 28".
Courtesy of Pamela Horowtiz and Julian Bond. Photograph by Tim Stamm.

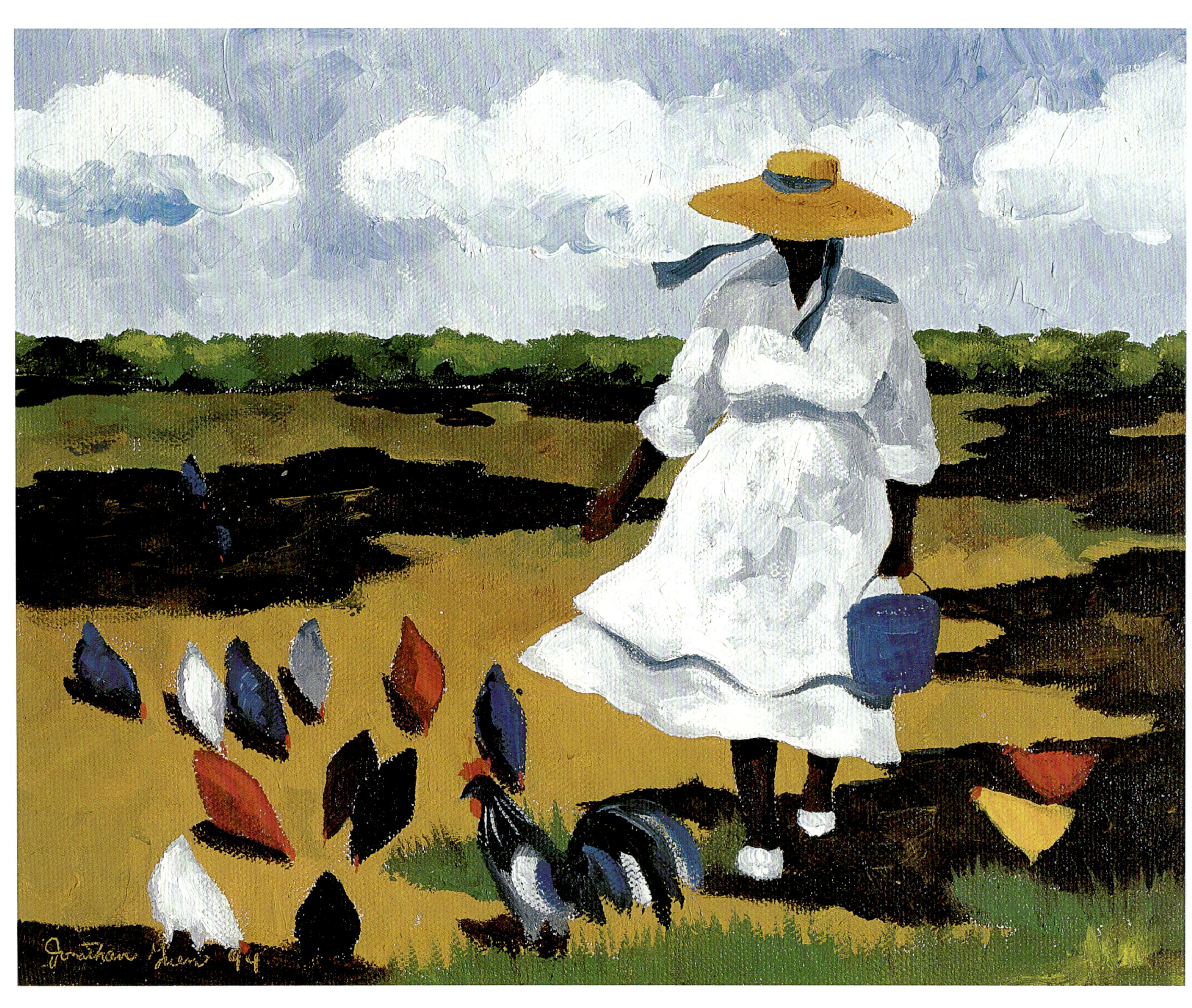

The Chicken Lady, 1994. Oil on canvas, 8 x 10".
Courtesy of Valerie Pilgrim Bell-Bey. Photograph by Tim Stamm.

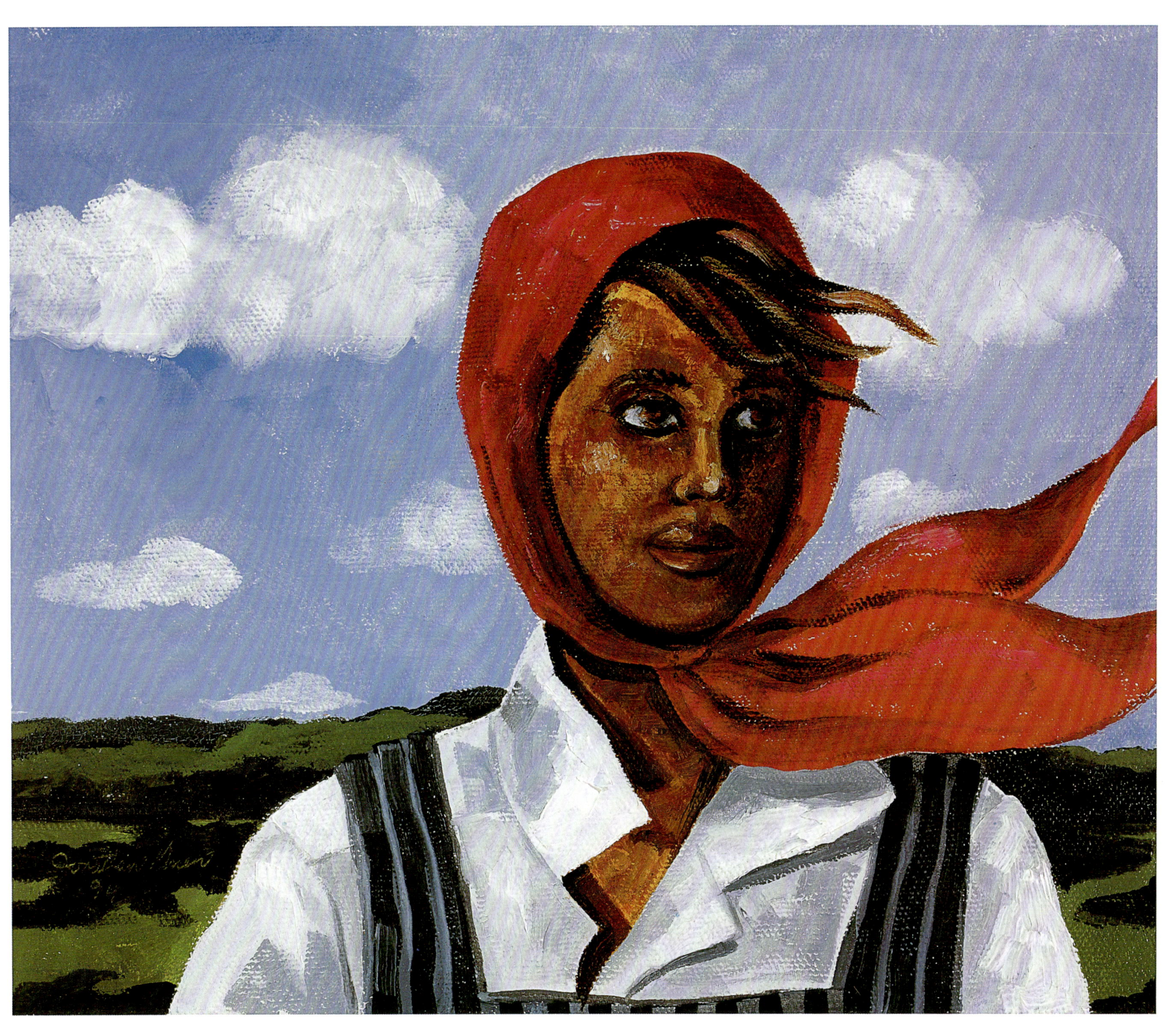

The Red Scarf, 1994. Oil on canvas, 8 x 10".
Courtesy of Robert, Charlotte, and Sarah Barrett. Photograph by Tim Stamm.

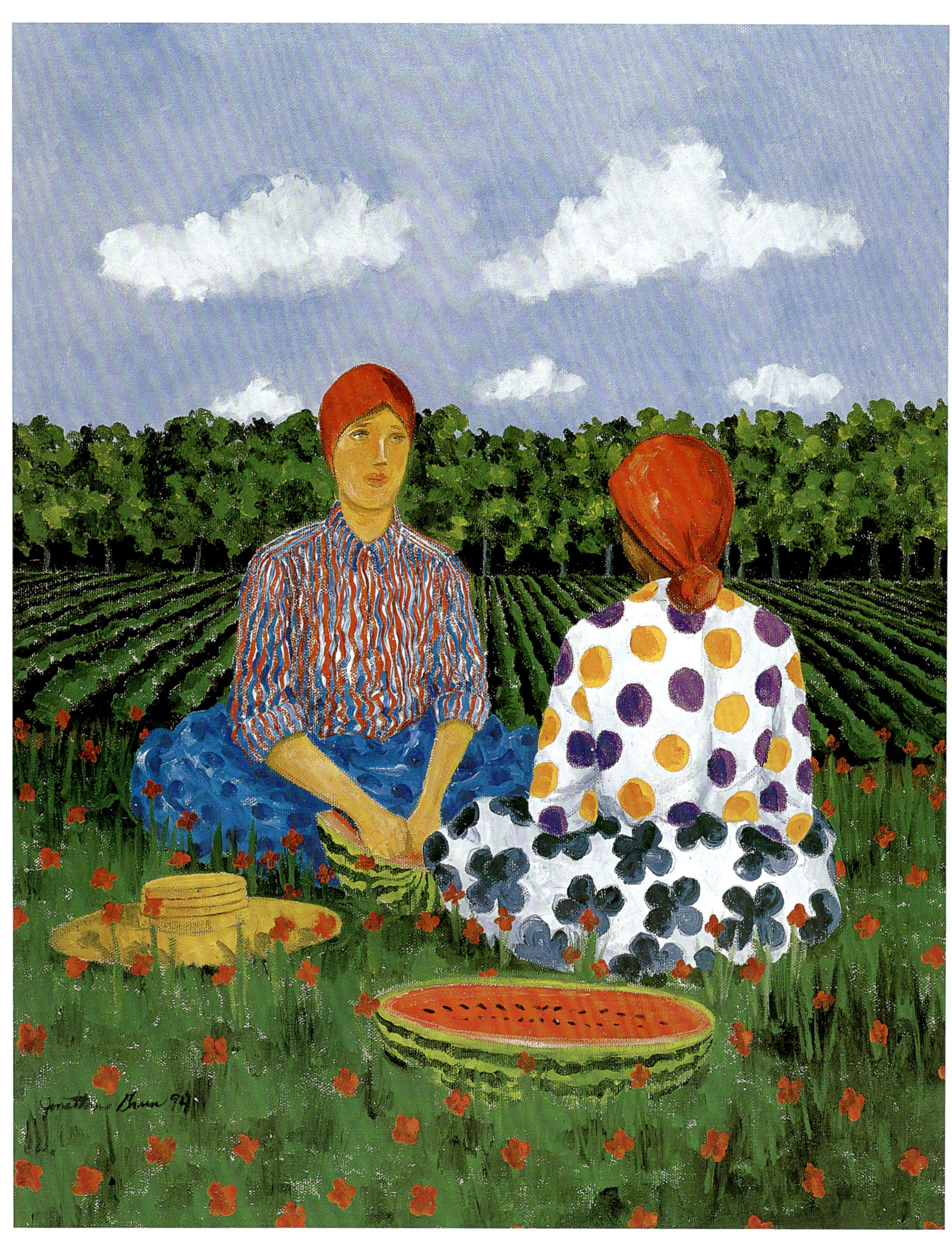

Watermelon Break, 1994. Oil on canvas, 20 x 16".
Courtesy of Wayne King. Photograph by Tim Stamm.

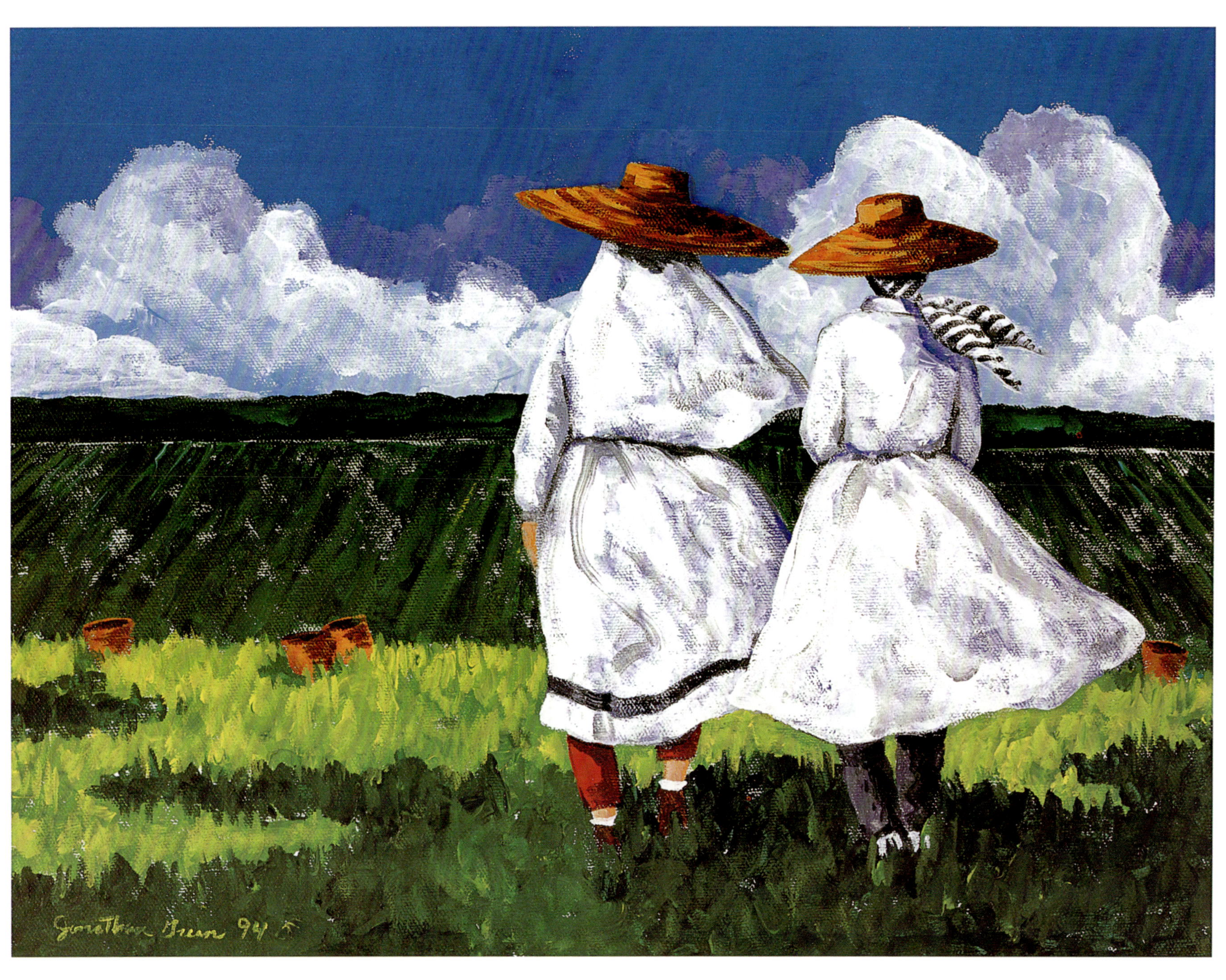

Two Friends, 1994. Acrylic on canvas, 12 x 16".
Courtesy of Dora D. Oheming. Photograph by Tim Stamm.

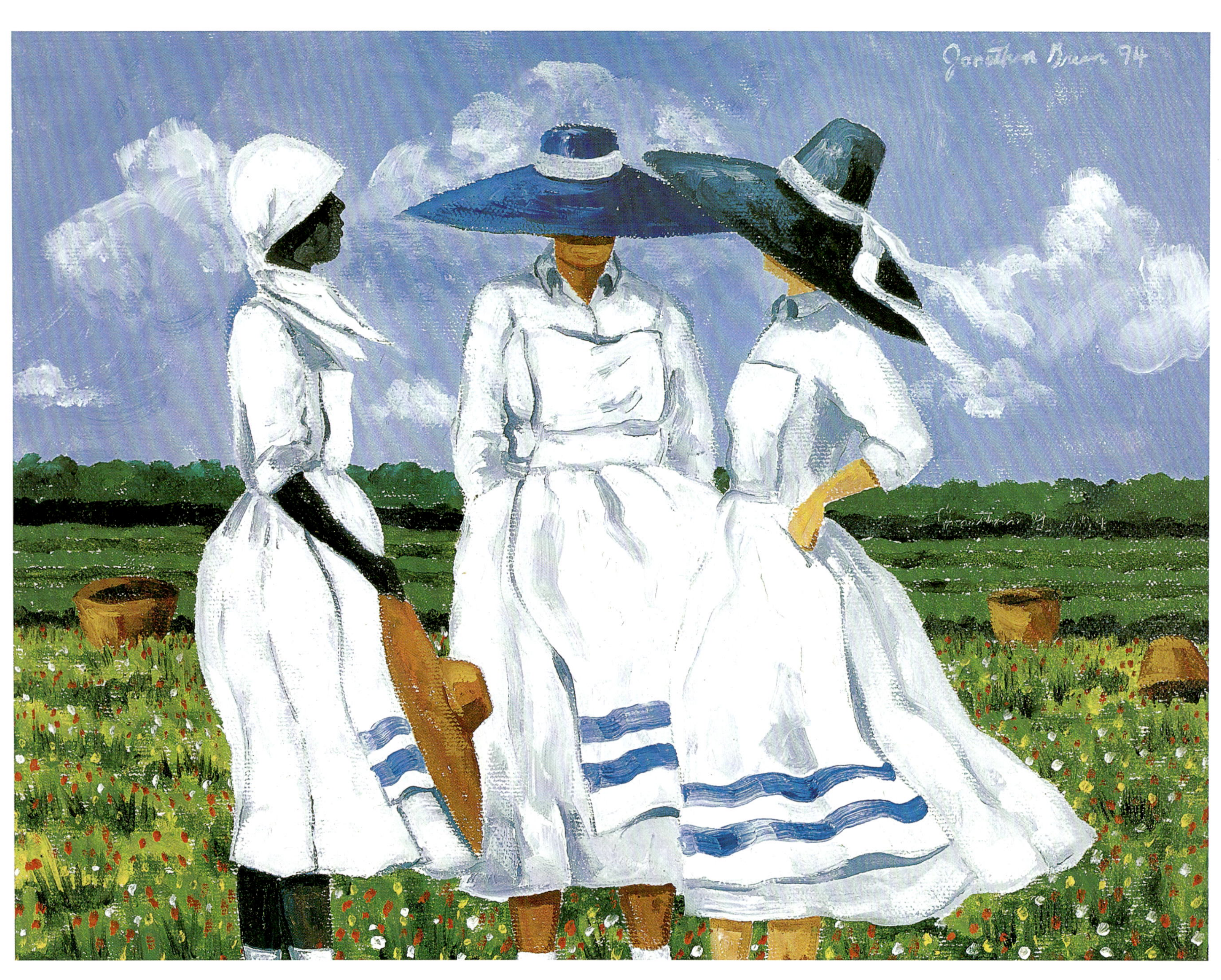

Three Hats, 1994. Oil on canvas, 9 x 12".
Courtesy of Melissa L. Langston. Photograph by Tim Stamm.

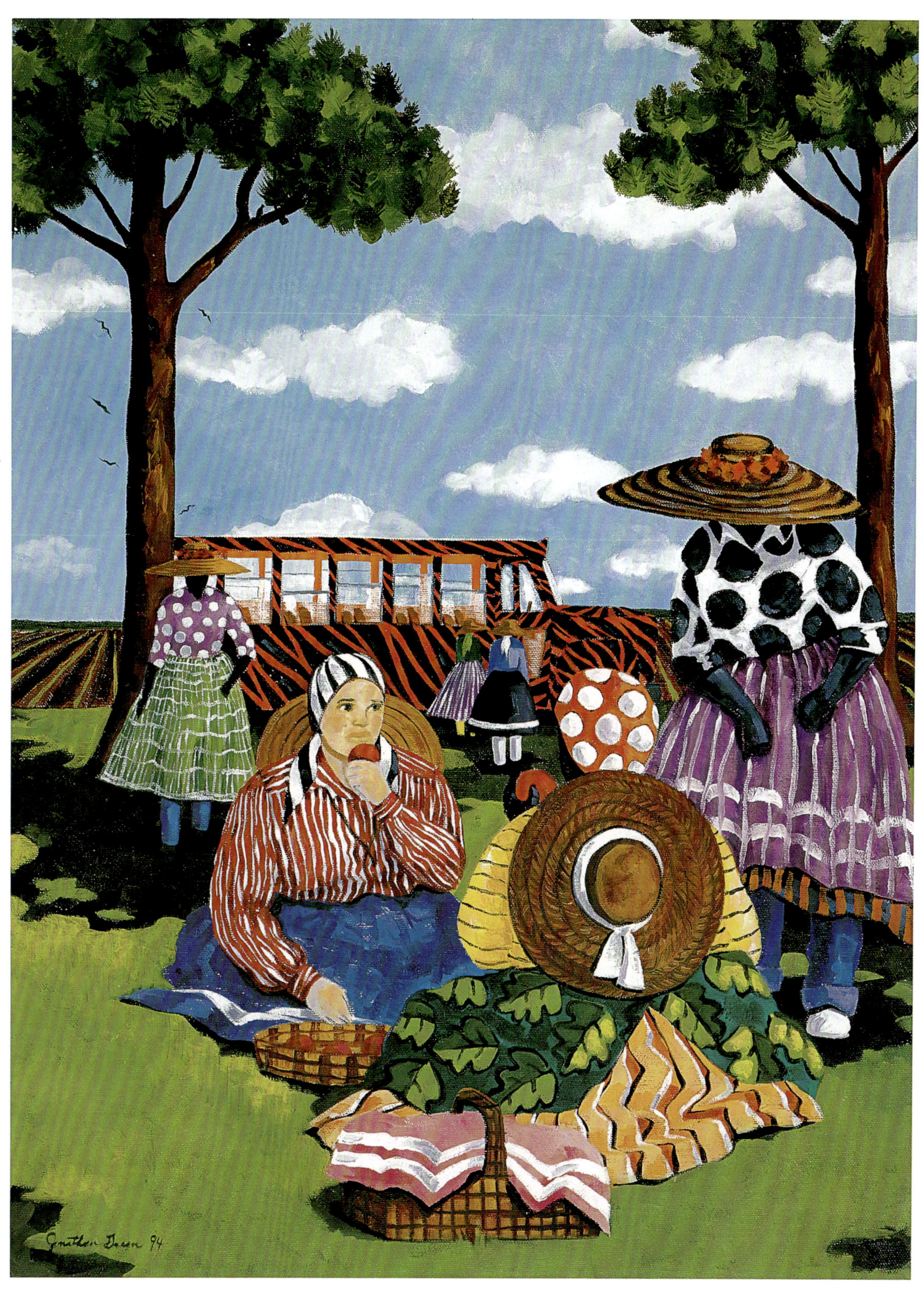

Tiger Farm Bus, 1994. Oil on canvas, 24 x 18".
Courtesy of Paul G. Langston. Photograph by Tim Stamm.

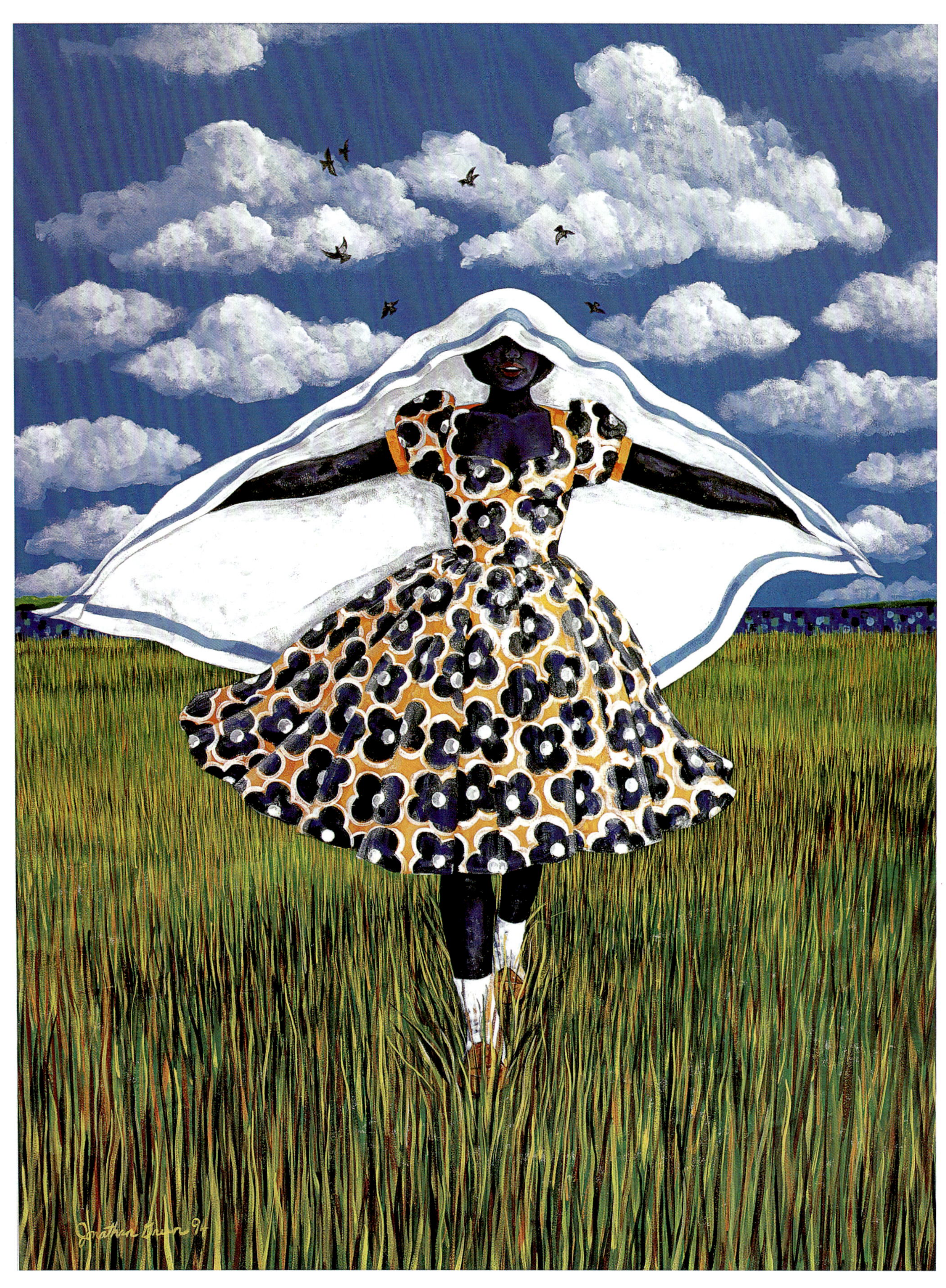

Skylarks, 1994. Acrylic on canvas, 48 x 36".
Courtesy of Christopher and Wendy Born. Photograph by Tim Stamm.

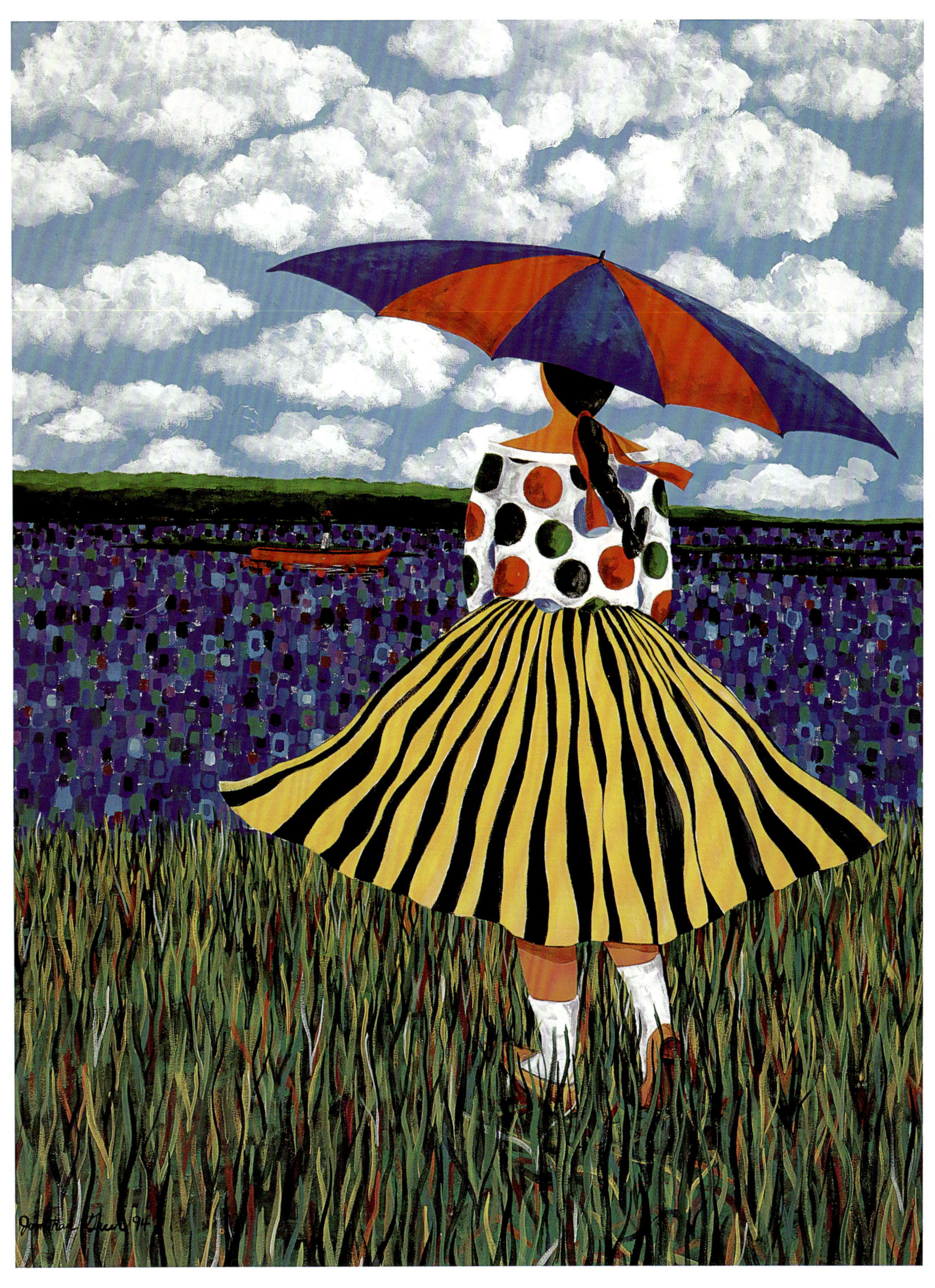

Passing Time, 1994. Acrylic on canvas, 48 x 36".
Courtesy of Sue A. Ofner. Photograph by Tim Stamm.

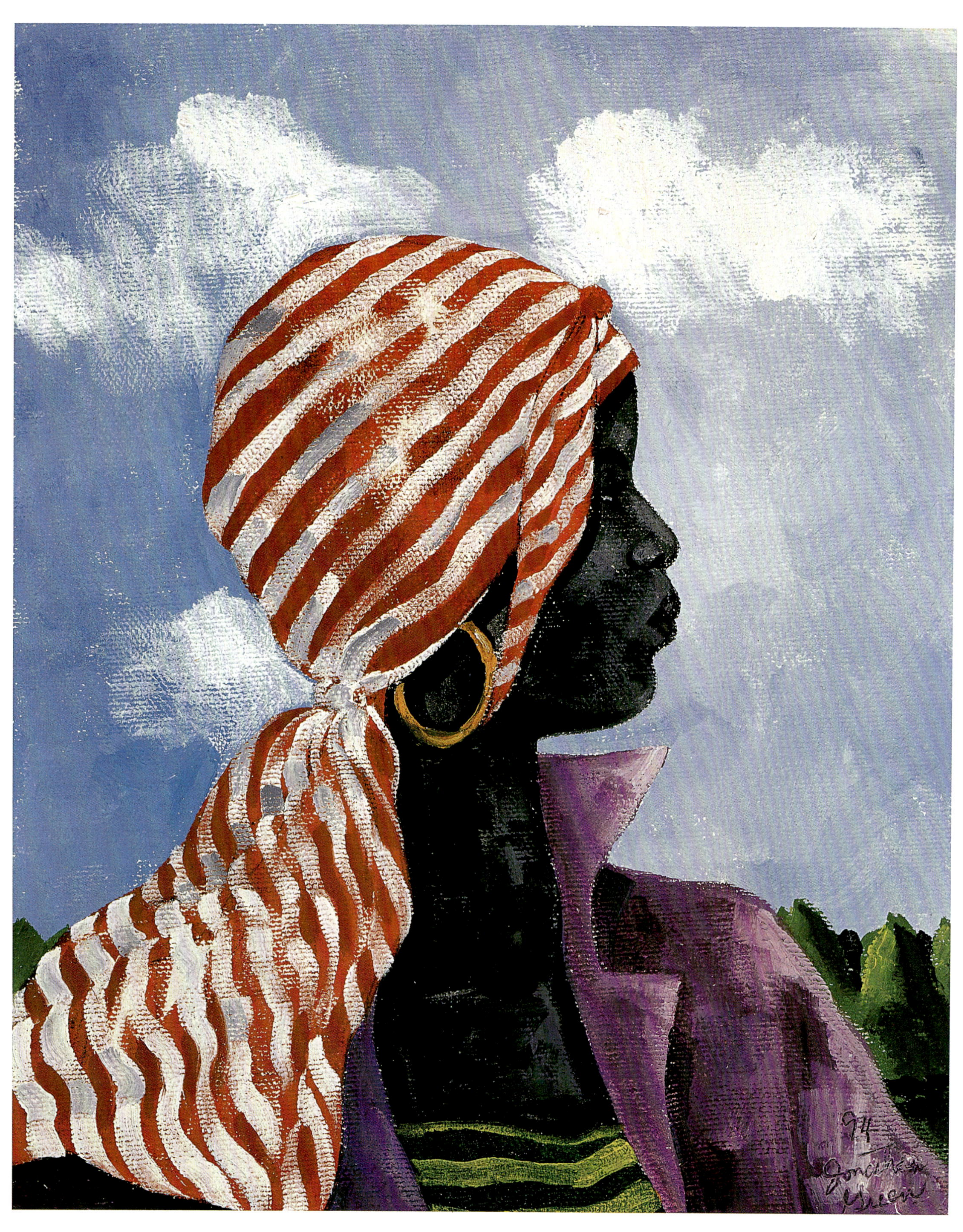

Queen, 1994. Oil on canvas, 10 x 8".
Courtesy of Paul G. Langston. Photograph by Tim Stamm.

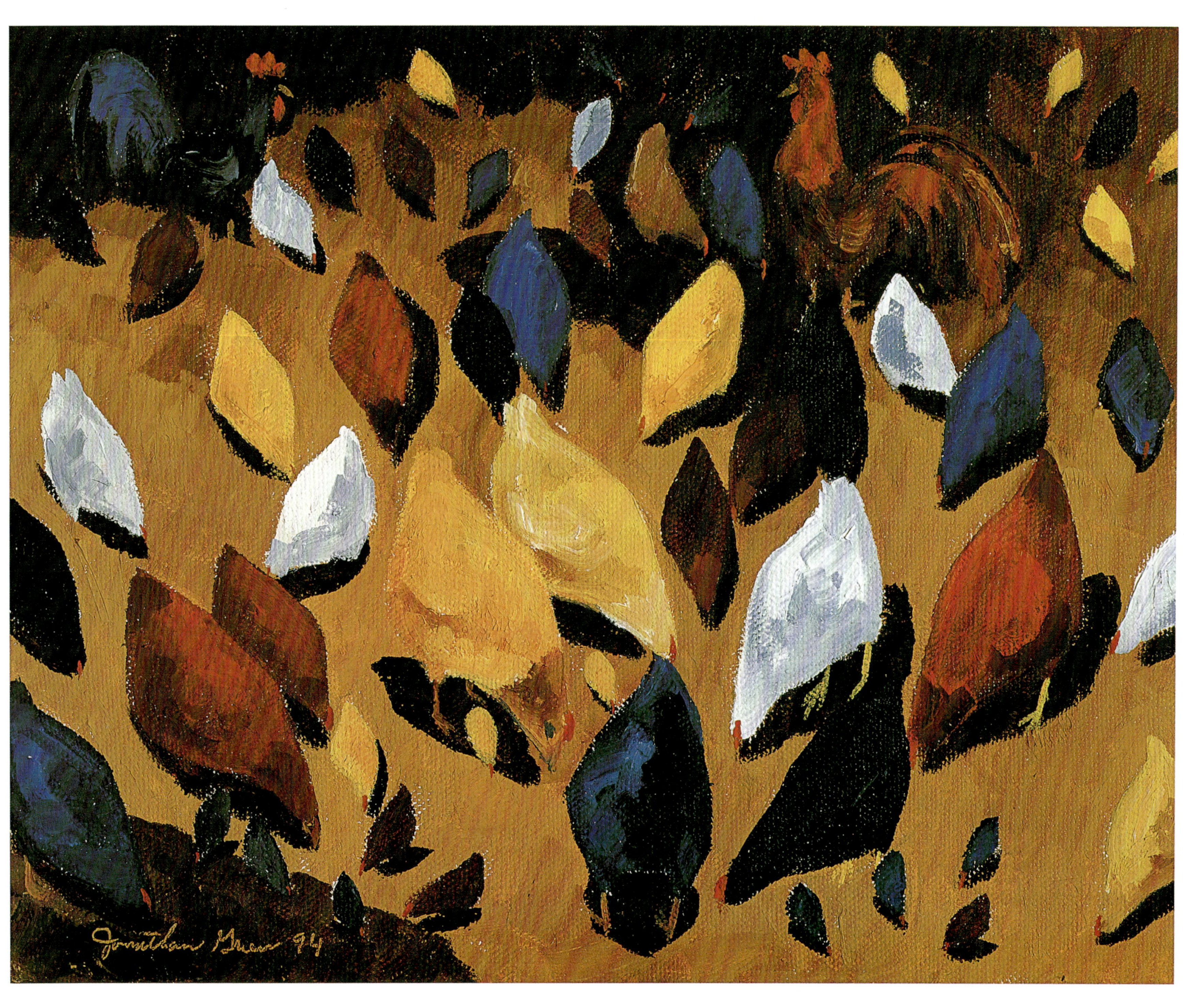

Chicken Flock, 1994. Oil on canvas, 8 x 10".
Courtesy of Karla Kaltenbrunner-Hoff. Photograph by Tim Stamm.

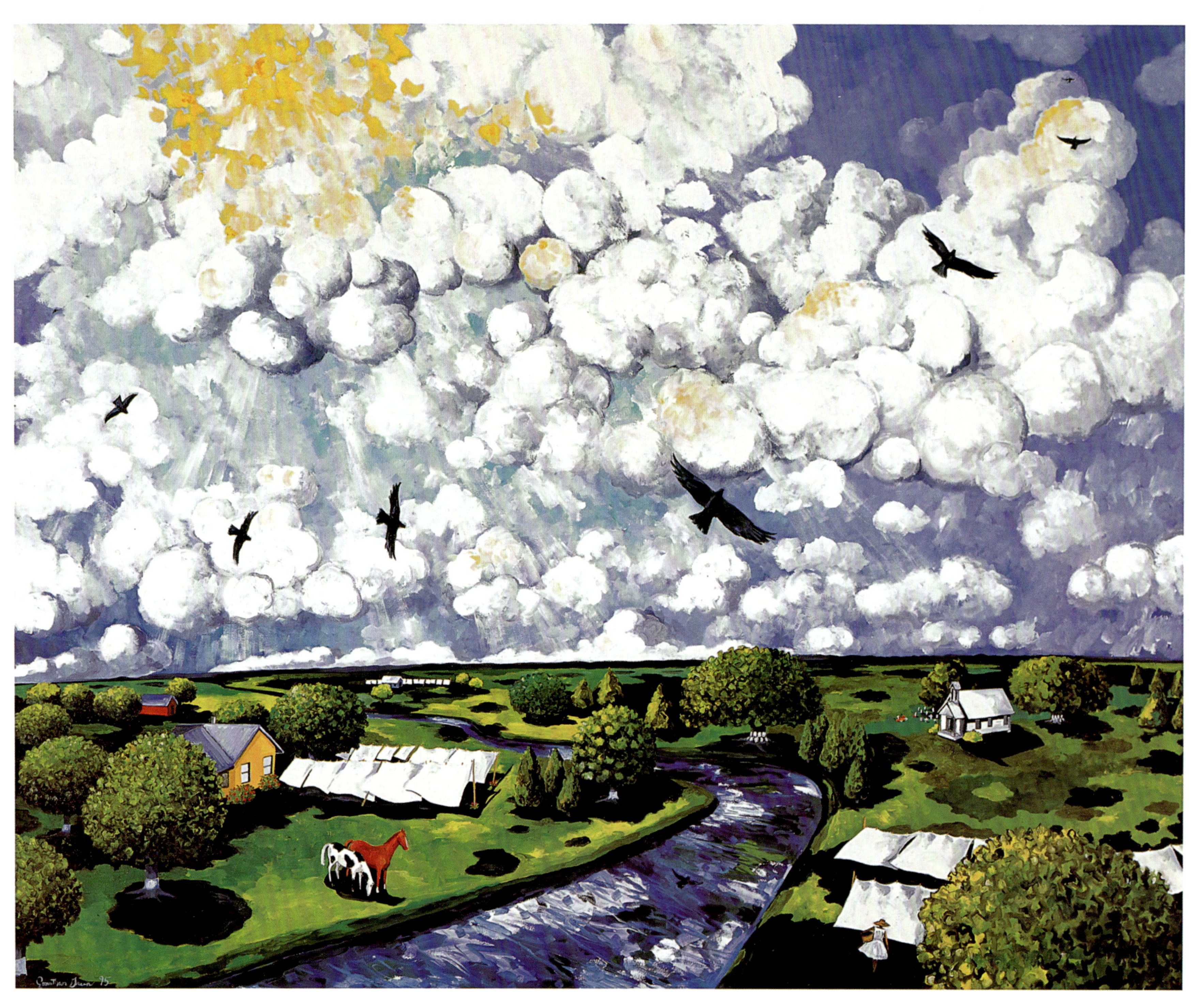

Stewart's Farm, 1995. Oil on canvas, 48 x 60".
Courtesy of the artist. Photograph by Tim Stamm.

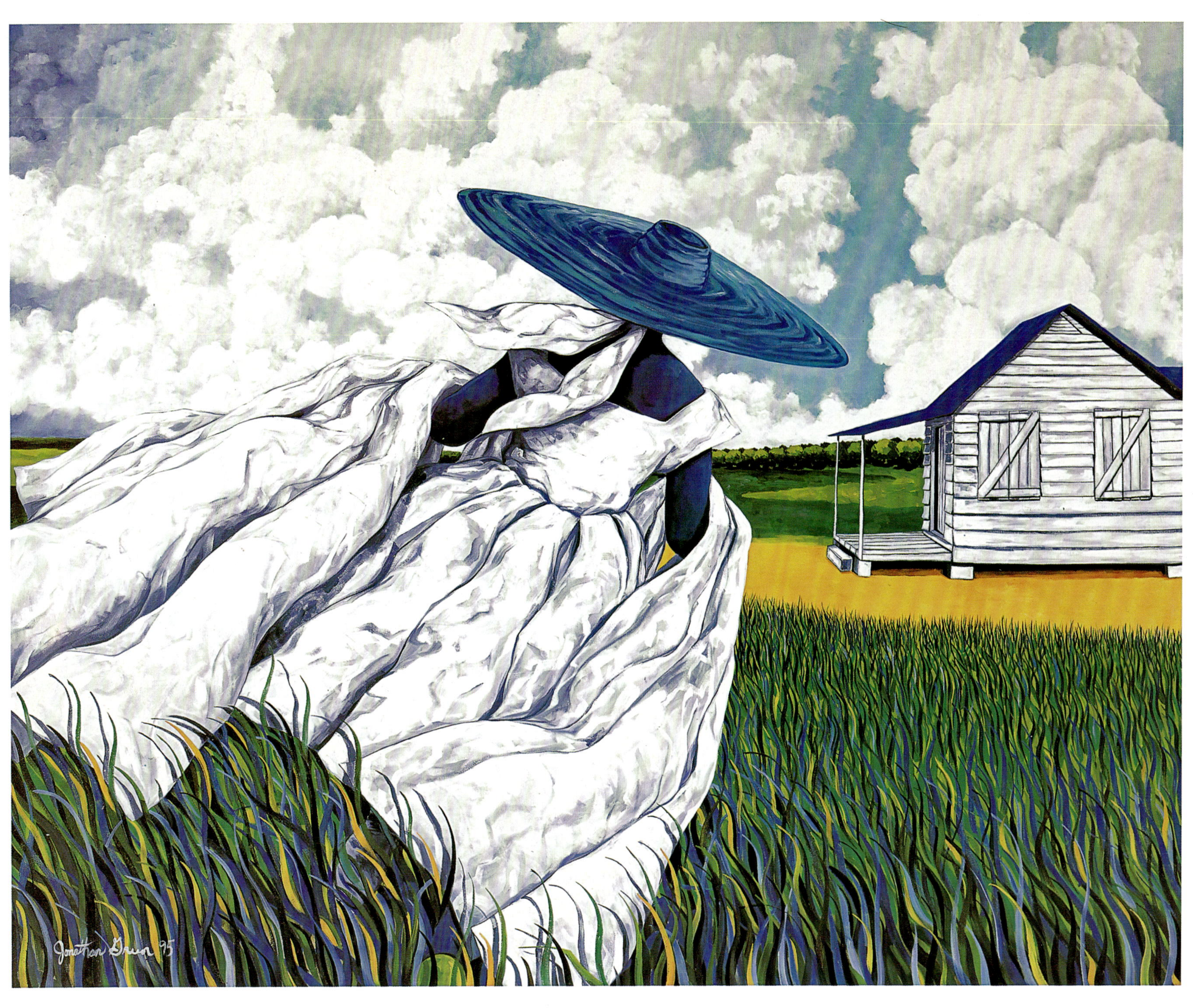

Broom Grass, 1995. Oil on canvas, 48 x 60".
Courtesy of Allison Powe. Photograph by Tim Stamm.

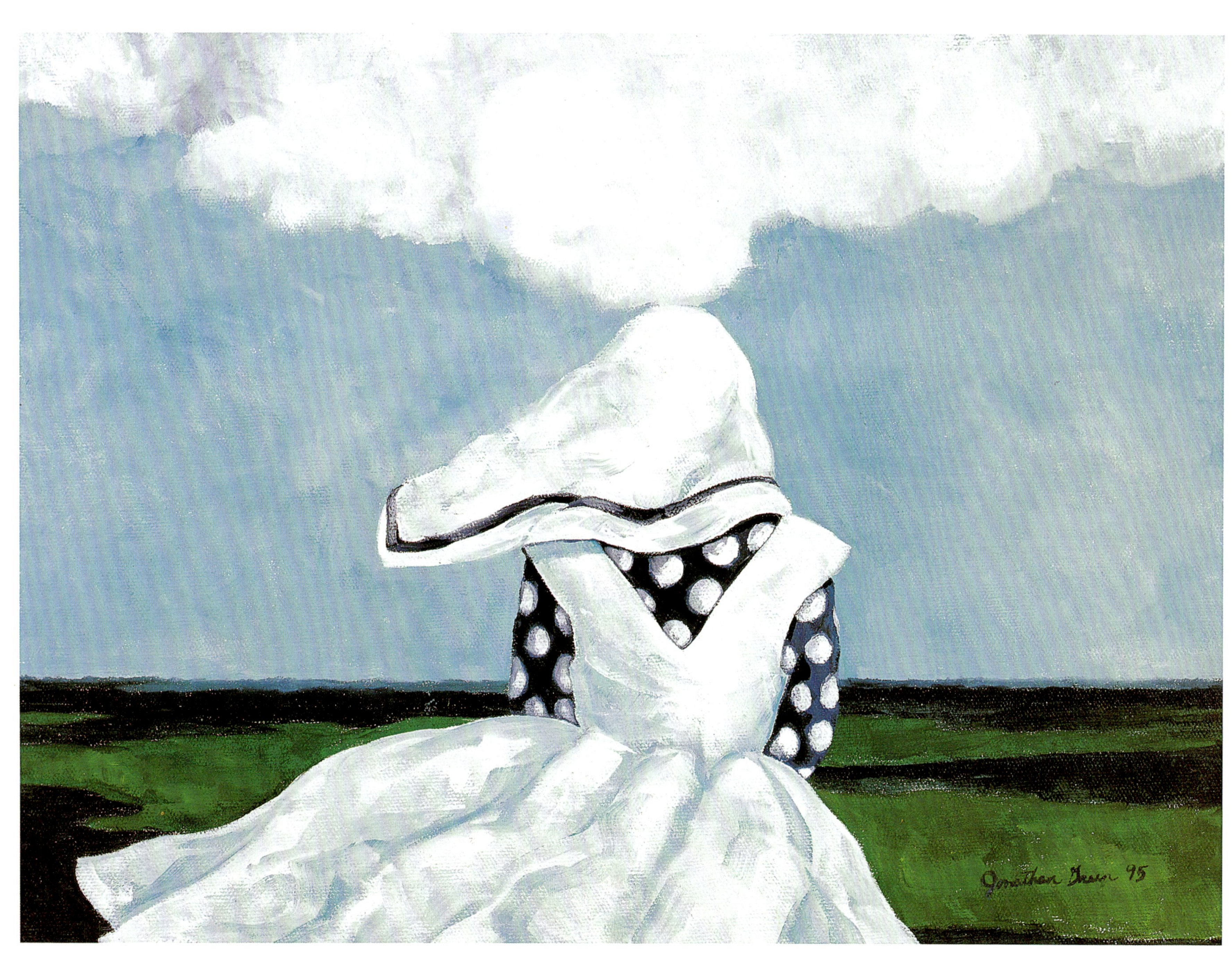

Solitude, 1995. Oil on canvas, 12 x 16".
Courtesy of Ronne Hartfield. Photograph by Tim Stamm.

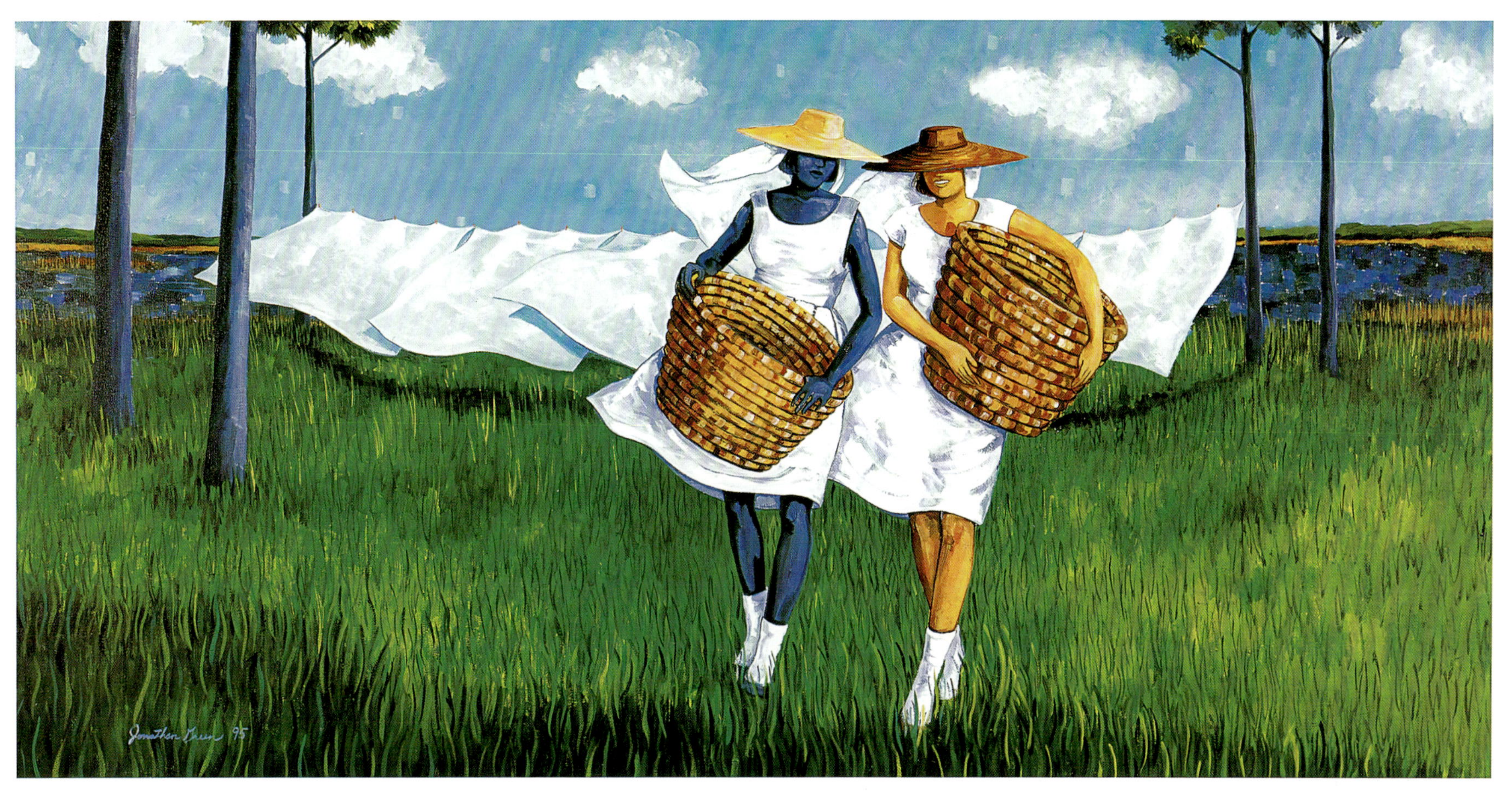

Two Girls with Wash, 1995. Oil on canvas, 24 x 47".
Courtesy of Miriam C. Brooke. Photograph by Tim Stamm.

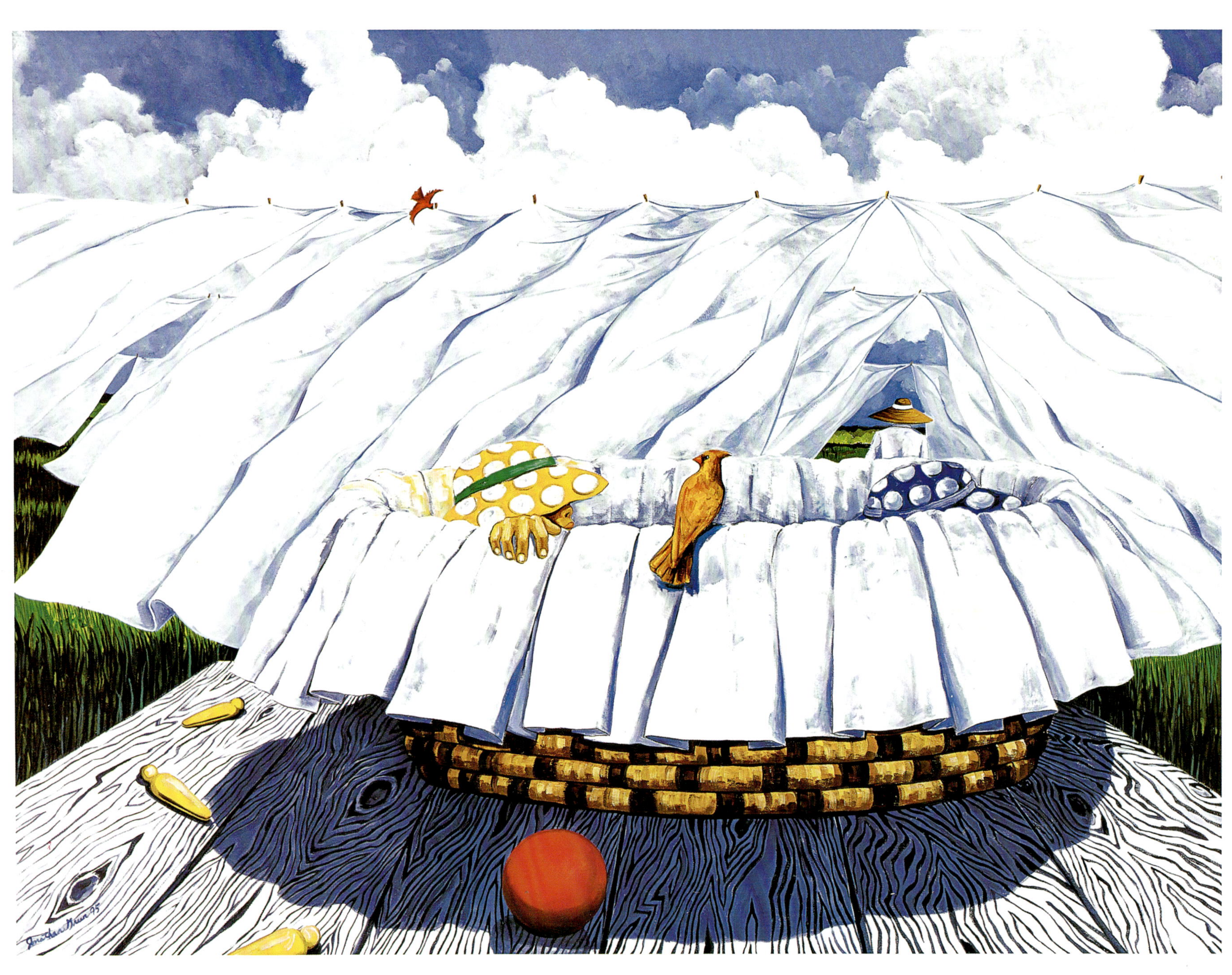

Sweet Grass Nursery, 1995. Oil on canvas, 36 x 48".
Courtesy of Terry and Thelma Harris. Photograph by Tim Stamm.

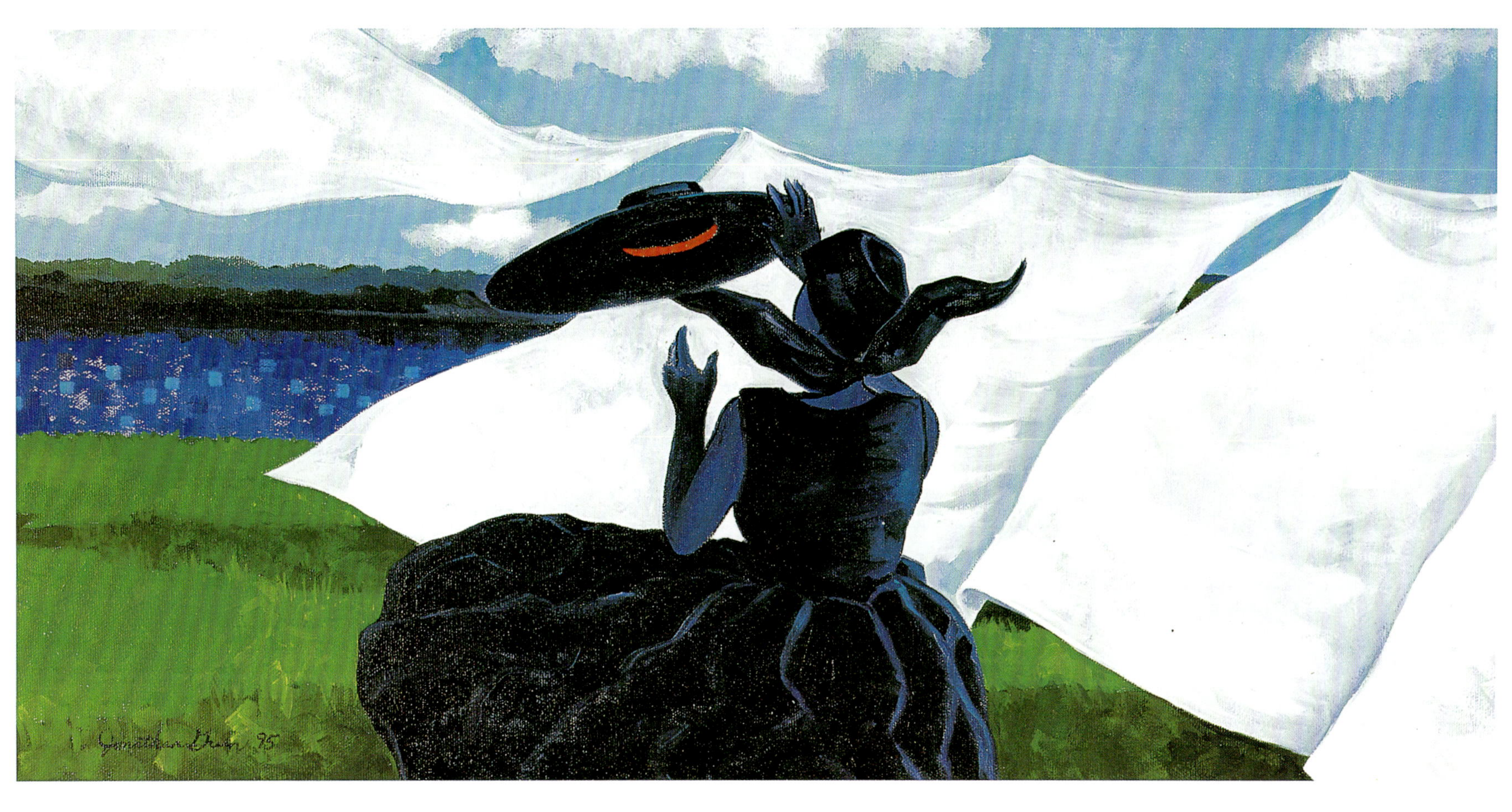

Widow Wash, 1995. Oil on canvas, 12 x 24".
Courtesy of Elizabeth C. Burke. Photograph by Tim Stamm.

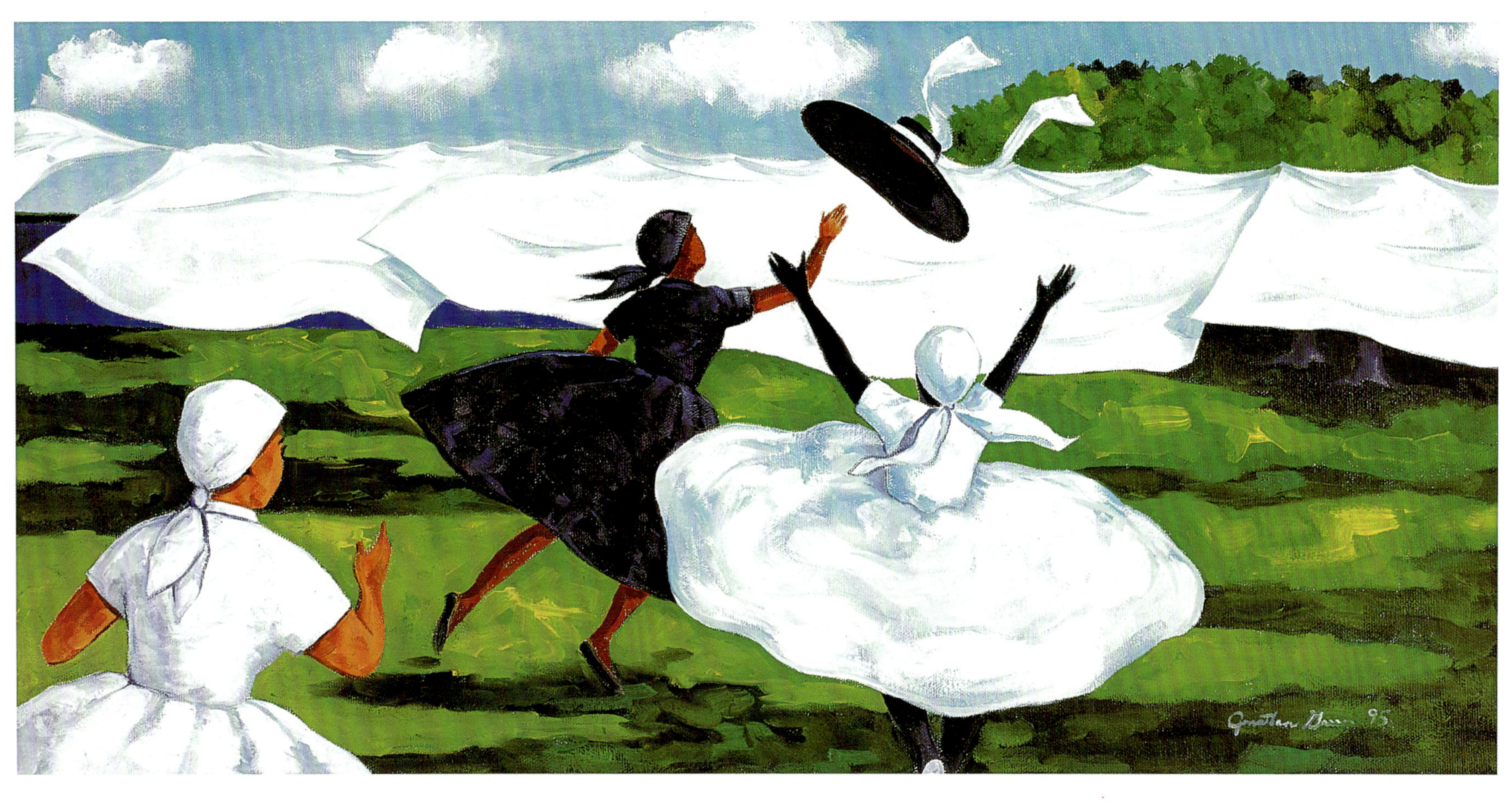

The Black Hat, 1995. Oil on canvas, 12 x 24".
Courtesy of Mac and Doris Williams. Photograph by Tim Stamm.

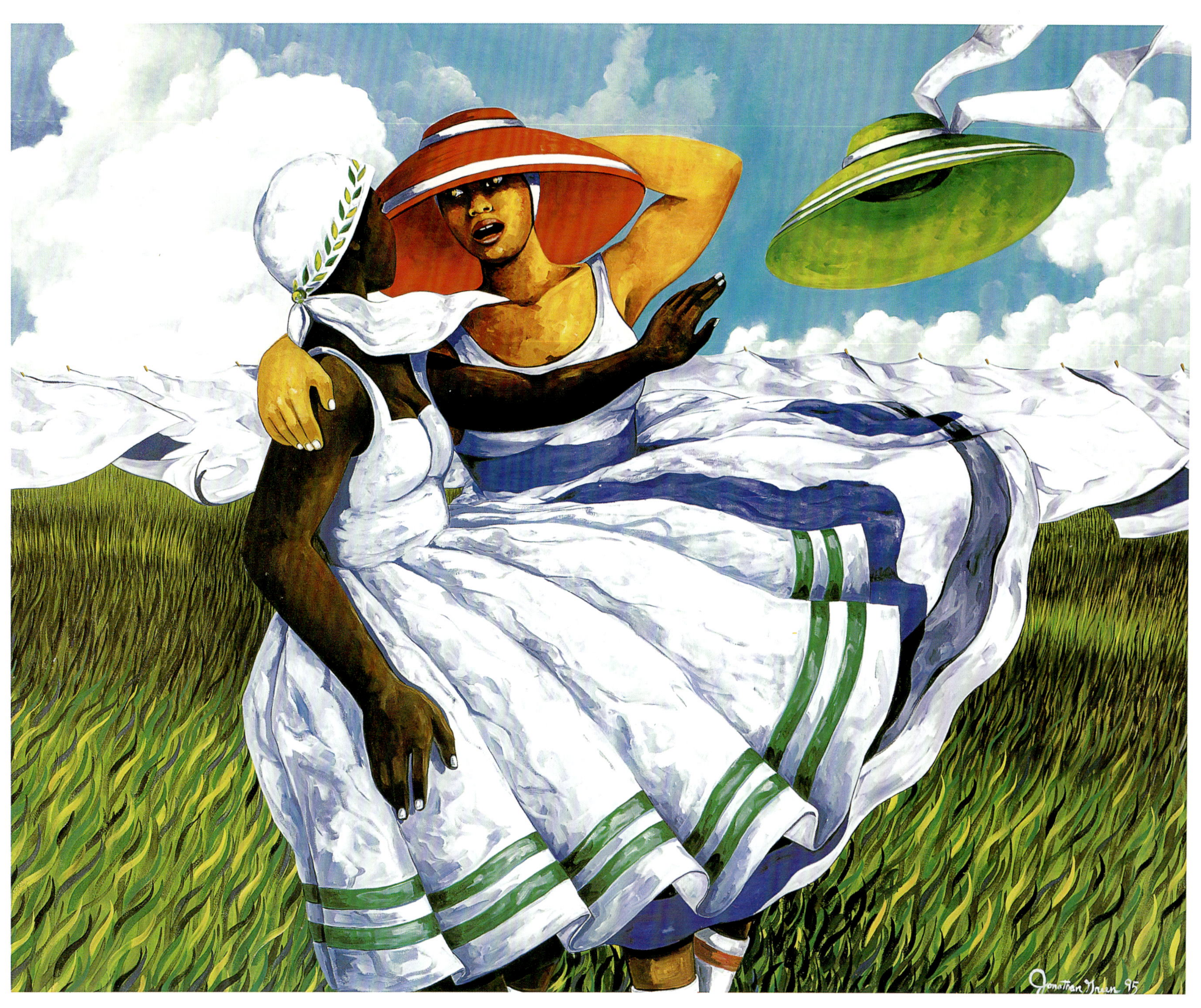

Flying Hat, 1995. Oil on canvas, 48 x 60".
Courtesy of Sandra Tuck. Photograph by Tim Stamm.

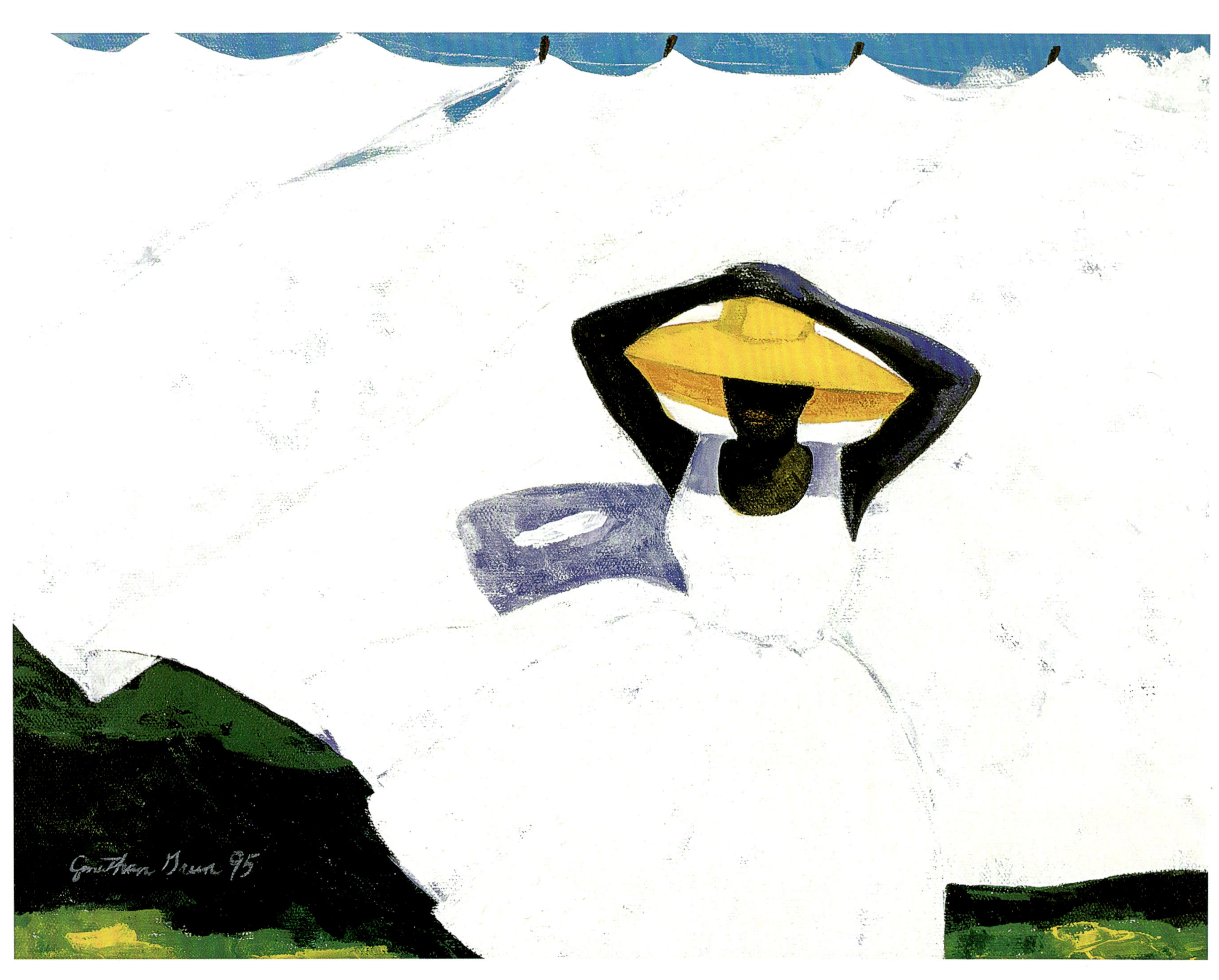

Canary Yellow Hat, 1995. Acrylic on canvas, 12 x 16".
Courtesy of Jill Farwell. Photograph by Tim Stamm.

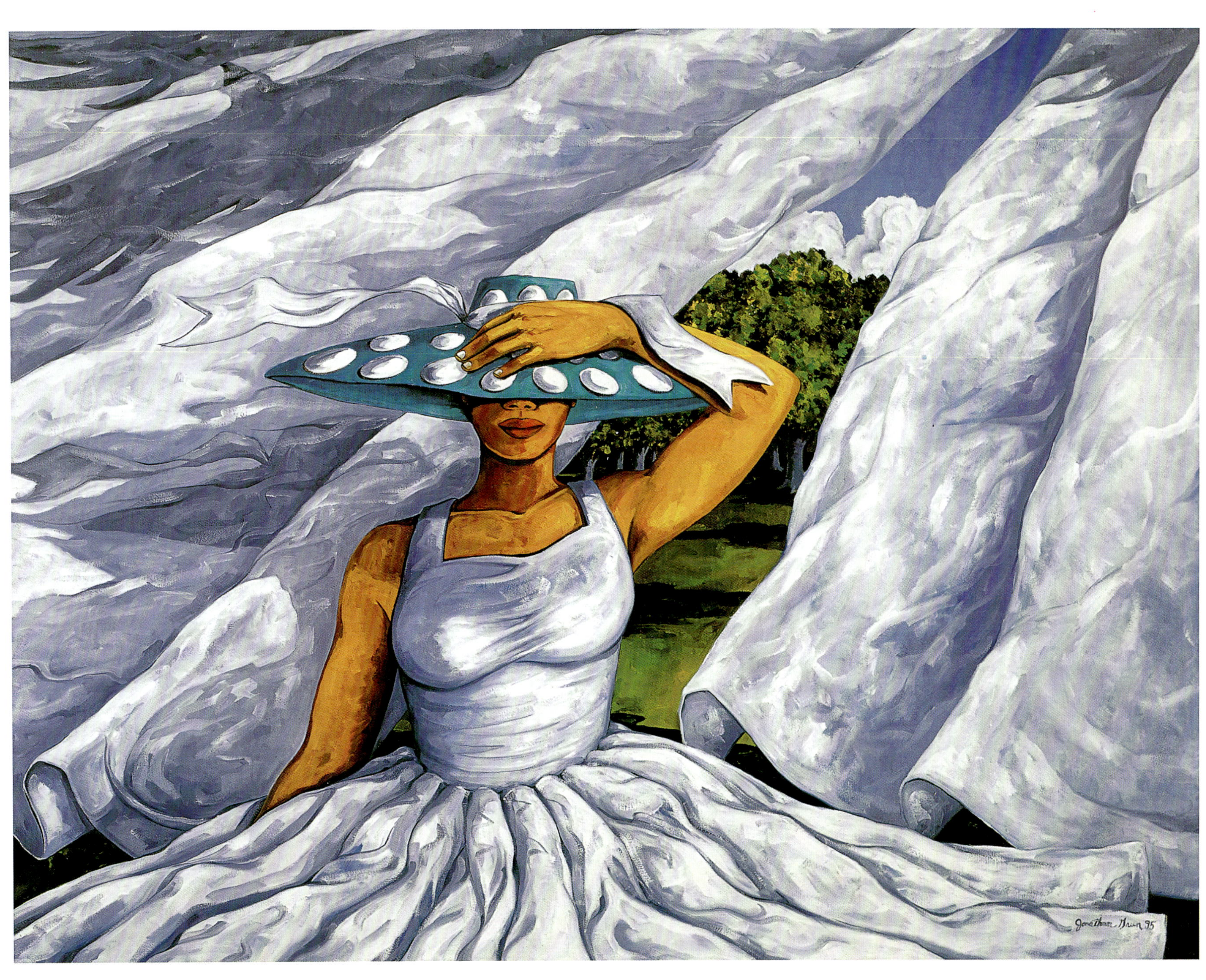

Blue Shadows, 1995. Oil on canvas, 36 x 48".
Courtesy of Laura Parsons. Photograph by Tim Stamm.

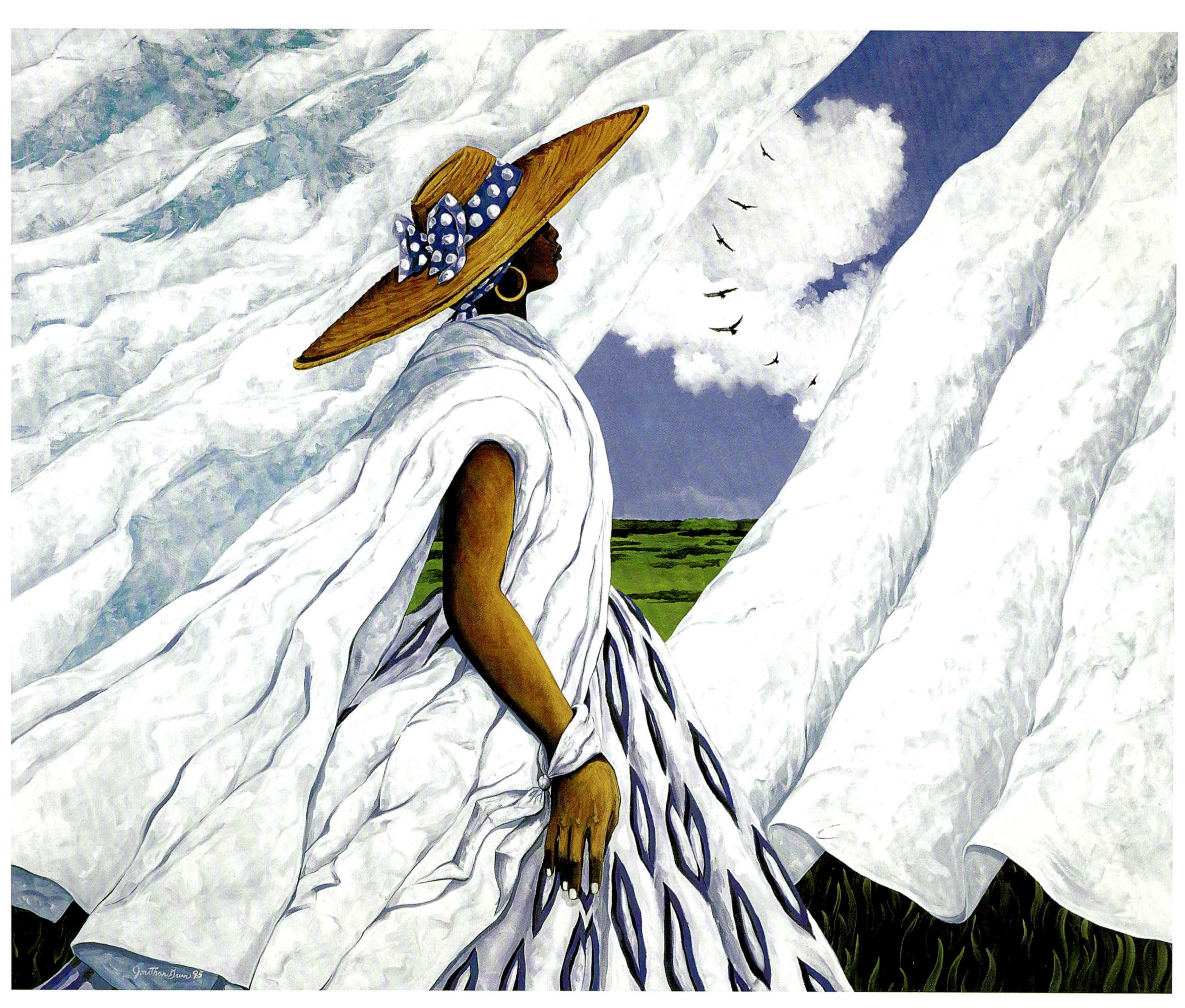

White Breeze, 1995. Oil on canvas, 48 x 60".
Courtesy of Gilbert and Elizabeth Ney. Photograph by Tim Stamm.

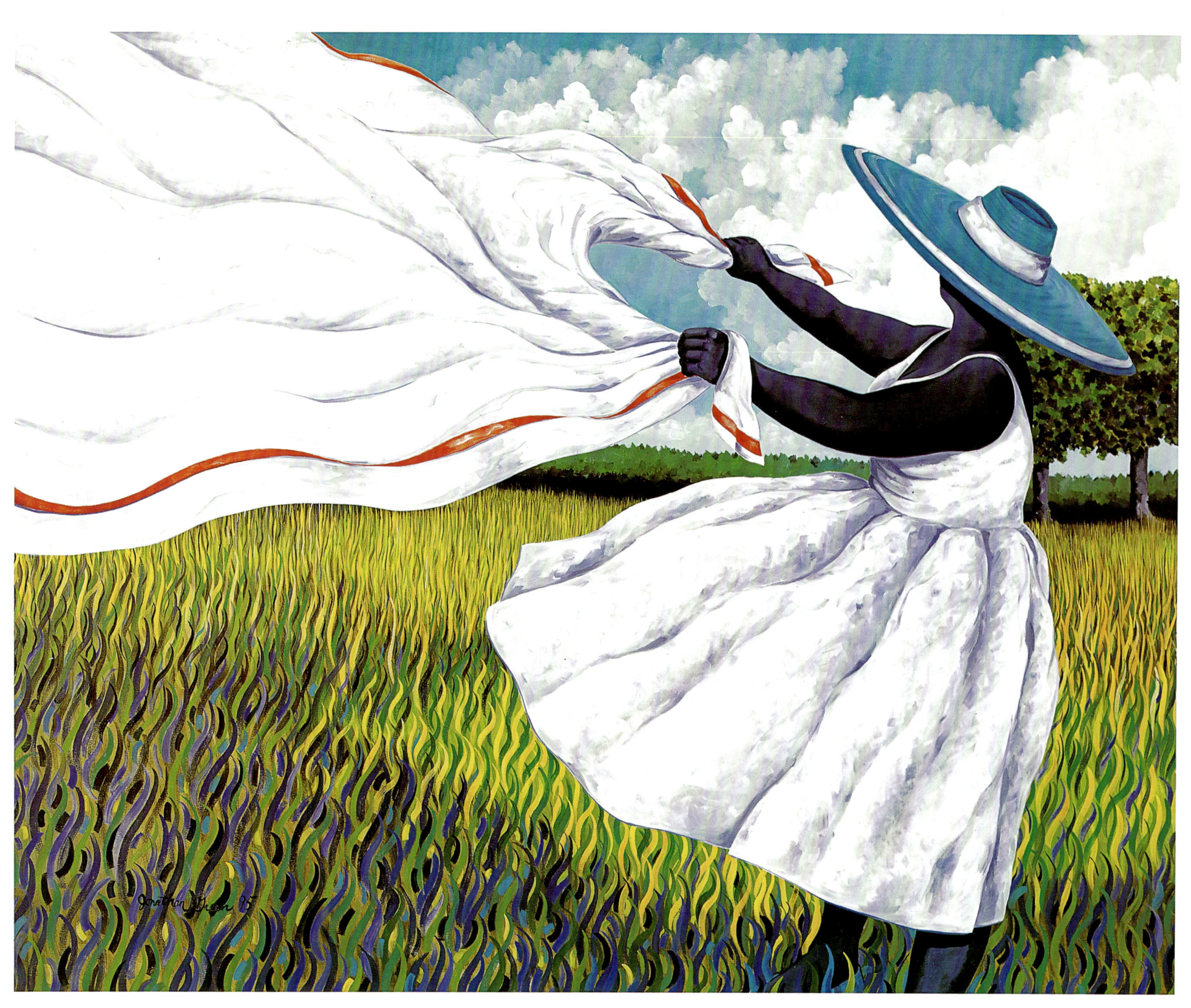

Wind Blown Sheets, 1995. Oil on canvas, 48 x 60".
Courtesy of Robert and Kathy Herrmann. Photograph by Tim Stamm.

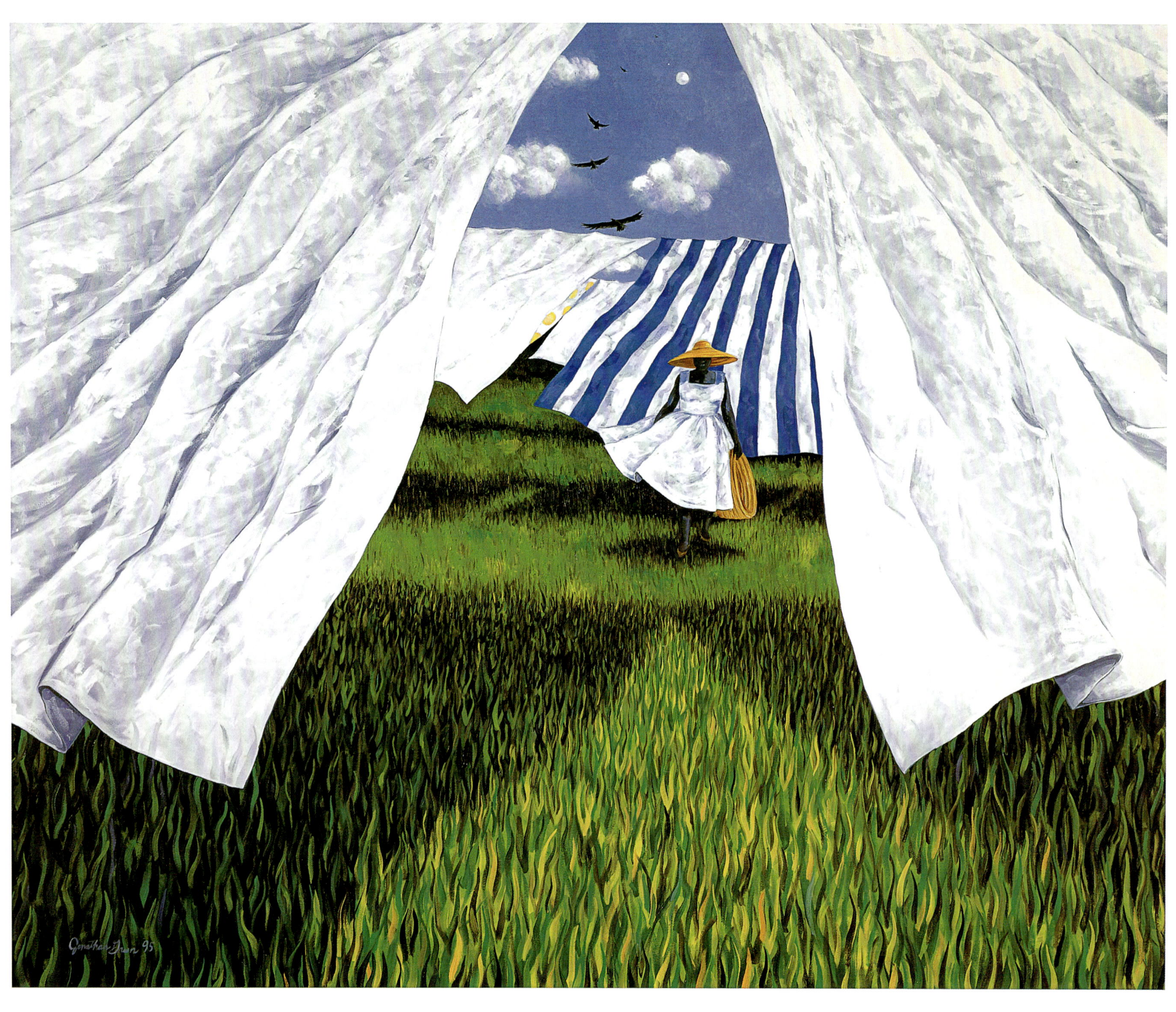

White Moon, 1995. Oil on canvas, 48 x 60".
Courtesy of Linda Sandrich. Photograph by Tim Stamm.

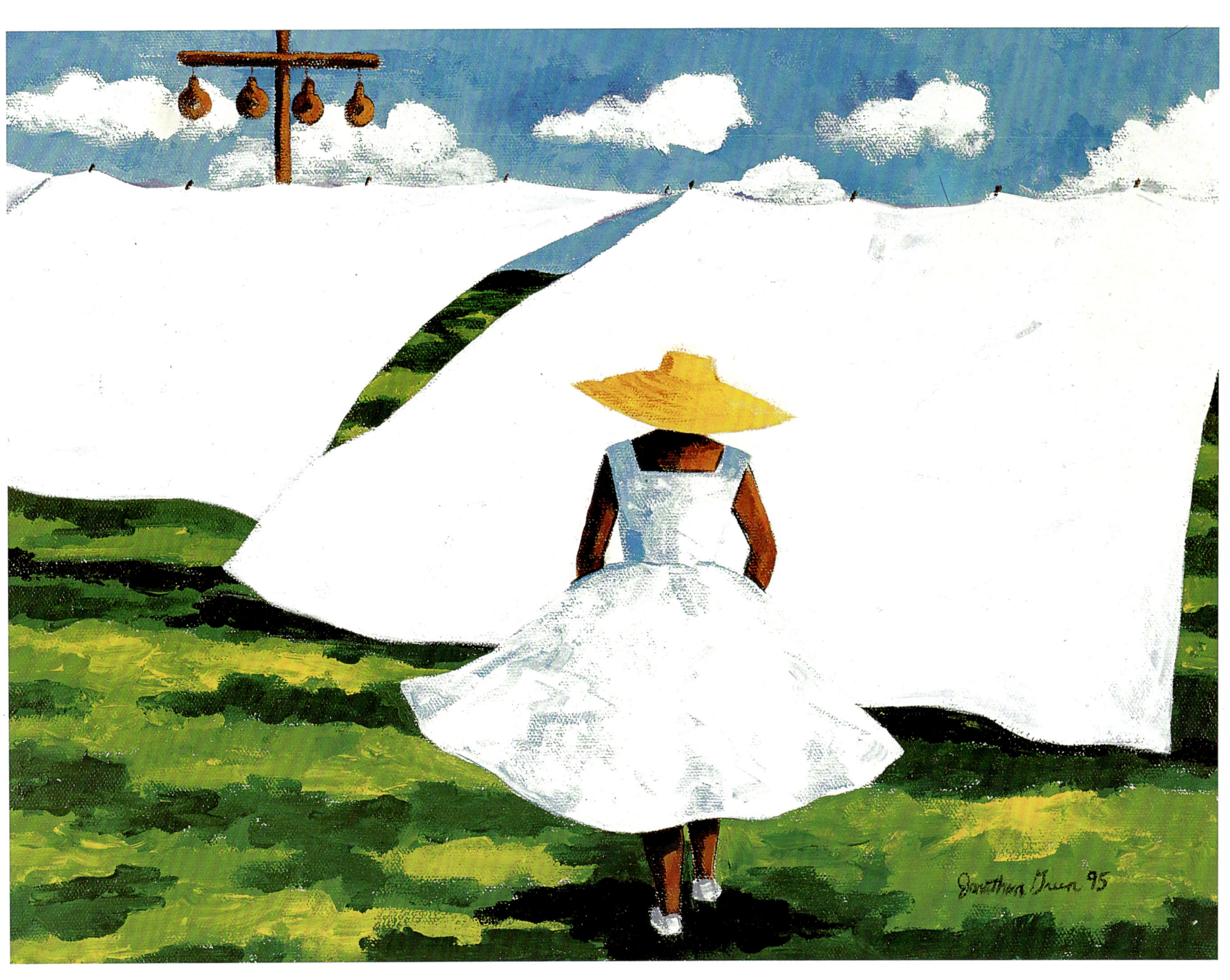

Viewing the Wash, 1995. Acrylic on canvas, 12 x 16".
Courtesy of Sandra Tuck. Photograph by Tim Stamm.

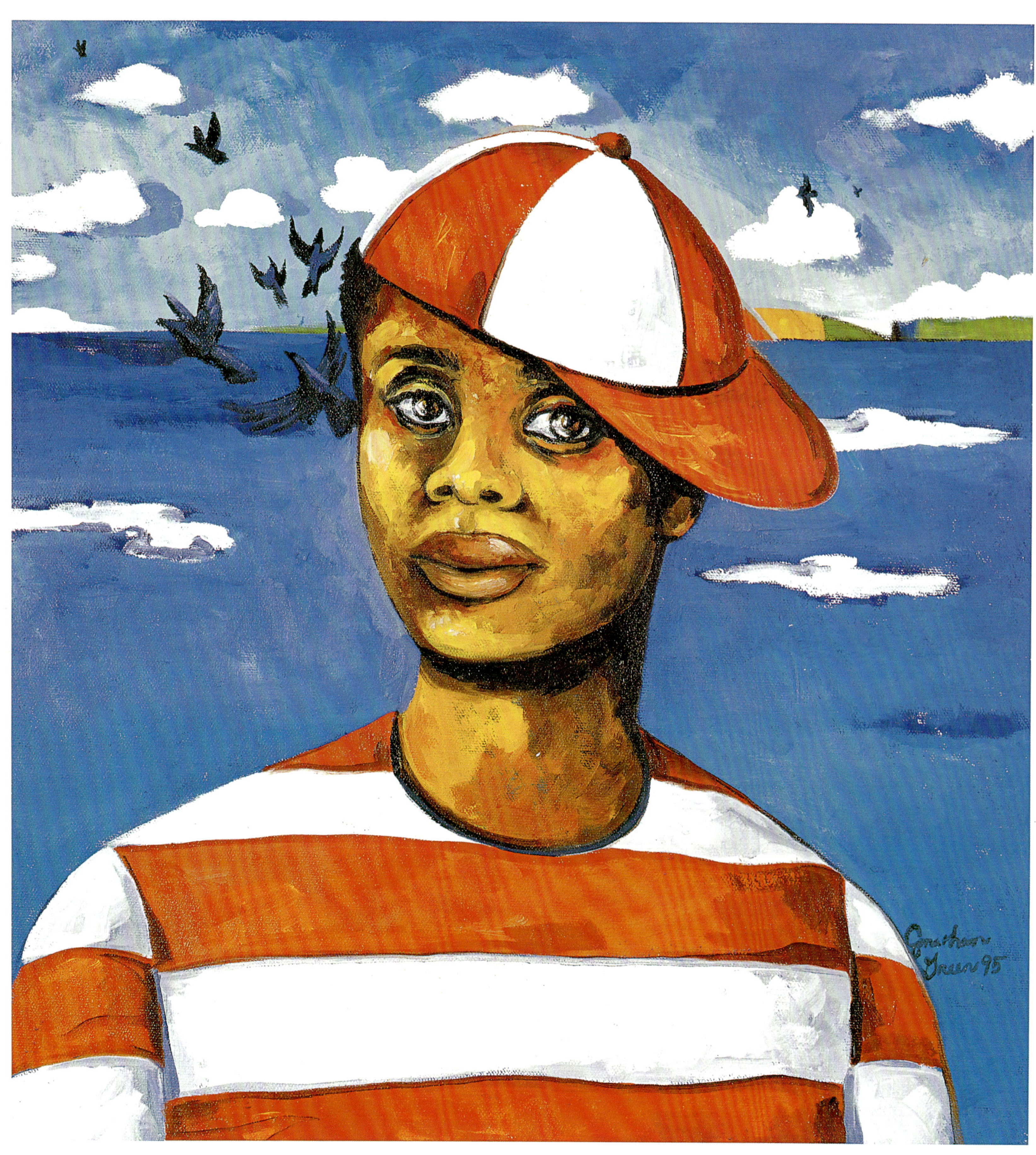

Boy by the Sea, 1995. Oil on canvas, 18 x 17".
Courtesy of Maxcine Ashcraft. Photograph by Tim Stamm.

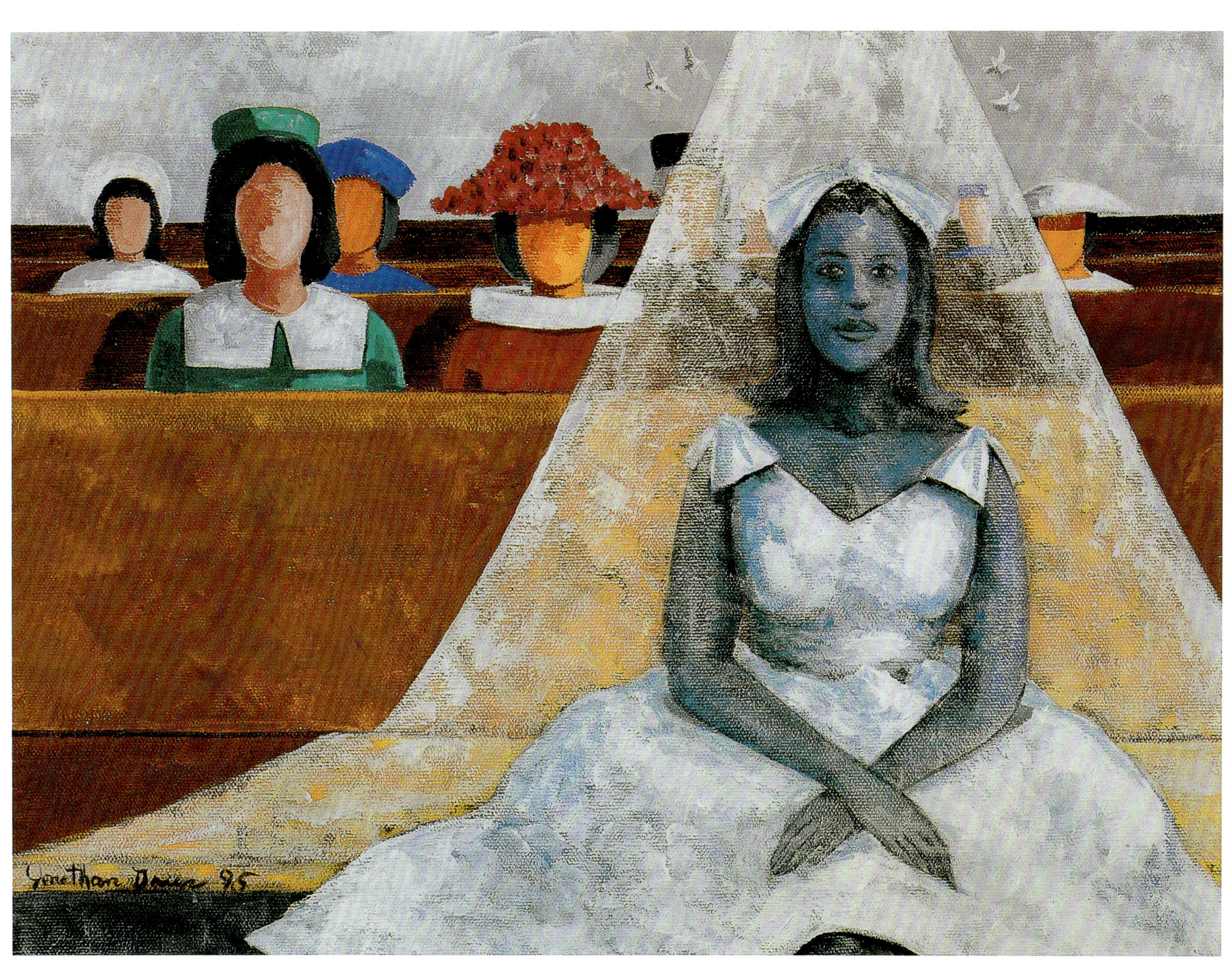

Angel, 1995. Acrylic on canvas, 12 x 16".
Collection of the artist. Photograph by Tim Stamm.

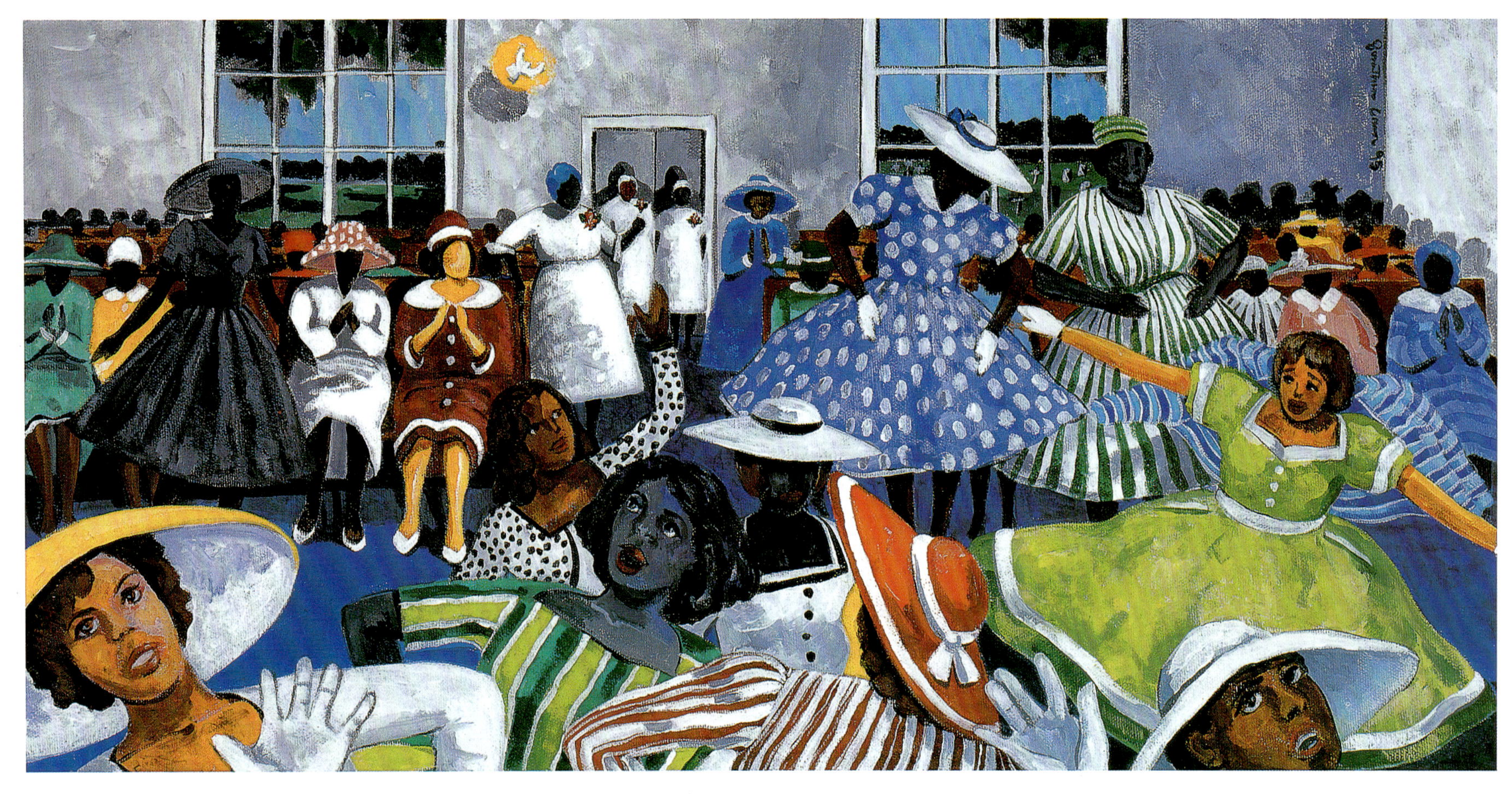

Huspah Spirit, 1995. Acrylic on canvas, 12 x 24".
Courtesy of Fabian and Carolynne Breaux. Photograph by Tim Stamm.

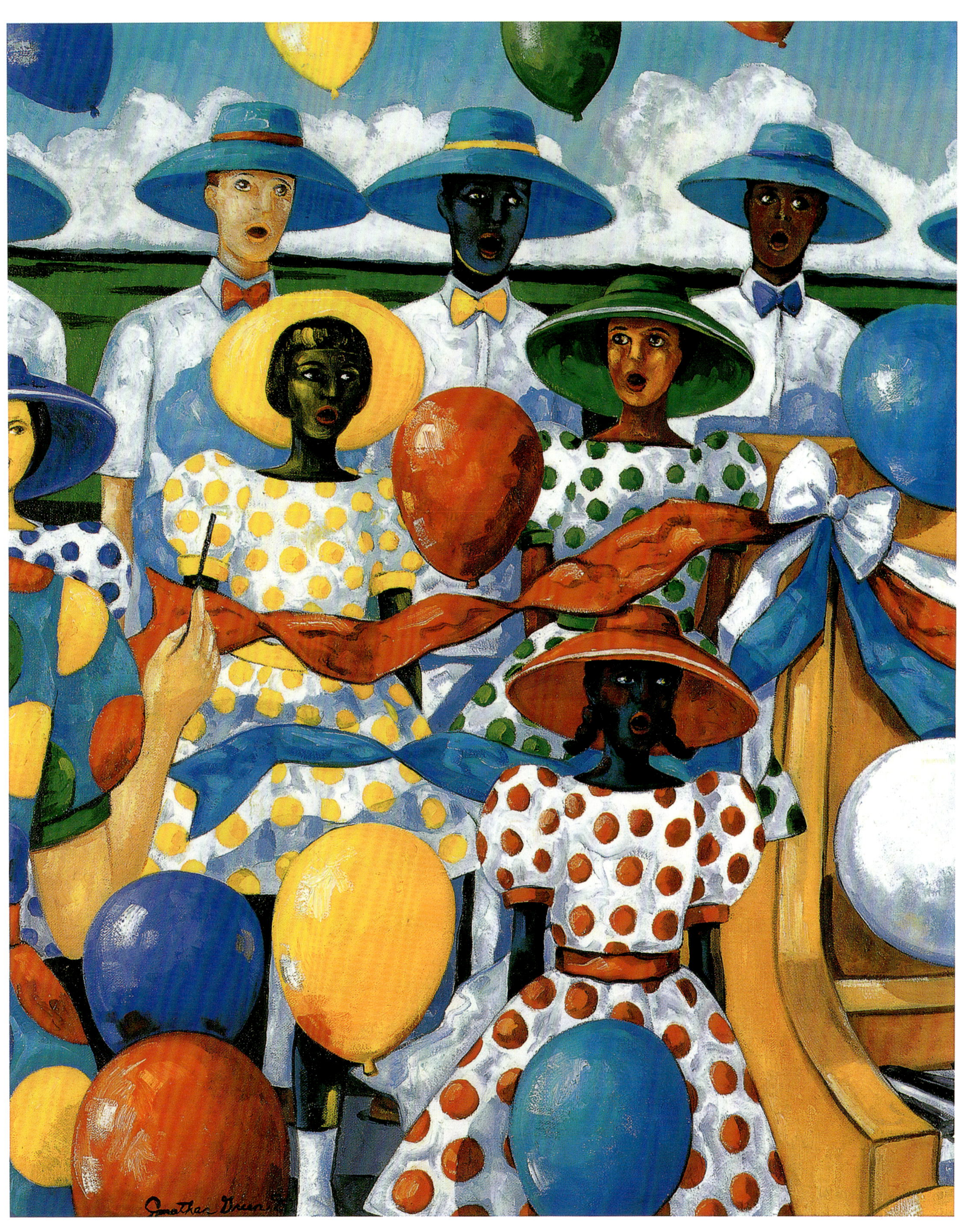

Dale School Choir, 1995. Oil on canvas, 23 x 19".
Courtesy of Robert, Charlotte, and Sarah Barrett. Photograph by Tim Stamm.

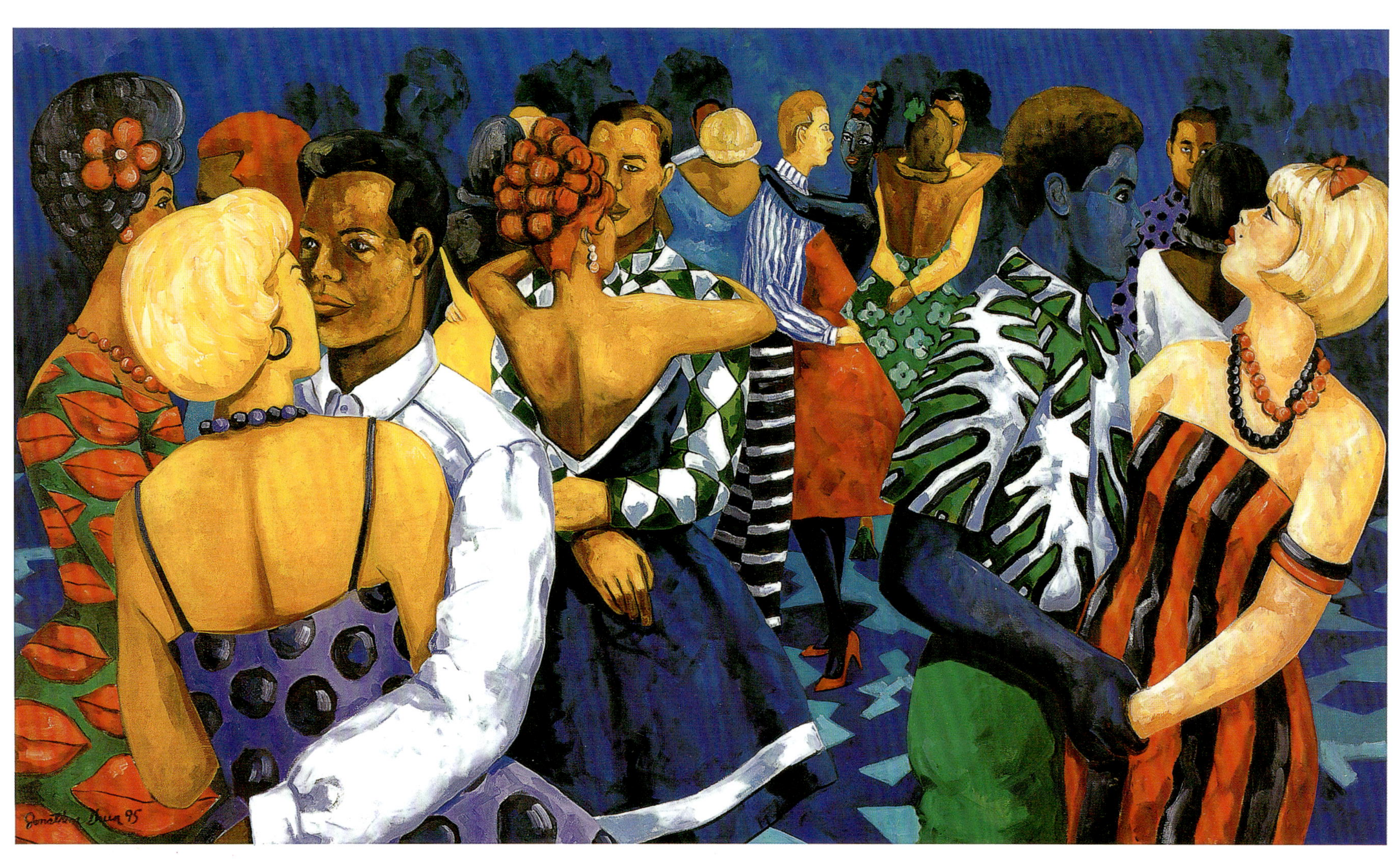

Small's Paradise, 1995. Oil on canvas, 30 x 52".
Courtesy of Carole A. Carter. Photograph by Tim Stamm.

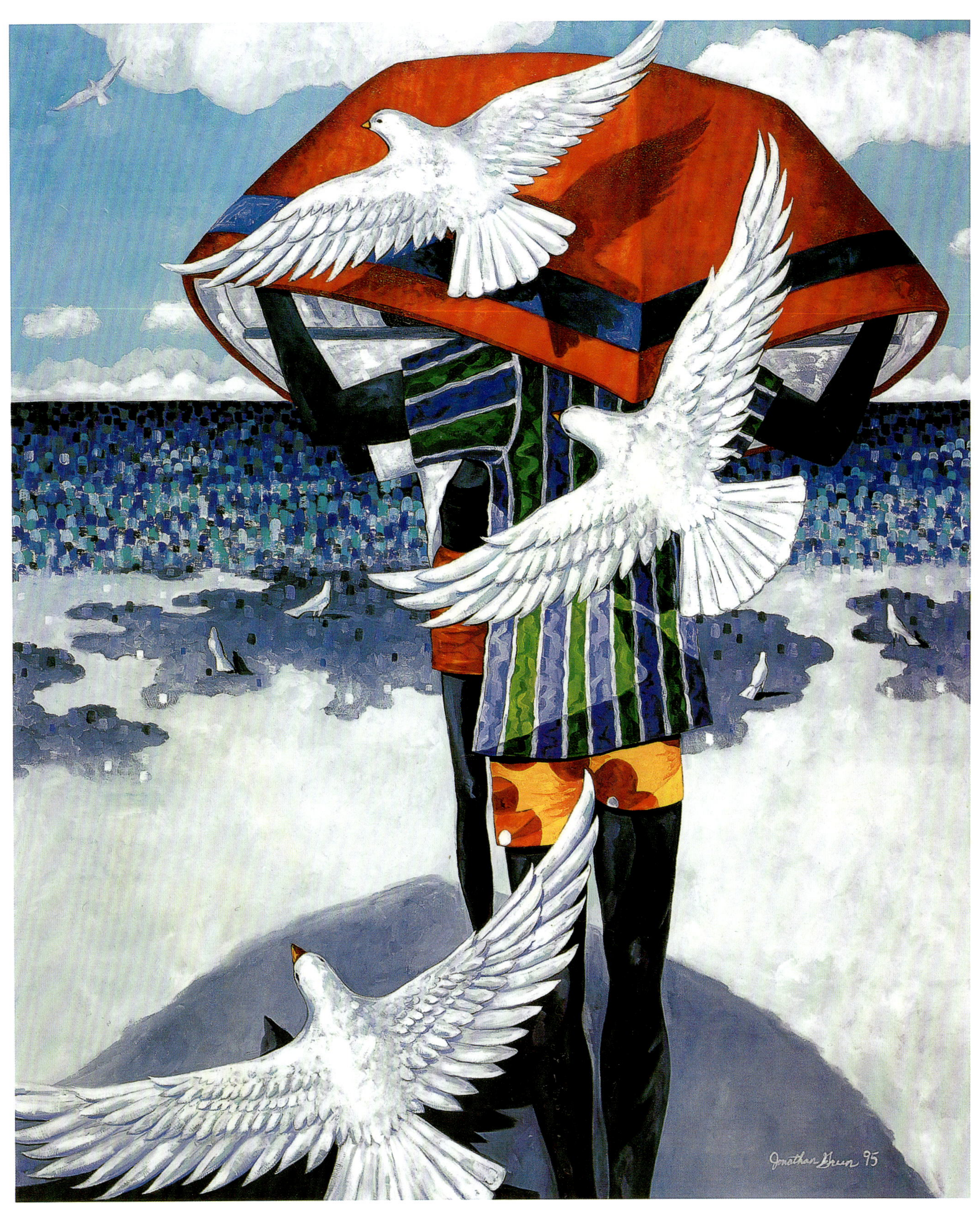

Dove Beach, 1995. Oil on canvas, 52 x 44".
Courtesy of Tom and Gloria Williams. Photograph by Tim Stamm.

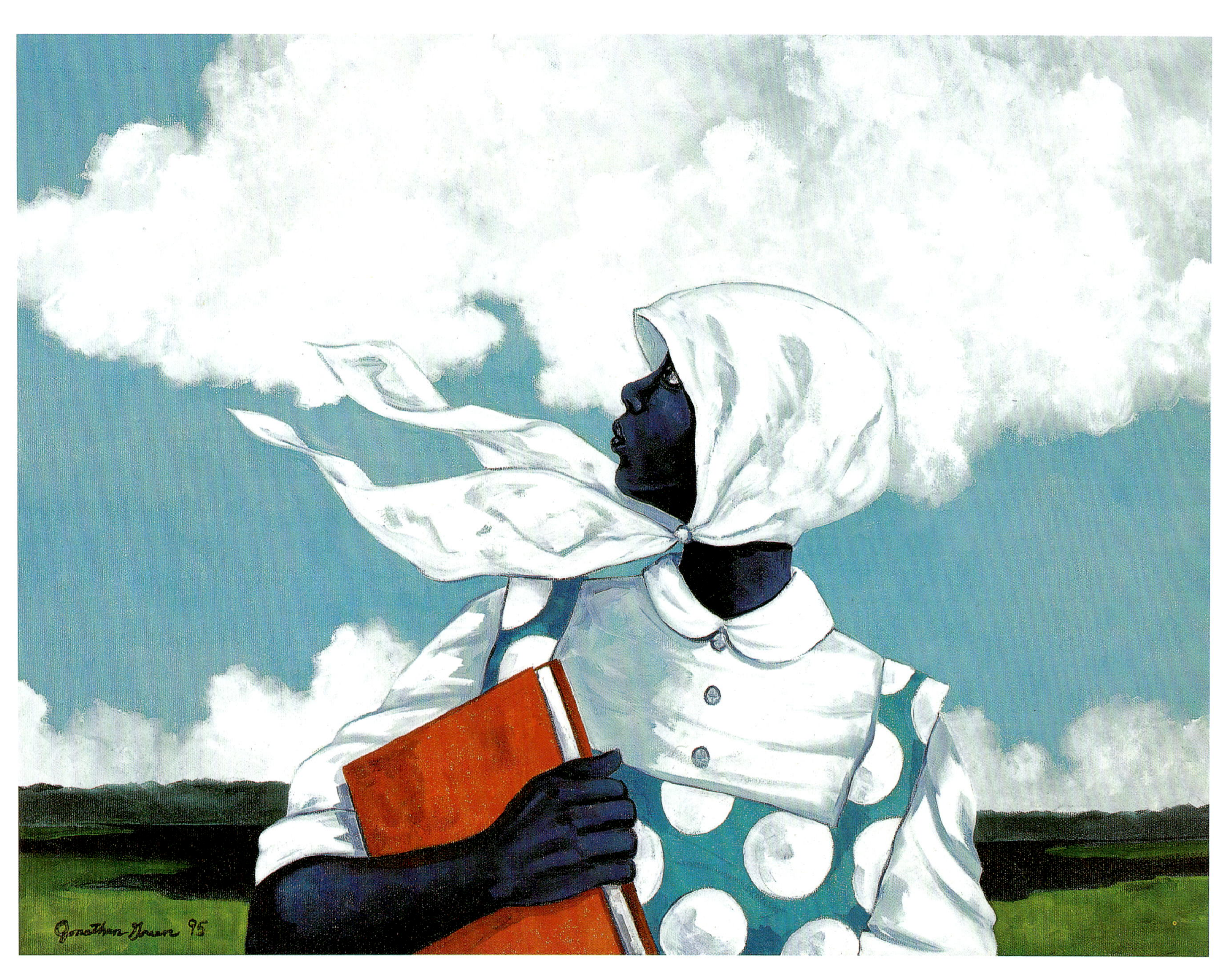

White Scarf, 1995. Oil on canvas, 18 x 24".
Courtesy of Dr. and Mrs. Robert Clymer. Photograph by Tim Stamm.

ACKNOWLEDGMENTS

This sensitive presentation of my work would not have been possible without the support and encouragement of many collectors, friends, and family members. The paintings in this publication serve as a conduit to a very personal and private world of passionate values that were influenced by my early emotional and cultural upbringing. Truly, the spiritual echoes of my grandmother Eloise (Sir Hand) Johnson; the gentle nurturing of my mother, Ruth Green, and her sister Corene; and the strength of my father, Melvin Green, are the cornerstones of my creative expression and hallmarks of my culture—a culture that instills in its children a profound respect for family, community, and the dignity and value of others. I grew up in a culture that uses visual, oral, and spiritual traditions to teach essential community values of cooperation and sharing.

It is with this spirit of cooperation and sharing that I am indebted to Ronne Hartfield, director of the Department of Museum Education at the Art Institute of Chicago, for her teaching skills and the direction given to me when I was a student at the School of the Art Institute. Her support, along with the assistance of my patron, friend, and studio manager, Richard Weedman, made the challenges of my formal art education and of the early stages of my career an exciting and rewarding adventure.

I am deeply grateful to Lynn Robertson and Alice Bouknight of the McKissick Museum for their skills in educating others about my art and culture through their efforts in sponsoring a three-year traveling exhibition of my work. Additionally, the insights and initial impetus of this publication would not have been possible without the sensitive encouragement of Robin Asbury, who helped formulate the concept of this book. The patience, skill, and professional discipline of Catherine Fry, director of the University of South Carolina Press, have been essential to the realization of this publication. I am very grateful to the University of South Carolina Press staff for working so diligently and patiently with me on the text and images chosen for this work, especially Peggy Hill, managing editor, Rebecca Blakeney, design and production manager, and Carleton Giles, designer.

I extend thanks also to Bettye J. (Mbitha) Parker Smith, vice president of the Florida Education Fund, for her sensitive essay about the South and the culture that is so much a part of me and my art. The commitment and support of the master storyteller Pat Conroy and the depth of his understanding of my culture will always be deeply respected.

J. G.

INDEX

Paintings are identified by date (in parentheses) and page number.